STRESS, COPING, AND DEVELOPMENT

STRESS, COPING, AND DEVELOPMENT
An Integrative Perspective

CAROLYN M. ALDWIN

Foreword by Richard S. Lazarus

THE GUILFORD PRESS
New York   London

To my father

© 1994 The Guilford Press
A Division of Guilford Publications, Inc.
72 Spring Street, New York, NY 10012
http://www.guilford.com

Preface to the Paperback Edition © 2000 The Guilford Press

Printed in the United States of America

This book is printed on acid-free paper.

Last digit is print number: 9   8   7   6   5   4

Library of Congress Cataloging-in-Publication Data
Aldwin, Carolyn M.
   Stress, coping, and development : an integrative perspective
Carolyn M. Aldwin.
      p.   cm.
   Includes bibliographical references and index.
   ISBN 0-89862-261-1 (hard)   ISBN 1-57230-543-6 (pbk.)
   1. Stress (Psychology)   2. Adjustment (Psychology)   3. Stress
(Psychology)—Research.   4. Adjustment (Psychology)—Research.
5. Developmental psychology.   6. Mind and body.   I. Title.
BF575.S75A42   1994
155.9'042—dc20   94-18295
                                                            CIP

Foreword

Coping research and theory now seem to be on a fast track, with many studies being done and debates taking place about how we should approach the topic, both in measurement and theory. To someone who was a pioneer in this territory, the widespread interest is gratifying, though I am not always especially pleased about what has been happening.

For example, I recently visited a well-attended symposium at an American Psychological Association meeting at which five coping researchers argued. Their main foci were centered on the contrast between coping inventories and more in-depth analyses, and between coping styles as a feature of personality and coping process. The treatment of the subject was often witty and trenchant but left me feeling that the contention was centered mostly on red herrings, with accusations abounding that this or that measurement style was inadequate. It was difficult to find evidence of agreement among the protagonists. Apparently, they could find little or nothing in common. It was not an edifying experience. I left feeling quite disappointed about finding a balanced, statesmanlike, and forward-looking treatment of so central a concept in the arena of human stress and adaptation.

More than stress alone, coping is a key concept helping us to grasp adaptation and maladaptation, because it is not stress alone that causes distress and dysfunction but how people manage stress. This idea is not new; the psychoanalytic concept of defense was a progenitor. However, in the late 1960s and 1970s formal attention began to be given to the measurement of coping and to how it worked. Since then, a fair amount of research has been reported in scientific journals publishing the work of several interested disciplines for whom coping is important.

What I find quite remarkable is that with all this research and ferment there has been no recent major treatment of the status of coping research and theory, which reviews what has been done since the early 1980s and analyzes the important issues that empower work on the coping process.

This new book by Carolyn Aldwin, whose training took place partly within the Berkeley Stress and Coping Project before it disbanded, and partly in a developmental program at the University of California at San Francisco, is impressive in its scholarship and gutsy in its forthright effort to address the major issues.

The outlook of the book is transactional, and the emphasis intra-individual and longitudinal, which I believe starts it off on the right track. It covers the history of thought about stress and coping, issues pertaining to the conceptualization of stress and coping, and design and measurement in stress research, which have long been topics of major contention.

By Chapter 5, having laid down the background, Aldwin is ready to address coping research itself, examining conceptual issues first, then moving to the measurement of coping, and reviewing coping scales themselves and arguments over how they should be formulated. Additional chapters deal with topics that are central to what motivates the study of stress and coping, such as recent and ongoing research and theory on coping and the impact of coping on health outcomes. The book also deals with a growing body of research on the coping process in children, as well as cultural factors in stress and coping, a topic that has hitherto received little attention. Throughout the book Aldwin takes a reasoned stand on most of the important issues in coping theory and research, not always the stand I might have taken, but one that warrants serious consideration by those interested in the subject matter. For anyone who desires to see coping research and theory brought together between the covers of a single book, and to have an opportunity to explore them in depth, this book comes none too soon.

The presence of Aldwin's book mitigates somewhat my own pessimism about the direction of present and future coping research, illustrated by my reaction to the symposium I mentioned at the outset. I hope the book will stimulate researchers to turn to the important issues and away from superficialities and convenient but uninformative types of studies of coping. I also hope it will encourage researchers to downplay simple normative studies of single stressful occasions and to increasingly emphasize prospective, preferably longitudinal, studies using more than one causal variable. And I hope that it will influence researchers to explore more than one adaptational outcome of coping, so that the role of coping in adaptation can be more fully evaluated. I believe researchers in a number of disciplines will find this book important. It fills a major need for a thorough review, analysis, and integration of the modern field of coping theory and research.

RICHARD S. LAZARUS, *March 1993*

Preface to the Paperback Edition

In the five years since the first publication of this book, there have been some interesting changes in the field. Perhaps the most noteworthy of these is the growing acceptance of the possibility of positive outcomes from undergoing major stressors. When I first presented a paper on the positive effects of combat at the International Conference on Social Stress in 1992, it was greeted with incredulity. One eminent sociologist went so far as to say that my respondents must have been lying—how could anyone find anything positive in such a horrendous experience? Four years later at this same conference, I reported a follow-up study on British veterans which paralleled the earlier findings, and now it was considered actually rather routine. The same scientist now said that, of course, people could development mastery and new coping skills in such circumstances—what else was new! Nonetheless, we are still struggling with many of the same issues that we were five years ago.

Interest in stress and coping research has remained very strong. A quick title word search of *Current Contents* showed that an additional 20,000 articles on stress and a more modest (but nonetheless daunting) 2,000+ articles on coping have been published in this period. While there is not sufficient time (or space) to do justification to the many fine studies that have been published since this book first appeared, I think a number of noteworthy trends have emerged, reflecting emphases in the book. These include recent advances in psychoneuroimmunology (PNI), greater acknowledgment of the positive aspects of stress, increased tension between short-term versus long-term assessment of stress and coping processes, and the often paradoxical effects of religious coping.

PSYCHONEUROIMMUNOLOGY

There is now no doubt that stress and coping processes affect both the occurrence and the course of illness, and also that psychosocial factors affect the immune system. However, definitively establishing the stress → immune → illness chain has still proven elusive, although the evidence is growing stronger. In part, this may be due to individual differences both in emotional reactions to stress and in immune system responses to emotional arousal. Kemeny and Laudenslager (1999) have recently edited a special edition of *Brain, Behavior, and Immunity* that specifically addresses the issue of individual differences in PNI processes. If true, identifying patterns of reactions would require much larger samples than are typically available in immune system research, as the costliness of immune assays often restricts sample sizes.

A series of ingenious studies by Kiecolt-Gleser and her colleagues (Kiecolt-Gleser, Page, Marucha, MacCallum, & Gleser, 1998) on stress and wound healing may help elucidate the PNI pathways between stress and health outcomes. In wound research, a standard paradigm is to create a series of small blisters and then remove their tops to create a row of small sores. By assaying one sore each day, the researcher can trace the trajectory of biochemical processes involved in wound healing over several days. Using this paradigm, Kiecolt-Gleser and her colleagues examined how stress affects the rate of wound healing. They were able to show that stress has a cascade effect on the healing process, sometimes delaying full healing by days.

However, psychoneuroimmunologists have yet to fully explore the circumstances under which stress can result in immune activation. Interestingly, biologists have begun to look into a related phenomenon they call "hormesis" (for a review, see Aldwin & Sutton, 1998). In hormesis, organisms are exposed to a sublethal dose of a toxic agent and allowed to recover. Thereafter, these organisms may be resistant to what would ordinarily be a lethal dose of this toxic agent. For example, it has been observed that people exposed to low doses of radiation may have lower than average chances of contracting cancer. Experimental studies have shown that flat worms exposed to high heat can survive a subsequent exposure that kills nonexposed worms in control groups. Similarly, plants "hardened" by short exposures to cold can endure colder temperatures than nonexposed plants. The proposed mechanism, however, is not through the immune system, but through activation of DNA repair agents within the cells. Temperature and radiation can directly affect DNA repair mechanisms. In other words, *physical* stressors can affect cellular processes directly, without necessarily going through the neuroendocrine system. While it is unlikely that psychosocial stressors would have these direct effects, neuroendocrine perturbations also impact DNA and other cellular-level repair mechanisms. It is important to begin exploring the effects of psychosocial stress (both positive and negative) at the cellular level, as well as the possible effects of stress moderators.

POSITIVE ASPECTS OF STRESS

As mentioned earlier, the positive aspects of stress on psychosocial and biomedical outcomes have begun to receive much more credence in the past five years. Several different terms for this phenomenon are now being used in the literature, including "perceived benefits of stress," "posttraumatic growth," and "thriving," and it is gratifying to see a growing interest in and acknowledgment of this possibility. Indeed, Ickovics and Park (1998) recently edited a special issue of the *Journal of Social Issues* on this topic (and both editors, I should mention, have very deservedly won early career awards).

A number of issues still need to be worked out, possibly the most critical of these being measurement. We need a reliable way of identifying the "pollyana" effect—that is, differentiating those individuals who genuinely benefit from undergoing a stressful episode from those individuals who are simply in a state of denial or in some other way deceiving themselves. Failure to do this may well be muddying the findings. For example, in our laboratory, Karen Sutton and I were analyzing data from a longitudinal follow-up to our earlier study on pathways to perceived benefits of stress (Aldwin, Sutton, & Lachman, 1996), and our preliminary analyses made very little sense. In the initial, cross-sectional study, we had found that individuals who used instrumental action were more likely to perceive positive long-term outcomes of stress and, in turn, they had higher levels of mastery and lower levels of depression. Those who used escapism, though, showed the opposite pattern: They were more likely to perceive negative long-term outcomes and had lower mastery and more depression. This makes theoretical sense. However, in our initial analyses of the longitudinal follow-up, the use of instrumental action was related to poorer outcomes, and escapism to better ones! This was just the opposite of what we had found before. Why would using alcohol and drugs result in more positive outcomes and increased mastery?

It turned out that we had inadvertently included in the analyses individuals who reported long-term outcomes even though they were still in the midst of an ongoing event (and thus couldn't possibly know what the long-term outcomes were!). Omitting these individuals from the analyses brought the findings more into line with previous outcomes, but this example emphasized the problem of reporting biases and premature assumptions in this area of research. Individuals who are in denial and are using escapist strategies may present overly optimistic outcomes, while individuals who are in the midst of working through problems may be unduly pessimistic. Thus, there are some serious issues in the timing of assessment, as well as in correcting for reporting distortions, that need to be addressed.

MEASUREMENT ISSUES

In terms of the timing of assessment of stress and coping, there is a growing tension in the field between those interested in microprocesses and the more "macro" researchers. For example, Arthur Stone and his colleagues (1998) are promoting what they call the "ecological momentary assessment" (EMA) technique (pioneered by Mihaly Csikszentmihalyi), in which individuals are given programmable watches that beep at random intervals and request immediate information on the wearers' stress levels, coping processes, and emotions. Stone et al. argue that this is a more accurate assessment of coping than even daily diary methods, and that any retrospective reporting—even daily, weekly, or monthly assessments—may be too flawed to be trustworthy. However, it is probable that EMA techniques may also include error—people may be too rushed to fill in the information accurately, or their sense of what actually happened may be improved by a little perspective. Nonetheless, EMA is an interesting technique that should be considered among the useful tools in the stress and coping field.

Daily diary methods are gaining in popularity, in part due to their sensitivity to fluctuations in both mood and pain. The sheer quantity of data generated by such techniques, however, proves rather daunting for analytical purposes, although the use of growth curve modeling may be a promising alternative analytic strategy (Almeida & Kessler, 1998). (Growth curve modeling generates a trajectory for each individual and can accommodate nonlinear trajectories, thus providing a useful summary of an individual's change over time.)

At the other end of the spectrum are the "macro" researchers who take a life course perspective on stress. These researchers analyze archival data or use retrospective reporting, usually of traumatic events, to examine the long-term effects of early life stressors on later outcomes. The outcomes of this research have been decidedly mixed, with some finding many and others very few long-term effects. While some have questioned the accuracy of retrospective reporting, new research suggests that it is likely that individuals are fairly accurate at reporting the occurrence of major events, although the details may get a little muddied (Quas et al., 1999). Our preliminary analyses of data from both the Normative Aging Study and the Davis Longitudinal Study suggest that the long-term effects of childhood stressors are modest at best, with emotional and physical abuse most likely to have long-term effects, and that some of these effects are mediated through personality (Aldwin, Cupertino, Levenson, & Spiro, 1998; Aldwin, Levenson, Cupertino, & Spiro, 1998). Certainly, more work is needed both to improve the accuracy of retrospective reporting, and also to examine the mediators through which trauma can have long-term effects.

RELIGION AND HEALTH

The relationship between religion and health, and especially the use of prayer as a coping strategy, has garnered a great deal of attention in both the scientific and the popular press in the past five years. While the popular press is quick to promote studies that show a positive relationship between religion and health, in truth there are nearly as many studies that show the opposite results—that is, greater religiosity and/or the use of prayer can often be associated with poorer health outcomes. Pargament (1997) has argued that there are different types of religious coping, two of which he calls "collaborative" and "deferring." Collaborative religious coping supports instrumental action; it relies on faith and prayer to show the individual the right course of action and/or provides a sense of support and respite, which can also facilitate action. In contrast, the deferring style of religious coping expects God to solve the problems without the necessity of individual action. (I also call the latter the "Janis Joplin" approach, in tribute to her song "Mercedes-Benz," in which she asks the Lord to buy her a series of goods, including color TVs and a Mercedes-Benz.) Interestingly, Pargament showed that standard measures of religiosity correlate equally well with both types of coping strategies, but that collaborative religious coping is associated with better health outcomes and the deferring style with poorer ones.

Of course, all of this may be confounded with other variables such as social status. The deferring style might be reflective of individuals in groups of lower socieconomic status who may subscribe to a more fundamentalist religion. Michael R. Levenson (personal communication, 1998) has suggested that the more fundamentalist religions may also be associated with high levels of authoritarianism, which is characterized primarily by hostility—and the relationship between hostility and poor health outcomes is well established.

It could be argued that the deferring style may not necessarily reflect (a hostile) passivity, but could (with the right items) also reflect patience and trust. Given that many problems are self-limiting, a "wait and see" attitude may be appropriate under many circumstances. A friend of mine relates an illustrative anecdote. When he visited Mother Teresa in the 1970s, she was feeding a phenomenal number of people every day, as many as 5,000. When he asked where she got all that food, she shrugged her shoulders and said, "I don't know. Everyday, it just comes. Everyday, it comes from a different place, but—it always comes!" Certainly, we need to learn more about the different types of religious coping, for whom they are most effective, and under what circumstances they provide the most benefit.

TEACHING

Finally, I wanted to mention a few words about this book's usefulness in teaching. The book was set up to reflect interdisciplinary interests, and it is gratifying to see that instructors from several disciplines, including psychology, sociology, and social work, have started adopting this book as a text.

I had sequestered methodological issues in their own separate chapter, assuming that most readers might not find these all that interesting. To my surprise, however, many people have told me that the methods chapter has actually been the most useful one to them, as it clearly lays out the nuts and bolts of doing stress and coping research. When I teach, I often cover methodological issues first so that students will be better able to interpret the subsequent studies, a technique that other instructors might find useful.

CAROLYN M. ALDWIN, *September 1999*

References

Aldwin, C. M., Cupertino, A. P., Levenson, M. R., & Spiro, A. III. (1998). Childhood experiences and health outcomes in later life. *The Gerontologist, 38.* [Abstract]

Aldwin, C. M., Levenson, M. R., Cupertino, A. P., & Spiro, A. III (1998). Personality, childhood experiences, and drinking patterns in older men: Findings from the Normative Aging Study. *Proceedings of the Fifth International Congress of Behavioral Medicine*, p. 82.

Aldwin, C. M., & Sutton, K. (1998). A developmental perspective on post-traumatic growth. In R. G. Tedeschi, C. L. Park, & L. G. Calhoun (Eds.), *Posttraumatic growth: Positive change in the aftermath of crisis* (pp. 43–63). Mahwah, NJ: Erlbaum.

Aldwin, C. M., Sutton, K., & Lachman, M. (1996). The development of coping resources in adulthoood. *Journal of Personality, 64,* 91–113.

Almeida, D. M., & Kessler, R. C. (1998). Everyday stressors and gender differences in daily distress. *Journal of Personality and Social Psychology, 75,* 670–680.

Ickovics, J. R., & Park, C. L. (1998). Thriving: Broadening the paradigm beyond illness to health. *Journal of Social Issues, 54*(Whole Issue).

Kemeny, M. E., & Laudenslager, M. L. (1999). Beyond stress: The role of individual difference factors in psychoneuroimmunology. *Brain, Behavior, and Immunity, 2,* 73–75.

Kiecolt-Glaser, J. K., Page, G. G., Marucha, P. T., MacCallum, R. C., & Gleser, R. (1998). Psychological influences on surgical recovery: Perspectives from psychoneuroimmunology. *American Psychologist, 53,* 1209–1218.

Pargament, K. (1997). *The psychology of religion and coping: Theory, research, practice.* New York: Guilford Press.

Quas, J. A., Goodman, G. S., Bidrose, S., Pipe, M. E., Craw, S., & Ablin, D. S. (1999). Emotion and memory: Children's long-term remembering, forgetting, and suggestibility. *Journal of Experimental Child Psychology, 72,* 35–270.

Stone, A. A., Schwartz, J. E., Neale, J. M., Shiffman, S., Marco, C. A., Hickcox, M., Paty, J., Porter, L. S., & Cruise, L. J. (1998). A comparison of coping assessed by ecological momentary assessment and retrospective recall. *Journal of Personality and Social Psychology, 74,* 1670–1680.

Preface

This book has undergone an interesting evolution. In 1984 and 1985, I taught a yearlong seminar on health psychology, behavioral medicine, and sociocultural aspects of health at the University of California, Irvine. At the time, I thought it would be fairly easy to turn my lecture notes into a book that sought to integrate these various perspectives on health and adaptation. However, over the course of time, the book has evolved into one that focuses more exclusively on the coping process, for several reasons. First, there has been a huge growth in the field, and the lack of an integrative work on the voluminous materials published since the mid-1980s was very apparent. Second, I had taken on a lot of reviewing responsibility for the coping field for several journals, and it was clear that basic conceptual and methodological issues in stress and coping research needed to be spelled out. Very basic distinctions between emotional reactions, coping styles, and coping strategies were often confused. Further, many researchers neglected elementary methodological concerns such as the timing of the measures. This is not to say that there have not been many fine and first-rate studies in the field, but that the basic practical knowledge of conducting coping research clearly needed to be spelled out in more explicit detail to a larger audience.

More troubling was a growing "Balkanization" of the stress and coping field. Many researchers were taking absolutist stands on the "best" ways of conceptualizing and measuring stress and coping, in a manner that seemed to me detrimental to the field. There seemed to be almost a centrifugal force driving apart those researchers who preferred trait assessments of coping and those who preferred contextual approaches, or those who felt that "objective" life events measures were the "correct" approach as opposed to the "hassles" researchers who felt that this was the only approach that made sense, and so forth. It seemed to me that the old story of the "Elephant in the Dark" best typified the field and that understanding the elephant as a whole was far too important to get bogged down in debates about whether it resembled a pillar or a fan or a hose. Thus, I thought it was time for an integrative approach, one which attempted to dispassionately examine the pros and cons of all the myriad approaches in the area, identifying their strengths and weaknesses and specifying the circumstances under which the various approaches were more or less appropriate.

Having said this, I should add that we all have assumptions and preferences, and no one can pretend to be totally dispassionate. As will be readily apparent, my own personal predilection is for the interdisciplinary, transactional approach. To me, this is absolutely necessary for understanding human adaptation. However, it seemed that a distressing countertrend back to reductionism was becoming more apparent in the field, as witnessed by the demise of some interdisciplinary programs and the charge that personality and social psychologists are only "folk" psychologists who will one day be supplanted by "real scientists" who will one day reduce all meaning and consciousness to the (rather random) firing of neurons. Thus, I felt that it was time once again to reaffirm the transactionist paradigm and the centrality of meaning for human experience.

Finally, there have been a number of ideas that I have been mulling over since graduate school, including the importance of culture for coping strategies and the role that coping with stress plays in adult development. This book seemed to me an excellent forum in which to develop those ideas, and I am grateful for the opportunity to finally put them into writing.

There have been many influences in my life that have played an important role in the development of this work. My undergraduate training at Clark University imbued in me an understanding of the absolute necessity for a theoretical grounding in any psychological endeavor, as well as a healthy respect for the phenomenology of meaning. My graduate training in the Adult Development and Aging Program at the University of California, San Francisco, taught me how to think in an interdisciplinary and integrative fashion, as did my postdoctoral training in the Social Ecology Program at the University of California at Irvine. My stint as a graduate student on the Berkeley Stress and Coping Project steeped me in the arcana of stress and coping theory and research, and I have fond memories of the heated (and often stressful) debates between me and my colleagues on the project, including Jim Coyne, Anita DeLongis, Susan Folkman, Alan Kanner, and Catherine Schaefer. The director of the project, Richard S. Lazarus, did something rather unique in the annals of graduate training: While providing the overarching framework, he allowed the graduate students to conceptualize and conduct the research project. Although this inevitably led to much conflict, the lively and heated debates (as well as the inevitable mistakes) forced us to confront theory and method in an exhaustive manner and resulted in a very fertile and creative group. Many of the ideas presented in this book stem from my musings during this time.

Other individuals have played an important role in my professional development. Dan Stokols, currently Dean of Social Ecology at the University of California at Irvine, taught me how to write psychological theory. When I was a postdoctoral fellow, he asked me to write a book review. Through three different drafts, he taught me how to present and develop ideas. Subsequently, we wrote a theoretical article (Aldwin & Stokols, 1988) that in many ways was a direct precursor to many of the ideas presented in this book. Tracey Revenson, another postdoctoral fellow at the University of California at Irvine, taught me the importance of meticulous presentation. By helping Bob Ornstein with a book while I was a graduate student, I learned both the mechanics of such a task and that it was possible for me to write a book. Dave Chiriboga, Chris Kiefer, and Richard Suzman spent many hours with me in graduate school, showing me how to view the world from psychological, anthropological, and sociological perspectives. Ray Bossé, Associate Director of the Normative Aging Study in Boston, provided an "intellectual space" within the Veterans Administration in which my colleagues, Ron Spiro and Rick Levenson, and I could play with ideas. From our fertile and usually humorous banterings, I honed my ideas, developing statistical sophistication by working with Ron and increasing my knowledge of "front-end methodology" (i.e., theory and measurement assumptions) by working with Rick.

A number of individuals provided direct help with this book. Paula Schnurr of the National Center for Post-Traumatic Stress Disorder read through two drafts of this book, providing invaluable comments, suggestions, and encouragement, for which I am extremely grateful. My colleagues at the University of California at Davis, Professors Larry Harper, Emmy Werner, and Brenda Bryant, provided very helpful reviews of portions of the manuscript, as did Professor Benjamin Gottlieb of the University of Guelph. The graduate students in my class on Adaptation and Aging at the University of California at Davis also provided lively commentary, including Leslie Aldag, Jennifer Brustrom, Charles Go, Carolyn Hughes, Kathy Kelley, Laurie Nickel and Karen Sutton. Karen also provided indispensable assistance with the many computer searches and tracking down references, as did another research assistant, Kent Kiehl. My research assistant in Boston, Gina Chiara, very competently took over much of the day-to-day management of my project on stress, coping, and aging, freeing up time for me to work on this book. We also coded together more that 1,000 interviews over the course of three years, and our struggles in this endeavor provided a number of valuable insights into the coping process. Diane Gilmer and Becky Parker, my graduate students working on their theses at this same time, provided much humorous support by entering into our friendly competition regarding who would finish first. My editor, Seymour Weingarten, exhibited almost inhuman patience through the many years (and missed deadlines) of this project. I am especially grateful to him for taking a chance on a young scholar and for providing me with the opportunity to develop my ideas. My husband and colleague, Rick Levenson, provided steadfast support during this time, reminding me of the importance of completing this work when my resolution flagged (and not complaining too much of the numerous stacks of books and reprints distributed liberally around our house!).

Finally, I must credit the many years of financial support from the federal government. My undergraduate training was financed through student loans, work study, and Veterans Administration and Social Security benefits (the latter program sadly now defunct for college students), and my graduate and postdoctoral training was supported through fellowships from the National Institute on Aging and the National Institute on Child and Human Development, respectively. The National Institute on Aging also granted me a FIRST Award (R29-07465), which provided not only the resources for the Stress and Coping in Aging project, but also partially supported this endeavor. The importance of continuing federal support for academic training and research cannot be understated.

CAROLYN M. ALDWIN, *January 1994*

Contents

Introduction and Purpose of the Book

Thomas Kuhn (1970) demonstrated that, from time to time, paradigm shifts occur in science and society—that is, a fundamental assumption about the nature of the world changes. The ascendence of the germ theory of disease represents one paradigm shift, relativity theory another. I believe we are currently undergoing another paradigm shift—from causal reductionism to transactionism. Simply put, in causal reductionism the occurrence of an event is reduced to its underlying cause, whereas in transactionism the occurrence of an event is understood to arise from the mutual influence of a number of factors. This paradigm shift has profound implications, not only for research and clinical practice, but also for the very fabric of society and how we conduct our everyday lives.

This shift is occurring in many different branches of science. It is most noticeable in studies on the relations between the mind and body and those between the person and the environment; but other disciplines, including ecology and subatomic physics, are also shifting to a transactionist paradigm. I will argue in this book that research into the psychological and physical effects of stress, and how they are modulated by coping efforts, has been instrumental in effecting this paradigm shift in the psychosocial and biomedical sciences. A primary focus of this book will be on bringing together literature from a variety of fields that examine transactions, both between the mind and body and between the person and the environment, within the context of stress, coping, and adaptation research.

MIND–BODY TRANSACTIONS

In the 17th century, René Descartes proposed a fundamental dualism between mind and body. The mind was held to engage in abstract thought and language, which was separate and distinct from the operations of the body (Eccles & Robinson, 1984). This Cartesian dualism has been a cornerstone of the reductionist paradigm underlying the biomedical sciences. It assigned the study of the physiological workings of the body to science, and consideration of the mind and soul to philosophy. It was further assumed that, being distinct, the mind and the body were influenced by completely different factors and that very little communication occurred between the two.

Cartesian dualism was expressed in the disease model of illness, or the basic biomedical model (Virchow, 1863). This model, prevalent for the last 150 years, has held that illness results from external agents that disrupt the body's normal functions, such as bacterial and viral agents, toxins, and carcinogens of various kinds. Research focused on the mechanisms by which external agents damaged health and on how that damage could best be repaired. This model was later expanded to include disruptions caused by internal agents, that is, faulty genes.

A corollary assumption underlying the reductionist model has been that of unidirectional causality — that is, $a \rightarrow b \rightarrow c$. In biomedical terms, this means that illness is caused by exposure to an agent a that disrupts the biochemical functioning of system b that in turn leads to symptoms c. These symptoms can only be abated by restoring the functioning of system b, either by eliminating the offending agent from the body (e.g., through antibiotics) or by restoring the biochemical balance. This assumption about causality focused research on the basic biochemical constitution of the body, and the amount learned has been tremendous. In Kuhn's (1970) terms, this paradigm has been extremely successful in advancing knowledge.

But any assumption holds within itself the seeds of its own limitations. As more and more was learned about physiology and biochemistry, the complexity of that information vastly increased. It became readily apparent that a simple causal model was inadequate to describe many phenomena (von Bertalanffy, 1969). Because physiological regulation of different systems involves a highly complex series of feedback loops among multiple variables, more and more conditions and limitations were placed upon simple causal models. Although invading germs or bacteria may create a *necessary* condition for a particular illness, they may not be *sufficient* to create the illness — rather, disease results from a highly complex interaction between host systems and disease agents.

For example, it can readily be demonstrated that tuberculosis results when a person is infected with tuberculin bacteria, which causes inflammation and consequent scarring of organs, especially the lungs. Characteristic symptoms include fatigue and coughing up blood and sputum. Eventually death ensues, as more and more of the target organs become damaged. These symptoms can be alleviated by a course of antibiotics, proper nutrition, rest, and, if necessary, surgery to remove the damaged parts of affected organs. However, epidemiological studies of tuberculosis and other illnesses demonstrated that many more people had been exposed to or actually carried the bacterial or viral agents than came down with the disease, and the disease model had to be expanded to include the concept of *host resistance*—that everyone was not equally affected by an invading agent. Investigation of host resistance to this and many other diseases resulted in the discovery of the immune system, the enormously complex system by which the body can destroy invading agents, isolate and break down toxins, and help repair damage to organs. In many instances, disease symptoms actually represent the body's attempt to repel the invading agents rather than any active damage by the agent.

Thus, simple causal models of illness are of necessity coming to be replaced by highly complex models demonstrating interaction among multiple agents. As Kuhn (1970) pointed out, the more conditions and limitations that are placed upon a model, the more unwieldy it becomes, and the more likely it is to be replaced via a paradigm shift.

But this heightened understanding of the complexity of interactions leading to disease states was not sufficient to effect the paradigm shift from physiological reductionism to mind–body transactionism. One can study any organ system in finer and finer detail without having to abandon Virchow's (1863) model. It is only when one begins to study interactions *across* levels of analysis that reductionism breaks down.

In other words, simple causal mechanisms assumed closed systems, to use von Bertalanffy's (1969) terms. That is, there is a circumscribed number of variables that are internally interacting and are relatively immune to outside forces. For example, classical textbook descriptions of the circulatory system detail its components, such as the heart, veins and arteries, capillaries and arterioles, and its regulators, such as the sympathetic and parasympathetic branches of the autonomic nervous system (ANS). But, as one begins to study the circulatory system and how it becomes diseased in greater detail, it becomes readily apparent that the circulatory system is not a closed system but an open one—consisting of a large number of components which are influenced by external forces. The circulatory system interacts not just with the ANS but also with the central nervous system

(CNS), via the neuroendocrine system and the immune system. It is also influenced by an individual's behavior—what he or she eats, smokes, drinks, as well as whether or not and how he or she exercises. Other influences include the level of stress in an individual's life and his or her personality, cognitive style, and social relations.

Thus, the very tools provided by the medical model and physiological reductionism that allowed us to understand in greater and greater detail the workings of the body also uncovered the limitations of that paradigm. No organ system is a completely closed system. Rather, all are subject to regulation by the brain via the neuroendocrine and immune systems (Ornstein & Thompson, 1984).

However, the psychological sciences imitated the biomedical ones in expressing Cartesian dualism as unidirectional, physiological reductionism—that is, psychological processes could be reduced to their neurophysiological bases. In the most extreme statement of this point of view, the mind was viewed as an "epiphenomenon" of the brain. While many more complex models do exist in modern psychiatric theories of mental illness, the dominant tendency is still to ascribe causality to biochemical mechanisms. For example, if one finds that depressives who commit suicide have much lower levels of serotonin than nonsuicides, the standard procedure is to ascribe the suicidal behavior to that neurotransmitter imbalance and to treat depressive disorders by restoring the neurotransmitter balance through drugs. However, equally plausible alternative explanations include the possibility that the suicidal ideation creates the serotonin imbalance or that there are mutually reinforcing feedback loops between the two.

Elegant arguments that the mind is not reducible to the brain have been proposed by Eccles and Robinson (1984), based upon the neuropsychology and linguistics literature, and by Walker (1970), based upon physics. Although Popper and Eccles (1977) proposed the term "dualist–interactionism" to describe the relationship between the mind and the brain, the construct of transactionism may be more appropriate in describing this relationship. According to transactionists such as Lazarus (1966; Lazarus & Folkman, 1984) and Appley and Turnbull (1986), dualist–interactionist models are incomplete because they imply that two agents are mutually creating a phenomenon but nonetheless remain independent and unchanged. Transactionism, on the other hand, assumes that the two agents are not independent but are mutually affected by the transaction.

Figure 1-1 illustrates the difference between physiological reductionism, interactionism, and transactionism, using emotions as the dependent or caused phenomenon. In the top section, the arrow indicates that the brain causes the emotions. For example, serotonin is hypothe-

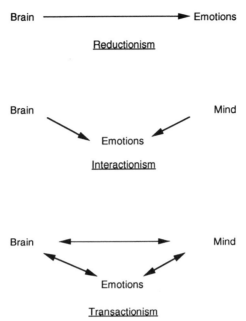

FIGURE 1-1. Comparison of physiological reductionism, interactionism, and transactionism.

sized to lead to depressive feelings, adrenaline to anxiety, noradrenaline to anger, and so on (Gray, 1971).

The middle part of the figure illustrates interactionism: that the brain and the mind (cognition) both affect emotions. Using stress terminology, one would say that the appraisal of a threat, combined with a genetic propensity to overproduce adrenaline, would result in excessive feelings of anxiety.

In transactionism, the dependent variable (in this case, emotions) in turn influences both the brain and the mind. Thus, through the medium of emotions, the brain and the mind *mutually affect one another*. From a transactionist viewpoint, the mind is no longer reducible simply to the workings of the brain, nor, as a colleague of mine once whimsically put it, is the brain a mere epiphenomenon of the mind. Rather, the state of mind influences the workings of the body, while the state of the body influences cognitive and emotional processes. Both can be changed as a result of the transaction. For example, continuing anxiety may affect both physiological functioning and appraisal processes.

Sperry (1993) suggested that this cognitive revolution in psychology has formed the basis for the current paradigm shift in the sciences in general. The seemingly simple addition of bidirectional arrows has enormous implications, not only for the manner in which science is conducted, but for much of everyday life. The body is no longer a mechanical device that sometimes requires repair. Psychological preparation for surgery, for example, may be as important to the healing process as the proper execution of the surgical procedure. People are now much more aware of the impact of psychological stress on their bodies, and may try to reduce that influence by a myriad of methods. In California, claims for stress-related disability or workman's compensation have increased dramatically in the last decade. On the other side of the equation, millions of Americans now avidly pursue physical fitness as a way of managing their psychological states. In short, the fabric of our lives has changed tremendously as a direct result of this paradigm shift.

A transactionist paradigm has greater implications also for the study of adaptation, which have not as yet been fully understood within psychology. It is extremely important for any scientific endeavor to examine its assumptions, understand their implications for how the world is thought to function, and formalize hypotheses. Studies of stress and coping form a laboratory, as it were, for examining the role of transactional processes in adaptation. Thus, an additional purpose of this book is to explore the implications of a transactionist paradigm for stress, coping, and development.

Two assumptions of transactionism are particularly relevant to stress and coping research. First, variables mutually influence each other, both within and across levels. If the mind and brain do transact, then, being regulated by the brain, organ systems are subject to influence by the mind, and, in turn, anything that affects the mind (e.g., society and culture). Thus, seemingly distinct levels of analysis— sociocultural, psychological, and biological—are all linked. Further, how a culture or society is structured has implications for an individual's physiological well-being, not only through the direct allocation of resources (Pearlin, 1989), but also through influencing characteristic psychological states and stress levels (Colby, 1987).

Second, transactionist models of necessity imply developmental processes, in that the focus of any transaction is change. Most stress theorists focus on the immediate situation and try to show, for example, how appraisal affects coping, which in turn affects both the outcome and appraisal processes. However, a transactionist model implies a strong possibility that both the mind and the body are altered as a result of their transaction. Theorists such as Schönpflug (1985) and Hobfall (1989) have implied this in their economic models of stress and coping as resource depletion–conservation. However, there is no reason to assume that a stress transaction has exclusively negative outcomes but rather may have positive ones as well, as is implied by Meichenbaum's (Meichenbaum & Cameron, 1983) stress inoculation theory and Dienstbier's (1989) construct of stress-induced "toughness." Aldwin and Stokols (1988) have presented various approaches to modeling change, whether positive or negative, short-term and long-term, which can result from stressful interactions.

PERSON–ENVIRONMENT TRANSACTIONS

Thus, transactionism has broad implications for the study of stress and coping in that it can link both environmental (e.g., sociocultural) and developmental perspectives to biomedical findings. Figure 1-2 presents the view of coping as seen from the reductionist, interactionist, and transactionist perspectives.

The top part of Figure 1-2 represents the reductionist, or stimulus–response (S-R), model of coping behavior. In this model, coping behaviors are viewed as simple responses to stressful environmental stimuli.

The middle part of Figure 1-2 represents the interactionist model.

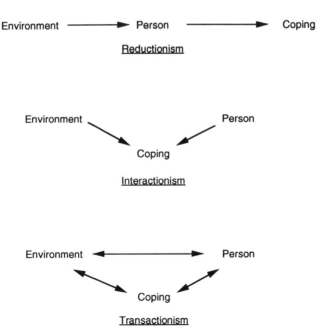

FIGURE 1-2. Comparison of reductionist, interactionist, and transactionist models of coping.

Coping is hypothesized to be a function of person and environmental characteristics. For example, the use of coping strategies is influenced by personality characteristics, such as emotionality (Bolger, 1990), as well as by the type of stressor or environmental demand (Mattlin, Wethington, & Kessler, 1990).

The standard transactionist point of view (see, e.g., Lazarus & Folkman, 1984) examines transactions only within the context of a single stressful episode. In this model, person and environmental variables influence appraisal, which determines the type of coping response. Coping outcomes, in turn, influence the appraisal process. Yet, inspection of the bottom part of Figure 1-2 suggests that coping outcomes not only influence appraisal processes within the stress context, but also may have effects on both the person and the environment. For example, how a person copes with a particular stressful situation may add to his or her coping repertoire or may alter a person's outlook on the controllability or uncontrollability of the environment (e.g., locus of control or explanatory style). Further, how an individual copes with a problem may alter the environment, affecting not only whether a particular problem is solved, but also whether and how the problem arises for other individuals. Legal action to resolve racial or sex discrimination cases, for example, may provide the means for other individuals to cope with similar problems. Thus, the implications of a transactionist viewpoint extend beyond the individual stressful context to wider developmental or social situations.

In stress and coping research, the environment has been viewed primarily in interactionist terms, that is, as a stimulus or source of stress, or less frequently as a source of resources for coping with stress (e.g., social support). However, a transactionist view suggests that the environment has a much more extensive role than simply its function as a stimulus or a resource. For examples, the role that the physical and social environments play in shaping coping strategies have received only scant attention (see, e.g., Mechanic, 1978; Thoits, 1986). Further, in most theories, coping is assumed to have some effect on the problem, but studies generally focus only on its effect on the individual's well-being. From a transactionist point of view, more attention needs to be paid to the effect of coping on the environment, whether its effect on the immediate problem or on others in the situation (DeLongis, Bolger, Kessler, & Wethington, 1989). If, as Mechanic (1978) so radically suggested, coping strategies are primarily a function of cultural patterns and institutions, then how an individual copes not only has an effect on the immediate problem, but also adds to the cultural repertoire of coping strategies (Aldwin, 1985).

ORGANIZATION OF THE BOOK

The book will explore the themes presented in this introduction from the perspective of the paradigm shift in the psychological and biomedical sciences. However, any paradigm shift is accompanied by much dissension and argument as various opposing factions argue for the status quo or for different directions of change. This dissension is obvious in the area of stress and coping. Rather than attempt to promote any one particular school or theory of stress and coping, we will take an "elephant in the dark" stance. That is, no one school or theory is complete and correct—the differing approaches all have strengths and limitations, and in some circumstances the approaches are not so much in conflict but are actually addressing quite disparate parts of the "elephant." By examining the historical context and conceptual assumptions underlying different approaches, we will attempt to clarify the nature of some of the debates in the field, and to show precisely where the conflict lies and how the differing approaches might be integrated, where possible.

It is also true that research methods have lagged far behind the theoretical conceptualization, especially in psychology. Thus, key methodological issues of relevance to both the conduct of research and its interpretation will also be considered. Again, rather than advocate any particular technique, we will discuss the strengths and weaknesses of the various ways in which stress and coping are measured and which techniques may be useful for differing research questions and contexts.

As with any scientific discipline, the field of psychology has gone down many blind alleys, in part because psychologists have made simplified assumptions for the sake of constructing theoretical models, but also in part because they have allowed their research—and to a certain extent, their clinical work—to become divorced from the realities of everyday life. In many ways, this divorce has been useful—the best of psychological research has often shown that "conventional wisdom" is markedly and decidedly wrong. But this divorce can also be responsible for pursuing assumptions down blind alleys, as when Watson tried to reduce thought to microscopic workings of the musculoskeletal system underlying speech or when Hull tried to reduce memory to muscle action. Thus, putting psychology into its everyday context is important not only as a check against wrong assumptions, but also as a didactic tool, a bridge for students to connect their own experiences to psychological theory.

These three concerns with theory, method, and relevance influence the structure of this book. Chapter 2 will discuss conceptual issues in stress research and why the construct of stress and how it is researched are important to our everyday lives. Chapter 3 will discuss the different definitions of stress and how the assumptions implicit in these definitions influence the type of research that is conducted. Chapter 4 addresses issues in stress measurement and methodology.

While the stress literature has been reviewed extensively, there have been surprisingly few exhaustive reviews of the coping literature; the subsequent chapters will attempt to fill that gap. Initially paralleling the construction of the chapters on stress research, Chapter 5 will address conceptual issues in coping research; Chapter 6 definitions of coping; and Chapter 7, the measurement of coping strategies. The Appendix will also include a partial, nonannotated list of coping measures, which should prove useful to both researchers and students. Chapter 8 will discuss some of the methodological and statistical issues in understanding the effects of coping, and Chapter 9 will review the literature on coping and health outcomes. Chapter 10 will present a brief look at how individuals cope with trauma.

A major limitation of stress research is that it has been almost strictly a psychological endeavor — that is, with few exceptions, the social and cultural contexts of stress and coping processes have been ignored. Chapter 11 will attempt to provide that perspective by reviewing the rather small body of research that demonstrates the interpersonal and social influences on appraisal and coping processes and that shows how work in medical anthropology might radically alter our view of how coping works.

This book will also place the study of stress and coping in a larger, developmental context. In part, this will be accomplished in Chapter 12 by reviewing the coping literature in special populations — children and the elderly. A larger, lifespan developmental perspective will be presented in Chapter 13. In our rush to document the negative aspects of stress, we may have overlooked its positive aspects — stress as an impetus for growth and development, and coping as the manifestation of a lifelong quest for greater mastery and understanding. Thus, Chapter 13 will review studies on the "anomalous" — positive — effects of stress. Chapter 14 will provide a summary of the various themes developed in this book and how they relate to the transactionist perspective espoused in this chapter. It will also examine deterministic versus nondeterministic models of adaptation.

In summary, within the field of stress and coping, this book will provide some insights into the nature of conceptual and methodological debates in the field, in order to allow researchers and students to best decide which particular approaches and assessment techniques are most relevant for them. In addition, integrating developmental psychology, especially adult developmental psychology, with an understanding of the nature of adaptation provided by stress and coping studies will enhance both fields. Adding a developmental perspective to studies of adaptation may provide an impetus to reconsidering the types of outcome measures that are used; adding an adaptation perspective to developmental psychology may provide greater insight into the role of the environment in promoting development, both in childhood and in adulthood.

CHAPTER 2

Conceptual Issues in Stress Research

The construct of stress is important on a number of levels. First, stress is intrinsically interesting, as a casual perusal of any bookstore, newspaper, or television news program indicates. Second, stress is highly relevant to psychosocial models of adaptation. As we shall see, a transactionist viewpoint subsumes many of the current models of mental illness. Third, stress is also relevant to biomedical models of adaptation, and may be transforming our notions of health, the maintenance of good health, and the treatment of illness.

INTRINSIC INTEREST

Stressful events are of almost unparalleled importance to people. For example, the evening news can be seen primarily as a means of transmitting information about stressful events—whether or not these events directly affect us. Television news focuses primarily on natural disasters, accidents and tragedies, economic dislocations, conflict between powerful individuals (generally politicians but sometimes movie stars or sports celebrities), deaths, crime, and punishment. Positive events are reported only rarely, and then often in the context of individuals who are struggling to overcome tremendous odds or handicaps.

A large percentage of our daily conversations focus on stressful events that happen to ourselves and others: deaths, divorces, job problems, car accidents, problems at school or work, illnesses (major or minor), and everyday "hassles" in general—missed buses, car problems, bureaucratic inconveniences, and the copying machine breaking down (again) at work. Certainly soap operas focus almost exclusively on the negative life events that happened to (or were provoked by) the characters.

One can only speculate on the reasons for this interest. Perhaps watching others struggling and grieving provides a form of catharsis, a way of discharging unhappiness and anger in a safe, nonthreatening context, as the ancient Greeks thought. Thus, it may be more comfortable to express anger over crooked politicians rather than to confront directly unethical practices in our own work contexts.

Perhaps interest in stress has an evolutionary function. McGaugh (1985) has demonstrated that heightened emotions enhance memory, that is, we are more likely to remember emotionally charged events. McGaugh has speculated that by remembering sources of trauma we may be more likely to learn from our mistakes and avoid dangerous situations in the future. Similarly, by attending to dangers and trauma that others face, we may learn of sources of danger in the hope of avoiding them or of vicariously learning about coping strategies, successful or unsuccessful, that others have used for dealing with problems.

Interest in stress can also be seen in a larger social context. Durkheim (1933) argued that emotional arousal in a group setting functions primarily to enhance feelings of community and group solidarity. Although usually applied to group rituals involving large crowds (such as football games), one could also argue that the arousal of emotion through news reporting of stressful events also can function to increase *communitas,* either directly or indirectly. For example, reports of major natural disasters also depict rescue efforts and directly invite participation by providing information on how the viewer can help (generally by providing money or goods to rescue agencies). At the very least, news reports of disasters provide a shared social context and topics of conversation for individuals in a community or nation.

Thus, the intrinsic interest in stress may stem from psychological, biological, and/or social causes. Whatever the reason, it is clear that stress, and how people cope with it, is intrinsically interesting for large numbers of people, both in the academic and general communities. Studies of stress have also had a major impact on psychosocial models of adaptation and on biomedical models of disease.

RELEVANCE OF STRESS TO PSYCHOSOCIAL MODELS OF ADAPTATION

Early models of mental illness focused primarily on internal processes as the source of psychological problems. Psychoanalysis, for example, related mental illness primarily to hidden or unconscious conflicts between the id, ego, and superego, stemming from early childhood fixation in psychosexual stages. Environmental events may trigger these conflicts, but the primary problem lies within the individual. Similarly, biomedical models try to relate symptoms to neurotransmitter imbalances, which are thought to be causal mechanisms underlying psychological distress. If a depressed person exhibits lower levels of serotonin, it is thought that the lack of serotonin causes the depressive symptoms. In both types of models, the cause or source of mental illness lies solely in the *individual's* makeup.

Sociologists and anthropologists, on the other hand, point to the major role that society and culture play in provoking both psychological distress and the way in which it is expressed. In other words, the origin of mental illness may lie, not so much within the individual, but within the environment, such as the social structure and the way in which strains are distributed within society (see, e.g., Totman, 1979). People who have marginal roles within a society, such as the poor, are more likely to exhibit signs of emotional and social disorder because of inadequate socialization to what are considered normative social roles and behavior (Howell, 1973).

Anthropologists point out that what constitutes abnormal behavior is a result more of cultural norms than of individual psychodynamics. What constitutes acceptable behavior in one culture may be considered abnormal and a treatable illness in another (Mead, 1928). To illustrate the importance of culture in the origin of mental illness, anthropologists also point to the existence of *culture-bound illnesses,* or disorders that are specific to particular cultures, such as running *amok* in the Philippines or "bear illness" among the Aleuts (see Kleinman, 1980). Thus, culture plays an important role in both the formation and expression of mental illness. (See Chapter 11 for further discussion of this issue.)

Models of stress and psychosocial adaptation can provide a link between these disparate viewpoints on the origin of mental illness. Stress models acknowledge the importance of environmental effects on mental health, but they also recognize that there are individual differences in vulnerability to stress. Thus, the onus for mental illness shifts from being solely the "fault" of the individual or simply a function of social roles and cultural norms to a recognition that there are multiple factors engendering psychological distress, some of which may be beyond individual control.

A good example of a causal environmental model of psychological distress is provided by Brenner (1973, 1979). Brenner related macro indicators of environmental stress, such as the unemployment rate, to macro measurements of psychological distress, for example, mental hospital admissions. Brenner found that a year after increases in the unemployment rate, admission to mental hospitals also increased. He concluded that social policies that result in increases in unemployment had adverse affects on the collective mental health status. Further, he proposed that the financial costs of such effects, as far as medical expenses and productivity losses are concerned, outweighed any financial gains derived from such manipulations of social policy.

However, others (Berg & Hughes, 1979; Spruit, 1982) pointed out that economic downturns did not necessarily causally increase psychological distress in the population; rather, poorly functioning individuals no longer had the "cushion" provided by a strong economy and were forced to turn to formal or institutional sources of support during hard times. For example, marginal employees, such as those with alcohol problems, may find themselves the first to be laid off during a recession. Thus, economic downturns may only reveal, not cause, individual distress (Catalano & Dooley, 1979).

Aldwin and Revenson (1986) examined this issue in a longitudinal-study of individual mental health during an economic recession. They found that neither model was complete. Rather, individuals in poorer mental health at Time 1 were more likely to be laid off during a recession, and these individuals also had more adverse reactions to economic stress. Nonetheless, economic stress resulted in increased psychological distress, even controlling for Time 1 mental health status. In other words, some individuals are more *vulnerable* to stress. For whatever reason, they may be more likely to experience stressful events, and they may also have more adverse reactions to them. Nonetheless, environmental stress may have negative impacts in even the strongest individuals.

Curiously, those higher in psychological distress at Time 1 seemed most distressed about the economy, even if they personally had not lost a job. And in keeping with the transactionist viewpoint, it should not be forgotten that individuals' attitudes toward the economy can deepen economic downturns. When consumer confidence is low and individuals save rather than spend money, their failure to buy goods can result in a further loss of jobs, as manufacturers cut back in response to decreasing economic demands. Thus, economic hardships can lead to feelings of consumer vulnerability, leading to the downward spiral of an economic decline.

The construct of *vulnerability to stress* is very important, because it can tie together a number of different approaches to adaptation. Vulnerability to stress may be either a function of personal or social characteristics. Personal vulnerabilities may stem from an individual's history, such as exposure to traumatic situations earlier in life or a biological propensity to manic depression. Thus, this construct can encompass both psychodynamic and biological approaches to mental health. However, vulnerabilities may also stem from one's position in the social environment, such as poverty, racism, few economic opportunities, and the like (see Pearlin, 1989). As in the economic stress study cited earlier, these characteristics may make it more likely that some individual will experience stressful events. They may have particularly adverse reactions to them and may take longer to recover. The construct of vulnerability nonetheless acknowledges that personal problems may indeed be due to one's social or physical environment and thus can also encompass environmental approaches to adaptation.

A corollary construct is *goodness of fit*. The same environment might be stressful to some persons because it requires capacities or preferences that they do not have, yet it might be a comfortable or challenging environment for other individuals who have those capacities or preferences. For example, one person may prefer a work environment with predictable, routinized tasks and might find it difficult to deal with a more unstructured environment with chaotic, unpredictable tasks. Another person may find the first environment boring and the second challenging and stimulating. Thus, the construct of goodness of fit recognizes the importance of *contextualism:* that there are very few causal absolutes in psychology. Environmental situations need to be evaluated by their effects on individuals, and individual adaptation needs to be understood in the context of particular environmental situations.

Thus, a stress and coping approach to psychosocial adaptation acknowledges the contribution of both the person and the environment, and seeks to understand the particular environmental context and personal skills and resources that provide for optimum adaptation. Further, a transactionist viewpoint emphasizes that the person and the environment are not independent contributors to stress and coping but, rather, mutually affect one another for good or for ill.

RELEVANCE OF STRESS TO BIOMEDICAL MODELS OF ADAPTATION

For over 2,000 years, philosophers and scientists have been debating whether the mind and body are separate or integrated entities and, if integrated, the nature of the relationship (see Eccles & Robinson, 1984).

The study of the effects of stress on physical health has been a great impetus to systematically investigating how the mind and body interact.

As discussed in Chapter 1, the standard medical model of disease, as enunciated by Virchow (1863), specified that individuals become ill due to external agents. Any illness can potentially be cured if the agent is known. A person gets a cold, a heart attack, or cancer, because an external agent (a germ or other toxin) infects the body, producing structural and physiological changes that are solely responsible for all symptoms. If the agent is identified and neutralized, the body recovers.

However, the study of stress suggests that this model may be simplistic. Not everyone who is exposed to a cold virus or tuberculosis becomes ill. Rather, the state of an individual's health reflects a dynamic interaction between environmental forces and physical resilience. There is increasing evidence that the latter is in part affected by psychological states: Undue stress or worry may increase vulnerability to illness (Cohen, Tyrell, & Smith, 1993). There is also evidence that the lack of close relations with others, or lack of social support, can increase the rates of morbidity and mortality (House, Landis, & Umberson, 1988).

The idea that stress can affect physical health is not at all new. In folk wisdom, people have been said "to die from a broken heart" or "to work themselves into an early grave." Similarly, people can be "scared to death," or fright can "turn your hair grey overnight." What is new is that we are beginning to discover the physiological pathways that mediate between stress and health. These pathways involve interactions between the neuroendocrine and immune systems. The field that studies these relationships is called *psychoneuroimmunology* (Ader, 1981; Ader, Felten, & Cohen, 1991).

Psychoneuroimmunology seeks to understand the relationships among the psyche, or mind, the neuroendocrine system, and the immune systems, as well as the role of these relationships in maintenance of health or vulnerability to illness. Figure 2-1 presents what might be called a basic, or generic, model illustrating the principles of psychoneuroimmunology. Stress activates negative affect, or emotions. We may feel angry, sad, or frustrated in response to a stressful episode. There are well-known physiological changes that accompany such emotions. Our hearts pound, we may breathe heavily (increase in heart and respiratory rates), we may turn beet red or deathly pale (changes in peripheral vasodilation), or we may feel "butterflies" in the stomach (decrease in parasympathetic system activation). Decades ago, both William James (1890) and Walter Cannon (1915) recognized the link between emotions and the neuroendocrine system, although they dif-

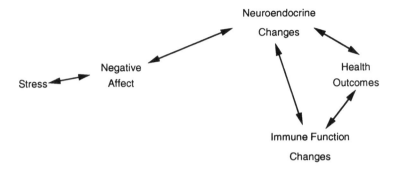

FIGURE 2-1. Basic psychoneuroimmunology model.

fered somewhat in their beliefs about causal directionality between the mind and the body (see Chapter 3). Thus, Figure 2-1 shows all relationships as bidirectional.

Figure 2-1 also shows stress and emotion affecting the immune system. Ader and Cohen (1982) made a remarkable discovery. Using classical conditioning techniques on laboratory mice, they paired a noise with injections of a drug that suppressed the immune system functioning. After a few trials, they then injected saline instead of the drug. The immune function still became suppressed when the mice heard the noise. Ader had demonstrated a stimulus–response association between the perception of a noise and immune system responses. In other words, the immune system was capable not only of learning, but also of responding to a psychological stimulus.

After that initial discovery, dozens of studies have demonstrated intimate links between the mind, the brain, and the immune system (for a review see O'Leary, 1990). For example, there are receptor sites for neurotransmitters and catecholamines on immune cells such as T lymphocytes (Smith, 1991). This suggests that the immune system is hard wired, so to speak, to respond to the mind and that this is not an accident but something that evolved for a reason.

From Cannon's (1915) point of view, it makes perfect evolutionary sense that the neuroendocrine system would respond in the manner that it does to strong emotion and stress. The "fight–flight" response, extreme activation, is extremely adaptive in that it allows an organism to respond more vigorously in stressful situations, to fight harder or to run faster. We've all experienced this: "I was so scared! I've never run so fast in all my life!" Stress may also increase beta endorphin levels, which may block the experience of pain, and allow people to function even while badly injured. However, why is it adaptive for the immune system also to respond to stress and emotions? Are we meant to become ill if we get upset?

This is a conundrum only if the effects of stress are understood solely in the context of immune system suppression. Stress also *activates* the immune system, at least initially (Monjan, 1981). Such activation is highly adaptive in that it may temporarily prevent a person from becoming ill at a time that calls for increased performance. (I have often observed that students get colds *after* final examinations, seldom *during* them.) If injured, an activated immune system can help to prevent infection and can also assist in repairs. Thus, immune system activation may be an integral response to adaptive challenges; and suppression may occur only later, after the stressful episode has passed, or in situations of chronic stress (see Chapter 13).

Thus, in order to respond optimally to challenges and threats, there must be a synchronized activation of the mind, the neuroendocrine and immune systems. Note that it is assumed in the field that emotions are the "glue," as it were, that ties the whole system together. As shown in Figure 2-1, stress is assumed to activate the emotions, which affects the neuroendocrine system, which in turn affects the immune system. Together, these influence the overall state of our health. However, these models may be simplistic. Work by Baum and his colleagues (Baum, Fleming, & Singer, 1983) on the Three Mile Island disaster has shown that the occurrence of stress can affect both neuroendocrine and immune system function independent of its emotional impact. Cohen et al. (1993) also found that the influence of stress on susceptibility to a cold virus did not appear to be mediated through negative affect. Either individuals are not accurately reporting their emotions, perhaps due to repression, or there exist other pathways between stress, and the neuroendocrine and immune systems. Thus, Figure 2-2 demonstrates alternative pathways, which may be interesting to investigate.

In summary, the study of stress is highly relevant to understanding biomedical adaptation. It is revealing how intimately the mind, the neuroendocrine system and the immune system are related, which suggests that a more holistic or multifactorial approach to understanding physical well-being is needed. It also provides support for the old Roman saying, *Mens sana, mens corpora,* or a healthy mind, a healthy body.

STRESS AS A UNIFYING CONSTRUCT

The most common complaint about the stress field is that the construct of stress is very amorphous. As we shall see in Chapter 3, different

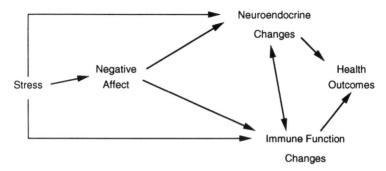

FIGURE 2-2. Modified psychoneuroimmunology model.

researchers use varying definitions of stress, depending upon their field of work and assumption system. Some, such as Kasl (1983), have gone so far as to suggest that the construct is so vague and so amorphous that it should be discarded.

Alternatively, it can be argued that the varying definitions of stress exist precisely because it is a very important construct with ramifications across a variety of endeavors. Different fields and philosophical traditions have come up with their own approaches to defining stress. Stress is a multifaceted and overdetermined phenomenon with ties to anthropology and sociology; developmental, personality, social, clinical, community, and environmental psychology; physiology and medicine. While this may create a certain amount of vagueness as the definition crosses disciplinary boundaries, it also provides an unparalleled opportunity for integrating different disciplines. While it is unlikely that a psychosocial Einstein will discover the "unifying field theory" of the behavioral and social sciences, the construct of stress does provide a common ground that can integrate scientific approaches in a variety of fields.

Thus, the construct of stress provides a framework in which the interplay between environmental, psychological, and physical factors can be seen. It thereby provides a bridge linking many different areas of scientific and clinical endeavors, thus providing a broader and more comprehensive understanding of human adaptation within a transactionist framework. As such, it may be one of the most important constructs in the clinical and social sciences today.

CHAPTER 3

Definitions of Stress

T he term "stress" is in such common usage that, at first glance, its meaning seems straightforward and in little need of definition, except perhaps for some minor clarifications here and there. After all, we all know what stresses us, what it feels like to be stressed — or "stressed out," in common parlance. Indeed, the *Oxford English Dictionary* assures us that the term has been in use since at least the 18th century. The problem is, of course, that the term has been in such common usage that it has taken on a variety of meanings. For example, it is both a noun and a verb. As a noun, "stress" can refer to external events or to an internal state. Similarly, the verb "stress" can be active, as in "to stress", or passive, as in "to be stressed."

If the term "stress" is understood to refer to external events, what type of events does it refer to? Should only negative events, such as being unemployed, be considered stressful, or can positive events, such as being promoted, also result in stress? Are only major events stressful, or can minor incidents also be troubling? Is stress to be understood as only those events that have negative consequences, or can stressful events sometimes have positive consequences? If the term refers to internal states, do we mean psychological states, as in emotional distress, or physiological ones?

Note that some researchers use the term "stressor" to refer to external events and use the term "strain" to refer to internal stressful states (Pearlin & Schooler, 1978). From a transactionist viewpoint, however, this distinction between external and internal states is hard to justify, given the importance of cognitive appraisal processes in the perception of stress.

Further, many disciplines have studied one aspect or another of stress — ranging from the biological sciences, such as physiology, biochemistry, and neurophysiology, through the psychological sciences, such as psychoanalysis, personality, learning theory, developmental psychology, and social ecology, to the social sciences, such as anthropology, sociology, and military history. Not surprisingly, the referents to the term "stress" vary across the fields, adding to the confusion. Studies of stress have included such diverse topics as men who are under battlefield conditions; mice that are rotating slowly on a drum; commuters who are languishing in traffic jams; pigs that are being shipped to market; students who are taking exams; people who are working on bomb squads; workers on assembly lines; the effect of drought on trees; massive dislocations of whole populations; and so on. It is not surprising that some have called for abandoning the term altogether, reasoning that by seeming to apply to almost everything, "stress" really is too amorphous a term and really does not apply to anything (Kasl, 1983).

For a number of reasons, this criticism of the term "stress" may be tantamount to throwing the baby out with the bath water. First, most researchers are quite precise about what they mean by "stress" in specific studies. Physiologists conducting studies on animal models of stress are almost always interested in the particulars of stress as a physiological state, focusing on the minutiae of neuroendocrine and immunological reactions. With notable exceptions, psychologists and sociologists generally concentrate on the definition of an external occurrence and on the individual's emotional reaction to it. Second, the fact that studies of stress are conducted at different levels of analysis should be cause for hope rather than despair. As mentioned in the previous chapter, stress can a common point for discussion across a number of disciplines, hopefully providing a pathway to integrate these disciplines. Indeed, the new field of psychoneuroimmunology is an attempt to do just that.

Although it is widely used, the term "stress" is not applied in a vague or ill-defined way. Nor is it a reified construct, an idea created by academics with little concrete referent to the real world. Rather, *stress refers to that quality of experience, produced through a person–environment transaction, that, through either overarousal or underarousal, results in psychological or physiological distress.* As we shall see, this overarching definition of stress incorporates most of the elements that researchers have used for identifying and studying the effects of this phenomenon.

COMPONENTS OF THE STRESS PROCESS

In order to sort through some of the confusion surrounding the use of the term "stress," Mason (1975) identified three definitions of stress, or three ways in which the term "stress" has been used. Stress can refer to (1) an internal state of the organism (sometimes referred to as "strain"); (2) an external event (or "stressor"); or (3) an experience that arises from a transaction between a person and the environment. Table 3-1 presents the various components of the stress process, based loosely on Mason's categorization. Note that the table should by read only as a set of sequential columns; sympathetic activation can attend trauma or chronic role strain; a hassle may be short-term or chronic, and so forth. The table is meant primarily as a heuristic device to indicate the enormous complexity of the stress process.

As indicated in Table 3-1, stress as an internal state of the organism refers both to physiological and emotional reactions. Studies of physiological reactions to stress focus on the peripheral and central nervous systems, as well as neuroendocrine and immune system function. While the common assumption is that stress has negative physiological effects, it would be more accurate to perceive stress as having an activating effect, which at times can be positive as well as negative, depending upon various personal and contextual factors (see Chapter 13).

Emotional reactions to stress generally refer to negative feelings such as anxiety, anger, and sadness, although shame, guilt, or feeling bored may also be considered stress reactions (Lazarus, 1991). While the focus in stress research is usually on negative affect, some attention has been paid to positive affect, generally in the form of *opponent processes*—that is, positive emotional states that arise as a sort of backlash to negative ones, as when a parachute jumper feels elated

TABLE 3-1. Components of the Stress Process

Strain		Stressor		Transaction	
Physiological reactions	Emotional reactions	Types of stress	Temporal dimensions	Cognitive appraisals	Intensity
Sympathetic activation	Negative affect	Trauma	Duration	Harm	Weak
Para-sympathetic suppression	Emotional numbing	Life events	Rapidity of onset	Threat	Moderate
	Positive affect	Aversive physical environments	Linkage	Loss	Strong
Other neuroendo-crine stimulation suppression		Chronic role strain		Challenge	Ambiguous
		Hassles		Benign	
				Concern for others	
Immuno-suppression–enhancement				Nuisance	

after initial feelings of terror (Solomon, 1980; see also Chapter 13). Emotional numbing, however, can also occur and is common with trauma or highly stressful life events such as bereavement or being diagnosed with a terminal illness.

[The second type of definition of stress refers to the external environment.] The earliest studies of stress focused on major trauma, such as combat and natural disasters. This characterization was later expanded to include major life events such as marriage, divorce, bereavement, or being laid off of or starting a new job. Other researchers have focused on noxious environmental characteristics such as noise, overcrowding, or pollution. Others prefer to focus on more common problems, such as the chronic role strain of a bad marriage or being impoverished, while some examine the hassles or daily stressors of everyday life.

There are a number of temporal dimensions of stress that deserve greater study, such as its duration, its rapidity of onset, and its linkage or spread. The animal literature indicates that the physiological effects of stress may be very different depending upon whether the stressor is short-term, chronic, or intermittent (Dienstbier, 1989), while the studies on bereavement suggest that the suddenness of death might also affect the severity of its negative effects (Parkes & Weiss, 1983). Finally, a stressor might have a limited, easily delineated effect, or it might start a chain reaction of events that reaches across domains. This chain reaction is termed "linkage" (Pearlin, 1989). For example, loss of a job could lead to long-term economic problems, which in turn could lead to a divorce, which in turn could lead to estrangement from children, and so forth.

Finally, stress can be characterized as an experience arising from transactions between a person and the environment, especially those transactions in which there is a mismatch between an individual's resources and the perceived challenge or need. In this schema, an individual's cognitive appraisal of stress—the recognition of harm, loss, threat, or challenge—must be present for any emotional or physiological reactions to occur (Lazarus & Folkman, 1984). These researchers have focused on how stress is perceived, or appraised, on its perceived characteristics (e.g., threat, harm, or loss), and on the severity of the problem.

Most (although not all) researchers would agree that these are the major components of the stress process. However, there are some fundamental disagreements between different schools of thought. These disagreements generally fall into one of two categories. First, regarding stress as an organismic state, researchers often disagree about whether there are general or specific reactions to stress—that is, whether all stressors evoke one general reaction or whether different stressors evoke specific reactions. Second, researchers emphatically disagree about the nature of causal directionality across the categories—that is, they disagree about which comes first: cognitive, emotional, or physiological reactions to stress. For example, do we first react physiologically to stress, then emotionally, or do emotional reactions drive both the physiological and cognitive processes? In addition, researchers also disagree about causal directionality between a person and the environment. Does the environment cause emotional and physiological reactions, or does an individual's internal state alter his or her perception of the environment and somehow evoke problems?

This section will review the major debates in the field concerning the conceptualization of stress using the framework that Mason (1975) first delineated. We will attempt to provide additional insight into various debates and, where possible, suggest means by which differing positions can be reconciled.

STRESS AS A STATE OF THE ORGANISM

Think of how your body might feel just before a big exam. Your face might be flushed or very pale, your palms might be sweaty, your hands might be trembling a little, and your mouth might be dry. These are *peripheral* nervous system reactions. You might also have "butterflies" in your stomach, your heart might be pounding, and you might start hyperventilating. These are *autonomic* nervous system reactions. Both are mediated by the actions of the sympathetic and parasympathetic nervous systems (see Table 3-2), in conjunction with the endocrine system (see Figure 3-1), hence the term *neuroendocrine* stress reactions.

TABLE 3-2. **Effects of the Autonomic Nervous System**

Sympathetic nervous system
  Increases blood pressure, heart rate, respiration rate, and perspiration
  Increases blood sugar and blood clotting
  Dilates pupils
  Causes piloerections (goose bumps)
  Decreases saliva, mucus, and gastrointestinal motility
  Diverts blood from intestines to brain and striated muscles

Parasympathetic nervous system
  Controls digestion
  Maintains and conserves bodily resources
  Decreases blood pressure, heart rate, respiration rate, etc.
  Generally opposes sympathetic activation but sometimes acts in consort

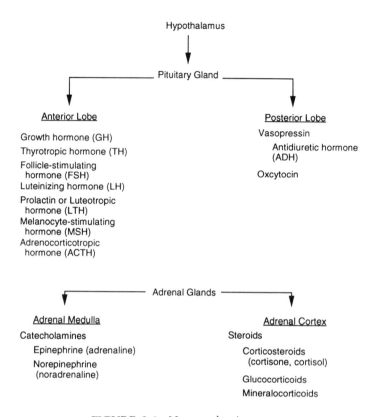

FIGURE 3-1. Neuroendocrine system.

Now think of how you might feel during final exams week. You might have a cold or gingivitis (a gum inflammation). Your allergies or ulcers might get worse, or you might develop a rash. These reflect *immune* system disturbances, also a common reaction to stress.

Thus, organismic responses to stress can generally be divided into two related categories: neuroendocrine and immunological. This section will briefly describe these physiological reactions to stressors and will also address two major debates within this field. In the study of stress and the neuroendocrine system, the first debate concerns whether there are general or specific physiological reactions to stress, that is, whether the body responds similarly to different types of stress or whether specific stressors evoke very specific patterns of response.

The second debate concerns issues in causal directionality in the stress–response chain. As we shall see, since the inception of this field, researchers have been arguing about whether emotional or physiological arousal is primary in stress reactions. By contrast, the field of psychoneuroimmunology is so new that the major debate is whether the immune system does react to psychological stress in a clinically meaningful fashion.

Neuroendocrine Responses to Stress

If you examine the functions of the sympathetic nervous system listed in Table 3-2, it is fairly obvious that increased arousal of the sympathetic nervous system prepares an organism for action. Blood is diverted from the intestines and other vegetative activity and transferred to the brain and the striated muscles. Blood pressure, heart rate, and respiration rate increase, allowing more oxygen to flow to the brain and muscles. The increase in blood sugar provides more energy, and the increase in blood clotting defends against cuts. These changes enable greater physical and mental effort on the part of the organism. (Piloerection is important for furred species. Hair standing on end makes a cat, for example, look much larger and intimidating, and also provides protection against bites.)

Walter Cannon (1939) named this type of sympathetic nervous system arousal the "fight–flight" reaction. In response to a threat or stress, the fight–flight reaction makes it possible for an organism to more effectively meet such challenges, through mobilizing mental and physical abilities. People often find that they run much faster when being chased than when out for their morning jog; athletes talk about "getting pumped up" or "getting the adrenaline flowing" to achieve peak performances.

Indeed, that is exactly what happens. As early as 1915, Cannon showed that when cats are exposed to barking dogs, epinephrine or adrenaline is released into their blood streams. Cannon hypothesized that the perception of a threat activates the thalamus (now we know it is the hypothalamus), which stimulates the pituitary gland to release hormones that activate the adrenal glands, which lie on top of the kidneys (see Figure 3-1). The adrenal medulla, or center, releases epinephrine (adrenaline) and norepinephrine (noradrenaline), which stimulate sympathetic nervous system activation — hence, the fight–flight reaction. Once the threat is removed, parasympathetic activation returns the body to *homeostasis* by decreasing blood pressure, heart rate, and respiratory rate, returning the body to a vegetative state that promotes gastrointestinal activity.

The effect of a sudden sympathetic nervous system arousal on someone with underlying cardiovascular disease may lead to a stroke or myocardial infarction (heart attack). However, prolonged sympathetic nervous system arousal can lead to serious physical problems and death in even relatively healthy individuals. Cannon described the case of an Australian aborigine who was cursed by a local "witch doctor" and who died a few days later of no obvious organic cause, such as disease. Cannon termed this phenomenon "voodoo death" and thought that it derived from overactivation of the sympathetic nervous system. Essentially, increased blood pressure decreases circulating blood volume by forcing liquids out of the vascular system and into the surrounding tissues. If this process goes on long enough, the blood volume is eventually insufficient to sustain adequate blood pressure levels, the arterioles dilate in an attempt to increase blood flow, and blood pressure can drop dramatically, leading to shock and cardiovascular arrest. This reaction may be aggravated by lack of food and drink (aborigines so cursed may stop ingesting food and liquids) but, nonetheless, is a direct effect of stress. Thus, one can be "frightened to death."

Cannon believed that any threat resulted in the fight–flight reaction and that such a reaction is a *general* response to any stress, physical or social. He believed that the body responds to all threats in a similar manner, *whether or not that manner is immediately relevant.* That is, we respond with the same sympathetic activation to negative performance evaluations from our supervisors as our ancestors did to carnivorous predators. In reacting to sudden physical threats, it makes a great deal of sense for the body to be able to run away very quickly, or even to challenge the predator with enhanced strength (and blood clotting ability). However, the same physiological response is not generally appropriate to social and verbal challenges (although increased blood flow to the brain should—but does not always—help with witty repartees). Physical violence is not an appropriate response to employers' chastisements (although work-related violence is unfortunately on the rise).

Dubos (1965) argued that the necessity to suppress direct physiological response to modern challenges results in *diseases of adaptation.* For example, increases in blood pressure and blood clotting, without the physical release of actually running or fighting, may eventually result in hypertension and cardiovascular disease. Thus, Dubos believed that the current epidemic of cardiovascular disease has resulted in part from the body's response to verbal and social challenges as if they were direct physical threats without the attendant release from physical activity.

Hans Selye's (1956) "physiology of dirt" expanded on Cannon's flight–fight proposal in two ways. First of all, Selye focused attention on the corticosteroids, which are released by the adrenal cortex, or top layer of the adrenal glands. He also expanded on Cannon's homeostatic process by describing three stages in reaction to stress. The first, or alarm, stage is similar to Cannon's fight–flight reaction but involves the adrenal glands as well as the hypothalamic–pituitary axis. However, Selye noticed that some organisms became inured to the stressor. In the second stage, adaptation, there is a return to physiological homeostasis, or perhaps augmented functioning. In the third stage, exhaustion, the organism may fall ill or die if the stress continues.

The models of Cannon and Selye are also similar in that they posit general or universal reactions to stress. Thus, heightened sympathetic reaction will occur regardless of whether the stressor is a physical predator or a college exam or whether the organism being stressed is a man or a mouse. More recent researchers, however, have suggested that there are more specific reactions to stress, which can vary depending on the stressor or the individual.

Specific Reactions to Stress

In many ways, the entire field of psychosomatic medicine is predicated upon individual differences in reaction to stress. Alexander (1950) proposed that different emotional states underlie different psychosomatic illnesses. For example, heart disease was thought to be related to underlying chronic patterns of hostility, while asthma involved unconscious anguish due to separation from the mother. Different types of environmental stress could result in particular emotional conflicts, which in turn provoked specific under- or overarousal of particular systems, eventually leading to organic problems.

Given the difficulty in establishing the presence of underlying unconscious conflicts, this psychosomatic theory developed the "weak organ" theory—namely that stress resulted in different illnesses, depending upon the physiological (genetic) weaknesses of the individual (see Wiener, 1977). In this model, stress is thought to result in either heart disease or asthma, depending upon the constitutional weaknesses of the individual. For example, individuals high in hostility exhibit greater increases in blood pressure under stress than those low in hostility, thus providing a possible mechanism through which hostility can result in heart disease (Hardy & Smith, 1988).

Work by Lazarus and his colleagues (reviewed in Lazarus, Averill, & Opton, 1974) have suggested that there are individual differences in physiological reactions to stress. They investigated the effect of stress on end organs, or the outward manifestations of sympathetic arousal. These include heart rate, respiratory rate, and galvanic skin response (GSR), which reflects the amount of perspiration on the skin. They found individual differences in the patterning of responses. For example, some individuals' heart rates increased in response to stress, whereas other individual's heart rates decreased though they perspired more. While sympathetic arousal did occur, the manifestation of this arousal varied across individuals. Thus, there may be individual differences in the pattern of physiological reactions to stress.

Further, there is some evidence that different types of stressors may evoke different physiological reactions. Mason (1971) subjected rats and monkeys to different types of stress, including hunger, inadequate nutrition, and cold. He found that there were "stressor profiles," such as specific neuroendocrine reactions that varied depending on types of stress, and concluded that reactions to stress were specific, not general.

Summary

In a very real sense, the approaches that emphasize general and specific reactions to stress are complementary rather than competing. Stress does involve mobilization of the hypothalamic–pituitary axis and the adrenal system. However, within that general framework, there may be variation due to individual differences in patterns of reactivity or to stressor characteristics. Which approach is correct — or, more precisely, appropriate — depends upon the specific stressors or responses to stress under investigation. Different types of problems or stressors require different levels of analysis.

For example, obtaining very precise neuroendocrine profiles in reaction to stress may be nearly impossible in a field setting. Confounding factors such as sleep patterns, nutrition, and activity level cannot be controlled. In such settings, more general measures of sympathetic nervous system arousal may be more appropriate. However, more precise physiological measurements may be necessary for studies that seek to define mechanisms between personality, stressors, and specific disease outcomes, such as hostility and coronary heart disease. Nonetheless, stress clearly affects the neuroendocrine system, and it is through that pathway that it may also affect other bodily functions, such as the immune system.

Immune Responses to Stress

The immune system is an extremely complex mechanism that regulates the body's reaction both to external threats and to internal malfunction (for overviews of this topic, see Ader et al., 1991; Guttmann et al., 1981). External threats include bacteria, viruses, parasites and toxins; internal threats consist of malfunctioning cells. "Antigen" is the common term for the protein, generally on the surface of the cell, that serves to identify the invader.

One of the great mysteries of the immune system is that it learns to differentiate between self and other. Once the immune system has learned to recognize an external invader, it somehow modifies its specific components to react to that specific antigen. For example, bacteria proliferating in the blood stream may be recognized by the immune system as a foreigner and then attacked. Viruses cannot proliferate on their own, but work by taking over the DNA or RNA of a cell to manufacture copies of themselves. Usually this results in a change on the surface of the cell membrane, which alerts the immune system to the invader. However, the AIDS virus is particularly deadly because not only does it take over an immune system component, the T cells, but it hides within the cell and does not appear to make easily recognizable membrane changes.

Further, the immune system has a memory. Once a specific type of immune response is learned, it remembers which components are necessary for combating the antigen, and it will manufacture more of that specific component when challenged. This is one reason why young children seem so susceptible to every infection that comes along—their immune systems are literally learning the "vocabulary" of bacteria and viruses, and until they have been exposed to a particular type of bacteria or virus, they will not have the appropriate antibody in their repertoire (unless they are nursing and can utilize their mothers' immune defenses).

Vaccinations work by administering either a dead or very weak version of a bacteria or virus so that a child's immune system can learn to make the correct antibodies without much risk of the child becoming seriously ill. Some vaccinations, such as gamma globulin shots for hepatitis, work by directly providing the immune system with copies of the appropriate antibody (IgG). However, viruses can mutate very rapidly, and the immune system must always be developing new antibodies for the mutations, which is why one needs to get a flu shot every year. Bacteria can also mutate rapidly, and the overuse and incorrect use of antibiotics may result in drug-resistant strains of bacteria. If a person does not take the full complement of antibiotics, for example, all of the bacteria may not be killed, and the surviving ones will be more drug-resistant. Further, if a particular strain of a bacteria or virus is provided with very hospitable *vectors,* or hosts, it can develop into a much stronger (or more virulent) version (Whiteside et al., 1993). For example, the homeless are very hospitable vectors for tuberculosis (TB). Due to nutritional deprivation, loss of sleep, and stress, the immune systems of the homeless are often weakened. The TB virus is airborne, and being exposed to coughs in a crowded shelter is often a perfect environment for the transmission of TB. Due to lack of medical care, the homeless may not seek treatment until the TB is fairly far advanced, and their chaotic living conditions may make it difficult for them to consistently take their antibiotics for the requisite number of months to completely destroy the infection. Some public health officials worry that our neglect of the health and well-being of the homeless may result in a dramatic increase in particularly virulent forms of TB (Villarino, Geiter, & Simone, 1992).

Thus, the immune system has to be constantly learning to recognize new enemies and manufacture new antibodies. However, errors can arise in learning, and the immune system may attack normal cells, resulting in autoimmune diseases such as rheumatoid arthritis. Sometimes viruses manufacture antigens that are very similar to a naturally occurring protein, and the immune system may get confused and attack a "good" protein. It is thought that multiple sclerosis (MS) and adult onset insulin-dependent diabetes mellitus (IDDM) are due to invading viruses that generate antigens that the immune system confuses with the nerve sheaths (in MS) or the beta cells that manufacture insulin (in IDDM). Thus, the viruses can disable an organism by getting the immune system to attack a crucial function.

There are a great many components to the immune system, and researchers are still identifying subcomponents. However, these components are generally categorized into two broad divisions: *humoral immunity,* which includes antibodies or immunoglobulins, and *cellular immunity,* which includes a variety of cell types that either directly challenge invaders (or malfunctioning cells) or mediate humoral immunity.

Antibodies

There are five major types of antibodies or immunoglobulins: IgA, IgD, IgE, IgG, and IgM. (I use the acronym MADGE to remember these, despite the contradiction in order of presentation.) Note that there are also many subtypes of each antibody. Antibodies are complex protein chains manufactured by plasma cells and lymphocytes, which are found in many parts of the body. Antibodies are generally specific to particular antigens, although if the molecular shape of antigens are similar enough, some *cross-reactivity* may occur. Sometimes an antibody may react to more than one antigen; this type of reaction is called *multispecificity.*

Antibodies generally work by agglutination—clumping together antigens—to help clear antigens from the body. Antibodies may also help by identifying antigens, or pointing them out to the cellular components, which then destroy the invaders by lysing, or splitting open, the invaders' cells.

Cellular Immunity

There are many different cellular components of the immune system. Mast cells, eosophinils, and macrophages generally work by surrounding the invading agent and destroying it. Two major classes of lymphocytes are B cells, which manufacture antibodies, and T cells, which are more generally involved in cytotoxicity. While both T and B cells derive from precursor cells in the bone marrow, T cells are matured in the thymus.

There are subsets of T cells. Two of these have figured prominently in stress research. CD4, sometimes known as helper T cells, function primarily to heighten immune response by helping B cells to identify and destroy antigens. CD8, also known as suppressor T cells, serve to dampen immune reactions. This is important because the immune system, like the neuroendocrine system, needs to maintain some sort of homeostasis. Too vigorous a response by the immune system can lead to autoimmune problems. Also, many of the symptoms that we commonly associate with an illness are actually immune responses to the invader. For example, the fevers, aches, runny nose, and lethargy commonly associated with colds are actually side effects of the actions of the immune system against the invading virus. Allergic reactions and asthma are caused by an inappropriate proliferation of IgE. Thus, the ratio of CD4 to CD8 cells may be better indicators of the healthiness of the immune system rather than of the absolute level of any one component. Remember that AIDS has its devastating effect by destroying T cells, which leaves the individual vulnerable to a host of diseases, as mentioned earlier.

Natural killer (NK) cells have been receiving increasing attention as an important immune system component. It appears that NK cells have a surveillance function to fight against tumor proliferation, and low levels of NK cells have also been associated with chronic virus infection and autoimmune disease (Whiteside, Bryant, Day, & Herberman, 1990). By a currently unknown mechanism, NK cells have the capacity to identify cells that are mutating into tumor cells. By destroying these cells, NK cells help fight against cancer. Depending upon the circumstances, precancerous cells arise very frequently, and thus a weakened NK cell system can have disastrous consequences.

Immune System Assays

There are two basic kinds of immune system assays, structural and reactivity measures. Structural assays refer to counts of the number of particular types of immune system antibodies or cells and constitute the most common and reliable way to assess immune function (Virella, 1993). However, simple counts of B and T cells may not be good indicators of immunocompetence; it may be more important to determine how well these cells are functioning. B cell functioning is generally determined by how many antibodies they produce when stimulated by mitogens (usually PHA or conA—hence, the term "conA proliferation assay"). Researchers determine what proportions of cells NK cells can lyse, and also examine CD4/CD8 reactivity. However, reactivity may be hard to quantify consistently, and some of the assays may be not only less than reliable but also subject to lab drift.

Stress and Immune Function

The relationship between stress and immune system functioning is complex, but stress and other psychosocial factors have been related to the functioning of various components of the immune system, including antigens, CD4/CD8 ratios, and NK cells (for reviews see Ader, 1981; Ader, Felton, & Cohen, 1991; Aldwin, Spiro, Clark, & Hall, 1991; Kaplan, 1991; Kemeny, Cohen, Zegans, & Conant, 1989; Kiecolt-Glaser & Glaser, 1989; O'Leary, 1990). Further, not every stress-related perturbation in immune function results in illness, and experimentally creating a stress–immune system–illness chain has proven difficult (Kaplan, 1991)—partly due to the difficulty of getting permission to expose human subjects to infections. However, Cohen, Tyrrell, & Smith (1993) conducted a carefully controlled experiment in which different types of stress were related to the "success" of a viral infection (how much the cold virus proliferated after exposure) and cold symptoms. However, most of the work, especially in humans, is correlational instead of causal—and thus must be viewed with caution.

While the mechanisms through which stress affects the immune system are not clearly understood at this point, the central nervous system and the immune system have complex, bidirectional relationships; and there is evidence, at least in animals, that the brain monitors immune system processes (Dunn, 1989). Given that the various components of the immune system need to communicate in order to function, it is not surprising that there are receptor cites for neurotransmitters on immune system cells. (Neurotransmitters may be more aptly named "communication peptides," since they are found in nearly every organ in the body and do not seem to be limited simply to transmitting neuronal commands.) Further, changes in the immune system may also have cognitive and psychological effects (for reviews see Dunn,

1989; Smith, 1991). Thus, stress-induced emotions, neuroendocrine functions, and the immune system may aptly be examined in a transactional framework.

STRESS AS AN EXTERNAL EVENT (mostly STRESSORS)

Historically, stress has been viewed as a noxious external stimuli impinging upon the organism. For millennia it has been common knowledge that people could die from stressful events or lifestyles. We say that someone was "scared to death," "died of a broken heart," or "worked himself into an early grave." External sources of stress may be either physical or sociocultural.

Physical Stressors

These include both trauma, which threatens immediate bodily harm (such as speeding cars, tornadoes, or fires) and aversive environmental conditions, which may have subtler but nonetheless harmful effects, such as pollutants, noise, and the like. A "sick building" is a good example of a subtle physical stressor. In buildings in which the windows are sealed, workers may be exposed to low levels of harmful chemicals such as formaldehyde (common in carpet backings and office furniture), paint residues, cleaning compounds, or fumes given off by copying machines, which may not be immediately noticeable but can result in headaches, irritated eyes, rashes, and increased susceptibility to viral infections. Migraine headaches can be triggered by flickering from improperly shielded fluorescent lights, and central heating and cooling systems that decrease humidity levels may result in irritated mucous membranes that in turn lead to nose bleeds and greater susceptibility to respiratory infections. Poor ventilation can also increase the concentration (and, thus, virulence) of infectious agents. Further, poorly designed work stations may result in mechanical stress leading to eye and muscle strain; typists, computer operators, supermarket checkers, and musicians may be particularly susceptible to repetitive motion injuries such as carpal tunnel syndrome.

An interesting study by Evans and Jacobs (1982) has suggested that physical stressors such as poor air quality may interact with social ones to result in increased symptomatology. Evans found that residents in the Los Angeles area who lived in highly polluted neighborhoods had more symptoms when they were exposed to stressful life events than did individuals who lived in areas with cleaner air.

Sociocultural Stressors

While stressful life events such as job loss or divorce are often seen by psychologists as occurring randomly or perhaps arising from an individual's psychological problems, sociologists are more likely to see the source of life events as embedded in the social structure. Pearlin (1989) has argued that stress arises as a function of the distribution of social resources, as well as an individual's status and roles. A lack of social resources either increases the probability of a stressful life event or enhance its stressfulness once it occurs. For example, having little disposable income can force a student to buy an older car with high mileage. This car may be more likely to break down (a stressful event), and the student may have little money to repair it, forcing him or her to make hard choices between rent, food, and car repair (to say nothing of leisure), thereby increasing the event's stressfulness. Furthermore, stressful life events may be linked; in Pearlin's terms, a primary event may lead to a secondary stressor. For example, our student may lose a much-needed job due to a lack of reliable transportation. Note that secondary stressors are not necessarily less stressful than primary stressors and may even be more distressing depending upon the circumstances.

One of the earliest studies of stress in the external environment was conducted by Calhoun (1962), who examined the effect of crowding in rats. He allowed rats to reproduce in a severely restricted environment. Under these conditions, social pathology among rats increased, typified by various measures of aggression, including fighting and rape. More important than crowding per se was restricted access to such basic necessities as food and water. Increased violence was most prevalent when there was only one narrow access to food; when multiple pathways to the same amount of food were provided, the negative effects of crowding were decreased. In other words, low levels of resources (as long as they are sufficient to sustain life) are not necessarily stressful; inequities in the distribution of resources are more problematic.

The structure of social roles may also provide opportunities for stress. Pearlin (1989) identified four types of chronic role strain. Role strain can consist of overload, as in having too much to do. Interpersonal conflict within roles (arguments with a spouse, child, or coworker) may be a source of role strain, as is interrole conflict (e.g., juggling parenting and work roles). Role captivity (such as being unable to quit an onerous job due to financial obligations) may be particularly problematic, as is role restructuring (e.g., a daughter who becomes a caretaker for her parents). There are also ambient strains, like living in poor neighborhoods, especially violent ones, and strains that may arise from informal or elective roles (arguments with friends or fellow members of a social organization).

Pearlin (1989) emphasized that the social and personal context is instrumental in determining the outcome of a stressor. Not all role exits or restructuring may be stressful. Exits from roles that are very stressful may be very positive. Leaving a job that one hates or a difficult marriage are good examples. Thus, stressors cannot be evaluated without a knowledge of both the social and the personal context.

Temporal Characteristics

There are a number of temporal dimensions of stress that deserve greater study: for example, its duration. As indicated earlier, the animal literature suggests that the physiological effects of stress may be very different depending upon whether the stressor is short-term, chronic, or intermittent (Dienstbier, 1989). This was brought home to me when I was piloting a combat exposure scale on men in the Normative Aging Study. The scale had been developed on the basis of the experience in Vietnam, and the length of exposure item only went up to about 24 months. One merchant marine veteran whom I interviewed explained that he had been at sea for over five years during World War II, and while he had only seen action a few times, the threat of German submarines was ever present. He was not sure how to respond—the amount of actual combat exposure was only about two weeks, but exposure to the threat of combat lasted over five years. Thus, this sailor had been subject to low level chronic stress punctuated by intermittent intense stress. Was this sailor more or less stressed than a Vietnam veteran who had served an 18-month tour of duty with moderate combat exposure? Did the intermittency allow for recuperation and restoration, as Dienstbier (1989) would hypothesize, or did the chronic, day-after-day, low-level stress of always having to be alert for U-boats lead to a state of exhaustion, as Selye (1956) might hypothesize?

Rapidity of onset is another interesting stress parameter. On the one hand, we know that the anticipatory phase of a problem is very stressful—waiting to be laid off, for example. A commonly voiced opinion is that it would be better to die quickly with a heart attack than to linger slowly with cancer. Yet, being able to anticipate a problem also means that we can prepare for it, both emotionally and practically. While experienced parachutists generally have only mild cardiovascular reactions to a jump, Epstein (1983) related the case of a professional who had fallen asleep in the plane. When he jumped, his heightened cardiovascular reactions resembled those of a novice. Epstein speculated that the nap resulted in a lack of preparation time; because the parachutist did not engage in his normal coping behavior, his reactions were more severe. Interestingly, a woman who runs a hospice told me that after going through their training program, volunteers expressed a preference for dying of cancer, which would allow them to prepare for their death and say goodbye to loved ones.

If the onset of a problem is too gradual, however, it may interfere with normal appraisal processes. Ecologists have coined the term "slow catastrophes" to refer to problems — such as overpopulation and the greenhouse effect — that begin very gradually but may have disastrous consequences in the long run. Thus, the temporal patterning may have very profound implications for both coping behavior and the effect of a stressor.

STRESS AS A TRANSACTION BETWEEN THE PERSON AND THE ENVIRONMENT

From Lazarus's point of view (Lazarus & Folkman, 1984; Lazarus, 1991), depicting stress merely as an external event ignores individual differences in the perception or appraisal of stress. What is stressful for one individual at one point in time may not be stressful for another individual or the same individual at another point in time. For example, losing a job may have a very different meaning or very different consequences for a teenager versus a middle-aged man. If a teenager loses at job at a fast-food restaurant, chances are very likely that he or she can easily find another at a different establishment. A middle-aged factory worker or manager, however, may have a very difficult time finding other work. Thus, the same life event, job loss, may be more or less stressful depending upon its individual and social context.

Thus, stress can also be seen as a combination of environmental demands and individual resources. In this model, cognitive processes are central. According to Lazarus, the perception of stress, or its *appraisal,* depends upon the extent of the environmental demand and the amount of resources that an individual has to cope with that demand. Theoretically, the person first recognizes that there is a problem and then determines what resources are required to meet that problem. Stress results from an imbalance between the requirements of the environmental situation and one's ability to cope with it. For example, for most people, a car breaking down is somewhat stressful, a more or less minor occurrence, which requires either the knowledge and ability to fix the car oneself or sufficient money to hire a mechanic to fix it. But for a homeless family who is living in the car, its mechanical failure may be an insurmountable problem creating extreme stress.

In the Lazarus and Folkman (1984) theory, five types of appraisal are generally identified: harm, threat, loss, challenge, or benign. However, there are other types that may also be important, such as concern over others' problems (Aldwin, 1990). In pilot testing a stress and coping instrument, I found that some hassles were simply nuisances—an annoying but harmless rattle in a car, for example. The other dimension of appraisal that is important is its severity, which may in part be related to what Folkman and Lazarus (1980) termed "secondary" appraisal. How severe a problem is thought to be is a function of the (mis)match between environmental demands and individual resources, as mentioned earlier.

Sociologically inclined researchers often object to the primacy of appraisal in this model. They point out that there are objective, external circumstances (such as the unemployment rate) that do not depend upon an individual's perception. Further, centering stress upon cognitive appraisal gives too much credence to rational cognitive processes and implies that stress is solely dependent upon subjective perception without much regard to objective factors (see Hobfall, 1989, for a review of this position).

However, it is mistaken to believe that a cognitive appraisal approach neglects environmental considerations. On the contrary, it seeks to understand how stress is a product of both the environment and the individual. Obviously, some environmental characteristics are so overwhelming as to result in a nearly universal experience of stress (as in major traumas such as wars, devastating earthquakes, etc.). However, most environments are more ambiguous and more subject to individual interpretations. Without an understanding of how this interpretation occurs, it is impossible to understand an individual's experience of and response to stress.

Hobfall (1989) tried to substitute the concept of resources for that of appraisal to derive a more "objective" understanding of stress. However, the comprehension of internal and external resources is, by definition, an appraisal process. Indeed, Lazarus defined secondary appraisal as the assessment of resources. (I suspect that there are profound individual differences in the appraisal of the availability of resources. It may be that adept copers are people who can divine the existence of resources that others may not be able to perceive and/or utilize.) Thus, substituting "resources" for "appraisal" does not turn a cognitive stress theory into an "objective," noncognitive one (*pace* Hobfall).

It could be argued that the centrality of appraisal processes may apply more to social than to physical sources of stress. Most people will react without thinking to an immanent source of physical danger of which they are at least minimally aware (e.g., jumping out of the way of a speeding bus). Further, subtle stressors, such as being in a sick building, may have negative effects without the individual even being aware of their source. However, it is also true that, given repeated exposure, individuals may learn to appraise immanent sources of physical danger very differently as they develop specific coping strategies. People drive on highways every day, in which the slightest wrong move can (and often does) result in death; Boston pedestrians learn to avoid without effort seemingly homicidal Boston drivers; parachutists come to love stepping out into empty space thousands of feet above the earth. It is also likely that a person with a chronic respiratory ailment such as asthma may find even very subtle problems with sealed buildings intolerable. And, as in Calhoun's experiment, the perceived access to physical resources may be more important than the actual level of resources, even in rats. Thus, appraisal processes may also play a role along with physical stressors.

Another major criticism of the appraisal model of stress lies in its emphasis on the primacy of cognition, as opposed to emotion. Several theorists have argued that emotions are primary—that one becomes aware that a problem exists because of one's emotional reaction to an event.

THE ROLE OF EMOTIONS AND COGNITION IN REACTIONS TO STRESS

James–Lange versus Cannon

The James–Lange hypothesis (James, 1890; Lange & James, 1922) held that the body's emotional (visceral) reaction to stress occurred prior to and resulted in conscious responses. We run, therefore we are afraid; we fight, therefore we are angry. Cannon (1929), however, believed that neural processing was primary (with pathways originating in the thalamus). Cannon pointed out that the viscera have very slow reaction times and that the perception of and reaction to stress takes place very quickly. Therefore, neural (e.g., mental) processing must occur first.

Schachter and Singer (1962) attempted to test the James–Lange hypothesis by injecting subjects with adrenaline in order to stimulate sympathetic nervous system arousal and then by putting them in either an aversive or a congenial environment. Subjects who had been injected with adrenaline showed stronger responses to the environment—and, thus, were said to "label" their emotions in the context of the environment. However, attempts to replicate this study have generally had little success (Marshall & Zimbardo, 1979).

Lazarus versus Zajonc

The James–Cannon debate has its modern counterpart in a similar debate between Lazarus (1982, 1984) and Zajonc (1984) as to whether cognitive or emotional reactions are primary in stress reactions. Lazarus argued that the cognitive processes of appraisal are central in determining whether a situation is potentially threatening or harmful, and thus cognition determines both the perception of stress and the individual's emotional reaction to it. Zajonc, however, argued that simple awareness should not be equated with cognition and that emotional reaction to stress occurs before and may be at odds with cognitive reactions.

The debate hinges on the definitions of emotion and cognition. Zajonc's implicit definition of cognition is similar to logical, conscious thought, whereas Lazarus's definition is closer to general awareness. It is true that one does need to become aware of a stress before one reacts to it. However, is that awareness primarily emotional or rational? In other words, do people become angry or afraid first and then impute a reason for their feelings, or do they define and recognize a situation as threatening and then emotionally react to it?

Put in these terms, it becomes clear that the answer is, both. On some occasions, we may react first and think later; on other occasions, we may not become upset until we fully realize the threat in the situation.

Implicit in this debate is the assumption that consciousness is unitary and that all neurological processing is sequential: *first* emotions, then cognition, or vice versa. However, current work in neuropsychology makes it abundantly clear that consciousness is not unitary—there are often multiple and parallel processing systems which may be more or less independent of each other (Gazzaniga, 1989; Ornstein & Thompson, 1984). If emotional processing is mediated more by the right hemisphere, and rational processing by the left hemisphere, then it should not be surprising that both mechanisms are involved and that one can inform the other in a noncausal sequence.

In short, critiques of the centrality of appraisal in stress theory are correct when they argue that people are not rational beings who coldly analyze environmental conditions and come to logical conclusions. However, I believe that this is a caricature of the appraisal process. The awareness of a stressful condition (whether it is harm, loss, threat, or challenge) may arise in a number of ways. We may intuit a problem, as when "a little voice" tells us that something isn't quite right, that danger is imminent, and that we must stop and find out what is wrong. We may also use logical analysis to determine that the present course of action will eventually result in harm of some sort. At other times it seems as if the body can react before the mind has a chance to recognize the danger, as when a soldier "instinctively" dodges a blow before he's even aware that one is coming. To my mind, all of these are examples of the appraisal process, whether it is conscious or unconscious, rational or arational. It seems to me a truism that a person must be aware of a problem before he or she begins to cope with it—however that awareness is defined, or comes about— again, with the exception of the imperceptibility of some nonetheless noxious physical stressors.

Indeed, Lazarus's recent work (1991, p. 153) underscores the widely held proposition that there are indeed two modes for imputing meaning to a situation, "one *conscious, deliberate, and under volitional control,* the other *automatic, unconscious, and uncontrollable*" (emphasis in original). Further, these two modes are understood to operate in an often simultaneous and parallel fashion, and may in fact be contradictory. This may be best illustrated with phobias. An individual may consciously be aware that accidents in an elevator or airplane are statistically unlikely but nonetheless be consumed with dread. Thus, cognition and emotion inform each other. People may use logical reasoning to calm themselves, or they may develop elaborate cognitive justifications (rationalization) for overblown emotional reactions.

SUMMARY

There is little argument about the various components of the stress process (see Table 3-1). Rather, differences among stress researchers arise primarily because of the varying degrees of emphasis put on individual components and because of disagreements about the causal ordering of the components. Sometimes the debate is healthy, and forces us to rethink our positions with greater clarity. At other times, however, feuds arise, passing on through generations of academics, usually over the ordering of two little boxes in a labyrinthine maze of boxes depicting what are actually rather similar views of the stress process.

A transactional framework is integrative, because it acknowledges the importance of all of these components. Stress is, indeed, partially a function of the environment, but it is also partially a function of the internal characteristics of the individual (whether psychological, hormonal, or immunological). It makes little sense to ignore one at the expense of the other. Rather, it is of greater importance to trace out the manner in which these transactions occur. Further, it is quite likely that, depending upon the context or the individual, differing components may assume more or less significance. The recognition of bi-directionality between the components also renders the exact causal sequencing less important. The important point is to understand clearly which components of the stress process are important in a given context and to make sure that the appropriate concepts and tools are being utilized, whether in research or clinical work.

Design and Measurement Issues in Stress Research

The sheer amount of research on the effects of stress in the past quarter century has been extraordinary. A review by Vingerhoets and Marcellissen (1988) counted nearly 10,000 articles published in the decade between 1976 and 1985 alone. Obviously, a review of all of this literature is beyond the scope of this book. However, there are a few general observations that can be made. Further, a number of extremely crucial research design issues have emerged, an understanding of which is essential to conducting adequately designed studies on stress. Finally, the different types of stress instruments will be briefly reviewed.

GENERAL OBSERVATIONS

It has been established, beyond doubt, that stress is associated with negative health outcomes in almost a bewildering array of illnesses, ranging from backaches and headaches to heart disease and, perhaps, cancer. (For reviews of the health effects of life events for various illnesses, see Brown & Harris, 1989a; Baum & Singer, 1987; Everly, 1989; Vingerhoets, 1985). The mechanisms for this broad spectrum effect of stress almost certainly lie within the neuroendocrine and immune systems, but the specific details are as yet still being worked out. A number of general observations, however, can be made.

Contrary to Holmes and Rahe's (1967) initial hypothesis, positive stressful events per se do not appear to have adverse health effects. Most research shows that negative or undesirable rather than positive events precipitate symptoms (Rabkin & Streuning, 1976). In fact, there are some studies suggesting that positive events may buffer or mitigate the adverse effects of negative or undesirable events, although there is a great deal of inconsistency in the findings (Reich & Zautra, 1981). Thoits (1983) cautioned that undesirable events may be better predictors of psychological symptoms, but total events may be better predictors of physical health symptoms. This may be because the so-called "positive" events may have many negative characteristics. A promotion or a new job may initially entail an increase in work load, or a new marriage may get off to a rocky start. In general, going through a negative event, like a divorce, may have more serious health consequences than experiencing a positive event like marriage.

Further, stressors that are thought to be uncontrollable are generally more distressing than those that are more likely to be under an individual's control (Reich & Zautra, 1981). For example, quitting a job may be less stressful than being fired. Similarly, initiating a divorce from a spouse may be less stressful than being divorced (Wilder & Chiriboga, 1991). The uncontrollability of the event may explain why natural disasters and other types of trauma are so stressful.

Perhaps the most important thing to remember about stress research is that the relations between stress and health outcomes, although broad in scope, are relatively modest in effect sizes. The correlations between stress and health outcomes are typically in the .20s and .30s. Overall, this is a positive finding, because it suggests as a species that we are rather resilient to stress. Unlike some laboratory rats, we tend not to become ill at the slightest bit of adversity!

However, the relatively modest relation between stress and health increases the difficulty in establishing a definitive causal relation between a stressor and a particular disease, because not everyone who experiences stress will become ill, and if they do become ill, the type of illness developed may depend upon the degree of exposure to pathogens, genetic propensities to disease, nutritional status, and so forth. It is much easier to establish a relation between stress and flare-ups of existing conditions, such as rheumatoid arthritis (Revenson & Felton, 1989), than it is to implicate stress in the etiology of a new illness (but see Cohen, Tyrrell, & Smith, 1991).

DESIGN ISSUES IN STRESS RESEARCH

There are additional problems to be considered in the design of any stress and health studies. First, what is the timing of the event under study, and what is the particular health outcome? Any specific disease, especially chronic illnesses such as heart disease or cancer, may take decades to develop. How reasonable is it to propose that a particular stressor may affect this etiology? Unless, of course, stress can be seen as a trigger that helps to precipitate full-blown disease from underlying preclinical pathologies, in which case it would be reasonable to expect a relation between stress and disease, if—and only if—there existed such pathologies. Similarly, it is also unreasonable to expect that illnesses with relatively short incubation periods, such as colds, will be greatly affected by an event that could have occurred up to a year earlier, unless that event has ongoing ramifications for day-to-day existence (which many do). Thus, for any study it is critical to consider issues regarding the timing of the stressor and the probable etiology of the particular illness under study.

The second major issue for consideration is whether the appropriate types of stressors have been identified for the particular age or ethnic group being studied. The inappropriateness of items to particular populations may lead to incorrect conclusions about the relation between stress and health outcomes in various groups. For example, an early review by Paykel (1983) found little relation between stress and health among the elderly, primarily because the types of events then studied were more relevant to younger groups than to older ones. Only when age-specific inventories were developed did the relation between stress and health emerge (Aldwin, 1990). Given that life stage, social structures, and cultural values may determine both the occurrence of particular types of stressors and the ways in which various events are perceived (See Chapters 9 and 10), it is imperative that the stress measure used in any given research project be both culturally and developmentally appropriate.

An additional issue that has as yet to be resolved is whether the effects of stress on well-being are cumulative (i.e., additive) or multiplicative. Most stress research assumes that stress is cumulative: There is a direct, linear increase in symptoms, negative affect, and so forth, with incremental increases in stress. This is indicated by the fact that we sum the number of life events checked or add up the ratings and then correlate them with an outcome measure. However, it is entirely possible that the effects of stress are multiplicative. That is, having two life events may multiply the stress effects by more than a factor of two. Early work by Rutter (1981), for example, found that most children could cope readily with one major stressful event, such as the death of a parent. However, the death of a parent in conjunction with other stressful circumstances, such as poverty or mental illness in the remaining parent, often proved overwhelming. (See Aldwin, Levenson, & Spiro, 1994, for a corroborating example of the nonlinear effects of combat exposure on mental health in later life.)

It is equally possible that stress may have an asymptotic effect, that is, after three or more stressors, the increase in symptoms would reach its maximum possible level. The point is that we simply do not know what the dose–response curve is between stress and various health outcomes, nor do we know how that curve varies among individuals, although recent studies by Brown and Harris (1989b) and Surtees (1989) have begun to address some of those issues.

Even the duration of stress effects is a matter of some debate. The general wisdom holds that the psychiatric effects of stressful life events usually dissipate within 6 months to one year (Depue & Monroe, 1986; Norris & Murrell, 1987), while the effects of hassles dissipate within a day or two (DeLongis, Folkman, & Lazarus, 1988). However, some of the trauma literature suggests that posttraumatic stress disorders may linger for decades, as with Pearl Harbor survivors (Wilson, Harel, & Kahana, 1989) and World War II prisoners of war (Page, Engdahl, & Eberly, 1991).

Much of the work in stress research has been directed toward the conceptualization and measurement of stress and, to a large extent, in overcoming barriers in the larger scientific community concerning the physiological effects of psychosocial phenomena. Thus, it is not surprising that such elemental questions as dose–response and timing of stress effects have not as yet been definitively delineated. In fairness, it should also be acknowledged that stress effects are highly probabilistic phenomena, being very dependent upon a myriad of contextual and personal factors. Thus, it literally may not be possible to develop clear-cut curves. At best, one can determine population risk rates, such as the temporary increase in deaths due to coronary heart disease (CHD) during the first year of widowhood documented by Parkes and Weiss (1983). However, it is also understood that generalizing from a population risk to an individual risk is not possible, at least not without committing the ecological fallacy.

PROBLEMS IN CAUSAL DIRECTIONALITY

One of the thorniest design issues in stress research remains the interrelations between stress, personality, and health. Despite the strong evidence that stress is related to health, assessing the causal direction-ality in this relation remains problematic. On the one hand, higher stress scores may reflect rather than cause poor health. Someone with a chronic, disabling illness, for example, may well experience more hassles in the struggle to do everyday chores; more role strain in rela-tion to finances, work, and marriage; and may even be subject to more life events. On the other hand, a serious problem in studies that rely primarily on self-reports of stress and health may be that a third fac-tor, personality style, is confounded with both types of assessment and creates a spurious association.

Both of these problems with causal directionality have resulted in a series of classical interchanges in the literature. Lazarus and his colleagues (DeLongis, Coyne, Dakof, Folkman, & Lazarus, 1982; Kan-ner, Coyne, Schaefer, & Lazarus, 1981; Lazarus & Folkman, 1984) have consistently argued that subjective appraisals of stress are more effective in predicting health outcomes because they take into account the *meaning* of the event to the individual. Individual characteristics (i.e., beliefs, values, and commitments) and contextual factors (i.e., the timing and duration of the stressor) may conjointly influence the degree to which any particular event may be stressful.

Due to a variety of factors, being laid off a job provides an excel-lent example of the lack of uniformity in stress effects. For example, the degree to which being laid off is stressful may depend upon per-sonal factors such as age and commitment to the lost job (e.g., losing a job at McDonald's when one is 16 years old is a lot less stressful than losing a managerial position when one is 50 years old). Or los-ing a job may be particularly stressful depending upon contextual fac-tors, such as a high general unemployment rate that may increase the duration of unemployment, the recent purchase of a house that has depleted one's savings, or a spouse who is also laid off. Thus, Lazarus argued that the so-called "objective" ratings of life-event stress that sum standardized life-change units do not take into account these in-dividual differences, and thus subjective ratings of stress are inherent-ly better predictors of health outcomes than objective ratings.

This emphasis on individual differences in the meaning of events was underscored by a recent prospective study of bereavement by Wort-man and Silver (1989). They found that nearly one third of bereaved spouses did not appear to be distressed at any point up to a year after the event, contrary to the general perception of the universality of ex-treme distress following conjugal bereavement.

In a challenge to this position taken by Lazarus and his colleagues, Dohrenwend, Dohrenwend, Dodson, and Shrout (1984) criticized as potentially confounded with prior mental health status subjective measures of stress that rely upon individual appraisals. That is, individuals who are depressed or who have high levels of emotionality, for example, may be more likely to perceive everyday occurrences as stressful. We all are familiar with individuals who "catastrophize" and overreact to very minor problems. Thus, the Dohrenwends have argued that subjective indices of stress such as hassles may be *reflecting* rather than *causing* mental health problems. Only objective stress measures could truly demonstrate that psychosocial stress causes problems in both psychological and physical health.

In response, Lazarus, DeLongis, Folkman, and Gruen (1985) had clinical psychologists identify the items that potentially reflected mental health problems and reanalyzed their data omitting these items. They still found that these "uncontaminated" hassles were better predictors of physical health than life events, a finding confirmed by Rowlison and Felner (1989).

In an escalation of the conflict, Schroeder and Costa (1984) attacked life events (and stress measures in general) for being confounded with personality characteristics as well as with preexisting health status. They separated "contaminated" life events—that is, those judged to reflect prior health status or personality—from "uncontaminated" ones. For example, "trouble paying bills" was judged to be contaminated by neuroticism, while "being laid off" was thought to be a more objective stressor. They found that only the "contaminated" life events were associated with health outcomes and concluded that "contamination factors . . . inflated the overall event-illness correlation" (p. 860).

In turn, Maddi, Bartone, and Pucetti (1987) attacked the Schroeder and Costa rating scheme for both its lack of theoretical rationale and its lack of clarity in the grouping procedure used. They pointed out, for example, that difficulty in paying bills may derive from being laid off—and, thus, terming one "contaminated" and the other as "uncontaminated" makes a spurious and insupportable distinction. They used their own grouping procedure and found that "uncontaminated" life events were actually better predictors of health, both cross-sectionally and longitudinally, than were so-called "contaminated" events.

The problem with both sets of arguments is, of course, that none of these studies actually assessed the factors with which the stressors were thought to be confounded, namely, prior mental health and emotionality. On the basis of self-report data, it is impossible to determine whether an event was due primarily to environmental happenstance or an individual's prior maladaptation. Someone may be laid off through no fault of his or her own but because his or her firm lost a big contract; another person might have had a problem with alcohol and the supervisor used an economic slowdown as an excuse to lay off the troublesome employee. Only longitudinal data with assessments of the putative confounding agent can answer the questions raised by the Dohrenwends and Costa and his colleagues.

My colleagues and I examined these issues in two longitudinal studies. In the first study, we examined the relationship between mental health and economic stress (Aldwin & Revenson, 1986). We had baseline measures of mental health and economic stress and obtained follow-up measures a year later, during which time the unemployment rate had risen by several points. We showed that people with poorer mental health at Time 1 were more likely to report economic strain at Time 2 when the economy had worsened, demonstrating that people with poorer mental health were more likely to experience stress. Nonetheless, even controlling for mental health at Time 1, economic stress did have adverse health effects at Time 2, especially if the economic problems appeared to be chronic. This demonstrated that stress could have adverse impacts in and of itself, not due to its acknowledged confound with prior mental health status.

A subsequent study also used longitudinal data to examine the issue of personality, stress, and mental health (Aldwin, Levenson, Spiro, & Bossé, 1989). Drawing upon the Normative Aging Study archives, we utilized a measure of emotionality assessed in 1975 and administered life events, hassles, and mental health measures in 1985 to a large sample of older men. We showed that both life events and hassles were correlated at about the same level ($\sim$.2) with the personality assessment 10 years earlier, partially confirming the concerns of Dohrenwends', Schroeder, and Costa. That is, individuals higher in emotionality were more likely to report hassles, even ten years later, but they were also more likely to report life events. Nonetheless, both life events and hassles contributed independent variance to mental health, even controlling for preexisting emotionality.

In other words, personality, stress and health are, to a certain extent, confounded with one another. While this confound needs to be recognized in studies, especially cross-sectional ones, longitudinal studies confirm that stress can cause negative health outcomes, regardless of prior personality and health status.

The debate over causal directionality between personality, stress, and health has also provided useful insights into the nature of the stress process. Rather than thinking of the stress process only in terms of confounds, the bidirectionality (or rather, multidirectionality) between personality, stress, and health actually provides strong support for the transactionist viewpoint. Once again, by focusing on unidirectional causality (does stress cause health problems or only reflect them? or is personality causing everything?), only parts of the process are being highlighted. Yes, the concerns of the Dohrenwends and the personality psychologists are real: The perception of stress is in part a reflection of prior personality and mental health. However, that is precisely the point of a transactionist perspective. Appraisal *is* a function of *both* the person *and* the environment. Nonetheless, that does not abrogate the very real and independent contribution that stress makes to mental and physical health—and, perhaps, even to changes in personality (see, e.g., Schnurr, Rosenberg, & Friedman, 1993).

The problem is that we are used to thinking in simple, reductionist terms: *a* causes *b,* and if a third element *c* intrudes, or if *b* sometimes causes *a,* then we assume that this nullifies the assertion that *a* causes *b.* However, life is not that simple, and a systems or transactionist approach rather than a reductionist one may be more reflective of reality. In a transactionist approach that allows for multidirectionality, all of the assertions are valid and do not necessarily nullify each other. The assertions simply shed more light on a very complex process.

Nonetheless, these issues in the design of stress research and causal directionality should be borne in mind as we consider the varying ways in which stress can be measured.

DIFFERENT APPROACHES TO STRESS MEASUREMENT

How a researcher chooses to measure stress depends upon both the research question and the way in which stress is conceptualized. Generally, researchers who define stress in terms of *environmental demands* study extremely stressful environments or individual life events, while those preferring definitions emphasizing the transaction between the person and the environment tend to study everyday stressors or hassles. Stress can also be studied in a laboratory situation, using standardized stressors such as mental math or cold pressor tests, in which pain is induced by immersing an arm in very cold water. The overall goals of the different approaches are usually similar—to determine the manner in which stress relates to some health outcome, whether it is physical or mental health, self-report or some physiological indicator of stress (except, of course, for those studies that seek to examine the precursors of stress or its distribution in a population).

In truth, the differences between various approaches to stress measurement are not necessarily clear cut, and there is much overlap at both the conceptual and measurement level. Not all researchers, for example, recognize a difference between trauma and life events. One sociological stress researcher discounted to me the whole notion of trauma, saying that her year of trying to get tenure was much worse than living through a hurricane. Clinicians who study posttraumatic stress disorder (PTSD) among combat veterans argue that there is a qualitative difference between the two categories, with trauma leading to a physiological state characterized by flashbacks, nightmares, and hyperreactivity, whereas life events "just" lead to depression and anxiety. Or are the differences simply a matter of degree of stressfulness? When is a car accident (or a sexual assault) a traumatic experience, a life event, or just a hassle? Further, the overlap between hassles, life events, and chronic role strain is also substantial.

In part, the various conceptions of stress can be differentiated using a two-dimensional space defined by duration on the x-axis and severity on the y-axis (see Figure 4-1). Traumas tend to be of relatively short duration characterized by life-threatening severity. On the other hand, conditions lasting for long periods of time that are not immediately life threatening can be considered chronic role strain. Some life circumstances such as living in a war-torn area or an impoverished, violent barrio are a combination of chronic stress punctuated by short

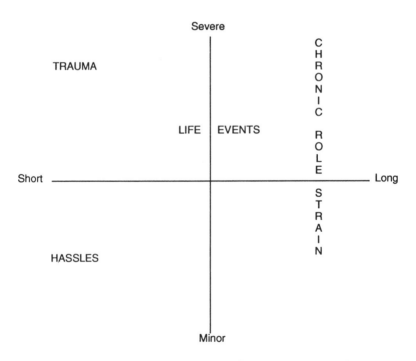

FIGURE 4-1. Relationships among different conceptions of stress.

periods of trauma. Life events may be of varying duration, but they differ from role strain in having clearly defined endpoints. Ongoing marital problems, for example, are role strain; divorce is a life event starting with separation and ending when the divorce papers are signed. Note that chronic role strain may well lead to a life event (and vice versa). A hassle is an event of short duration that is usually minor; however, a hassle may be embedded in the context of an ongoing life event or role strain that may increase its severity. Waiting in a restaurant for a spouse who is a little late may be a hassle; if, however, the spouse is chronically late and this is a major bone of contention in the relationship, that hassle may be experienced as very stressful and may even precipitate a life event (i.e., separation).

The following is not an exhaustive list of all stress indices, or ways in which stress is assessed. It is simply meant to be a guide to some of the most basic approaches to stress. The emphasis is on indices used in quasi-experimental research, that is, self-reported stress. However, laboratory research will also be briefly discussed.

TRAUMA

Trauma can be divided into three types, natural and technological disasters, war and related problems such as famine, and individual trauma.

Natural and Technological Disasters

Natural disasters include events such as tornadoes (Wallace, 1956), major fires (Lindemann, 1944), and earthquakes (Nolen-Hoeksema & Morrow, 1991). Technological disasters include nuclear reactor problems, such as that at Three Mile Island (Baum, Fleming, & Singer, 1983) or Chernobyl (Giel, 1991), and the Buffalo Creek flood, which was caused by improper storage of industrial waste on a massive scale (Erikson, 1976).

There are a number of shared characteristics of major disasters. First, there is often little or no warning that the event is about to occur. Disasters, whether created by nature or technology, may often happen very rapidly and with little notice, such as the Loma Prieta earthquake of 1989, which occurred at the very beginning of a World Series game. Even when there is adequate warning, as with such meteorological disasters as floods or hurricanes, people are often quite adept at ignoring or minimizing such warnings (Janis & Mann, 1977).

Second, disasters generally occur in a relatively short time frame. Earthquakes, tornadoes, volcanic eruptions, or nuclear disasters generally take place in a defined, discrete span of time. The aftermaths of disasters obviously may extend over much longer periods, but disasters tend to be focal stressors. (Long-term environmental disasters may be better conceptualized as chronic stressors—see below.)

Third, disasters involve extreme threat, up to and including loss of life. Not only is the individual and his or her family threatened, but survivors may witness the deaths of others, often on a immense scale. Needless to say, this involvement with death creates massive trauma.

Fourth, natural and technological disasters provide individuals with very little chance to exercise personal control. There is usually not very much that one can do in an earthquake or massive flood except to try to escape, if possible. Interestingly, people who attempt to exercise control, primarily by engaging in rescue or relief efforts, often after the event itself, may show the least psychological trauma after the event (Erikson, 1976).

Finally, disasters happen to many people simultaneously. Rather than an individual or isolated event, a disaster may feel like generalized chaos. It is not unusual for victims of such catastrophes to feel that the whole world is coming to an end. While this may initially create a great deal of stress, it also provides the opportunity for community support subsequent to the event. After a disaster, people often talk about how supportive everyone was, how they just pulled together, or how they were in awe of heroic efforts that people made to help others. A good example is the Loma Prieta earthquake. Most loss of life occurred because a freeway ramp collapsed in Oakland in a very poor neighborhood. There was heavily televised coverage of ordinary citizens risking their own lives to rescue people trapped in automobiles. Of course, there are circumstances under which such community cohesion does not occur, as when the physical and social structure of a community is damaged and people are dispersed (Erikson, 1976). Nonetheless, the group nature of disasters is a key characteristic that sets them apart from individual life events.

War

War shares some characteristics with at least technological disasters in that war occurs on a massive scale, to a general community, and involves extreme threat and exposure to death. On the other hand, there is usually ample warning (except, of course, in the case of surprise attacks). War also differs from other disasters in that it usually occurs over a relatively longer span of time. Further, soldiers (and sometimes citizens) engage in purposeful activity designed either to defend themselves or to attack the enemy, which may produce a sense of control. This purposeful activity is often coordinated with other soldiers in the unit, which can generate extremely close social ties.

While no one would dispute the traumatic nature of combat and its deleterious effect on both soldiers, civilians, and the environment, one very curious phenomenon is the positive effects that combat can have on individuals. Elder and Clipp (1989) were among the first to study these effects, which included increased sense of mastery, enhanced self-esteem, improved coping skills, and the development of leadership skills and close personal friendships (see also Wilson et al., 1989). Indeed, the extent to which veterans could construe their military experience as positive appeared to decrease the likelihood of experiencing symptoms of PTSD in later life (Aldwin et al., 1994). Further, moderate combat exposure may actually improve psychological functioning in the long run (Schnurr et al., 1993). (A more in-depth discussion of the positive aspects of stress will be presented in Chapter 13).

Individual Trauma

Unlike disasters or wars, sometimes life-threatening trauma happens to only an individual or a few people. Trauma includes things like major accidents, and violent crime such as rape and incest. Again, only those accidents or crimes involving severe injury and (perceived) threat to life should be classified as trauma. There is a qualitative difference between having a purse snatched, on the one hand, and being beaten to within an inch of one's life, on the other; between having too many drinks at a party and going further with a date than one intended, on the one hand, and being kidnapped and raped repeatedly at gun point, on the other; and between having an uncle who is a little too friendly, on the one hand, and being molested repeatedly by one's father and brothers, on the other. Failing to differentiate between hassles, life events, and trauma in dealing with individual problems leads only to trivializing very real traumatic episodes and blowing minor ones out of proportion. For example, a recent survey of Canadian physicians classified "admiring glances from patients" as a form of sexual harassment! Since there is good evidence that trauma per se can have lifelong consequences (see Chapter 10), there is good reason to keep this distinction in the literature.

Measurement of Extreme Stress

Studying natural and technological disasters can often provide extremely interesting insights into human behavior under extreme stress. Wallace's (1956) descriptions of the similarity of behavior when people are in shock is a particularly good example. However, disasters are, by definition, extremely rare. There are few instruments that provide standardized measurements of the extent and nature of disasters (although, of course, researchers may use standardized instruments to assess the effects of disasters on individuals).

An exception to this lack of standardized measurements is the Combat Exposure Scale (Keane et al., 1989). This instrument attempts to quantify aspects of this stressor by identifying different components of the combat experience (see Table 4-1). These include being subjected to enemy fire, seeing dead comrades, killing others, and so forth. Not only are different stressful characteristics of combat identified, but an attempt has been made to quantify the intensity and duration of such characteristics. Obviously, this approach to detailing precise environmental aspects of this type of technological disaster may be generalized to other disasters, but, to our knowledge, no one has as yet published such a scale.

An alternative approach is to assess generalized trauma, which is usually defined as the lifetime exposure to extreme stressors, such as combat, rape, or natural disasters. Norris (1992) has developed a simple checklist, which does not attempt to assess the environmental characteristics or psychological impact of the trauma, but serves primarily as an extremely useful epidemiological tool to assess the extent to which populations have experienced various traumas. Interestingly, the trauma that was the largest source of cases of posttraumatic stress disorder was not war or a natural disaster but an automobile accident.

A slightly different approach is being taken by Jessica Wolfe and her colleagues at the National Center for Post-Traumatic Stress Disorder at the Boston Department of Veterans Affairs Medical Center. They are developing a scale that not only assesses exposure to trauma

TABLE 4-1. Questions from the Combat Exposure Scale

1. Did you ever go on combat patrols or have other very dangerous duty?
2. Were you ever under enemy fire?
3. Were you ever surrounded by the enemy?
4. What percentage of men in your unit were killed, wounded, or missing in action?
5. How often did you fire rounds at the enemy?
6. How often did you see someone hit by incoming or outgoing rounds?
7. How often were you in danger of being injured or killed (i.e., pinned down, overrun, ambushed, near miss, etc.)?

TABLE 4-2. Items from the Life Stressor Checklist

The respondents are asked a series of questions about experiences particular trauma, such as:

1. Have you ever been in a natural or manmade disaster (e.g., a flood, tornado, fire, earthquake, or chemical spill)?
2. Have you every had a very serious accident and/or accident-related injury?
3. When you were young, were you ever put in foster care or put up for adoption?
4. Have you ever had an extended or permanent separation from your child (e.g., the loss of custody or visitation; kidnapping)?
5. Have you every been robbed, mugged, or physically attacked by someone you did not know?

For each trauma that the individual experienced, four additional questions are asked, concerning the person's age at the time of the event, the degree to which the event was upsetting at the time, how much it affected the person's life in the past year, and whether the person felt that his or her life was threatened.

---

but also seeks to assess the psychological impact of the event. Respondents are asked about 28 different events in four major categories: accidents and natural disasters, personal experiences (including childhood traumas, pregnancy, and parenting), physical violence and assault, and sexual violence and assault. For each episode actually experienced by the respondent, he or she is asked to answer four additional questions concerning the person's age at the time of the event, the degree to which the event was upsetting at the time, how much the event affected the person's life in the past year, and whether the person felt that his or her life was threatened (see Table 4-2).

General trauma is a relatively new and exciting area of research. There is some indication that incidence of lifelong trauma may be a better predictor of health outcomes and mortality than either more general life events or personality (Felitti, 1991; Hallstrom, Lapidus, Bengtson, & Edstrom, 1986; Scherg & Blohmke, 1988), but much work remains to be done in this area.

LIFE EVENTS

Life events are generally thought of as major events—such as bereavement, divorce, or job loss—that happen to individuals. A cardiologist named Wolff (1950) asked his patients to maintain diaries and observed that they often reported experiencing a stressful life event six months to a year before becoming ill. He suggested that *any* change, whether positive or negative, requires adaptational energy and thus predisposes an individual to illness. An example of a positive event would be a new job or marriage; the corollary negative event would be a job loss or divorce.

Holmes and Rahe (1967) sought to systematize and quantify this observation through the development of a standard list of events, the Schedule of Readjustment Rating Scale (SRRS)(see Table 4-3). Several hundred respondents rated the amount of adaptation or "life change units" (LCUs) that each event was thought to entail. On a scale of 500, respondents on average thought that the death of a spouse required the most amount of life change and thus assigned the highest number of LCUs to this life change. Individuals with more than a certain number of LCUs in the past year are considered at risk for developing disease. Holmes and Rahe (1967) also developed a simple checklist, the Schedule of Recent Events (SRE).

MEASUREMENT OF LIFE EVENTS

Since the development of the SRRS by Holmes and Rahe, the number of stressful life event inventories have mushroomed. Widely used inventories include the Psychiatric Epidemiological Research Interview (Dohrenwend, Krasnoff, Askenasy, & Dohrenwend, 1978), often used in community surveys, and the Life Experiences Survey (Sarason, Johnson, & Siegal, 1978), most often used in college settings. Others have developed scales for use in specific populations, such as children and

TABLE 4-3. Sample Items from the Social Readjustment Rating Scale

Rank	Life event	Mean LCU value
1	Death of spouse	100
2	Divorce	73
3	Marital separation	65
4	Jail term	63
5	Death of close family member	63
6	Personal injury or illness	53
7	Marriage	50
8	Fired at work	47
9	Retirement	45
10	Marital reconciliation	45
11	Change in health of family member	44
12	Pregnancy	40
13	Sex difficulties	39
14	Gain of new family member	39
15	Business readjustment	39

adolescents (Coddington, 1972), Hispanics (Cervantes, Padilla, & de Snyder, 1990), African-Americans (Watts-Jones, 1990), and the elderly (Aldwin, 1990; Krause, 1986; Murrell, Norris, & Hutchins, 1984).

These inventories share a number of characteristics, including being relatively short (generally less than 100 items), while still covering a broad range of types of stressors. The inventories may be simple checklists or may consist of stress rating scales. Checklists ask respondents simply to indicate whether a particular event happened during the time period under study (often a year), whereas stress rating scales ask respondents to rate how stressful the problem was for them, often using four- or five-point scales, ranging from "not at all stressful" to "extremely stressful."

A major debate in the history of stress research has been whether to use "objective" ratings (i.e., weights developed by judges to show how much change or stress an event is presumed to entail [presumed stress]), checklists, or stress rating scales (perceived stress) (see, e.g., Chiriboga, 1992). Basically, which strategy is used depends upon whether the researcher is interested in the respondent's subjective experience of stress or wishes to focus on some relatively "objective" indicator of stress levels (see discussion above on causal directionality in stress research).

Generally, the period of time covered by life event scales ranges from 6 to 18 months, which has led some researchers to question the accuracy of individuals' memories. Stressful life event inventories are self-report measures and are thus subject to questions of reliability and validity—that is, will individuals respond in a similar fashion to multiple administrations of the questionnaire, and do the measures fairly accurately reflect the stresses in individuals' lives?

To the extent that they assess environmental change, however, reliability and validity may be difficult to assess. Measures of internal reliability such as Cronbach's alpha are not appropriate for life event measures. To the extent that life events are properties of the environment, they should not correlate highly with each other. Death, divorces, and jail terms, for example, are likely to be orthogonal. Further, in studies examining test–retest reliability, it may be very difficult to determine whether responses on the inventory have changed because respondents experienced a new stressful life event or because the one previously reported no longer falls into the time scale. Still, there is no doubt that the memory of stressful life events may be fairly inaccurate (Jenkins, Hurst, & Rose, 1979; Raphael, Cloitre, & Dohrenwend, 1991).

Kessler and Wethington (1986; cited in Brown, 1989) have identified three sources of inaccuracies in life event reporting. The respondent may not realize the level of information required by the researcher; the respondent may be embarrassed to reveal certain problems; or the respondent may genuinely forget. Brown (1989) has argued that a semistructured interview that he developed, entitled the Life Events and Difficulties Schedules (LEDS), surmounts those difficulties in life event reporting by providing a supportive context and a series of probes that encourage self-revelation.

Given these difficulties, it is not surprising that other researchers have attempted to find alternative ways of assessing stress and its effects. Four very different approaches have been tried: role strain, hassles, clinical interviews, and laboratory experiments.

ROLE STRAIN

Sociologists, community psychologists, and social ecologists often examine stress as a systematic, contextual phenomenon rather than as more or less random events occurring to individuals. Sociologists in particular are interested in how the structural characteristics of a particular society or culture result in stress experienced by individuals or even changes in macrolevel indicators of pathology (Mechanic, 1974; Pearlin, 1989). For example, in the past decade there has been a great controversy over the extent to which changes in the economic structure, such as increases in the unemployment rate, cause changes in social indicators of pathology, such as increases in suicide rates, commitments to psychiatric hospitals, and deaths from cirrhosis of the liver (Brenner, 1973). Linsky and Straus (1986) computed a social stress index (SSI) composed of macro indicators of economic, family, and other stressfors. Economic stressors consisted of such items as business failures and initial unemployment claims, family stressors included divorce rates and abortion rates, and other stressful events were typified by items assessing requests for disaster assistance, the high school dropout rate, and the number of welfare recipients. The states with the highest aggregate stress levels were Nevada, Alaska, and Georgia, while those with the lowest stress levels were the Dakotas, Iowa, and Nebraska.

Controlling for a number of demographic variables, the SSI strongly correlated with a number of indicators of social pathology, such as domestic violence, alcohol problems, suicides, and motor vehicle accidents. Curiously, the SSI was related to death from peptic ulcers and asthma for women, but respiratory diseases for men, and was unrelated or negatively related to heart disease. This effect appeared to be independent of the contribution of individual life events to health outcomes, thus establishing social, structural stress as a construct independent of individual-level stress.

Work Stress

Stress relating to the workplace has been a special focus of role stress research for sociologists. Stressors may involve workload; speed of work; dangerous or toxic working conditions; poorly designed environments; interpersonal discord with supervisors, employees, colleagues, or clientele; discrimination based on ethnicity or sex; and frustrations related to the social organization of the workplace. The Work Environment Scale (Moos & Moos, 1983) is a good reference for examples of the types of stressors that people face in the workplace. Much work has been done in the past decade delineating the types and consequences of work stress.

As in studies of life event stress, some researchers have focused on particular types of occupations while others have examined broader work role issues. A classic example of studies of specific workplace stress is Rose's (1978) research on air traffic controllers. Monitoring tasks tend to be very stressful because they involve a great deal of effort expended on maintaining alertness. Air traffic controllers not only must monitor and coordinate the activities of multiple planes, but also must bear in mind that the consequences of error are very severe. One small error in judgement or lapse in attention could potentially result in several hundred deaths. Thus, it is not surprising that Rose found evidence of higher rates of stress-related disorders, such as elevated blood pressures, stomach ulcers, and so forth. One can only speculate as to whether these studies, emphasizing the stressfulness of that particular occupation, influenced the fatal decision of the air traffic controllers union to strike in the early 1980s, demanding such things as higher wages, shorter working hours, and better equipment.

Early studies such as this one focused on the environment as the source of stress independent of an individual's characteristics or life circumstances. The source of the problems lay, not in the individual's perceptions or neuroses, but rather in the environmental characteristics that would presumably be noxious to most people. More recent work focused on the interaction between the person and the environment. A good example of such research was conducted by Carrere, Evans, Palseme, and Rivas (1991) on San Francisco bus drivers, who were shown to have very high stress levels. Not only must they deal with urban traffic and congestion on a daily basis, but they also must handle a sometimes hostile and even dangerous public, all the while adhering to a very rigid time table with severe penalties if they are off by even a few minutes. However, not all bus drivers reacted to the stressors in the same way. Bus drivers with Type A personalities were found to perceive their work environment as more stressful and to have higher levels of urinary catecholamines.

A central construct in the work stress literature is that of control. Over a decade's worth of research by Frankenhauser and her colleagues (1980) in Sweden on assembly-line working conditions have clearly demonstrated that workload is not nearly as problematic as the inability to control the pace of one's work. Workers given even the illusion of control had lower levels of harmful urinary catecholamines than those who worked at the same pace but believed that they had no control over the pace of the assembly line.

Work by Karasek and Theorell (1990) provides a good example of an attempt at a more generalizable theory of workplace stress. Building on the studies on control, Karasek has hypothesized that the experience of stress arises from an interaction between two factors, responsibility and control, also specifically termed "job latitude" and "psychological demands." High strain jobs are those in which the individual has a great deal of responsibility but little control over the way in which tasks are done, the lot of many secretaries, waitresses, and factory workers.

Active jobs are very demanding, but also allow for a great deal of control. These are the high-prestige jobs of physicians, lawyers, and executives. There are a few occupations with high control but relatively low demands, such as the occupations of scientists, repairmen, and architects, which are thought perhaps to be the least stressful of positions. Passive jobs, such as those for watchmen and janitors, provide few opportunities for control but also place low psychological demands on the worker. These jobs are thought to be about average in stressfulness, but boring and "mind-deadening" in nature. Karasek and his colleagues have completed several longitudinal studies that strongly suggest that high-responsibility–low-control workers are more likely both to develop coronary heart disease and to die from it (for reviews see Cottington & House, 1987; Karasek & Theorell, 1990).

Thus, work role stress may involve physical, social, and psychological demands that without adequate resources to cope with this stress, may have deleterious consequences. However, most researchers agree that unemployment per se is generally more stressful than work stress. Further, Coyne and DeLongis (1986) have argued that relationship stress may have more deleterious consequences than work stress.

Chronic Role Strain

Rather than focus on one role, Pearlin and Schooler (1978) have argued that chronic role strain, defined as enduring problems related to specific social roles, is a better indicator of the stressfulness of an individual's life than isolated life events — and, thus, should be a better predictor of well-being. They have focused on four primary roles, including marital, parental, occupational, and household economics, and have devised scales assessing both the strains that occurred in those domains and the coping strategies specific to those types of problems.

In Pearlin and Schooler's scales, three categories of items defined marital strain: nonacceptance by spouse, nonreciprocity in give and take, and frustration of role expectations. Categories of parent strain items included failure of a child to live up to parental standards of behavior, nonconformity to parental aspirations and values, and disregard for parental status. Four categories of items defined occupational strain: inadequacy of rewards, noxiousness of work environment, depersonalization, and role overload. Finally, household economic strain was defined by difficulty in acquiring the necessities of life and paying monthly bills.

Pearlin and Schooler found that role strain was a good correlate of emotional distress related to that specific role. Further, subsequent studies (Pearlin, Lieberman, Menaghan, & Mullan, 1981) have demonstrated that the effect of life events is primarily mediated through changes in role strain. In other words, Pearlin and his colleagues believed that life events have deleterious effects because they cause disruptions in peoples' ongoing relations with their spouses, children, jobs, or finances.

Some roles are inherently stressful and provide a good opportunity to study adaptation to chronic stress. In particular, caregiver burden (Zarit, Todd, & Zarit, 1986) and hassles (Kinney & Stephens, 1989) have been studied extensively in the past few years. Many elderly people have some form of chronic illness, and some problems, such as dementia, pose serious caregiving problems. Interestingly, there is some evidence that, over time, caregiving roles may come to be perceived as less stressful if successful adaptation can occur (Townsend, Noelker, Deimling, & Bass, 1989).

Often it is a combination of problems in several roles that may contribute to difficulties in individual adaptation. For example, Brown and Harris (1978) found that women who were most likely to be depressed were single parents who had young children under the age of five and who had financial difficulties making ends meet. Similarly, most people do not find retirement that stressful; however, those that do usually have other problems, such as financial difficulties, major health problems, or bereavement which render that role problematic (Bossé, Aldwin, Levenson, & Workman-Daniels, 1991). Retirement may become problematic if there is not enough money to cover basic expenses in retirement or if one's dreams of a retirement life are shattered by the death of a spouse or by an illness.

Other researchers have focused on the extent to which stress in one role "bleeds" over into stress in another role, or on whether the domains are relatively independent. In general, work stress appears to affect marital relations for men, while for women, marital stress appears to create strain at work (Coyne & DeLongis, 1986).

Role strain approaches are interesting because they suggest that there may be systemic, social causes of psychological distress. Rather than being related to neuroticism, as some personality psychologists have suggested (McCrae & Costa, 1990), stress is viewed as resulting from the way in which our lives are organized by our sociocultural milieu. The failure to understand this may lead to some unfortunate gaffs. For example, during the Los Angeles riots, a clinical psychologist on a local news program suggested that if the rioters had learned better coping skills they would not have expressed their frustration in violence. This statement blithely ignored the loss of 80,000 of 115,000 manufacturing jobs in south central Los Angeles and the massive unemployment problem caused by structural changes in the economy. For the most part, stresses arising from collective behavior may be effectively coped with only by collective action, not by individual coping efforts, unless the individual has sufficient power to effect structural change. This issue will be addressed further in Chapter 11.

HASSLES: DAILY STRESSORS OR MICROSTRESSORS

Lazarus and Folkman (1984) have argued that an individual's appraisal of a situation is primary in determining whether it is stressful and that everyday stress or hassles have a greater effect on health than relatively rare life events. These include environmental problems (noise, pollution), mechanical malfunctions, standing in line for errands, and the like. Sample items from the Brief Hassles Inventory (DeLongis et al., 1988) are presented in Table 4-4.

Hassles are assessed using a daily diary method. Rather than ask an individual to recall events that may have happened several months ago, individuals are asked to record the number and severity of hassles that occurred that day. Typically, the time period under study is a week or longer. This technique was developed precisely to preclude

TABLE 4-4. Sample Items from the Hassles Scale

Problems getting along with fellow workers.
Hassles from boss or supervisor.
Planning or preparing meals.
Too many things to do.
Not enough time for entertainment and recreation.
Too many interruptions.
Troublesome neighbors.
Not enough time for family.
Rising prices of common goods.
Side effects of medication.
Not getting enough sleep.
Being lonely.
Inability to express oneself.

the types of recall difficulties seen with life event inventories. Further, it is also acknowledged in this methodology that any given episode may have both positive and negative aspects. Thus, individuals are asked to rate "uplifts" as well as hassles.

Several studies have suggested that hassles are better predictors of both psychological and physical health outcomes than life events are (DeLongis et al., 1982; Holahan, Holahan, & Belk, 1984; Kanner et al., 1981; Rowlison & Felner, 1989; Weinberger, Hiner, & Tierney, 1987). That is, when both life events and hassles are entered into the same regression equation, the contribution of hassles to health outcomes weakens or even obliterates the relation between life events and health outcomes.

However, these studies need to be viewed with some caution, given the different statistical distributions of life events and hassles scales. Life events being rather rare, life events scales typically have very low means (generally between 1 and 2 items) and, thus, usually have Poisson distributions (i.e., most people report between 0 and 2 items, with a rapid drop after two life events). Hassles scales, on the other hand, do tap more widespread problems and thus tend to have much better variances and distributions. Statistically speaking, the scale with the better variance is usually going to be a better correlate than another scale with a highly skewed variance (depending, of course, on the distribution of the outcome variable). So the strength of hassles versus life events in predicting health outcomes may in part be due to a statistical artifact. It is difficult to believe, for example, that losing a spouse has fewer health effects than being stuck in traffic a few times.

However, there may also be systemic patterns in hassles that would truly provide superior predictive power for health outcomes. As with chronic role strain, the effect of life events on health outcomes may be mediated through an increase in hassles (Aldwin et al., 1989; Wagner, Compas, & Howell, 1988). It is also possible that chronic hassles may prove to be more enervating than life events. Indeed, recent work by Lazarus (1990) has equated daily hassles with chronic role strain.

WHICH MEASURE TO USE?

While life events, chronic role strain, and hassles appear to be conceptually and statistically related, they are nonetheless distinct constructs, and either equating them or saying that one should be measured at the expense of the other may be ill advised. In terms of employment, for example, being laid off a union job with higher wages (life event) may force an individual to take a lower paying job with no health benefits (role strain) that also requires a longer commute (hassles). These cascade effects between different levels of stressors may make them statistically confounded but nonetheless conceptually distinct constructs. (Interestingly, this cascade could conceivably go in other directions: Too long a commute may lead a person to leave one job and take another that turns out to be less suitable.)

Rather than using simple multivariate regression techniques, in which one variable is pitted against another, studies using path analysis or structural equation modeling (SEM) that allow the examination of the joint (rather than competing) effects of life events and hassles on health outcomes have generally found these alternate stress measures to be correlated with one another, but nonetheless to contribute separate variance to health outcomes (Aldwin et al., 1989; Zautra, Reich, & Guarnaccia, 1990). The same appears to be true for life events and chronic role strain (Pearlin et al., 1981). (To my knowledge, no published studies have sought to relate all three types of stress measures.) Thus, at this stage of our knowledge, it is probably useful to retain as many ways of examining stress as possible, until we have clearer conceptions of exactly how they work.

CLINICAL INTERVIEWS

Some have argued that self-report stress questionnaires in general are inaccurate. As mentioned earlier, people are often unwilling to reveal what are often very private problems, they may not understand exactly the types of information that the researcher is looking for, or they may have compartmentalized their emotions so well that it simply does not occur to them to report something. Brown (1989) developed a semistructured interview entitled the Life Events and Difficulties Schedules (LEDS), which provides a supportive context and a series of structured probes which may allow for more complete reporting.

With mail surveys, it is my experience that about 25% of any community sample reports that they do not have a problem, whether minor or major, in the past month. When I piloted a stress and coping self-report questionnaire with the men in the Normative Aging Study, I found that a similar proportion of the men said that they had no problems. In interviews, however, many of these same men did reveal problems. Sometimes they had resolved a problem—and, therefore, no longer considered it to have been a problem. Other men were dealing with chronic role strains such as being the primary caretaker for a dying wife; as long as there had not been a recent flare-up or crisis, it did not occur to them that they had a "problem." By switching to interviews rather than a self-report mode, we were able to decrease to less than 10% the number of men who reported "no problems" (Aldwin, Chiara, & Sutton, 1993).

Clinical interviews may be especially useful when exploring a new area about which relatively little is known, when studying potentially very sensitive subjects like AIDS or incest, or when dealing with a population that might have very different views of what constitutes stressors, either owing to culture or age (children, the elderly). For example, typical stress questionnaires do not include items assessing worry about "La Immigré," breaking cultural taboos, offending ancestors, or whether your unmarried daughter has lost her virginity—all potent sources of stress in different cultures. Interviews may also help in getting a better idea of the stress process—how a problem unfolds over time, whether or not it "bleeds" into different domains, and so forth. However, lists of stressful events or hassles are often useful in prompting recall; in an interview, unless one has very complete probes (which can become tedious), if the respondent does not mention something, it may not be clear whether it did not occur or whether the respondent simply did not report it. Further, regarding the time and personnel it takes to administer the interviews and the time it takes to code them, interviews are usually much more expensive to administer than questionnaires. Consequently, one is often limited to very small samples. Thus, like any technique, stress interviews can be very useful, but they also have certain limitations.

LABORATORY STRESSORS

Controlled laboratory experiments are one way of addressing causality in biopsychosocial phenomena (Aronson, 1980). While the bulk of laboratory stress experiments are conducted with animals, some studies are also conducted on humans. The types of stressors utilized in human research in a laboratory include mild electric shock, mental arithmetic, or a cold pressor test. In this procedure, the subject's arm is submerged in cold running water, which rapidly becomes very painful but which does no harm (to noncardiac patients, that is). Another procedure is to mimic an everyday life situation, as in Frankenhauser's (1980) studies using assembly lines, or by showing films that have distressing contents, such as circumcisions or industrial accidents (Lazarus, Speisman, Markoff, & Davison, 1962).

The advantages of studying stress in a laboratory is that the stressors are clearly defined and delimited, and specific responses of the neural, endocrine, and immune systems can be carefully investigated. Laboratory studies are also very useful in examining specific elements of the stress process, for example, whether Type A persons show greater physiological reactivity to stress.

A classic example of the usefulness of laboratory research is an early study by Lazarus and his colleagues (Lazarus et al., 1962). They showed undergraduates very stressful films and manipulated the types of appraisals used. For example, some people were asked to empathize with the subject of the film, and others were urged to use clinical detachment. Lazarus was able to demonstrate that physiological reactions to stress were affected by the types of cognitive processes that people used.

However, there are ethical limits to the amounts and types of stress that individuals (and animals) can be subjected to in a laboratory setting. Ader (1981) has argued forcefully that placing laboratory mice on a slowly rotating drum is sufficiently stressful to evoke changes in neuroendocrine and immune function and that more stressful procedures, such as electric shock, restraint, food deprivation, social isolation, and swimming until nearly (or actually) drowned, are unnecessary. In addition, serious questions remain about the generalizability of laboratory studies to actual stressful episodes. If Type As do not show greater increases in blood pressure than Type Bs when doing mental arithmetic, does this mean that the two types will also react equally calmly to being cut off in traffic?

Among the relatively new technology being tested in field assessments of physiological reactivity are portable heart monitors, telemetry devices, and so forth. The respondent may carry a beeper and at random intervals may be asked to write down what he or she is doing at the moment. In this way, physiological reactions, such as heart rate to actual field stressors, can be monitored. There are some obvious limitations to this technique. There are problems with compliance; there are times when it is simply not possible to stop what one is doing and write something down, field notes get lost, and so forth. Also, only a limited range of physiological reactions can be assessed; those that require urine or blood samples, for example, cannot be utilized in such studies. Thus, at the present moment, laboratory studies are indispensable for examining the neurophysiology of stress.

SUMMARY

Given the variety of types of stress measures, the question of what type of stress should be assessed in any given study is a matter of some debate. There are cogent arguments for assessing individual stressful episodes, life events, hassles, chronic role strain, as well as for conducting laboratory experiments. Which procedure should be assessed depends in large measure upon the specific research question and on the type of health outcome. Obviously, a laboratory study will do little toward examining regional differences in stress levels. In some ways, the "cleanest" studies relate one particular event to a specific health outcome (e.g., bereavement and heart attacks). However, such particular events tend to be rare, and clearly there is a more general relation between stress and health.

The temporal parameters of the study and the type of health outcomes being assessed should guide the choice of stress measure. In studies that assess fluctuating and immediate health outcomes, such as blood pressure or immune measures, one should use more process orientation (e.g., daily stressors) or a laboratory experiment in which the timing, severity, and duration of the stressor can be controlled. One should not expect that a major life event that might have occurred at some point during the past year will necessarily affect ongoing physiological process measures. However, when assessing major health outcomes such as disease, it is less likely that a relatively minor stress will eventuate in, say, a heart attack or cancer, and such studies should focus on more major life events, chronic role strain, or trauma.

The point is that all of these procedures are valid and, to a certain extent, overlapping indicators of the general construct we call stress. As in the tale of the elephant and the blind man presented in Chapter 1, each type of procedure allows us to examine only one segment of a much larger issue. To argue whether one should only assess life events or hassles or only chronic role strain or conduct laboratory experiments is analogous to arguing that in order to understand the elephant one should only examine its trunk, ears, legs, or tail. Obviously, we need as many different ways of assessing stress as possible, in the hope that one day we will be able to construct an entire elephant.

While the evidence that stress has adverse impacts on health is firmly established, it is also true that not everyone becomes ill or even distressed when faced with a stressor. Individuals have differing resources and vulnerabilities when facing stress in their lives, which can moderate the effects of stress. There is increasing evidence that how one copes with stress, even major trauma, may be more important for at least mental health outcomes than the occurrence of the stressor itself. How one copes with physical illness may also affect its outcome; some coping strategies appear to hasten death, whereas others can delay it. Thus, the remainder of this book will be devoted to examining the ways of coping, exploring the various ways in which it has been conceptualized; examining measurement, design, and statistical issues, examining their relations to outcome and how the context may modify those outcomes; and lastly, examining cultural influences on coping and how it develops.

CHAPTER 5

Conceptual Issues in Coping Research

Ionce had occasion to look up the definition of the term *cope* in the 1955 revised edition of the abridged *Oxford English Dictionary* (OED). To my surprise, the venerable OED provided the following definitions of the word *cope:* "1. A long cloak or cape. . . . 2. An [ecclesiastical] vestment. . . . 3. Anything resembling a cloak, canopy, or vault. 4. The outer portion or case of a mould" (p. 391). The word could also mean "to furnish with a cope"; "to strike," or "come to blows". The term also had relevance to animal husbandry, in that the verb *to cope* could mean "to cut the beak of a falcon" and "to tie or sew up the mouth of a ferret." It could also refer to the shock of combat, or an encounter. The term *coping* referred primarily to masonry or brickwork.

Embedded among these myriad definitions was only a hint as to what could be considered to be current usage: "To be or prove oneself a match for," or "to contend successfully with." To indicate how much the culture and usage of the term has changed, the 1980 *Oxford American Dictionary* gives "to manage successfully" (p. 189) as the primary definition of the word *cope*.

Contemporary American culture has become nearly obsessed with stress and how to cope with it. Examples of this interest can be found in the most cursory inspection of any of the media. Self-help books abound, providing sage (or not so sage) directions on the best ways to cope with personal shortcomings, the opposite sex, work, illnesses, parents, children, and so forth. Every day millions of people avidly read the advice columns in newspapers, where various pundits attempt to resolve problems for people in a variety of areas, including personal problems, disputes between family members or coworkers, problems with etiquette, pets, plants, elderly parents, health, finances, and so forth. The *Boston Globe* regularly runs a column entitled "Confidential Chat," in which people write in with problems and solicit advice from other readers. The advice that is sought ranges from minor problems, such as how to locate a particular pattern for knitting a shawl, to major problems, such as how to handle a hyperactive child or whether to move to another state.

The same phenomenon can be seen on the broadcast media. The talk shows, such as "Oprah" and "Donahue," often deal with everyday problems, which can range from the relatively mundane, such as problems with retirement, to the bizarre and titillating. The panels generally include "formal" experts, such as psychologists or lawyers, and "informal" experts, such as individuals who have gone through such an experience. Television also broadcasts numerous "illness-of-the-week" movies, which depict individuals and families coping with a variety of illnesses, usually life threatening or disfiguring. Soap operas not only depict people in trying circumstances but also provide role models for coping with problems (usually in the most negative way possible—lying, cheating, stealing, and seeking revenge).

People also turn to formal sources of support, such as psychiatrists, psychologists, social workers, and religious figures. Time-honored custom also leads individuals to turn to folk advisers, such as hair dressers, bartenders, astrologers, fortune tellers, mediums, channelers, and so forth.

This interest has been paralleled in the academic literature. Since Coelho, Hamburg, and Adams's (1974) seminal book entitled *Stress, Coping, and Adaptation,* some 7,800 articles on coping have appeared in the literature, as indicated by a computer search of Psychlit. These studies range from general works on the structure of coping to very specific articles on how individuals cope with particular stressors, usually chronic illnesses. (See Chapter 9 for a review of this literature.)

This explosion of interest in coping has its roots in several domains. As with stress research, the importance of studying how people cope with stress can loosely be divided into three areas: intrinsic interest; relevance for psychological models of adaptation; and relevance for biomedical models of adaptation. We will explore the reasons for the interest in coping in each of these three domains.

INTRINSIC INTEREST

Studying how people cope with stress is intrinsically interesting. Since stress is so much a part of everyday life, how people successfully manage stress has immediate personal relevance. As mentioned earlier, the widespread depiction of coping strategies in the media signal their importance. It is as if individuals, in their quest for mastery and control in their own lives, have insatiable interest in acquiring new strategies by observing the coping strategies of other individuals, whether real or fictional.

Intrinsic interest in coping stems in part from its mythopoetic roots—the ideal of the hero who braves tremendous odds to accomplish some crucial task. However, the rapid change in common usage of the term *coping* and the explosion of interest in the construct noted above suggests that this preoccupation may also be driven by social changes—namely, changes in the demands of social roles, as well as possible changes in social character.

Mythopoetic Roots

The construct of "coping with stress" is rooted in a basic interest in heroic action under adversity. Heroes are people who have braved harsh circumstances in their search for some higher goal, which can be either personal or collective. In fairy tales, a young prince must conquer dragons and demons in his quest to win the beautiful princess. King Arthur's knights fought bravely against villainous knights and invading Saxons. Heroes have also been "founding fathers" or revolutionary leaders, military figures such as Robert E. Lee or George Patton, or people associated with extraordinary personal characteristics, such as saints or religious leaders. Modern heroes can be grouped into three basic types: those who brave physical hardships, those who provide leadership during times of social upheaval, or those who cope with personal trauma in ways that, for whatever reason, prove inspiring to others.

Heroes who brave physical hardships include explorers, astronauts, war heroes, and test pilots. These men (and a sprinkling of women) have demonstrated fearlessness and resolve in the face of life-threatening danger—and have survived when most would not. Chuck Yaeger's ability to escape from exploding experimental supersonic jets and to survive despite a burning parachute and jumpsuit is a notable example (Yaeger & Janos, 1985). Interestingly, television, after having substituted rock stars and actors for heroes for so many years, may be generating more interest in real life-heroes. The Public Broadcasting System has been showcasing an adventure–action series, depicting real-life quests in foreign lands, which often entail a high degree of danger. Another network has instituted a new program, "Super Cops," that reenacts the exploits of police officers who have won various honors, generally with the officer explaining his or her behavior. It will be fascinating to see if the construct of heroics becomes reintroduced to contemporary popular culture.

Some heroes have the courage and integrity to combat social ills or to provide leadership in times of social upheaval, despite grave personal risks. In this country, individuals such as Martin Luther King and Robert Kennedy led the fight against institutionalized racial prejudice—and were assassinated for their efforts. In the Soviet Union, men such as Andrei Sakharov and Natan Sharansky suffered terribly in their public fight against totalitarian repression. Sharansky's (1988) recent work, *Fear No Evil,* is a remarkable account of the coping strategies that he used to maintain his personal integrity in Soviet gulags.

Others' heroics stem from facing physical limitations and life-threatening illnesses with strength and dignity. Lou Gehrig was a famous baseball player who developed a disabling and fatal disease, amyolateral sclerosis. His farewell speech to his fans at Yankee Stadium is perhaps the best-known example of fortitude and steadfastness in the face of certain disability and death, although Gehrig's speech is certainly rivaled by Magic Johnson's admission that he was infected with the AIDS virus.

I would argue that a large part of the interest in how people cope with stress is due to its connectedness with such admired traits as courage, integrity, and fortitude. Yet, academic studies of coping are but a pale reflection of such interests. Neither the terms *strength, courage, fortitude,* and *bravery* nor attempts to operationalize these constructs appear in our scientific research. Instead, we cautiously examine problem-focused and emotion-focused strategies, such as making plans of action or using wishful thinking, with appropriate caveats about how little we actually know about the process. As Aldwin and Revenson (1987) have pointed out, we have become fairly proficient at identifying coping strategies that are associated with poor outcomes, but we know relatively little about strategies that are associated with positive outcomes. In Chapter 13, I will argue that academic studies need a reinfusion of interest in positive coping strategies that reflect heroic attributes—attributes that are displayed not only by "larger-than-life" heroes but also by people who cope with everyday problems.

Changes in Social Roles

The very avidness of interest in coping suggests that people are having profound difficulties in dealing with personal problems. This interest in coping may be a reflection of the major social upheavals of the last two decades. As we will argue later (see Chapter 11), the general manner in which individuals cope with stress is largely dependent on social norms that indicate the acceptable ways of coping with particular problems. With social change, those norms often become inapplicable, and new ways for handling both new social problems and old ones must be generated. Unfortunately, this generation is usually done at the individual level—that is, individuals must work out new ways of coping with problems and then seek to bring about changes in the social or legal system to reinforce those new patterns of coping.

In the past 50 years, there has been a massive change in social roles that has created new problems and has required new ways of coping with old problems. The entry of women into the workforce, social mobility, racial integration, and changes in family structure have created new problems for which there are no socially prescribed and routinized methods of coping. People must learn new ways and generate new solutions; thus, it is not surprising that they seek information in as many different ways as they can.

Consider the position of the first African-American in a managerial position or a woman as the first female law partner. The standard methods of dealing with problems in a work setting may simply not be appropriate for these individuals. They may not easily fit into expectations of corporate culture, and their very existence in nontraditional roles may generate new problems that require novel solutions. A study of women in the health professions schools done in the mid-1970s, for example, found that many schools simply did not have the infrastructure to cope with female students—for example, there were neither surgical gloves in the appropriate sizes nor on-call rooms for female interns and residents (Women's Action Program, 1976). Common assumptions about the capacities of African-Americans and women and the most appropriate method of social interactions had to be confronted and changes had to be made in the interaction styles of pioneer individuals and their coworkers.

For example, an influx of women into the workplace created new difficulties in terms of separating work and personal lives. Thirty years ago among middle-class women, jobs were held primarily by young, unmarried women who often used the workplace as a means of meeting potential husbands. Now women mostly separate their work from their personal lives and often refuse to date coworkers in order to avoid complications deriving from attempting to work with former lovers. Thus, women needed to learn new ways of coping with unwanted sexual advances and have instituted changes in the legal structure. For example, a woman (or a man) can use the threat of a law suit for sexual harassment in the workplace. Similarly, African-Americans and other minorities have had to discover new ways of coping with bigotry, both conscious and unconscious, and have also used the courts as ways of both legitimizing new forms of adaptation and providing new resources for coping. Thus, changes in social roles have created new problems for which we are still trying to come up with new ways of coping, both on an individual and societal level.

Changes in women's roles also presaged changes in family structure. Elder and Caspi (1988) have argued that the entry of women into the labor force during the Great Depression and World War II had a massive effect on expectations for marital roles, which eventually led to an increase in the divorce rate. Thus, the old modes of relating between spouses changed as women gained more economic leverage, and this same leverage made it possible to leave unhappy marriages. The role expectations that men and women had of married life, based upon observing their parents' interactions, were no longer appropriate; and people had to forge new modes of coping with changes in role requirements and the resultant conflicts. The extremely high divorce rate is one indication of the difficulty that individuals face in developing new modes of interaction within the family.

In turn, the change in marital roles and the divorce rate created new difficulties in raising children. The capacity to manage day care arrangements even in intact families with two working parents requires new skills. Solutions include such diverse options as drafting the grandmother, hiring in-house help, sharing one full-time job, taking jobs on different shifts, using family-based or institutional day care, starting a home-based business, or some combination thereof.

In divorced families, things may become even more difficult. Estimates are that as many as half of the nation's children are likely to experience the divorce of their parents in this generation (Spanier & Glick, 1981). How does one help a child to deal with divorce when this is the first generation to have to cope with this problem on such a massive scale? How does one learn to be a "weekend father", maintain civil relations with an ex-spouse in a joint custody situation, or introduce a new spouse into a family? Given these massive changes in social roles, it is not surprising that people seem to have lost their bearings. They are forced to cope with new problems caused by social changes for which there are no ready or pat answers, and they thus turn to each other and the media for examples.

Changes in Social Character

The widespread interest in coping may also reflect changes in social character. According to Riesman (1961), there has been a shift in American national character, from an "inner-directed" population, "whose conformity is insured by their tendency to acquire early in life an internalized set of goals," to an "outer-directed" population, "whose conformity is insured by their tendency to be sensitized to the expectations and preferences of others" (p. 8).

I would argue that not only goals but also preferred adaptive strategies are implanted at an early age in inner-directed types. The old strategies were manifested in adages such as "Honesty is the best policy," "Keep a stiff upper lip," and "Count your blessings." These adages reflected preferred modes of dealing with problems — adherence to certain codes of honor, such as honesty, suppression of emotion (especially in men), and the acceptance of responsibility for problems. When one was confronted with life's problems, these "internal gyroscopes" often spelled out what were the right actions: obedience to authority, loyalty to country and family, and the avoidance of lying, cheating, or stealing.

With the growth of outer directedness, individuals look more toward the behavior of others in similar situations and what their peers deem acceptable strategies. The "internal gyroscopes" have been replaced by situationalism and an acute sense of relative values. Rather than an internal guide of what should be the morally correct behavior in a situation, an outer-directed individual may be more concerned with the opinion of others in the immediate setting and the immediate consequences of his or her actions. *Thus, each problem becomes unique and requires its own individual solution,* vastly complicating adaptational processes.

The benefit of an outer-directed stance is its flexibility and frequent sensitivity to the needs of others in the situation; the disadvantage is that it leaves individuals unduly subject to peer pressure and requires constant choice or decision making. No wonder individuals seek to increase the size of their coping repertoires and (of necessity) turn to others for advice on strategies.

RELEVANCE OF COPING TO PSYCHOSOCIAL MODELS OF ADAPTATION

In Chapter 2, two contributions of the construct of stress to psychosocial models of adaptation were identified: (1) its ability to combine environmental and personal factors with the development of mental illness through the construct of vulnerability to stress, and (2) the notion of goodness of fit— namely, that psychosocial adaptation is in part a match between the demands of a situation and the capacities of an individual.

Coping research also combines environmental and personological perspectives by showing that how individuals respond and deal with stress is a combination of multiple factors. This overdetermination of coping behavior allows for flexibility in adaptation. People modify what they do in order to take into account both environmental exigencies and personal preferences. How well one copes is also in part a matter of "goodness of fit" between environmental demands and individual resources.

Some believe that individuals can be categorized as "good" or "bad" copers. They assume that competence in one domain is a personological characteristic that will generally be manifested in other domains. Aldwin (1982) examined this assumption in an early study of coping among middle-aged men and women in different domains: work and family. The men, generally middle managers, exhibited good coping skills in work situations, relying mainly on an array of very sophisticated problem-focused strategies. In family situations, however, they appeared to feel much less competent and would say things like, "I don't deal with crying babies. I let my wife handle it." The women, on the other hand, were adept at dealing with family problems; but the few women who did work, mainly lower-level secretaries and clerks, were far less skilled and were more likely to use emotion-focused strategies in work situations. Thus, whether one is a "good coper" or a "bad coper" depends greatly upon the types of skills that one brings to a particular environmental context.

Thus, the construct of coping with stress reemphasizes these two contributions of stress models, but it also extends our understanding of psychosocial adaptation in two important ways. First, the addition of the construct of coping to the stress paradigm emphasizes that people are neither passive responders to environmental circumstances nor are they guided solely by inborn temperament. By actively responding to environmental circumstances, individuals can learn to adapt to and overcome adversity. Not only do people change themselves, but they can also learn to modify their environments.

Second, this last characteristic of coping actions—that they are learned behaviors—also has implications for the treatment of psychological problems. In many cultures, including our own, psychological problems and mental illness are stigmatized, and people who have sought such help are often deemed suspect. In the 1970s, Senator Thomas Eagleton was disqualified from the vice-presidential candidacy because it was revealed that he had at one time been treated for depression. This stigmatization is a logical outgrowth of the view that psychological abnormalities are due to innate physiological or psychological problems and can be a barrier to the seeking of treatment for problems.

Rather than suggest that some individuals are inherently defective, a stress and coping approach argues that some individuals do not have the appropriate skills needed to cope with particular sets of problems. Therapists such as Minuchin (1974) have argued that some individuals have learned maladaptive ways of coping with problematic situations that serve to maintain rather than eliminate problems, but with appropriate intervention, new strategies can be learned. In the 1992 presidential campaign, both Clinton and Gore admitted to having been in family therapy, one for treatment of his brother's alcohol abuse and the other for help in dealing with a son's serious illness, and little or no stigma was attached to this.

By destigmatizing emotional or psychological problems, the stress and coping approach to psychosocial adaptation allows more people access to the skills they need to cope with their particular set of problems. After all, everyone "has stress," and there is little stigma attached to increasing coping skills. For example, tens of thousands of individuals have enrolled in stress management courses, and telephone counseling services for parents at risk of abusing their children are called parental stress hotlines. Certainly, some individuals are more vulnerable than others. But it is much easier for a person to acknowledge that he or she may need help in handling a specific type of problem than submit to a label of neurotic, hysteric, or depressive.

This is not to say that the learning of coping skills is the only purpose of therapy — far from it. Obviously, therapy includes many other dimensions, including medication and self-knowledge. However, by focusing on coping skills, therapy may become more accessible to individuals who would not otherwise risk the potential stigmatization of psychotherapy.

Thus, the construct of coping with stress is preferable in that it allows for an innate flexibility in psychosocial adaptation. Inasmuch as stress arises from the interaction (or transaction) between the person and the environment, the management of problems and the attendant negative affect is also a function of multiple factors. Adaptation may require both environmental and personal change. The strength of the concept of coping lies in its flexibility — its ability to respond both to the requirements of the situation and to personal needs. Adaptive strategies are thus malleable — people can learn new skills, either in self or environmental management, which can allow them to transcend difficult problems.

RELEVANCE TO BIOMEDICAL
MODELS OF ADAPTATION

It is commonly observed that stress accounts for only a modest amount of the variance in health, with correlations between stress measures and self-report physical health typically ranging in the .20s and .30s.

In other words, not everyone succumbs to illness under stressful conditions, or, more precisely, every experience of a stressful episode does not lead to ill health. While this fact is often interpreted as a problem in stress research indicative of the weakness of the construct, another interpretation is that this relatively low correlation is actually positive — it is a tribute to humans' adaptive capacity that, unlike some laboratory mice, we do not become ill with every stressor.

The problem, then, becomes one of trying to determine why stress sometimes results in ill health and at other times does not. Obviously there are a number of factors that are relevant. One is physical hardiness: some individuals may not be genetically susceptible to particular illnesses, others may be in good physical condition, which much research has shown is protective against the adverse effects of stress (e.g., Roth & Holmes, 1985). Nutritional status and immediate state of health (e.g., how tired one is) are also factors.

The impetus for the study of coping strategies is a direct result of this recognition of individual differences in response to stress. The idea is that somehow coping mitigates the adverse effects of stress. (See Chapter 8 for a discussion of coping strategies as mediators, moderators, and buffers.)

However, we have yet to work out exactly how stress buffering happens; indeed, only a handful of studies have actually demonstrated it. Studies that look at the mitigating effects of coping often use psychological outcomes, while studies with good physical health measures simply assume that individuals who do not become ill are "good copers," with little or no attempt to assess the recent coping strategies actually used. Further complicating the issue is that, according to Pearlin and Schooler (1978), it is unlikely that researchers will find a "magic bullet" coping strategy that is good for all people under all circumstances. Instead, we will need to define a taxonomy of coping actions and determine what works under disparate circumstances and for which individuals. Nonetheless, if we can demonstrate a relation between coping and physical health, this would open up exciting possibilities for preventive medicine. Individuals may be able to protect their health by learning to deal effectively with stress.

The second way in which the construct of coping is important for biomedical adaptation involves how individuals cope with illness. That is, once individuals become ill, it is necessary to face certain adaptive tasks. In the case of chronic or other serious illness, these tasks include following medical regimens, maintaining emotional stability, and establishing workable relationships with medical personnel. Individual differences in the course of illness may be due in part to how successful individuals are in coping with these adaptive tasks (Moos

& Schaeffer, 1984). Indeed, Greer, Morris, Pettingail, and Watson (1981) have shown that length of survival after breast cancer is due more to women's emotional coping styles than to tumor size and grade.

DIFFERENTIATING BETWEEN ADAPTATION, COPING, AND EMOTIONAL RESPONSES

Adaptation is an overarching construct that includes concepts such as defenses, mastery, and coping strategies (White, 1974). Further, it is also important to differentiate between general adaptation or management skills, coping strategies, and emotional responses.

Everyone develops certain management skills to help them deal with life. We brush our teeth to prevent cavities and gum disease, develop a morning routine that enables us to get to school or work on time, manage driving on the freeway or negotiate the subway to get to work, develop a routine for dealing with common tasks at work, learn how to comfort a small child, and so forth. To the extent that these become routinized and everyday skills that forestall stress, they are no longer coping strategies per se but management skills. As White (1974, p. 48) pointed out, "Nobody has chosen going to school for the sixty-third time as an occasion for coping." Management skills may have developed out of learning to cope with a problem but, once routine, are no longer considered coping *strategies,* although they may be coping *resources,* or what Antonovsky (1979) has called generalized resistance resources. (As we shall see in Chapter 7, management skills are different from coping styles. Coping styles are considered to be characteristic ways of handling problems; in contrast, management skills refer to situation-specific skills used to forestall or avoid problems.)

Some strategies such as *anticipatory coping* straddle the boundary between management skills and coping. Anticipatory coping involves action which is designed to prevent or minimize problems that are likely to occur. For example, making sure one has sufficient gas in the tank before driving late at night is preferable to running out of gas and having to call a friend to come and get you. Again, to the extent that such activities become part of our everyday routine (e.g., always filling up the tank on Saturday afternoon for the next week's commute to avoid waiting in line Monday mornings), it is a management skill. However, when an anticipatory action is undertaken for a relatively novel problem, or when its outcome is uncertain, then it becomes more of a coping strategy. Anticipatory coping is surprisingly little studied, with the exception of medical procedures (Bush,

Melamed, Sheras, & Greenbaum, 1986) and laboratory studies of anticipated shock (e.g., Thompson, Dengerink, & George, 1987). However, it may be a very important adaptational strategy — and one which is deserving of greater attention.

On the other hand, involuntary emotional reactions should also not be considered coping strategies. Gasping with pain because you stepped on a nail is not generally considered to be a coping strategy per se, and being sad or depressed is generally considered to be an outcome of the stress and coping process. However, *expressing* emotions (having a good cry, yelling at someone, moaning and groaning with pain) may be either emotion- or problem-focused coping (or both), since it has a purpose. Admittedly, this distinction can become rather arbitrary, since the difference between voluntary and involuntary emotional reactions can become rather blurred at times. However, it is important to distinguish between coping strategies and their purported outcomes; if they are confounded at the outset, we will never be able to get objective indicators on which strategies "work" in which situations (Lazarus, 1983).

Coping strategies are thought to consist of both cognitions and behaviors that are directed at managing a problem and its attendant negative emotions (Folkman & Lazarus, 1980). In a transactional scheme, stressors arise because of a perceived shortfall of resources needed to deal with a problem; once the resources have been developed, the situation is no longer perceived as stressful — unless, of course, the situation (or its meaning) somehow becomes altered and the routines are no longer adequate. Consider driving on the freeway. For the novice driver, this is a highly stressful procedure: The person must maintain awareness, figure out how to merge in traffic, learn how to read the intentions of other drivers, and so forth. Once a person has mastered the task, driving on the freeway becomes more of a management skill than a coping behavior — unless, of course, something changes that increases the difficulty of the task, such as hazardous driving conditions. A meaning change may also require coping strategies: Routine traffic congestion, which ordinarily requires simple management skills, may become suddenly stressful if it threatens to make a person late for a crucial appointment. The hallmark of coping strategies is that they require effort — whether conscious or unconscious — in their task of managing negative affect and stressful situations, whether temporary or chronic.

SUMMARY

The study of coping is fraught with difficulties. As we shall see in the next chapters, there are many unanswered questions about to how to conceptualize and measure coping, and, indeed, some believe that the study of coping should be replaced with an examination of stress–personality interactions. However, the study of coping strategies is important in and of itself. Not only is there is a great deal of intrinsic interest, but focusing on stress and coping behaviors has implications for the flexibility of the adaptational process and destigmatizes seeking help for problems.

Further, the study of stress and coping processes represents a methodological breakthrough for psychology. Most prior research has focused either on self-reported personality, attitudes, and feelings, on the one hand, or observed behaviors in experimental settings, on the other. This is the first time that there has been a concerted effort in the field of psychology to have people systematically *self-report on their own cognitions and behaviors in specific contexts*. As we shall see, the introduction of self-report questionnaires has created a number of conceptual and methodological difficulties but is exciting in its implications for psychology as a whole.

CHAPTER 6

Theoretical Approaches to Coping

As we saw in the previous chapter, the study of coping has its roots in the recognition that there are individual differences in reactions to stress—that is, similar stresses may have varying effects on different people. For example, individuals can respond in many different ways to a reprimand by a supervisor at work. Some people may shrug it off; others may argue with the supervisor, trying to convince him or her that the evaluation is faulty. Some people may react with tears and spend the rest of the day complaining to coworkers, others may become angry and quit the job or threaten the supervisor with violence. Some may acknowledge the problem and resolve to improve their job performance. Yet others may become involved in office politics and seek to sabotage the supervisor in some way.

The purpose of studying coping strategies is to understand why people differ so greatly in their responses to stress and how differing responses relate to well-being. The theoretical orientation of a researcher or clinician directs the types of factors that he or she considers in studying influences on coping. Simply put, a clinician will focus on such person factors as personality characteristics, values, and commitments if he or she believes that the origin of coping strategies lies with the person. In the example given above, one explanation for the differences in the hypothesized coping strategies is that these individuals differ in their personality characteristics, such as emotionality; those low in emotionality may simply shrug off the confrontation with the supervisor, those high in emotionality may react with tears or aggression, either verbal or physical. In contrast, those who acknowledge problems and respond in a socially appropriate manner (assuming we can tell what that is) are thought to be more mature or higher in ego strength. (The Machiavellian style depicted in the last example is rarely investigated in the stress and coping literature.)

The astute observer will note that a strictly person-based approach implicitly assumes *environmental constancy*—namely, that all of the individuals in the above example are responding to the same situation: a reprimand from the supervisor. A situation-based approach would argue that environmental demands or situational characteristics evoke differing coping strategies. This approach argues that stimulus characteristics need to be considered. For example, we do not know whether the reprimand is justified. If it is, acknowledgment is appropriate, however, if it is not, anger may be understandable.

Given that this is an interpersonal situation, the characteristics of the other individuals may affect the type of coping strategies used. The individual who responded hysterically may have been previously subjected to sexual harassment by the supervisor and is now being unduly criticized in an attempt to get her to quit. By spending the day talking to people, she may be trying to determine whether there is enough support in the office from her fellow coworkers to file charges.

Finally, macrocharacteristics of the situation, such as the structure of the working conditions, also should be considered. The person who responded with Machiavellian scheming might be working in a federal agency. The supervisor may be incompetent and adversely affecting the functions of the office. However, in an entrenched bureaucracy, it is nearly impossible to directly effect changes in personnel; therefore, otherwise perfectly upstanding individuals may resort to Machiavellian scheming in order to indirectly oust people by making their working conditions unbearable.

Borrowing from the discussion in Chapter 1, a person-based approach assumes that person → coping. A situation-based approach assumes that situation → coping. The interactionist approach that most stress and coping researchers accept is that the person + the situation → coping. Thus, the person who responds with anger to his supervisor's reprimand could be both high in hostility and reacting to an unjustified reprimand.

As we noted in Chapter 1, there is a fourth approach: the transactionist approach. In this instance, the person, situation, and coping mutually affect each other in a process that evolves over time (see Figure 1-2). This approach requires a larger, or more contextual, view of the situation and specifies that coping behavior may change in response to its effects on the situation (Lazarus & Folkman, 1984). In the federal bureaucracy example above, an incompetent supervisor has unjustifiably rebuked the employee. From the employee's point of view, the supervisor has become an impediment to the smooth running of the office and the completion of tasks. By resorting to Machiavellian scheming, however, the employee sets off a bureaucratic firestorm that uses up a great deal of the office's resources—that is, the personnel spend most of their time engaging in office politics and very little on the actual tasks at hand. Thus, the coping strategy has made the situation worse, and has further increased the employee's distress, at least in the short run. At this point, the employee may reassess his or her coping strategies and decide whether to continue on that course of action or modify it in some fashion. Thus, the person, situation, and behavior become enmeshed in an admittedly circular process.

This chapter will review both person- and environment-based theories of coping and will address basic issues in coping research, such as consistency and change across situations.

PERSON-BASED DEFINITIONS OF COPING

Person-based approaches to the study of coping posit that personality characteristics are primary in determining how people cope with stress. Person-based approaches can be loosely divided into three schools: psychoanalytic, personality trait, and perceptual styles.

Psychoanalytic Traditions

The study of coping strategies has its roots in psychoanalytic descriptions of defense mechanisms, which are directed primarily toward internal conflicts. According to A. Freud (1966), defense mechanisms are the ways in which the ego wards off anxiety and exercises control over impulsive behaviors, affects, and instincts. Basically, anxiety arises from unconscious conflicts between the id and the superego. The ego, with its primary emphasis on reality testing and mediation between environmental and internal demands, tries to defend against this overwhelming anxiety by distorting reality or metamorphosing instinctual demands. Defense mechanisms are manifested primarily as symptoms and are characterized by automatic, rigid reactions.

Vaillant (1977, p. 10) identified five major functions of defense mechanisms:

1. to keep affects within bearable limits during sudden life crises (e.g., following a death);
2. to restore emotional balance by postponing or channeling sudden increases in biological drives (e.g., at puberty);
3. to obtain a time-out to master changes in self-image (e.g., following major surgery or unexpected promotion);
4. to handle unresolvable conflicts with people, living or dead, whom one cannot bear to leave. . . ; [and]
5. to survive major conflicts with conscience (e.g., killing in wartime, putting a parent in a nursing home).

A. Freud (1966) identified several major defense mechanisms, including suppression, denial, projection, reaction formation, hysteria, obsessive–compulsive behaviors, and sublimation. Tart (1987) has an excellent discussion of these mechanisms. Briefly, suppression and denial involve varying forms of the refusal to acknowledge an event or feelings. To return to our example of the confrontation with the supervisor, an individual suppressing the episode may try not to think about it; someone who is in denial will literally "forget" that it ever happened and deny it if queried. In contrast, rather than forget the event, the hysteric will inappropriately focus attention on it, thus magnifying the problem — by spending the day crying in the bathroom, for example. An obsessive–compulsive will also focus attention, but in a different manner. The next time the supervisor requires the employee to perform a task, the employee may spend so long checking and rechecking every step of the project that he or she misses the deadline.

Projection and reaction formation are similar in that they both involve casting off one's own feelings about an event. In projection, an aggressive coper might think that the reprimand was unjust and may feel that the work is fine; the supervisor just had it in for him or her. This individual has attributed his or her own feelings of anger to someone else. In reaction formation, a person inverts his or her own feelings, turning anger into admiration, for example. But this person may later react inappropriately, either by not bothering to actually improve performance or by becoming overly upset at the inevitable emergence of flaws in the supervisor. On the other hand, the "mature" coper could also sublimate by using the anger to accomplish the next task better. If this individual were a reporter, he or she could write a scathing political exposé; if this person were on the maintenance crew, he or she could work off anger physically by scrubbing things harder.

In this model, the type of coping behavior used has very little to do with either the actual environmental stimulus or what the individual does to solve the problem. Rather, the focus of defense mechanisms are to regulate emotions—to reduce anxiety by whatever means possible. Thus, behaviors, feelings, and cognitions evoked by a stressful situation are determined by the individual's personality structure, which was developed in early childhood and is thus not readily mutable.

Defense mechanisms can be used fleetingly and only under conditions of great trauma, or they can be become habitual. For example, a common initial reaction to the sudden death of a loved one is denial. Confronted with the death of a son in a car accident, an understandable reaction is to think, "Oh, no, they've made an error. That's not my son in the morgue—it's someone else." Denial, however, may become habitual, as in the case where the mother refuses to believe that her son is dead and continues to set a place for him at the dinner table every night. In this model, both the fleeting and permanent denial are caused by personality structure.

Shapiro (1965) posited that people can become characterized by their predominant use of a particular mechanism. Shapiro focused on four major styles. The obsessive–compulsive style is characterized by rigidity, distortion of the experience of autonomy, and the loss of reality. Paranoids also suffer from a loss of reality, but are primarily characterized by suspicious thinking. The hysterical style is characterized by both repression and hyperemotionality, while the impulsive style is characterized by rapid, thoughtless action and a lack of planning.

One limitation of this approach is that it focuses primarily on poor adaptation—individuals who are thought of as "neurotics." Several psychoanalytic thinkers have attempted to circumvent this approach by suggesting adaptive hierarchies, either by positing more or less adaptive defense mechanisms (Vaillant, 1977) or by including defenses in a larger adaptive hierarchy (e.g., Haan, 1977).

Defensive Hierarchies

One problem with understanding coping efforts primarily in terms of defense mechanisms is that these mechanisms are, by definition, maladaptive in that they distort reality. However, most of us are not that maladaptive—at least most of the time. Vaillant (1977) attempted to deal with this limitation by redefining defense mechanisms in terms of adaptive styles, with the explicit assumption that some defense mechanisms can be healthy and adaptive.

Vaillant (1977) utilized data from the Grant Study (begun in the 1930s), a longitudinal study of college men who were judged "mentally healthy." His primary focus was on the adaptive mechanisms used by these men at various points in their lives. Although Vaillant recognized that adaption requires people to "alter themselves and the world around them" (p. 13), he concentrated on the regulation of emotion and the preservation of ego integrity.

Vaillant arranged the defense mechanisms in a hierarchy from projective through mature mechanisms (see Table 6-1), which also doubled as a developmental progression across the lifespan. He broke from traditional psychoanalytic theory in recognizing that the use of defense mechanisms is not inherently pathological but serves to maintain ego integrity under difficult circumstances. The higher categories, however, are considered more effective and adaptive than lower ones.

As Table 6-1 indicates, Vaillant identified four levels of defense mechanisms: projective, immature, neurotic, and mature. The hierarchy is based primarily upon how much distortion of reality is involved in each mechanism, with the lower mechanisms involving more distortion and, thus, more pathology. Returning to our example, the aggressive coper who attributes his own anger to his supervisor is the

---

TABLE 6-1. Vaillant's Hierarchy of Defensive Mechanisms

Level I	Projective mechanisms
	Denial
	Distortion
	Delusional projection
Level II	Immature mechanisms
	Fantasy
	Projection
	Hypochondriasis
	Passive–aggressive behavior (turning against the self)
	Acting out
Level III	Neurotic mechanisms
	Intellectualization (isolation, obsessive behavior, undoing, rationalization)
	Repression
	Reaction formation
	Displacement (conversion, phobias)
	Dissociation
Level IV	Mature mechanisms
	Sublimation
	Altruism
	Suppression
	Anticipation
	Humor

Adapted from Vaillant (1977). Copyright 1977 by G. Vaillant. Reprinted by permission.

using an immature mechanism, the person who turned his or her anger into unrealistic admiration is using a neurotic mechanism, while the person who sublimates is using a mature mechanism. In Vaillant's scheme, the projective mechanisms involve major delusions, such as denial—the inability to acknowledge that the episode even occurred. Delusional projection would involve a paranoid fantasy, for example, that the supervisor has been working for years to destroy the employee. Such paranoia may be accompanied by extreme reactions such as physical violence.

Vaillant then applied this hierarchical categorization to the interview materials acquired over thirty years of study with the Grant Study men, graduates from a particular class at an Ivy League school. He demonstrated that as people grow from young adulthood to midlife, their characteristic defensive styles often change from immature to more mature. The men who used more immature mechanisms in later life were judged less adaptive or successful, defined primarily in the context of career achievement and marital stability.

Vaillant has presented a very compelling and highly entertaining picture of how defensive styles change over the lifespan. He was also one of the first individuals to study coping processes in everyday life rather than maladaptive strategies exhibited by individuals seeking therapy. Thus, he was forced to consider adaptive as well as maladaptive processes and sought to modify psychoanalytic theory to take into account these adaptive processes. However, the assumptions inherent in psychoanalytic theory—that is, the primacy of affect regulation that is chiefly unconscious in nature—led to some difficulties with this theory. If coping–defenses are mainly unconscious, how is it that development occurs? By what means do people shift from immature to mature defenses? Further, emotion regulation is only half of the adaptive process. Are there also consistent changes in problem-focused coping across the lifespan?

While Vaillant goes beyond traditional psychodynamic theory in recognizing that the use of defense mechanisms is not inherently pathological, his insistence on the unconsciousness of adaptive strategies is somewhat inconsistent with the notion that they nonetheless reflect developmental processes. If, as he states, defense mechanisms do not appear to be linked to childhood factors, nor can one "consciously acquire them," how do they develop? He reiterates throughout the book that one cannot "will" or "consciously acquire" adaptive strategies (see pp. 61, 875). But in his description of how defenses evolve, it becomes clear that the men whom Vaillant studied did consciously attempt to modify their adaptive styles. For example, the adaptive style of one respondent, Jefferson, was initially characterized as reaction formation, he aggressively rejected anger and hostility. However, "as soon as Jefferson discovered how to inject pleasure into reaction formation, it evolved into the more mature defense of altruism" (p. 107). Throughout the book are other examples of individuals trying different adaptive strategies, suggesting that some form of conscious development occurs.

The lack of interest in problem-solving techniques is also a limitation of Vaillant's early work. While dealing with unconscious material is undoubtedly important in coping, emotions are not the only component to stressful situations. Thus, how problem-solving strategies and styles evolve over the life course was not addressed.

In a recent revision of his theory, Vaillant (1993) addressed more explicitly the ways in which the ego matures. He presented three models: neurobiology, social learning theory, and assimilation–imprinting. From a neurobiological standpoint, neuronal maturation processes are hypothesized to continue into adulthood, allowing individuals to develop such higher ego processes as becoming more tolerant of paradox, being able to use sublimation, and so forth. Such a model would obviously have a hard time explaining the great variation in ego development in adulthood, although Vaillant suggested that systematic poisoning of the nervous system, through drug or alcohol abuse, may retard ego development.

From a social learning viewpoint, we learn more mature defense mechanisms through both learning processes and social support. As Vaillant (1993) concluded: "Learning as well as heredity plays a major role in our choice of defenses. Sublimation hurts less than masochism; altruism is better paid than reaction formation; humor wins us more friends . . . than wit" (p. 332). In addition, social support facilitates the maturation of defenses by enhancing a sense of safety and self-esteem and reinforcing the use of more mature defenses.

However, Vaillant thought the assimilation model of ego development was more complete. From his case histories, he felt that "what was most critical to resilience was not social supports but the ability to internalize those supports" (p. 332). He identified several ways in which adults internalized loved ones, ranging from very immature incorporation and introjection to more mature idealization and identification. Basically, in incorporation or introjection, people unconsciously take in "undigested" significant others—Norman Bates's taking on the identity of his deceased mother would perhaps be an extreme example. In more mature identification or idealization, we can recognize and integrate both the positive and negative aspects of loved ones. "Compared to internalization, identification is a more flexible, reversible, neutralized, differentiated, choice-determined way of taking another person in . . . With identification we can say to ourselves, " 'He did it and, if I choose, I can do it too' " (p. 351).

Yet Vaillant still insisted that defense mechanisms are unconscious—even those involving planning and anticipation. As he put it, "Paranoids cannot become altruists by an act of will" (pp. 103–104). Yet he went on to say, "But, through therapy, maturation, and loving relationships people learn more mature styles of self-deception" (p. 104). Thus, Vaillant is very ambivalent about what is conscious and unconscious in adaptation; on the one hand, his eloquent case histories are convincing demonstrations of unconscious processes in adaptation: on the other hand, they equally and clearly demonstrate that development and use of more mature coping strategies occur at least partially through conscious effort.

Haan (1977) had a more straightforward approach to the problem of what is unconscious and conscious in adaptation. She also sought to integrate the idea of adaptive processes with defense mechanisms in a largely psychodynamic framework. In contrast to Vaillant's approach, however, Haan maintained that defense mechanisms are inherently pathological and constructed a hierarchy of adaptation based upon the extent to which the strategies used reflect conscious or unconscious processes. She identified ten basic, or generic, ego processes that can be expressed in three modes (see Table 6-2). The first mode, coping, is conscious, flexible, and purposive, and permits moderate expression of emotion. The second mode, defensive, is compelled, negating, and rigid and is directed toward anxiety rather than the problem. The third mode, fragmentation, or ego failure, most clearly distorts "intersubjective reality" and is automated, ritualistic, and irrational.

The ten generic processes are further divided into four functions: cognitive, reflexive–intraceptive, attention-focusing, and affective-impulse regulation. Note that these ego processes not only are directed toward anxiety reduction (the last category), but also function to regulate cognitive processing, to provide self-reflective capacity, and focus attention.

In Haan's scheme, a particular generic process can be expressed differently and with varying levels of pathology in the three modes. As Table 6-3 illustrates, the third cognitive function, "means–ends symbolization," can be seen as a problem-focused strategy, at least in the coping mode. In this mode, means–end symbolization is expressed in logical analysis of the problem, a process underlying most attempts to resolve problems. In the defense mode, means–end symbolization becomes rationalization, or an attempt to justify one's actions. In the fragmentation mode, however, means–end symbolization degenerates

TABLE 6-2. Haan's Description of the Properties of Coping, Defense, and Fragmentation

Coping processes	Defense processes	Fragmentary processes
Appear to involve choice and are, therefore, flexible, purposeful behavior	Turn away from choice and are, therefore, rigid and channeled	Appear repetitive, ritualistic, and automated
Are pulled toward the future and take account of the needs of the present	Are pushed from the past	Operate on assumptions that are privatistically based
Are oriented to the reality requirements of the present situation	Distort aspects of present requirements	Close the system and are nonresponsive to the present
Involve differentiated process thinking that integrates conscious preconscious elements	Involve undifferentiated thinking and include elements that do not seem part of the situation.	Are primarily and unadulteratedly determined by affect needs
Operate with the organism's necessity of "metering" the experiencing of disturbing affects	Operate with the assumption that it is possible to magically remove disturbing feelings	Flood the person with affect
Allow various forms of affective satisfactions in an open, ordered, and tempered way	Allow gratification by subterfuge	Allow unmodulated gratification of some impulses

Adapted from Haan (1977). Copyright 1977 by Academic Press. Reprinted by permission.

into confabulation, when someone simply makes up a story in an attempt to defend him- or herself.

According to Haan, people cope when they can and defend when they must:

> Coping processes are likely to be employed . . . when assimilation and accommodation are either quite evenly matched or the person experiences no pressure about the imbalance, for example, he's enjoying his daydreaming or he wants very much to acquire a new skill . . . Defensive strategies are needed when marked imbalances between assimilation and accommodation occur. . . . Fragmentation, as a retreat to privatistic assimilatory modes, occurs as an accommodation to stress and as a solution to a situation or to a likely developmental movement, where and when the required accommodations are not only beyond the person's capability, but also irrefutably contradict and confuse his self-constructions and make intrasubjective reality preferable. (p. 49)

TABLE 6-3. Haan's Taxonomy of Ego Defenses

Generic processes	Modes		
	Coping	Defense	Fragmentation
Cognitive functions			
1. Discrimination	Objectivity	Isolation	Concretism
2. Detachment	Intellectuality	Intellectualizing	Word salads, neologisms
3. Means–ends	Symbolization	Logical analysis rationalization	Confabulation
Reflexive–intraceptive functions			
4. Delayed response	Tolerance of doubt	Immobilization	Ambiguity
5. Sensitivity	Empathy	Projection	Delusion
6. Time reversion	Regression	Ego regression	Decompensation
Attention-focusing functions			
7. Selective awareness	Concentration	Denial	Distraction, fixation
Affective-impulse regulations			
8. Diversion	Sublimation	Displacement	Affective preoccupation
9. Transformation	Substitution	Reaction formation	Unstable alternation
10. Restraint	Suppression	Repression	Depersonaliza-tion, amnesia

Adapted from Haan (1977). Copyright 1977 by Academic Press. Reprinted by permission.

In other words, if the situation is not very stressful, the ego will cope, which is described as being purposeful, flexible, adhering to intersubjective reality, and permitting affective expression. But under stressful circumstances, the ego preserves integrity by greater or lesser distortion of reality. Defensive strategies are compelled, negating, rigid, and are directed toward anxiety rather than toward the problem. Fragmentation most clearly distorts intersubjective reality. It is automated, ritualistic, and irrational, and adheres to privatistic (e.g., idiosyncratic) formulae. Successful ego processes are not defined by their content or effects, but are defined a priori by which processes are used. However, these modes are not orthogonal; Haan admits that generally a mixture of coping and defensive strategies is used. Development consists of gaining progressive control over behavior, shifting from defensive to coping modes.

Haan's theory has some very positive and interesting aspects. She departs from traditional psychoanalytic theory in positing a constructivist rather than reactivist view of adaptation—that is, people actively construct their environments rather than passively react to them. Haan's hierarchy also doubles as a developmental theory. Its basic assumption—that development consists of progressive control over one's behavior—is extremely promising.

Nonetheless, there are several limitations to Haan's theory. The main problem lies in her a priori categorization of the three modes into adaptive and maladaptive processes and in the conditions under which the three modes are used. In part, Haan's theory is too neatly categorical. For example, she believes that people can use rational, coping modes when not under too much stress, and defensive modes when the stress is too great—an extension of classical Freudian hydraulics. However, as can be noted by any casual observer, people can and do act in a rational, focused manner under situations of extreme environmental demand—during combat and disasters, for example (see Chapter 10).

Further, some have argued that defensive processes are not necessarily pathological. For example, Lazarus (1983) has argued that, under certain limited circumstances, denial can have beneficial effects by granting a brief respite that allows an individual to gather strength. Horowitz (1976, 1986) has described the sequelae to extremely stressful events in terms of the phases of denial and numbness of affect alternating with intrusive memories. Horowitz believes that this process, while unconscious and probably defensive, is not pathological in that it provides a means of working through or adjusting to the event. This allows the information to be gradually incorporated so as not overwhelm the person.

The primary problem with hierarchical, teleological systems is that they tend to be expressions of the dominant cultural mode, and, as such, may be limited to that culture. For example, as future-oriented, differentiated thinking and as the "open, ordered, and tempered" expression of affect, Haan's criteria for coping is clearly culture bound. As we shall see in Chapter 11, some cultures have very different modes of regulating affect, preferring either indirect expressions of affect or decidedly "nontempered" ones.

Integrated Models of Coping and Defense

Rather than view coping and defense as separate hierarchies, other clinicians have envisioned defense mechanisms as supporting more general coping and/or adaptive processes directed at managing the environment. For White (1974), adaptation includes defense, mastery, and coping, defined simply as adaptation under difficult circumstances. Coping has three important functions (White, 1974, p. 55):

1. keep securing adequate information about the environment;
2. maintain satisfactory internal conditions for both action and for processing information; [and]
3. maintain [the organism's] autonomy or freedom of movement, freedom to use its repertoire in a flexible fashion

White's contribution is thus to recognize the importance of obtaining information about the environment. He perceived defense processes as necessary prerequisites for gathering information and acting upon the environment. Individuals who are overwhelmed by their emotions are unable to adequately deal with environmental problems, and defensive processes are seen as a means of supporting problem-solving activities. These problem-solving activities, in turn, are not ends in themselves but function to maintain the individual's autonomy and freedom, as well as his or her self-esteem. Thus, White's schema is also inherently hierarchical. However, defensive processes are seen as a necessary rather than pathological component of adaptation, and adaptive processes are thus both developmental and since they are directed toward the higher goals of autonomy and freedom.

Murphy (1974; Murphy & Moriarty, 1976) studied adaptation over time in a panel of children who were followed from infancy through adulthood. Murphy's techniques were primarily based upon observation of the children interacting with their parents and peers, and interviews about how they coped with both minor problems and major life crises.

Murphy (1974, p. 77) divided adaptation into four components:

1. Reflexes (built in mechanisms) and instincts (broader built-in patterns);
2. Coping efforts (to deal with situations not adequately managed by reflexes);
3. Mastery resulting from effective and well-practiced coping efforts;
4. Competence as the congeries of skills resulting from cumulative mastery achievement.

Coping is defined as having two components: active efforts directed toward the environment (Coping I) and defense mechanisms (Coping II). Coping is defined as "efforts to deal with environmental pressures that could not be handled by reflexes or organized skills [involving] struggles, trials, persistent focused energy directed toward a goal" (Murphy, 1974, p. 71).

Menninger (1963) envisioned coping as a means of tension-reduction and problem-solving. His focus was on conscious attempts to cope with problems and the ability of individuals to draw upon large coping repertoires:

> Faced with an increased task of adjustment and sensing the increased tension, the ego seems capable of overexerting itself. It makes special efforts, and it has at its disposal many techniques for solving the problem and diminishing the tension. It can suppress, it can repress, it can permit some gratification or effect more sublimation. It can direct some behavior toward altering the external circumstances, perhaps focusing some aggressive energy directly against the threat or danger; it can sidestep the issue, or it can provide some antidote. It can direct a withdrawal of the personality from the danger situation, or it can invoke help from external sources. . . . The ego of our relatively healthy-minded individual will have to make some choices and resort to some expediencies. (pp. 133–134)

Menninger provided an early and engaging description of coping in everyday life. One of the earliest ways of relieving distress is through touch: turning to the mother for hugging and rocking. Later, verbal reassurances become important. Food and alcohol consumption reduce tension, as does affective discharge through crying, swearing, or "laughing it off." Fantasizing may reduce tension, as does withdrawal through sleep and dreaming. However, one may also exercise self-control, talk to other people, or think through a problem. Individuals also work off excess energy through working, playing, or physical exercise. People engage in active problem solving and attempt to alter the environment, or they may also engage in pointless overactivity.

The key emphasis in this system is flexibility. Menninger quotes from an early study by Visotsky, Hamburg, Goss, and Lebovitz (1961) of poliomyelitis patients: "Frequently we see an interlocking or alternation of protective strategies. If coping pattern A does not work, then pattern B is brought to bear on the problem. If A and B together do not work, then pattern C is brought into play, and so on" (quoted in Menninger, 1963, p. 133n.).

While these strategies are seen as regulating or discharging tension and restoring an individual to homeostasis, Menninger's theory also had a developmental cast. Menninger recognized that there may be long-term outcomes of coping with everyday problems. On the one hand, adaptations made in coping with stress may "make for a less flexible, less resourceful personality than we would wish, with less capacity for adaptation to change and to new stresses" (Menninger, 1963, p. 147). On the other hand, there may be positive outcomes to adap-

tive processes: "A degree of resiliency and sturdiness may be engen-
dered by the successful weathering of many such crises" (Menninger,
1963, p. 147). Healthy outcomes to stressful episodes are those resulting
in a flexible, resourceful personality that allows for satisfactions, sublimation, outlets for controlled and neutralized aggression, and attachment to significant others.

Thus, Menninger, White, and Murphy described coping as
processes that unfold over time and that are directed toward both the
environment and, in the form of defense mechanisms, toward the person. Adaptation is both conscious and unconscious and is inherently
developmental in nature in that individuals develop resources and vulnerabilities. Menninger clearly identified different types of coping
processes, whereas for Murphy anything that involved effort in novel
situations could be defined as coping.

Summary

Psychoanalytic studies of coping that focus on defensive strategies have
several assumptions. The primary function of defense mechanisms is
to control negative affect, primarily anxiety. These mechanisms are
assumed to be rooted in personality, primarily in unconscious conflicts stemming from childhood trauma. Being expressive of personality, coping styles are assumed to be consistent across situations,
although, as we have seen, the use of defense mechanisms may be transitory.

Psychoanalytic theories are denoted by their use of hierarchies.
With some theorists, notably Haan and Vaillant, hierarchies are characterized by their assumptions of pathology. In Vaillant's case, defense
mechanisms can be ordered according to the degree to which they distort reality, with more mature mechanisms being the least distorting.
For Haan, conscious coping processes are inherently more adaptive,
while defensive processes are more pathological.

In contrast, psychodynamic theorists who integrate models of coping and defense are more likely to recognize environmental contingencies. These theorists tend to define defensive processes as attempts to
control emotions in order to engage in more problem-focused strategies. For Menninger in particular, defenses only become pathological
when they interfere with coping processes and/or the general enjoy-
ment of life. Menninger's theory clearly anticipates many more modern
approaches.

Psychoanalytic approaches tend to be based on case studies and
intensive interviews or observations over relatively long periods of time.
This can provide fascinating material for a developmental, growth-

oriented study of adaptation (e.g., White, 1961). Unfortunately, these types of designs tend to be highly labor intensive, and only Haan has attempted to operationalize her schema into easily usable instruments.

Nonetheless, psychoanalytic theories of defense, coping, and adaptation are unique in their focus on development. For White and Murphy, stressful episodes are important in that individuals can develop their coping repertoires and develop a sense of mastery. The primary focus is on the individual, and the case studies presented by the various psychoanalytic authors are fascinating and often insightful. This focus on the individual, however, tends to neglect environmental considerations in coping and, as we shall see in the next chapter, presents difficulties in developing generalizable measurement techniques.

Coping as Personality Traits

Early studies asked, "How do people differ in their responses to a particular type of stress?" and grouped individuals into different adaptational types or coping styles. A very early example of this is a study that characterized different ways of adapting to retirement (Reichard, Livson, & Peterson, 1962). In this qualitative study, retirees were classified into five different types. "Rocking-chair men" were content to sit in their rocking chairs on the porch, passively watching the world go by, whereas the "armored men" took a very active stance toward life — for example, by getting involved in community activities or going on trips — and in general were overactive, primarily to ward off anxieties. The "angry men" were extremely discontent, spending most of their time complaining about things, while another complaining group was labeled the "self-haters." Finally, the "mature men" accepted themselves and had few regrets. From these descriptions, one can easily imagine that these men responded in these ways to most things in their lives, not just to retirement.

Similarly, Wortman and Silver (1989) characterized four stable coping styles following bereavement. Surprisingly, there were individuals who never appeared distressed, while others could be classified as acute grievers, chronic grievers, and those who experienced a delayed reaction.

Millon (1982) stated: "Personality styles characterize the more or less everyday manner in which people approach the events of their lives. It is these typical ways of coping . . . that may contribute to illness and the manner in which individuals deal with it" (p. 11). Based on earlier work by Lipowski (1970) and Leigh and Reiser (1980), Millon described eight ways in which individuals characteristically deal with health problems. Individuals who use the introversive style of coping tend to be "emotionally flat," using a cognitive coping style called minimization. These individuals tend to ignore, deny, or rationalize their problems and are often quiet and untalkative. They can be oblivious to the implications of their illness and primarily wish to be left alone.

In contrast, individuals using the cooperative style follow advice religiously, as long as they do not have to assume responsibility for themselves. They need care and reassurance and may see illness as a "relief." People using the sociable coping style tend to be talkative, outgoing, and charming, although undependable. They are disinclined to deal with serious problems, viewing illness as a strategy to gain attention.

Individuals who are highly motivated to regain their health are sometimes characterized as having a confident style. The sick role signifies a major threat to their self-image as independent and invulnerable. They are unduly concerned with status and may display arrogance and a disdain for others.

A similar stratagem is the forceful style, wherein individuals are aggressive, hostile, and domineering. They are also unwilling to accept the sick role and forcefully attack the problem, sometimes to the extent of ignoring the seriousness of their injuries (e.g. by inappropriately exercising an injured limb or climbing stairs during a heart attack).

Individuals using a respectful style may also see illness as a weakness and may want to conceal or deny problems. In contrast to the hostile style, these individuals are unduly responsible and conforming, becoming "model" patients. However, these people may have rigid routines and inflexible daily schedules, which makes coping with the disruptive aspects of illness difficult.

Finally, individuals characterized by a sensitive style may be "long suffering" and "self-sacrificing." They may be difficult patients in that they are likely to reject reassurance and to complain a great deal.

In some ways, this characterization of coping styles is preferable to simple approach–avoidance dichotomies (see below), in that it allows for a more complex description of the ways in which people behave in an illness situation. Such characterizations may also be clinically useful and do not necessarily entail the sort of pathology attendant upon descriptions based upon defense mechanisms. Nonetheless, most of these styles are described in ways inclusive of pathology — perhaps individuals who are coping well with physical illnesses do not come to the attention of clinicians. However, it is also possible that a clinician utilizing this schema may tend to "pigeonhole" people in inappropriate ways. Depending upon the sensitivity and skill of the staff, the same patient may be self-reliant or complaining, denying or compliant. In other words, strict personality approaches ignore environmental demands that may shape an individual's behavior.

Coping as Perceptual Styles

In contrast to psychoanalytic conceptions, the perceptual style approach to coping focuses less on how individuals deal with emotions and more on how they deal with information. The earliest typology was called repression–sensitization (Byrne, 1964). Repressors were defined as individuals who avoid or suppress information, sensitizers were individuals who seek or augment information. This dichotomy has appeared in the literature in many different guises, including nonvigilant–vigilant (Averill & Rosenn, 1972), selective inattention–selective attention (Kahneman, 1973), reducers–augmenters (Petrie, 1978), blunting-monitoring (Miller, 1980; Miller & Mangan, 1983), and rejection-attention (Mullen & Suls, 1982). Currently, the terminology most commonly in use is approach avoidance (for a review of this construct, see Roth & Cohen, 1986).

Lazarus, Averill, and Opton (1974) provided three major criticisms of the repression–sensitization typology. First, measures of repression–sensitization are highly correlated with anxiety. Second, there appears to be little consistency of perceptual style across situations. Finally, general measures of repression–sensitization do not predict actual coping behavior (Cohen & Lazarus, 1973), although situation-specific measures have been shown to be useful in particular circumstances (see Miller & Mangan, 1983).

Further, one could argue that there are patterns rather than styles in how one processes incoming information. Horowitz (1976), and Lazarus (1983) have argued that individuals alternate between phases of denial and intrusiveness. Pennebaker, Colder, and Sharp (1990) refer to these types of coping theories as "stage models of coping." For example, a violent trauma may first threaten to overwhelm the ego, and denial or blunting may serve a very useful purpose in protecting the individual. However, too much denial can prevent a person from taking appropriate action, as in the case of the middle-aged man with chest pains who runs up the stairs to prove that he is not having a heart attack rather than go to the emergency room. In the intrusive phase, images and memory come flooding back, as when combat veterans or rape victims experience flashbacks.

While some people have very sharp swings between denial and intrusion, others simply use denial as a way of maintaining hope. As Lazarus (1983) recounted, persons with terminal cancer may be planning the next year's vacation on one day and crying the next because they know that they only have a few weeks to live. People may also vary in the extent to which they use approach or avoidance processes in different areas of their lives. In my dissertation on middle-aged men and women (from an earlier generation), I found that men very often used problem-focused coping at work, and emotion-focused or avoidant coping at home, whereas women used opposite tactics. Perhaps people use approach strategies in situations in which they have adequate coping resources and in which they feel comfortable in dealing with problems, and perhaps they are more likely to use avoidant strategies in situations with which they feel less comfortable. Thus, rather than coping *styles* per se, one could refer to approach–avoidance as coping *modalities* that are differentially used, depending upon the interaction or transaction between the person and the situation; only a few individuals may be consistently characterized by one or the other.

Dichotomizing coping strategies into two broad modalities provides certain benefits: It is simple and elegant and can be used to classify a broad number of different strategies. Currently, some have argued anew for dividing coping strategies into two or three broad categories (Amirkhian, 1990; Endler & Parker, 1990). However, this runs the danger of oversimplifying the construct. After all, if one is truly interested in understanding what constitutes efficacious coping, then knowing simply that someone "approached" a problem is insufficient. We would need to know the *quality* of that approach: Was it organized or disorganized, hostile, compliant, or assertive? When people avoided a problem, did they do so by going on a week-long drinking binge or by reading a book to get their minds off it for a little while? Further, as we have seen, approach and avoidance are not mutually exclusive categories. The conjunction of how they are used is undoubtedly critical. For example, one may blunt emotions by denying responsibility but still engage in problem-focused coping (Aldwin, 1991). Thus, the construct of approach and avoidance can be a useful informing organizing principle, but our understanding of coping should not be forced into such a procrustean bed.

SITUATIONAL DETERMINANTS OF COPING

In contrast to personality theories, proponents of the situational determinant approach to coping argue that the types of strategies that individuals use to cope with problems depend highly on environmental demands. That is, the characteristics of different types of stresses "pull for" different types of solutions and coping processes.

To take examples at random, the way in which an individual copes with the death of a spouse could be very different from the way in which that same person deals with the limitations imposed by rheumatoid arthritis or the strategies used in finding a new job after being laid off.

Early studies often conducted in-depth observations and detailed empirical descriptions of individuals dealing with problems of particular interest such as disasters. The focus was on broad, general adaptive responses to a major life change or problem rather than specific behaviors in everyday situations. In some ways this is not dissimilar to psychoanalytic approaches in that such research typically involved the intense observation of small numbers of individuals and relied upon interviews and personal observations. It differs, however, in being empirically rather than theoretically oriented. That is, such researchers often did not try to develop a general model of human behavior that is applicable across a range of contexts and problems, but rather simply ask, "How do people respond to this particular stressor?"

This approach has produced many classical works, including Wallace's (1956) description of psychological responses to a tornado, Lifton's (1968) study of the survivors of Hiroshima, and Erikson's (1976) examination of the Boulder Creek disaster. Of course, this simple question generally evokes complex answers, and these authors in particular sought to identify general processes that give insight into human nature.

There is a fair amount of evidence showing that individuals do respond in varying ways to different types of stressors (for a review see Mattlin, Wethington, & Kessler, 1990). There are a number of ways in which situations can be categorized. One way is to determine whether the situation has already had harmful effects (such as a loss), has the potential for future harm (e.g., entails a threat), or has potentially positive outcomes (i.e., it can be seen as a challenge) (Brown & Harris, 1978; Lazarus, 1966; McCrae, 1984). Alternatively, a researcher can classify the stressors according to their content types, such as illness, death, interpersonal or practical (Billings & Moos, 1984; Folkman & Lazarus, 1980; Mattlin et al., 1990). The general research strategy is to ask individuals to relate multiple problems and compare coping responses across problems. Such studies are often longitudinal. For example, the Folkman and Lazarus study followed individuals every month for a year and asked them to relate problems each month. In general, individuals utilize coping strategies that are directed more toward the emotions in loss circumstances, such as illnesses or deaths, whereas coping strategies are directed more toward problems that are practical and interpersonal, involving threat or challenge appraisals. Thus, individuals alter their coping techniques depending upon the demands of the situation.

Pearlin and Schooler (1978) categorized stressors according to five major social roles: work, marital, parental, household economics, and health. They found that distinctly different coping strategies are used in different social roles. Strategies, such as disciplining a child, that are used in coping with parental problems are simply not appropriate in other social roles, such as difficulties with a supervisor at work. Further, even similar strategies may have differential effects across situations. For example, Pearlin and Schooler found that problem-focused strategies might relieve psychological distress with interpersonal problems but would have little effect at work.

COGNITIVE APPROACHES

Cognitive approaches to coping are based on four assumptions. First, how an individual copes with a problem is largely dependent upon his or her appraisal of the situation. Generally, appraisal is considered to be a conscious evaluation of whether a situation is benign, threatening, involves a harm or a loss, or constitutes a challenge (Lazarus & Folkman, 1984). If a situation is benign, no coping is needed. Theoretically, a situation that is threatening or challenging will evoke attempts to solve or ward off the problem (problem-focused coping), whereas a situation that involves harm or loss will be more likely to evoke palliative coping, which attempts to decrease or assuage the negative emotions evoked by a stressor. Thus, in cognitive models, adaptation is *conscious*—that is, individuals appraise the type of problem and its severity and decide how to cope with problems based on prior experience.

Secondly, cognitive approaches assume that individuals are flexible in their choice of coping strategies and modify their strategies according to the demands of the particular problem. That is, they assume some degree of situational specificity; individuals are not uniformly consistent in how they approach problems, but rather take into account environmental contingencies. The term "coping styles" is anathema to such theorists because it implies that coping is consistent, a function of personality, rather than a blend of personal preferences and environmental demands. Thus, cognitive theorists believe that one must tie any reports of coping strategies to a particular problem.

The third assumption is that coping efforts include both problem- and emotion-focused strategies that are directed at the problem and at the emotions, respectively. Cognitive theorists do not attempt to arrange coping efforts hierarchically. Although controlling the emotions might facilitate efforts to solve or manage a problem, it is also likely that solving or managing a problem satisfactorily is one of the best ways of managing emotions.

(Note that the construct of individuals who consciously seek to regulate their emotions has some very interesting implications for theories of adult development. In psychodynamic theories, affect is automatically regulated by the ego via the unconscious mechanisms of defense. By contrast, in the cognitive model, the self is actively and consciously trying to manage both internal and external processes. As we shall see in Chapter 14, this construct of self-determination in the management of stress has interesting implications for theories of adult development.)

Finally, cognitive theorists also do not assume a hierarchy of adaptiveness. Rather, they take an empiricist approach: The task is to identify which coping strategies are used in specific situations and the conditions under which the strategies do or do not promote positive adaptation. For example, rather than assume that denial is of necessity maladaptive, Lazarus (1983) described conditions under which denial can be a useful tool—for example, by allowing individuals to maintain hope in seemingly hopeless situations.

It would be safe to say that the majority of coping researchers currently have adopted at least some aspects of the cognitive approach —that is, they rely upon self-descriptions of coping behaviors, generally in the form of checklists. However, many researchers, either implicitly or explicitly, continue to regard the use of coping strategies primarily as a function of personality, either by simply not specifying a target situation or by inadequately doing so (e.g., McCrae & Costa, 1986). And, indeed, the extent to which coping strategies are a function of both the person and the environment is a matter of some debate. To my knowledge, no one has done a study of the amount of variance in coping strategies contributed by personality and situational factors. Researchers have shown that coping varies by situation (Mattlin et al., 1990), and that personality influences the use of coping strategies (Bolger, 1990; Holakan & Moos, 1985), but the relative proportion of the variance that the two factors contribute has not been examined.

In part, this problem of relative proportion stems from the difficulty in adequately specifying the relevant situational factors that are thought to affect coping. No one has developed an adequate theory of what the ecological psychologists refer to as "environmental affordances" for coping behavior (Aldwin & Stokols, 1988). The term "environmental affordances" refers to the characteristics of the environment that evoke specific behaviors. Thus, a chair affords the behavior of sitting better than an angled surface does; a bed affords sleeping behavior better than a rock pile does (Barker, 1968). At best, we characterize situations in terms of roles, for example, work versus family problems (Folkman & Lazarus, 1980; Pearlin & Schooler, 1978). But all work problems are not equivalent; how one copes with difficulties with a supervisor could be very different from strategies used with peers or assistants. Similarly, dealing with a two-year-old's temper tantrums requires different strategies from those used for dealing with the temper tantrums of an adolescent.

To adequately examine the relative contribution of personality and environment requires adequate specification of environmental characteristics. However, determining the dimensions of environmental affordances vis-à-vis coping behavior in a naturalistic setting is an overwhelming and probably too complex task. While some researchers do expand the assessment of appraisal to include perceptions of controllability of the stressor (Moos, Brennan, Fondacaro, & Moos, 1990), self-reports cannot adequately distinguish personality contributions to this appraisal. Thus, laboratory research may be needed before attempting to appropriately develop such a theory. Approach–avoidance researchers such as Amirkhan (1990) have provided an example of such work in studies of the interaction between ambiguity, predictability, and personality.

Other central assumptions of this approach remain untested. For example, it is unclear what proportion of coping efforts are unconscious, and if unconscious it is unclear how these can be assessed in the self-report format. If an individual is actively using denial, for example, how are self-report inventories going to assess this? Second, the extent to which individuals vary in their coping strategies over time is also unclear. To what extent do people vary their approaches, or are they likely to rely on certain characteristic coping styles across situations and time? Are some strategies more stable than others? Folkman, Lazarus, Dunkel-Schetter, Gruen, and DeLongis (1986) assessed coping over five occasions and found that emotion-focused coping was moderately stable, whereas secondary appraisal (and presumably problem-focused coping) was much more variable. Aldwin and Revenson (1987) suggested that emotion-focused coping may be more influenced by personality characteristics, whereas problem-focused coping may be more affected by the situation, a hypothesis supported by Long and Sangster (1993).

Third, if we do not begin with a priori definitions of adaptive and maladaptive coping, by what criteria should the outcomes of coping strategies be assessed? For example, most studies have examined the ability of coping to moderate the effect of stress on psychological or physical symptoms. However, most of the coping studies to date have found that some strategies, especially emotion-focused ones, increase or magnify psychological distress rather than buffer the effect of stress per se (Aldwin & Revenson, 1987). Perhaps we need to examine the ability of coping strategies to maintain positive psychological states, as well as mitigate negative ones. Further, coping strategies could also affect not only the individual's physical and psychological well-being but also the resolution of the problem, the well-being of others in the situation, and perhaps even the larger society (Aldwin & Stokols, 1988).

Finally, the cognitive model assumes that coping grows out of appraisals of situations and personal experience. However, social and cultural influences on coping strategies are seldom examined. Are there cultural or social differences in what constitute preferred or effective coping strategies?

SUMMARY

Coping is defined as the use of strategies for dealing with actual or anticipated problems and their attendant negative emotions. While individuals actively attempt to handle problems, their emotional responses and strategies may not always be fully conscious. The social and cultural environment can influence both the appraisal of stress and the use of coping strategies in both direct and subtle ways. Thus, coping is an overdetermined phenomenon. Assessing coping strategies used by individuals presents unique challenges, and, as we shall see, no one scale attempts to measure all of the facets of coping.

CHAPTER 7

Measurement of
Coping Strategies

Tₕe most controversial issue in the field today is how to assess coping. While nearly everyone agrees that coping is a (or even the) crucial variable in understanding the effect of stress on health, nearly everyone disagrees on how it should be measured. I think this is due to the fact that we are in the midst of developing a new technology in psychology and the social sciences. Traditionally, psychology has relied upon three basic techniques. With the first technique, experimental or laboratory-based research, the stimulus and the response are clearly defined and measured in a specified or controlled setting. The second technique, personality research, has traditionally relied upon "paper and pencil" tests of personality (and values), in which individuals self-attribute characteristics (e.g., "I am usually kind and patient") or state various preferences indicating values (e.g., "I would prefer to go sea kayaking rather than read a book"). In personality research, psychometric properties such as internal and cross-time reliability are critical, and external validity is most often tested against other paper and pencil instruments. The third technique, qualitative research, studied what people actually thought and did in real situations and was primarily used by clinicians such as Coles (1977) and Lifton (1968) or qualitative sociologists such as Erikson (1976). These researchers conducted field studies by interviewing people and relying upon their native intelligence or simple coding techniques to make sense of this information.

In stress research, we ask individuals for standardized self-reports of events that they experienced which, as we have seen, has involved many problems in reliability and validity. In coping research, we ask people to tell us not only what they did, or how they behaved, in a particular circumstance, but also what they thought and how they handled their emotions, using a standardized format. In other words, we are combining two different techniques, borrowing from both personality research and qualitative field studies, and exactly how one goes about constructing these measures and evaluating their reliability and validity is unknown. In many ways, the assumptions underlying the two techniques and their goals conflict, as do the research strategies. Hence the controversy.

There are several basic (albeit related) debates that fuel this controversy. First, should we assess coping *styles*, which are thought to be stable characteristics of individuals, or coping *processes*, which are fluctuating strategies that change in response to demands by the person or the environment? Second, should the content of items be general enough to apply to a variety of situations or should they be specific to particular kinds of situations? Third, do we want very rich, complicated descriptions of coping strategies (which are often psychometrically messy) or should we try to identify simplifying dimensions that are thought to underlie more complex characterizations and that are psychometrically much more satisfying (i.e., approach–avoidance)? Fourth, should we use rating for scale items that assess coping effort or simply dichotomous items to indicate whether or not a particular coping strategy was used?

Finally, there is one issue that everyone acknowledges but then avoids (like the plague): If people do use defense mechanisms in coping with stress—which means that coping strategies are at least partially unconscious—how can they be assessed? Do self-report inventories miss a whole realm of coping that may be crucial in understanding the relation between stress and health? Can interviews reliably tap these strategies?

This chapter will address each of those issues in turn. In addition, Appendix A lists many of the various coping inventories currently in use, grouped according to the typologies delineated in the previous chapter.

COPING STYLES VERSUS COPING PROCESSES

The study of coping is rooted in the widespread observation that there are individual differences in how people react to and deal with stress. Since Stouffer's (1949) early study of American soldiers and combat fatigue, now called posttraumatic stress disorder (PTSD), researchers have known that some people simply do not have the resources to deal with major trauma and that they therefore succumb to psychiatric disorders very quickly under stress. For example, nearly one third of combat casualties in World War II were psychiatric in nature (Friedman, 1981). Since then, the search has been on to identify the person and environmental factors that lead to adverse stress reactions, which can be divided into three basic (and often conflicting) orientations.

Clinical and personality psychologists focus on the personality factors associated with vulnerability (or resilience) to stress. These are assumed to be stable characteristics of the individual and are often referred to as coping styles. In contrast, sociologists and social psychologists are more likely to examine the ways in which the environment is organized which can lead to vulnerability or resilience on the part of individuals, that is, structural barriers in accessing resources.

The transactional or process approach seeks to combine these two orientations, and posits a dynamic transaction between the person and the environment (see Chapter 6). In other words, coping is thought to vary within individuals, depending upon the situational context, and within contexts, depending upon individual differences. Coping strategies are hypothesized to be complex and dynamic, changing in response to their effects on the environment.

What can be confusing is that, methodologically speaking, these approaches at first glance appear to be very similar. Most rely on "paper and pencil tests," questionnaires that list a variety of coping strategies. *The measurement distinction between these points of view lies primarily in the accompanying instructions on the coping questionnaire to the respondents,* a point often overlooked by many researchers.

As we have observed, coping styles or trait approaches assume that there are stable characteristics of the individual that account for differences in reactions to stress. Thus, these approaches traditionally use a standard personality trait format of self-descriptors to infer coping styles (Haan, 1977). More recent approaches ask the respondent what he or she *usually* does to handle problems *without referring to a specific problem* (Carver, Scheier, & Weintraub, 1989; Endler & Parker, 1990). Thus, the coping style approach assumes consistency within individuals across stressors, without regard to environmental demands.

In contrast, sociologists such as Pearlin and Schooler (1978) have assumed that the choice of coping strategies is primarily a function of the social context, specifically role demands. They may ask questions such as, "How do you cope with problems with your spouse?" or "How do you cope in raising your children?" Thus, social approaches link specific role-related behaviors to role strains, for example, trying to establish better communications with a spouse or restricting privileges when a child is disobedient. This approach assumes consistency within role domain, but inconsistency across roles.

The process approach does not assume consistency either within or across situations or roles. Rather, it asks respondents to recollect what they did in a particular stressful episode, usually occurring during the past week or month, although some researchers simply tie the coping to a life event in the past year (e.g., Moos, Brennan, Fondacaro, & Moos, 1990). Some researchers use a diary approach, which asks respondents to fill out questionnaires each evening concerning problems during the day (Stone, Neale, & Shiffman, 1993). Process approaches permit the examination of both the person and the environmental influences on coping strategies.

There are a number of methodological problems with all of these approaches toward assessing coping. Approaches based upon coping styles make three assumptions that have yet to be empirically demonstrated. The first is that generalized self-descriptors of coping styles translate reliably into actual behaviors in a specific situation. This notion has been challenged by Lazarus and his colleagues. For example, early work by Cohen and Lazarus (1973) demonstrated no relation between trait measures of repression–sensitization and actual approach–avoidance behavior in coping with surgery, although more recent strategies that ask individuals to describe more specific approach–avoidance behaviors in medical settings may prove a little more accurate (Miller, 1980). There is also some suggestion that people high in neuroticism may use more emotion-focused coping in stressful circumstances (Bolger, 1990). However, there is as yet no indication that coping strategies in general may be mapped onto specific personality traits in a one-to-one fashion. To get around this, some researchers will ask how a respondent *generally* copes with problems, which leads us to the second assumption.

The second assumption is that individuals do cope consistently with different problems. This is as yet unproven. The handful of published studies that have examined coping at two points in time have generally found rather modest correlations, mostly in the .20s and .30s (Fondacaro & Moos, 1987; McCrae, 1989), and studies that look for situational differences in coping behaviors always find them (e.g., Folkman & Lazarus, 1980; Mattlin, Wethington, & Kessler, 1990). Further, how individuals cope with a given problem such as exams (Folkman & Lazarus, 1985) or breast cancer (Heim, Augustiny, Schaffner, & Valach, 1993), also changes over time, depending upon the varying situational demands.

Ogrocki, Stephens, and Kinney (1990) examined the relationship between state and trait coping measures. In this study of caregivers of relatives with Alzheimer's disease, respondents were asked to state how they usually coped with caregiving problems in two settings: at home and at the nursing home. State–trait measures were moderately correlated, ranging from .25 to .47. Not surprisingly, the trait measures were more strongly related to a global measure of well-being. However, examining across situations, the *state* measures were more strongly correlated with each other than were the *trait* measures. This suggests that the state measures may be more accurate assessments of coping behaviors than the trait measures are. Carver and Scheier (1994) also found that coping style and coping process measures were only weakly related to each other.

Ipsative studies are needed that assess patterns of stability and change in coping behaviors in individuals across time and situations. Some early and unpublished analyses that I did using the Berkeley Stress and Coping data, which assessed up to ten coping episodes over a year, suggested that there are marked differences in patterns of stability and change. Some individuals demonstrated rather consistent patterns of approaches emphasizing negative affect (e.g., avoidance and self-blame) or positive affect (e.g., growth-oriented coping), and others simply shifted their strategies according to situational demands. Thus, while many people make the not unreasonable assumption that coping styles exist, at this point we simply do not have adequate empirical evidence for cross-situational consistency in coping strategies — although emotion-focused coping may be more consistent than problem-focused coping (Folkman et al., 1986). Dunkel-Schetter, Feinstein, Taylor, and Falke (1992) found that over half of the sample of cancer patients were very evenhanded in their coping efforts — that is, they did not greatly emphasize one strategy at the expense of others.

It is true that persons routinely respond to questionnaires that ask them how they usually cope with problems, which would seemingly be prima facie evidence for the existence of coping styles. However, there are marked concerns over whether individuals' *generalized* descriptions of coping styles accurately describe *specific* coping behaviors (Folkman & Lazarus, 1980; see also Carver & Scheier, 1994). Anecdotal evidence leads many researchers to suspect that persons who believe they do one thing actually do quite another. Individuals may overestimate their own performance, thinking that, in general, they only use strategies that they think are adaptive. One 80-year-old respondent could not understand why I bothered to study how individuals cope with stress. "Everyone knows," he said, "that what you do is sit down and analyze the problem and then solve it calmly and rationally." At that point, his wife of 50 years burst out laughing and said, "You've never done that in your life!" Sadly enough, when this man's wife died a few months later, his primary coping behavior was first to engage in a mad whirlwind of activities to ward off depression (he took six concurrent courses at a local junior college) and then, when that failed, he went to bed for several months with a bottle of alcohol and had to be hospitalized. Not all problems are amenable to rational analysis, and how individuals think that they usually cope could be very different from their actual behavior under stress.

Process approaches attempt to solve this problem by asking the respondents to recollect a very specific (and preferably very recent) episode and to recount their cognitions and behaviors in coping with that one episode. The (albeit untested) assumption is that this is a more accurate technique, which minimizes distortions in self-presentation. Using this technique, people have clearly been shown to modify their coping strategies in response to different types of problems (Billings & Moos, 1984; Folkman & Lazarus, 1980; McCrae, 1984; Mattlin et al., 1990). Manifestly, we use different strategies depending upon situational demands. For example, simple reflection on our own behaviors reveals that how we deal with a small child crying is very different from the strategies used to study for an exam.

However, reliance upon a recent stressful episode as the mechanism for evoking self-reported coping cognitions and behaviors unleashes another set of difficulties, with one of the primary difficulties being diversity in the types of problems that evoke the behavior. For example, in one survey that we did the type of problems reported by the respondents ranged from a tiff with a boyfriend to the murder of grandchildren in a restaurant robbery (Aldwin & Revenson, 1987). Trying to examine individual differences in coping strategies in this context is inevitably confounded with variability in stressors. One can mitigate this problem by controlling for situational characteristics, such as perceived stressfulness of the problem, general type of problem (e.g., relating to health, bereavement, work, or interpersonal conflict), or appraisal characteristics such as a threat to well-being or actual harm already done (McCrae, 1984). In doing so, however, there is still the problem of variability in the stimulus. Even with a broad category such as work stressors, there may be distinct dissimilarities in problem characteristics that may affect the choice of coping strategies. Dealing with an irate supervisor, for example, may require strategies different from those used in dealing with a broken machine.

One way of getting around this difficulty is to study individuals who are all undergoing a similar stressor, such as surgery or a specific chronic illness. A favorite stressful context for stress and coping researchers is midterms or finals, for the obvious reason that in a university setting it is easy to find subjects. Using this technique, researchers have shown that coping is clearly a fluid process, influenced by both personality characteristics (Bolger, 1990; Friedman et al., 1992; Long & Sangster, 1993), situational demands (Folkman & Lazarus, 1986; Heim et al., 1993; Mattlin et al., 1990), and even the social and physical characteristics of the setting (Mechanic, 1978).

The key criteria in determining whether to use a process or style measure must be the research question at hand. If one wishes to know how well a student is going to perform on a specific test, then knowing how the student prepared for that particular test (a process measure) is critical. However, if one is trying to predict a student's overall grade point average, knowing how the student usually copes with tests (a style measure) might be better. Similar to the debate between life events and hassles research, process measures might be better for predicting immediate outcomes while style measures may be better for predicting long-term outcomes. Carver et al. (1989) tried to straddle this fence by developing a state–trait measure of coping, which can be worded for general or specific strategies, depending on the instruction to the respondents.

My particular preference is for process measures, given my mistrust of people's generalized descriptions of their behavior. A good example of this is that depressed persons often present themselves and their situations as helpless and hopeless. However, when one examines actual strategies used in stressful situations, depressed people have been shown to use more strategies than those who are not depressed (Coyne, Aldwin, & Lazarus, 1981; Folkman & Lazarus, 1986). However, I certainly would not try to predict who would come down with cancer from an examination of only one episode of coping 10 years earlier, given my belief in the variability of coping across situations. Thus, the issue devolves, to a certain extent, upon matters of personal and disciplinary preference and, as always, the specific question that a researcher has in mind.

Psychometric Issues

In response to the advocates of process-oriented coping instruments, researchers who prefer the simplicity of coping styles argue that process measures of coping are simply too psychometrically messy. Specifically, several researchers (Amirkian, 1990; Edwards & Baglioni, 1993; Endler & Parker, 1990) have criticized the most generally used process measure, the Ways of Coping Scale (WOCS) (Folkman & Lazarus, 1980; Folkman et al., 1986) for having an unstable factor structure and poor internal reliability on the subscales. By this reasoning, any change that appears to occur across situations using process measures of coping is primarily due to the unreliability of the instrument rather than to any important contribution of the situational context per se. By focusing only on approach–avoidance coping, Amirkian as well as Endler and Parker have been able to demonstrate that their measures of coping styles are psychometrically superior to process measures and have thus argued that trait measures are generally superior to process measures.

The problem with this line of reasoning is that these researchers are taking the criteria for what constitutes good personality instruments and inappropriately applying it to field instruments. Personality traits are supposed to tap stable characteristics of the individual. Thus, these traits should have high test–retest reliability. Further, personality measures assume some inaccuracy in self-description and are thus highly redundant, using several different items to tap one construct, which in turn generates good internal reliability.

Process instruments designed to be used in a field setting, however, are designed precisely not to be stable. These instruments are meant to tap variability and change, making them almost by definition unreliable. Further, a certain amount of vagueness in the wording of items was done purposefully so that the items would be applicable across situations. Thus, it is not surprising that the meaning of the item may change across situations; therefore, factor structures may also shift a bit. But it can be argued that this is a result of the instruments' accurate reflection of reality rather than of poor scale construction. For example, in problems involving interpersonal tensions, making a plan of action may appropriately include going and talking to the person who caused the problem. However, in dealing with a strictly practical problem such as changing a bicycle tire, going and talking to the person who caused the problem is simply not appropriate (assuming that the flat tire was due to natural causes and not malicious tack strewing). Thus, it is not surprising that items could cluster slightly differently depending on the characteristics of the situations with which people are coping.

Actually, changes in factor structure across situations can tell us a great deal about the types of demands of a situation. For example, the factor structure of the WOCS may change systematically when the target population consists of patients undergoing serious illnesses, such as rheumatoid arthritis (RA) or cancer (Dunkel-Schetter et al., 1992). This demonstrates that the characteristics of serious illness change coping patterns, but it does not mean that the WOCS is defective.

Factor structures and internal reliability may also vary because coping is a process that can change over time. While it is true that pen and paper instruments do not tap the process of change in strategies over time, in that people do not tell you, "First I did this, and then I did that" (Coyne, 1992), the very unreliability of the instrument may actually reflect the process of coping. Examination of any one checklist of coping strategies tied to a particular episode will almost invariably reveal what appear to be marked inconsistencies in individuals' accounts of what they did. For example, respondents often check off "Made a plan of action and followed it" and "Decided nothing could be done." In reality, these may not be contradictory statements. The strategies may be sequential—that is, individuals first tried to solve the problem, failed, and then decided that nothing could be done, or their initial assessment of the problem was that nothing could be done, but then they looked more closely and found possibilities for active intervention. Or the statements might refer to different aspects of the problem. A husband may come to the painful realization that nothing can be done about the fact that his wife is dying but still may take active measures to ameliorate her pain and discomfort. Thus, checking off both active and passive strategies on a coping instrument may not be contradictory at all, but it certainly wreaks havoc on the internal reliability of subscales and the orthogonality and stability of the factor structure!

Obviously, there are limits to the amounts of vagueness and unreliability that should be built into a scale, and attempts clearly need be made to eliminate double-barreled items (i.e., "Made a plan of action and followed it"), as well as those items that are impossibly imprecise ("Did something in hopes that it would help"). Further, there are questions about individual differences in how respondents interpret both the time period and the response ratings typically used in self-report coping questionnaires (Stone, Greenberg, Kennedy-Moore, & Newman, 1991). Nonetheless, it is invalid to hold process measures that are used in field settings to the same psychometric criteria as personality measures. They have different purposes and functions, and, unfortunately, field work (and reality) are very messy, changeable, and imprecise. Insisting on methodological purity at this stage in the research process would be akin to throwing out the baby with the bath water!

General versus Specific Coping Strategies

A related issue concerns the generalizability or specificity of items in a coping measure. If a scale is devised that is highly specific to a given circumstance, it may work very well in that situation, but not be generalizable to other situations. On the other hand, if a scale is devised in which the wording is vague enough to be relevant to many situations, the scale may not "fit" a particular situation very well. For example, "Made a plan of action and followed it" is sufficiently vague to apply to many situations, but its very vagueness may make it less than useful in any given situation. On the other hand, "Replaced buttons with velcro" may be a highly useful strategy for individuals coping with rheumatoid arthritis but would be completely inapplicable in most other situations.

Obviously, coping style researchers prefer coping instruments with items that are worded in a very general fashion. It would be hard to assume that substituting velcro for buttons is directly a function of personality (as opposed, say, to suggestions by a nurse or fellow member of a self-help group). On the other hand, approaching problems rationally and persevering in trying to find solutions to problems may well be a personality characteristic. However, one person's perseverance is another person's perseveration, or someone may think that she is being persistent when, from another person's point of view, she gave up on the problem far too early. Thus, trying to get specific instances of behavior may be a more accurate assessment of actual coping behavior used.

This is particularly important when trying to identify strategies that are useful in coping with very specific problems. For example, a clinician may be developing a manual to be used in helping clients deal with very particular problems, for example, a chronic illness such as rheumatoid arthritis. While exhortations to perseverance may be motivational, specific suggestions may be more meaningful, such as coming up with different ways of opening cans and bottles or substituting velcro for buttons.

On the other hand, very specific instruments cannot be used for examining some of the basic questions in coping research, such as stability and change in coping strategies across situations. Further, being able to compare the efficacy of coping strategies across situations (and studies) may also require a more generally worded scale. However, this may sacrifice predictive validity, as we have seen.

Lazarus (1990) has suggested an intermediate approach — namely, that individuals use a general coping scale such as the WOCS, but modify it to fit particular situations. Theoretically, this would allow some degree of comparability across studies while minimizing the loss of predictive validity for any one study. However, Endler and Parker (1990) have criticized this on methodological grounds: Item substitution or addition could affect the factor structure of the scale, thus increasing the difficulty of arriving at a consensus on the structure of coping strategies.

On the contrary, it is my observation that the factor structure for the WOCS is markedly robust, given the fact that there have been so many modifications of the scale in individual studies. The same basic factors keep reemerging in a host of different studies, even though individual items may shift around a bit, depending upon the population, type of stressor, and modifications made to the scale. Whether these same seven or eight factors universally define all possible coping strategies is yet another question.

However, the methods used in any particular research design must always defer to the research question. This point cannot be overemphasized. Thus, whether one assesses very specific or very general coping items in any particular study depends entirely upon the purpose of the study.

Diversity versus Simplicity

As we have seen in Chapter 6, early personality-based approaches to coping focused on two or three discrete and opposing dimensions, which have variously been called repression–sensitization, blunting–monitoring, and approach–avoidance. This approach has the benefit of a long theoretical history, both behaviorist and psychodynamic, and allows for good, clean psychometrics, which endears it to personality-oriented researchers. It is generally used in studies focusing on coping styles, and approach–avoidance measures most often utilize items that are couched in general rather than specific terms. By its very generality, it can provide an overarching theoretical framework with which to integrate many of the findings in the stress and coping literature. In other words, if one is willing to equate problem-focused coping with approach, on the one hand, and emotion-focused coping with avoidance, on the other, one can examine approach–avoidance strategies across studies—and, thus, across situations—and draw general conclusions concerning the utility of these two coping styles. Not surprisingly, approach is generally associated with positive outcomes, and avoidance with negative ones (Mullen & Suls, 1982).

Critics argue that this approach is simply too simplistic to adequately reflect the myriad of coping strategies used by people in everyday circumstances. The approach also impossibly amalgamates strategies that could be either adaptive or maladaptive, depending on the context. Other strategies, such as cognitive reappraisal, can be categorized either as avoidant or as a strategy that can facilitate approach strategies. In some situations, neither categorization fits cognitive reappraisal very well. For example, such stressors as bereavement are simply not amenable to approach-based coping strategies. In those situations, cognitive reappraisal efforts are appropriate and effective. That is, a widow may comfort herself with the idea that the death of her husband was actually welcome, given the amount of suffering that her husband had gone through in the few months (or sometimes years) before his death. This cannot be interpreted as an avoidant strategy. On the other hand, cognitive reappraisal may be a way of avoiding problems: A necessary confrontation with a boss or a coworker may be avoided by saying, "Oh, it really doesn't matter anyway." However, in the long run the lack of efforts to resolve the situation can result in a worsening of problems. Finally, cognitive reappraisal may facilitate problem-focused efforts. A young athlete might be unduly anxious about an upcoming contest, putting undue meaning on it by thinking, "If I don't win, I won't get the scholarship, and I'll never go to college, and my life will be a failure". In this circumstance, a little judicious cognitive reappraisal might enable the athlete to relax enough to perform really well. "Hey, what have I got to loose? If I win, great. If I don't, I'll figure out some other way to get to college."

Thus, the same overarching strategy — cognitive reappraisal — may be an approach strategy, an avoidance strategy, or simply the only possible thing to do in a situation. Further, its effectiveness is also dependent on the situation. Mattlin et al. (1990) found that reappraisal was most effective in dealing with losses such as bereavement but was counterproductive in dealing with everyday problems if reappraisal was not accompanied by problem-focused coping. Thus, the combination of coping strategies could influence the efficacy of any one particular strategy.

This is also true of many other emotion-focused strategies — distraction, for example. Distraction may be a very useful time-out strategy. Reading a book, going to a movie with a friend, or even watching television may serve a recuperative function that enables further and more effective problem-focused efforts. Distraction used to the point of obviating attempts to solve the problem, however, is maladaptive.

A student in a class once objected to my description of escapism as a maladaptive coping strategy. He pointed out that escaping the rigors and stressors of studying by engaging in pleasurable activities, such as going to a movie, was absolutely necessary for him. I assured him that he was correct — that this was a useful strategy. However, taken to an extreme, it could be very dangerous, and I used the example of Woody Allen's *The Purple Rose of Cairo*. In this film, the main character spends most of her free time in the movie theater, seeking to avoid her failing marriage and miserable job. She eventually loses touch with reality, falling in love with a celluloid character. She tries to win her way back to reality by falling in love with the actor and abandoning the character. However, in the last scene, after her marriage has failed, she's been fired from her job, and abandoned by the actor, she retreats to watching her films. Thus, judicious use of an avoidant strategy may be helpful, but avoidance to the exclusion of problem-focused efforts is clearly not appropriate.

The same thing may be said for many coping strategies, including accessing social support or deferring action on a problem. Getting advice and help from family, friends, and colleagues may be one of the most useful and necessary strategies that a person can use; spending all of one's time complaining to friends about a problem and never trying to do anything may be one of the least useful strategies. Similarly, deferring action on a problem until one has all the information necessary to make an adequate decision is often the best policy; delaying making a decision until all opportunities for intervention are gone is foolish.

Thus, an approach–avoidance dichotomy is too simplistic to realistically capture coping efforts. It amounts to the too general observation that trying to solve your problems is useful and avoiding them is not useful. It cannot capture how people go about solving problems, how they pace themselves and their efforts, what is an effective use of time-out strategies, what are useful ways of dealing with negative emotions, and so forth.

An additional problem with the approach–avoidance dichotomy is that it categorizes all emotion-focused coping as avoidant, when in actuality this type of coping could serve to facilitate problem-focused coping. A similar criticism can be made about Folkman and Lazarus's (1980) early dichotomization of coping into problem- and emotion-focused efforts. Manifestly, there are many different ways of handling problems and emotions, and failure to discriminate among these different ways hampers our ability to truly identify efficacious and nonefficacious coping efforts.

This reasoning led to the first factor analysis of the WOCS in an attempt to identify different types of problem- and emotion-focused coping (Aldwin, Folkman, Coyne, Schaefer, & Lazarus, 1980). This early study identified seven factors: instrumental action, escapism, exercising caution, growth-oriented coping, seeking social support, self-blame, and minimizing threat. Generally, this factor structure has held up reasonably well over time, with most subsequent factor structures identifying from five to eight dimensions (Aldwin & Revenson, 1987; Dunkel-Schetter et al., 1992; Felton & Revenson, 1984). While the factor structure shifts slightly, depending upon modifications to the scale and the types of problems being evoked, the same coping themes reemerge.

Moos and his colleagues have recently tried a compromise method that combines approach/avoidance with the more multifaceted process approach (Moos et al., 1990). In this method, the overarching approach–avoidance dichotomization is maintained, but both emotion- and problem-focused subcategories within each of the overarching categories is maintained. In other words, within approach strategies there are subscales reflecting both cognitive and behavioral efforts, thereby resolving the criticism above that simple approach–avoidance dichotomies failed to differentiate between those emotion-focused strategies that obviate and those that support problem-solving efforts. Similarly, there are also cognitive and behavioral subscales within the avoidant category, thereby recognizing that some behaviors also serve as ways of avoiding problems (e.g., alcohol or drug consumption).

On the other hand, some researchers have criticized the WOCS because it is too simple, does not include every possible strategy, and actually might exclude some very important ones. As Coyne and Smith (1991) have pointed out, the WOCS (and the other checklists as well) has often treated coping as a heroic, individualistic endeavor, when in reality much coping takes place in an interpersonal context. That is, how an individual copes with a problem is profoundly influenced by what other individuals in the situation are doing. This is true of both appraisal and coping processes (Mechanic, 1978), as well as decision-making processes (Janis & Mann, 1977).

Further, the WOCS does not include items that assess many important interpersonal strategies, such as capitulating to others' demands, trying to deceive or manipulate others, or trying to dominate people (Hobfall & Dunahoo, 1992). DeLongis, Bolger, and Kessler's (1987) approach to this problem was simply to add more interpersonal items to the existing WOCS rather than crafting a new instrument.

Thus, it is not surprising that a second generation of coping scales has arisen. Some have tried to simplify coping assessment by limiting the number and type of strategies assessed (Amirkian, 1990; Endler & Parker, 1990; Moos, 1990), while others have tried to expand the coping universe by including different items (DeLongis et al., 1987). Others have simply tried to refine the original WOCS (Dunkel-Schetter et al., 1992; Vitaliano, Russo, Carr, Maiuro, & Becker, 1985).

There is a problem in the overreliance on factor analysis to identify basic coping strategies. The results of such analyses rely heavily on the initial choice of items for a scale. For example, on the Berkeley Stress and Coping Project, none of the original items for the WOCS included prayer. Inspection of the "other" category revealed that this

strategy was mentioned frequently. Thus, for the revision we included an item assessing prayer as a coping strategy. However, it did not
load on any of the factors, so we dropped our focus on it. Does the
failure of prayer to load on a factor mean that prayer is not an important coping strategy? No, it means that we needed to include multiple
items assessing prayer in order for it to form its own factor. In the
development of the California Coping Inventory (Aldwin, 1994), I included three items that assess the use of prayer as a coping strategy;
these items form their own independent factor. Thus, the initial base
of items strongly influence what the final factor structure is.

The biggest problem with our coping scales is that they have not
been theoretically driven. Until we develop a theory of how and why
coping strategies mitigate or increase stress, factor analyses claiming
to be the definitive identification of coping strategies should be viewed
circumspectly. Just as there is are multiple personality instruments, there
will in all likelihood be multiple coping instruments. Again, which one
"should" be used depends upon the research question.

RATING SCALES

Coping scales can either be simple checklists of dichotomous items,
requiring respondents to indicate whether a particular strategy was used,
or they can have some sort of rating scale attached to each item, requiring respondents to indicate the extent to which each strategy was
used. Each approach has its strengths and limitations.

Dichotomized items provide very little information about the way
in which a strategy was used. As we have seen above, how much a
particular tactic is used may strongly influence whether it is effective
or maladaptive. For example, a little bit of distraction may be helpful; overreliance on it may be harmful. Scales with dichotomous items
also have less variance and are more likely to be skewed or kurtotic,
which limits their predictive validity. Further, the internal reliability
of scales with dichotomous items also tends to be lower than those
using rating scales.

Using a rating scale entails certain advantages, both with internal reliability and with predictive validity. There are also disadvan-
tages. The items on coping strategy scales are almost invariably a
heterogeneous mix of cognitions and behaviors, and the same rating
scale may need to be interpreted differently depending on the afford-
ance characteristics of the item. In a very elegant study, Stone and his
colleagues (1991) criticized the rating scale on the revised WOCS because the wording ("To what extent did you use each of the following

strategies: Not at all, a little, somewhat, and a lot") can be interpreted in four ways: frequency, duration, effort, and usefulness. For example, talking to someone who could do something about the problem could have been done several times, or it could have been done once but for a long time. Or the individual could have put a lot of effort and planning into one talk. Under each of these conditions, respondents could have indicated "somewhat" or "a lot". From Stone and his colleagues' point of view, this is unacceptable, because it means that people are not necessarily interpreting the rating of each item in the same way:

> For some people and some items, extent means one thing, and for other people and other items it means one of several other things. Our concern is the obvious one: what is the meaning of combined ratings of duration, frequency, usefulness, and effort? A single scale measuring differing dimensions in unknown ways may result in a scale that is not interpretable. . . . Imagine that 2 different subjects each spoke to an aggressive and antagonistic landlord for 5 min [sic] to complain about a rent increase. When these subjects rate the extent to which they "approached the person who caused the problem" on the WOC, the 1st subject might give this item a low rating because the conversation was of short duration. On the other hand, the 2nd subject might give this item a high rating, reflecting the great deal of effort that it took to approach this difficult landlord. In this scale, the scale would reflect more coping on the part of the 2nd subject than the 1st, whereas, in fact, their actual coping behaviors were topographically similar. Thus, the problem of subjects using different dimensions to rate coping items is a serious one when specific thoughts and behaviors are being evaluated. (p. 657)

I am reminded of the scene from Woody Allen's *Annie Hall* in which the two antagonists are both seeing their respective therapists. Annie Hall complains that they have sex too much—at least three times a week. Annie Hall's lover complains that they almost never have sex—only three times a week. The exact same behaviors may have widely discrepant meanings to different individuals.

The transactionist approach is predicated upon the fact that knowing whether something happened is less important than the meaning of the occurrence was to the individual. From the therapists' point of view, knowing exactly how many times Annie Hall and her lover had sex each week is less important than knowing that one felt burdened and the other felt deprived. Similarly, although both subjects in Stone's example may have talked to their respective landlords for five minutes, the second respondent may have been much more reticent, and it may have been much harder for this student to talk to the landlord than it was for the first student. Thus, even though the duration of the coping efforts was identical, the effort, mobilization, and probably the outcome were not identical. The student for whom the task was more difficult probably expended more emotional energy—and, thus, it would be appropriate to rate the coping strategy as having more effort. Further, one could also hypothesize that the second student's blood pressure and catecholamine responses were much stronger, which would be in keeping with using higher coping ratings.

I was a member of the Berkeley Stress and Coping Project when it was decided to switch from a dichotomous to a four-point rating scale. We agonized for some time over how to word the rating scale. We considered using wording that variously reflected frequency, duration, or effort. But we had to reject each one, given that some were more appropriate than others to different items. As Stone and his colleagues have correctly pointed out, effort, frequency, and duration are overlapping but not identical constructs. What if an individual used a coping strategy only once but for a very long time or very intensely? We could not untangle this Gordian knot, and thus fell back on using the admittedly very subjective and vague term "extent to which you used each strategy." However, we felt strongly enough that the amount of coping effort expended was too important to ignore, despite the fuzziness that it added to the scale.

In part, the difficulties in assessing anything are due to Heisenberg's famous Uncertainty Principle. In essence, the measurement process in and of itself distorts the thing it is measuring. Using dichotomous items may be more objective in that individuals may more reliably indicate whether they used a strategy, but this distorts the picture that one obtains of coping by not assessing the extent to which the coping strategy was used. As we have seen, using a little distraction or cognitive reappraisal may be very different from using too much. On the other hand, attaching a rating scale distorts the picture because it is a much more subjective assessment. However, one could argue that its subjectivity provides a more complex and perhaps more accurate picture of the coping effort involved and enhances its predictive validity. Having used both simple scales with a few dichotomous items and more complex scales with many subjectively rated items, I generally find that the latter are simply better predictors of psychological and physical outcomes.

Nonetheless, the idea of using an "elastic ruler" in scales is not a comfortable one. But I cannot help wondering whether the same sort of elasticity would not emerge if one applied Stone's very elegant design to rating scales in general (or even dichotomous items). As we have seen, even simple frequencies may be interpreted in many varying ways by different individuals, and even dichotomous items may be subject to divergent interpretations. For example, what if the two students mentioned above had fleeting thoughts of taking revenge on their landlord. One student is more compulsive than the other and dutifully checked off "Had unrealistic fantasies about how the situation may turn out." The other student may not have felt that he actually did this, because it was so fleeting. Given the vagueness of many cognitive coping strategies, what is the threshold for saying that, yes, one actually did this? Or, for that matter, saying, "Yes, this is generally true of me" or "No, this is not usually true of me" on coping styles measures?

My hypothesis is that there always are individual differences in how people interpret the response formats to items on psychological testing in general. If true, a strict positivist would argue that this would call into question all of psychological testing. However, a pragmatist would argue that this is simply a form of noise in the assessment instrument. All assessment instruments, whether used by psychological, biological, or physical scientists, have tolerances for various degrees of noise — or uncertainty, to use Heisenberg's terminology. Obviously, an important goal is always to minimize noise. However, there are often various sources of noise, and sometimes trying to minimize one source increases another. Psychologists try to decrease noise by using multiple items that assess the same underlying construct. But psychology, especially personality and cognitive social psychology, by definition deals with subjective experiences. Sometimes this should be exploited, not minimized.

HOW CONSCIOUS IS COPING?

Earlier models of adaptation focused on unconscious and/or conditioned responses. From a behaviorist perspective, people respond automatically with conditioned responses to environmental demands. From a psychoanalytic perspective, people respond unconsciously with defense mechanisms to environmental and/or internal demands. One benefit of the coping process paradigm is that it shifted the view of persons passively responding to environment demands to a proactive viewpoint, in which people consciously anticipated problems and manipulated the external environment (and their internal environment) to respond to problems in order to achieve certain goals. The very term "coping strategies" reflects conscious, rational decision making.

This cognitive perspective has been criticized by some clinicians who have severe misgivings about the rationality of the coping process.

From their perspective, many coping responses are automatic and not under conscious control (Scheier & Kleban, 1992). For example, the woman who denies that the body of the accident victim is her son is not consciously deciding not to recognize him; rather, she is frantically denying reality in an attempt to maintain her sanity. Our first emotional response may well be automatic and, even under the best of circumstances, many individuals' coping appears neither rational nor even thought out. The "did–didn't" arguments between children (and sometimes academics) are a prime example of this.

Given that defense mechanisms are held to be unconscious processes, assessments of them must necessarily be indirect. Generally, these assessments are based upon detailed clinical interviews. Perhaps the best example of this technique is provided by Vaillant (1977) in his book *Adaptation to Life*. This book presents case studies based upon multiple interviews with the men in the Grant Study, as does a 1993 follow-up book entitled *Wisdom of the Ego*.

Again, a major limitation of such approaches is their focus on emotional regulation, to the neglect of active attempts to solve the problem. In addition, interrater reliability of interview ratings of coping and defense tends to be low in both Haan's system (Morrissey, 1977) as well as in Vaillant's (see Vaillant, 1977, p. 329, although his most recent rating system appears more reliable, if somewhat convoluted; see Vaillant, 1993, pp. 369–370).

Joffe and Naditch (1977) attempted to systematize the measurement of Haan's coping and defense mechanisms by using items from the California Psychological Inventory. In this approach, respondents indicate to what extent the items are true or false with regard to themselves. This allows more flexible research methods (e.g., they presumably can be used in surveys as well as in face-to-face interviews), and the scale has been successful in discriminating between different adaptive groups. However, if defensive mechanisms are really unconscious, presumably their use cannot be reported by the individual. For example, if someone denies that a problem exists, they presumably cannot report on either the problem or their denial processes. This limitation, however, is shared by all self-report inventories.

If coping is primarily an unconscious process, this would call into question all self-report coping inventories. However, I suspect that unconscious mechanisms are used only by a small minority of individuals in most everyday coping circumstances. This is based upon having coded over 1,000 interviews over two different samples of men and women of all ages. Generally, we found very few instances in which it was clear that the respondents had little or no access to the way in which they had coped with the problem. In 100 interviews in which the focus was on the most recent low point in the respondents' lives, there were only two or three instances in which we suspected the use of defense mechanisms, given the difficulty of determining what the respondent actually did. In a second study that focused on a problem in the past week, we devised a reasonably reliable way of determining the existence of denial. In this study of over 1,000 men from ages 45 to 90, we asked individuals to rate the stressor on a seven-point scale (where 7 represented the most stressful problem ever experienced), and then we asked separate questions about strategies used to manage the problem, about the emotions experienced, and then about the strategies used to manage the emotions. If the respondents rated the stressfulness of the problem as a 4 or greater, reported only coping mechanisms when we asked for emotions, and said that they had no emotions, we coded that individual as using denial. For example, say a man's problem was caretaking for a terminally ill wife. He rated the problem as a 5, indicating that this was reasonably troubling to him. However, when queried about emotions, if he replied, "Oh, I just don't think about things like that" and reported "None" when queried about emotion-focused coping mechanisms, that person was thought to be in denial. Using these criteria, only 1% of the men were coded as using denial. Note, however, that 15% of the men reported suppression, or "tried not to think about it."

Why is this rate of denial so low? I suspect that this occurred for several reasons. First of all, this latter study focused on a recent episode, whether major or minor, and unconscious mechanisms may be more likely to be activated during extremely threatening problems. Second, coping is indeed a process. Although initial reactions to an extreme stressor may be unconscious defenses, over time the vast majority of individuals come to a more realistic assessment. For example, at first it may be completely natural to deny the reality of the death of a child. However, most people eventually confront this reality, even though they may go in and out of a state of denial for some time (Lazarus, 1983). Very few people outside of mental institutions go into complete states of denial in which a death is never acknowledged. Thus, people may be able to report the use of defense mechanisms because they are no longer in a defensive state.

In a more troubling vein, the identification of defense mechanisms may be relatively rare because, if actually working, the individual may not ever report having a problem. This is a serious issue for most stress and coping studies. As I indicated in Chapter 4, self-report stress surveys tend to have fairly high rates of false negatives—many of the people who report having no stress on a questionnaire do reveal problems in an interview setting. Most of the men who reported no problems using self-report inventories were not, strictly speaking, in a state of denial. Rather, this was more reflective of cognitive restructuring processes. For some, if a problem had been resolved, it was not really a problem. For example, once I pilot tested a self-report stress and coping instrument in a federal housing facility for the elderly. One 80-year-old man asserted that he had had no problems whatsoever in the past month, even though he was manifestly in a rather frail condition. A social worker overheard his stringent denials to my gentle probings for a problem and said, "Why, Mr. So-and-so, don't you remember? You had a big fight with your wife last week, and she threw a knife at you!" To which the elderly gentleman replied, "Yes, but she missed me, so it really wasn't a problem!" (Aldwin, 1992).

Other individuals may not see chronic, ongoing stressors as "problems" as long as there was not a crisis during the specified time period. For example, in the pilot interviews mentioned in Chapter 4, two of the men who reported on questionnaires that their lives were "completely fine, no problems" revealed in the interviews that they were the primary caretakers for terminally ill wives. These men were actively providing both emotional and instrumental support for their wives, doing housework, overseeing medication schedules, taking them to the doctors, and so forth. They could report their anguish and worries for the future in the interviews and also provided information on strategies that they used for managing their emotions, usually distracting themselves with chores, work, or gardening. However, their wives' health had been stable in the past week, so they did not consider themselves to have "had problems." Clearly, these men were not in a state of denial. They recognized the existence of the problem, used active strategies to manage both their wives' illness and their own emotional reactions. They tried not to burden their children by hiding the seriousness of their wives' condition. Yet, to the outside world, they would say, in apparent honesty, that their lives were fine, with no problems. In part, these men were compartmentalizing rather than denying, but the social custom of not discussing problems can also be in evidence.

One 85-year-old man said that he had no problems because he "wasn't the sort of person to have problems." He admitted to having "concerns" (in his case, trying to get his 90-year-old sister to agree to living in a nursing home after two falls at home) but not to having "problems." These men managed to dissociate their public self-presentation from their private selves. By defining themselves as not having "problems," they were using social conventions to regulate their self-presentations (and probably their emotions, as well).

This coping strategy can result in the underreporting of the existence of problems, and if the respondents do not report problems, the researcher cannot assess their coping strategies. (I was once called in to consult on a study of coping and retirement that was obtaining absolutely no results. The problem was that most of the respondents had reported no problems with retirement, but the researchers had them go ahead and fill out the coping inventory anyway.) We resorted to interviews since one goal of this research project was to link coping strategies with blood chemistries; thus, it was absolutely necessary to get as accurate an assessment of stress and coping processes as possible. However, interviews are a very expensive and time-consuming procedure. It is imperative that future researchers come up with ways to penetrate this dissociation between public self-presentation and the private self in a self-report format. Nonetheless, interviews may be the only good way to understand what proportion of individuals' coping efforts are unconscious.

SUMMARY

As we have seen, the assessment of coping strategies is currently a matter of great contention. Coping style theorists prefer assessing a small number of strategies, which are presumed to be stable across situations and time and which may or may not be unconscious. Sociologists and social psychologists tend to look at multiple strategies that are often situation-specific and assume that coping is proactive, conscious, and a matter of socialization. Process theorists try to straddle these two approaches, seeking to identify several strategies that might be applicable to specific situations, and believe that coping is largely conscious. As such, process theorists are criticized by the clinicians for paying insufficient attention to personality traits and by the social theorists for paying insufficient attention to situational demands. It remains to be seen if the process theorists can adequately combine these two approaches.

APPENDIX: COPING SCALES

In 1987, Aldwin and Revenson counted over 20 coping scales in existence and provided a list of those scales to researchers. For this book, I have updated this list and have included it as an appendix to this chapter.

The following is a partial list of published or presented coping scales as of 1994. This list is meant to be more illustrative that comprehensive. It is organized by date into three categories: psychodynamic and/or interview approaches, coping style or personality approaches, and situation-based approaches. Occasionally review articles are included that specify more scales than can be economically presented in this list.

Well over 2,000 articles on coping have been published in the past five years, and at times it seems like nearly all of them have developed their own assessment strategies. To try to manage this burgeoning area, I developed a few exclusionary strategies. First, scales were limited primarily to those published in English-language psychological journals, although I had to include sociological journals for occupational coping and occasionally included a presentation as well. Some coping studies have been published in foreign language journals, but the difficulty of accessing and assessing them precluded their inclusion. Many coping assessments are also published in nursing journals, and those wishing detailed examination of pediatric issues in coping should consult those journals. Second, I excluded some inventories that appeared to be assessing attitudes toward efficacy, mastery, helplessness, locus of control, and so forth, rather than toward actual coping strategies per se. Sometimes it was difficult to distinguish between these and coping style questionnaires, and my apologies to anyone who felt their scale should not have been excluded for this reason. Even with these exclusions, over 70 scales are included in this list.

Psychodynamic and/or Interview Approaches

Andrews, G., Singh, M., & Bond, M. (1993). The Defense Style Questionnaire. *Journal of Nervous and Mental Disease, 181,* 246–256.

Bond, M., Gardiner, S. T., & Siegel, J. J. (1983). An empirical examination of defense mechanisms. *Archives of General Psychiatry, 40,* 333–338.

Brown, G., & Harris, T. (1978). *Social origins of depression: A study of psychiatric disorder in women.* New York: Free Press.

Diaz-Guerrero, R. (1979). The development of coping style. *Human Development, 22,* 320–331.

Gleser, G., & Ihilevich, D. (1969). An objective instrument for measuring defense mechanisms. *Journal of Consulting and Clinical Psychology, 33,* 51–60.

Horowitz, M. J., & Wilner, N. (1980). Life events, stress, and coping. In L. Poon (Ed.), *Aging in the 1980s* (pp. 363–374). Washington, DC: American Psychological Association.

Joffe, P., & Naditch, M. P. (1977). Paper and pencil measures of coping and defense processes. In N. Haan (Ed.), *Coping and defending* (pp. 280–297). New York: Academic Press.

Vaillant, G. (1977). *Adaptation to life.* Boston: Little, Brown.

Vaillant, G. E. (1993) *The wisdom of the ego.* Cambridge, MA: Harvard University Press.

Wiedl, K. H., & Schottner, B. (1991). Coping with syptoms related to schizophrenia. *Schizophrenia Bulletin, 17,* 525–538.

Zeitlin, S. (1980). Assessing coping behavior. *American Journal of Orthopsychiatry, 50,* 139–144.

Coping Styles or Personality Approaches

Amirkhian, J. H. (1990). A factor analytically derived measure of coping: The Coping Strategy Indicator. *Journal of Personality and Social Psychology, 59,* 1066–1074.

Beckham, E. E., & Adams, R. L. (1984). Coping behavior in depression: Report on a new scale. *Behaviour Research Therapy, 22,* 71–75.

Brandstäter, J., & Renner, G. (1990). Tenacious goal pursuit and flexible goal adjustment: Explication and age-related analysis for assilmilative and accomodative strategies of coping. *Psychology and Aging, 5,* 58–67.

Bugen, L. A., & Hawkins, R. C. (1981, August). *The coping assessment battery: Theoretical and empirical foundations.* Paper presented at the Annual Meeting of the American Psychological Association, Los Angeles.

Byrne, D. (1964). Repression–sensitization as a dimension of personality. In B. A. Maher (Ed.), *Progress in experimental personality research* (Vol. 1, pp. 170–220). New York: Academic Press.

Carver, C. S., Scheier, M. F., & Weintraub, J. K. (1989). Assessing coping strategies: A theoretically-based approach. *Journal of Personality and Social Psychology, 56,* 267–283. (Note: This can be scored in terms of coping styles or situation-based coping strategies.)

Cohen, C. I., Teresi, J., Holmes, D., & Roth, E. (1988). Survival strategies of older homeless men. *Gerontologist, 28,* 58–65.

Endler, N., & Parker, J. D. A. (1990). Multidimensional assessment of coping: A critical evaluation. *Journal of Personality and Social Psychology, 58,* 844–854.

Feifel, H., Strack, S., & Nagy, V. P. (1987). Degree of life-threat and differential use of coping modes. *Journal of Psychosomatic Research, 31,* 91–99.

Hall, D. T. (1972). A model of coping with role conflict: The role behavior of college educated women. *Administrative Science Quarterly, 17,* 471–487.

Kaiser, D. L. (1991). Religious problem-solving styles and guilt. *Journal for the Scientific Study of Religion, 30,* 94–98.

Marcus, G., & Forster, J. (1988). Assessing self-efficacy during marital separation. *Journal of Divorce, 11,* 77–85.

Martin, R. A., & Lefcourt, H. M. (1983). Sense of humor as a moderator of the relation between stressors and moods. *Journal of Personality and Social Psychology, 45,* 1313–1324.

Miller, S. M. (1980). When is a little information a dangerous thing? Coping with stressful events by monitoring versus blunting. In S. Levine & H. Ursin (Eds.), *Coping and health* (pp. 145–170). New York: Plenum.

Millon, T., Green, C. J., & Meagher, R. B. (1979). The MBHI: A new inventory for the psychodiagnostician in medical settings. *Professional Psychology, 10,* 529–539.

Mullen, B., & Suls, J. (1980). The effectiveness of attention and rejection as coping styles: A meta-analysis of temporal differences. *Journal of Psychosomatic Research, 26,* 43–49.

Rosenbaum M. (1980). A schedule for assessing self-control behaviors: Preliminary findings. *Behavior Therapy, 11,* 109–121.

Situation-Based Approaches

General

Aldwin, C. M. (1994, August). *The California Coping Inventory.* Paper presented at the Annual Meeting of the American Psychological Association, Los Angeles, CA.

Amirkhan, J. H. (1990). A factor analytically derived measure of coping: The Coping Strategy Indicator. *Journal of Personality and Social Psychology, 59,* 1066–1074.

Edwards, J. R., & Baglioni, A. J., Jr. (1993). The measurement of coping with stress: Construct validity of the Ways of Coping Checklist and the Cybernetic Coping Scale. *Work and Stress, 7,* 17–31.

Kottke, J. L., Cowan, G., & Pfahler, D. J. (1988). Development of two scales of coping strategies: An initial investigation. *Educational and Psychological Measurement, 48,* 737–742.

McCrae, R. R. (1984). Situational determinants of coping responses: Loss, threat, and challenge. *Journal of Personality and Social Psychology, 46,* 919–928.

Moos, R. H., Cronkite, R. C., Billings, A., G. & Finney, J. W. (1982). *Health and daily living form manual.* Stanford, CA: Social Ecology Laboratory, Department of Psychiatry and Behavioral Sciences, Stanford University School of Medicine.

Pearlin, L., & Schooler, C. (1978). The structure of coping. *Journal of Health and Social Behavior, 19,* 2–21.

Sidel, A., Moos, R. H., Adams, J., & Cody, P. (1969). Development of a coping scale. *Archives of General Psychiatry, 20,* 225–233.

Stone, A. A., & Neale, J. M. (1982). A new measure of daily coping: Development and preliminary results. *Journal of Personality and Social Psychology, 46,* 892–906.

Tobin, D. L., Holroyd, K. A., Reynolds, R. V., & Wigal, J. K. (1989). The hierarchical factor structure of the Coping Strategies Inventory. *Cognitive Therapy and Research, 13,* 343–361.

Ways of Coping Scale (Original—includes references regarding scoring)

Aldwin, C. M., Folkman, S., Schaefer, C., Coyne, J., & Lazarus, R. S. (1980, September). *Ways of coping: A process measure.* Paper presented at the Annual Meeting of the American Psychological Association, Montreal.

Folkman, S., & Lazarus, R. S. (1980). An analysis of coping in a middle-aged community sample. *Journal of Health and Social Behavior, 21,* 219–239.

Parkes, K. R. (1984). Locus of control, cognitive appraisal, and coping in stressful episodes. *Journal of Personality and Social Psychology, 46,* 655–668.

Vitaliano, P., Russo, J., Carr, J., Maiuro, R., & Becker, J. (1985). The Ways of Coping checklist: Revision and psychometric properties. *Multivariate Behavioral Research, 20,* 3–26.

Vitaliano, P., Maiuro, R. D., Russo, J., & Becker, J. (1987). Raw versus relative scores in the assessment of coping strategies. *Journal of Behavioral Medicine, 10,* 1–18.

Ways of Coping Scale
(Revised—includes references regarding factor structures)

Aldwin, C., & Revenson, T. A. (1987). Does coping help? A reexamination of the relation between coping and mental health. *Journal of Personality and Social Psychology, 53,* 337–348.

Dunkel-Schetter, C., Feinstein, L. G., Taylor, S. E., & Falke, R. L. (1992). Patterns of coping with cancer. *Health Psychology, 11,* 79–87.

Folkman, S., & Lazarus, R. S. (1985). If it changes it must be a process: A study of emotion and coping during three stages of a college examination. *Journal of Personality and Social Psychology, 48,* 150–170.

Folkman, S., Lazarus, R. S., Dunkel-Schetter, C., DeLongis, A., & Gruen, R. (1986). The dynamics of a stressful encounter: Cognitive appraisal, coping, and encounter outcomes. *Journal of Personality and Social Psychology, 50,* 992–1003.

Coping Scales for Specific Situations or Populations

Occupational Scales

Cooper, C. L., Sloan, S. J., & Williams, S. (1988). *Occupational stress indicator: Management guide.* Windsor, England: NFER–Nelson.

Latack, J. C. (1986). Coping with job stress: Measures and future directions for scale development. *Journal of Applied Psychology, 71,* 377–385.

Nowack, K. M. (1990). Initial development of an inventory to assess stress and health risk. *American Journal of Health Promotion, 4,* 173–180.

Osipow, S. H., & Spokane, A. R. (1983). *A manual for measures of occupational stress, strain, and coping.* Odessa, FL: PAR.

Schonfeld, I. S. (1990). Coping with job-related stress: The case of teachers. *Journal of Occupational Psychology, 63,* 141–149.

Wilder, J. F., & Plutchik, R. (1982). The AECOM coping scales. *Annals of Stress Research.*

Medeiros, M. E., & Prochaska, J. E. (1988). Coping strategies that psychotherapists use in working with stressful clients. *Professional Psychology Research and Practice, 19,* 112–114.

Child and Adolescent Scales

Compas, B. E. (1987). Coping with stress during childhood and adolescence. *Psychological Bulletin, 101,* 393–403.

Dise-Lewis, J. E. (1988). The Life Events and Coping Inventory: An assessment of stress in children. *Psychosomatic Medicine, 50,* 484–499.

Elwood, S. W. (1987). Stressor and coping response inventories for children. *Psychological Reports, 60,* 931–947.

Fanshawe, J. P., Burnett, P. C. (1991). Assessing school-related stressors and coping mechanisms in adolescents. *British Journal of Educational Psychology, 61,* 92–98.

Frydenberg, E., & Lewis, R. (1990). How adolescents cope with different concerns: The development of the Adolescent Coping Checklist (ACC). *Psychological Test Bulletin, 3,* 63–73.

Harter, S. (1982). The Perceived Competence Scale for Children. *Child Development, 53,* 87–97.

Jorgensen, R. S., & Dusek, J. B. (1990). Adolescent adjustment and coping strategies. *Journal of Personality, 58,* 503–514.

Patterson, J. M., & McCubbin, H. I. (1987). Adolescent coping styles and behaviors: Conceptualization and measurement. *Journal of Adolescence, 10,* 163–186.

Ryan-Wenger, N. M. (1990). Development and psychometric properties of The Schoolagers' Coping Strategies Inventory. *Nursing Research, 39,* 344–349.

Spirito, A., Overholswer, J., & Stark, L. J. (1989). Common problems and coping strategies II: Findings with adolescent suicide attemptors. *Journal of Abnormal Child Psychology, 17,* 213–221.

Spirito, A., Stark, L. J., Grace, N., & Stamoulis, D. (1991). Common problems and coping strategies reported in childhood and early adolescence. *Journal of Youth and Adolescence, 20,* 531–544.

Spirito, A., Stark, L. J., Williams, C. (1988). Development of a brief checklist to assess coping in pediatric populations. *Journal of Pediatric Psychology, 13,* 555–574.

Stark, L. J., Spirito. A., Williams, C., & Guevremont, D. (1989). Common problems and coping strategies I: Findings with normal adolescents. *Journal of Abnormal Child Psyychology, 17,* 204–212.

Wertlieb, D., Weigel, C., & Felstein, M. (1987). Measuring children's coping. *Journal of Orthopsychiatry, 57,* 548–560.

Geriatric Scales

Feifel, H., & Strack, S. (1989). Coping with conflict situations: Middle-aged and elderly men. *Psychology and Aging, 4,* 26–33.

Quayhagen, M. P., & Quayhagen, M. (1982). Coping with conflict: Measurement of age-related patterns. *Research on Aging, 4,* 364–377.

Family Scales

McCubbin, H. I., Dahl, B., Lester, G., Benson, D., & Robertson, M. (1976). Coping repertoires of families adapting to prolonged war-induced separations. *Journal of Marriage and the Family, 38,* 461–471.

McCubbin, H. I., Olson, D. H., & Larsen, A. S. (1982). Family Crisis Oriented Personal Scales. In D. Olson, H. I. McCubbin, H. Banes, A. Larsen, M. Muxen, & M. Wilson (Eds.), *Family inventories* (pp. 101–120). St. Paul: University of Minnesota, Family Social Science.

Coping Scales for Clinical Situations

Burt, M. R., & Katz, B. L. (1988). Coping strategies and recovery from rape. *Annals of the New York Academy of Sciences 528*, 345–358.

Butler, R. W., Damarin, F. L., Beaulieu, C., Schwebel, A. I., & Thorn, B. E. (1989). Assessing cognitive coping strategies for acute postsurgical pain. *Psychological Assessment: A Journal of Consulting and Clinical Psychology, 1,* 41–45.

Coyne, J., & Smith, D. A. F (1991). Couples coping with a myocardial infarction: A contextual perspective on wives' distress. *Journal of Personality and Social Psychology, 61,* 404–412.

Felton, B. J., & Revenson, T. A. (1984). Coping with chronic illness: A study of illness controllability and the influence of coping strategies on psychological adjustment. *Journal of Consulting and Clinical Psychology, 52,* 343–353.

Lipowski, Z. J. (1970). Physical illness, the individual, and the coping process. *Psychiatry in Medicine, 1,* 91–102.

Manne, S. L., & Zautra, A. J. (1990). Couples coping with chronic illness: Women with rheumatoid arthritis and their healthy husbands. *Journal of Behavioral Medicine, 13,* 327–342.

Prochaska, J. O., Velicer, W. F., DiClemente, C. C., & Fava, J. (1988). Measuring the process of change: Applications to the cessation of smoking. *Journal of Consulting and Clinical Psychology, 56,* 520–528.

Regan, C. A., Lorig, K., & Thoresen, C. E. (1988). Arthritis appraisal and ways of coping: Scale development. *Arthritis Care and Research, 1,* 139–150.

Rosensteil, A. K., & Keefe, F. J. (1983). The use of coping strategies in chronic low back pain patients: Relationship to patient characteristics and current adjustment. *Pain, 17,* 33–44.

Other Specialized Scales

Shek, D. T. L., & Cheung, C. K. (1990). Locus of coping in a sample of Chinese working parents: Reliance on self or seeking help from others. *Social Behavior and Personality, 18,* 326–246.

Statistical Issues
in Coping Research

There are some critical methodological issues concerning the mechanism of the relation between stress, coping, and health. As such, some of the stress and coping literature can be statistically very complex. Not only are there key constructs that need to be addressed, but understanding the statistical means by which the constructs are tested is crucial. Very often, researchers simply assume one particular model, or assume that coping must be working in a particular way, without actually having adequately tested different models. Thus, before reviewing the literature on coping and health, some understanding of what the different models are and how they are tested is important and is the *raison d'être* for this chapter.

MECHANISMS OF COPING EFFECTS

There are three possible ways in which coping can affect well-being. First, there may be *direct* effects on health outcomes. Second, the effect of coping on health may be *mediated* through another variable, such as medical compliance. Third, coping strategies may *moderate* or *buffer* the effect of stress on health. (For a discussion of mediating and moderating effects in the social sciences, see Barron & Kenney, 1986). The statistical mechanisms for investigating these effects will be reviewed in the following section.

Direct Effects

Most studies of coping and well-being implicitly assume a direct effects model; by simply using a correlational paradigm, such studies assume that particular coping strategies are simply linked to particular types of outcomes. That is, the more that problem-focused coping is utilized, the lower the psychological or physical distress. This is a simple, bivariate approach to the problem and assumes that the nature of the relation between coping and well-being looks like that demonstrated in Figure 8-1.

In short, coping is assumed to have direct, causal effects on whatever outcome variable is under study. Thus, if a coping strategy or style is correlated with lower blood pressure levels, shorter hospital stays, or better affect, it is assumed that somehow the coping strategy has directly affected on physiological or psychological processes. While this is certainly a possibility (and, to my mind, probable in some instances), this simplistic assumption is probably incorrect in many cases and may account for the often quite modest effect size of coping in such studies.

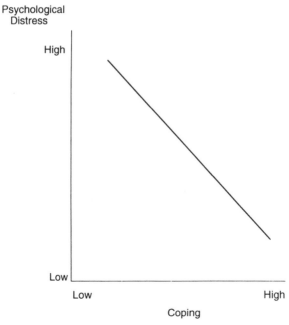

FIGURE 8-1. Direct effects model of coping on psychological distress.

Mediating Effects

Some of the effect of coping with health problems may be mediated or indirect rather than being a direct effect. In other words, coping strategies may not directly affect physiology (e.g., lower cholesterol levels) but rather may indirectly affect health outcomes through a change in a health behavior habit (e.g., quitting smoking), which in turn leads to decreases in cholesterol. For example, it has been observed that women diagnosed with breast cancer who use more active forms of coping live longer than women with more passive coping styles (Greer & Morris, 1975; Morris, Greer, Pettingale, & Watson, 1981). The conclusion that many people jump to is that coping directly affects immunocompetence, which is why these women live longer. However, it is also plausible that actively coping women do other things, such as quit smoking, start exercising, improve their nutrition, and faithfully adhere to their medical regimen, all of which are known to affect immunocompetence. Thus, coping may not have a direct effect on physiology but only an indirect or mediating effect by leading to other things that do directly affect physiology.

For example, one 80-year-old woman I know had severe osteoporosis. Her spine had broken so many times that her ribs were resting on her hip bones. Her physician told her that there was nothing he could do and that she should simply go home, go to bed, and await death. "Doctor," retorted this spunky woman, "I *refuse* to accept your diagnosis. There *must* be *something* that I can do." Laughing, the physician told her that he liked her spirit and said that he would recommend her for an experimental program at the local research university. This retired nurse adhered faithfully to the regimen of injecting herself periodically with calcium and a special form of Vitamin D, and her bone density did increase, thus extending her lifespan. In this instance, there would be a statistical association between active coping style and bone density, but it would be a mistake to assume that the link was direct and that coping affected calcium metabolism and, thus, longevity. Rather, this effect was *indirect* because this woman's active coping style led her physician to recommend her to an experimental program that did affect her calcium metabolism and, thus, her quality and length of life. There can be an association between coping strategies and physiological outcomes that are not direct but mediated through practicing health behavior habits, taking advantage of medical opportunities, and adhering to medical regimes. Unfortunately, few studies test for mediating effects of coping strategies.

Moderating Effects

Most of the literature on moderating effects, also known as buffering effects, involves the effects of social support on health outcomes (e.g., Dooley, 1985; Finney, Mitchell, Cronkite, & Moos, 1984). However, the observations in that area are directly relevant to coping mechanisms as well. The resolution of this argument is the key not only to determining whether coping is largely based on personality characteristics or interactions between the person and the environment but also to discovering how coping affects psychological and physical health.

As we have seen, the direct effects model proposes that coping will be associated with a given outcome, regardless of the level of stress. In this model, active or direct coping will always be associated with good outcomes, no matter how stressful the problem. In contrast, the buffering model posits that coping has an effect on outcomes only to the extent that coping moderates the effect of stress on the outcome. That is, active coping will affect outcomes only because it reduces the negative effects of stress, especially at higher stress levels.

Why is this question of direct versus buffering mechanisms important? In social support research, it is thought to be important because it reveals something about the underlying mechanism of how social support relates to health outcomes (House et al., 1988). For example, we know that married men tend to live longer than single men. If this is because having a spouse helps reduce stress, then we suspect that social support from a spouse enhances physical health by reducing the deleterious effect of stress—in which case, there should be a significant statistical interaction effect between marital status and stress on health. In other words, unmarried people or those with poor marriages will experience more symptoms under high stress, while those with good marriages will not have more symptoms, because they are *protected* from the negative effects of stress by social support. If, on the other hand, being married has only a direct effect, then we may suspect that social support per se is not that important, but rather that healthier people are more likely to be married. Thus married people might have better health regardless of the stress level.

This is especially important in quasi-experimental designs, that is, naturalistic studies which use surveys or interviews to assess existing levels of social support. In these studies, social support is thought to have a direct, causal effect on health only if there is an interaction effect between stress and social support on health outcomes. If there is only a direct effect, then it is entirely possible that social support is confounded with something else (like personality or health), which may be the key causal link. Obviously in experimental studies social support can be shown to have causal effects regardless of the existence of any interaction, because one can externally manipulate the social support variable. Lynch's (1979) studies of the effects of a nurse's touch on the heart beat of patients in cardiac intensive care units is a good example of the latter.

In coping research, the interpretation of direct versus buffering effects may be more complex. Aldwin and Revenson (1987) suggested that direct effects support the idea of personality-based coping, whereas interaction effects support a model of coping based on person–situation interactions. In other words, if a particular strategy such as avoidant coping shows only direct effects and no interaction effects, then people who use this strategy often are more likely to be distressed regardless of the external environment, which suggests an underlying problem in psychopathology. On the other hand, if coping has a moderating effect, then this suggests that what an individual does *in a particular situation* may decrease (or enhance) the effect of stress. In other words, deducing the mechanism through which coping affects health outcomes aids in answering the more basic question of whether coping is primarily a function of personality or is a joint expression of the effect of both the person and the situation.

It is also possible that direct versus moderating effects can be interpreted vis-à-vis the causal effects of coping on health in the same manner as social support and health. For example, let us suppose that expressing emotions is associated with increased blood pressure. If threat minimization results in lower blood pressure regardless of stress level, then one could argue that the relationship between threat minimization and blood pressure is simply a function of preexisting personality characteristics; calm, phlegmatic people may have lower blood pressure in general. However, if threat minimization is associated with lower blood pressure levels primarily under conditions of high stress, one could argue that this coping strategy serves to buffer the effect of stress on high blood pressure and thus may have causal effects regardless of personality. It is also true that in a quasi-experimental setting, it may be impossible to totally rule out the preexisting effects of personality. In this instance, a better study would involve an experimental design in which people are taught how to use a particular coping strategy and then observe its effect on physiological outcomes (e.g., Lazarus et al., 1962). Nonetheless, an interaction effect provides some evidence that coping has a causal effect on health outcomes. If true, this means that people may be taught to cope in ways that can enhance their health, which is one reason why the study of coping is so important.

Summary

Most studies of coping and health outcomes are quasi-experimental in nature. Many researchers simply use pen and pencil questionnaires to relate coping to self-reported mental and physical symptoms; others study medical patients and associate coping styles with health outcomes. *Simply associating coping with health outcomes through correlational or group differences techniques tells us nothing about the all-important question of the mechanism(s) through which coping affects health. Only by examining moderating and mediating effects can we begin to understand such mechanisms and thus examine the nature of the link between the mind and the body.* However, coping research is still in its infancy, and most researchers are simply working on demonstrating an association, in and of itself a difficult task. Additionally, many researchers are put off by what appears to be overly complicated statistics and are not guided by any sort of theory as to when the use of such statistics is appropriate. Thus, the following section includes a simplified explanation of some of the statistical techniques involved.

STATISTICAL MODELS OF MEDIATING AND MODERATING EFFECTS

Early studies of coping illustrated moderating very simply by dividing respondents into "bad" or "good" copers (e.g., Locke et al., 1984). Among the "bad" copers, there would be shown a positive correlation between stress and outcomes, whereas in the "good" copers there would be little or no relationship. In other words, "good" coping buffered or reduced the negative effects of stress on an outcome. The coping mechanisms were thus thought to protect an individual against the adverse effects of stress.

In more recent research, direct versus buffering models are usually tested with hierarchical regression equations (Finney et al. 1984; see Kenny & Judd, 1984, for ways to include interaction effects with latent variable models). This mitigates against the problems associated with dividing people (more or less arbitrarily) into groups (Cronbach & Snow, 1977). In a hierarchical regression model, first the stress variable, then the coping strategy, and then the interaction term are entered into the equation in separate steps. The interaction term is generated by multiplying the coping variable by the stress variable.

Hierarchical regression equations generate two very useful statistics that allow one to determine whether the direct or buffering model best fits the data. In general regression equations, R^2 refers to the amount of variance in the dependent, or outcome, variable accounted for by the independent variables. If, for example, the R^2 term for the equation is .25, we know that our independent variables account for 25% of the variance in the outcome measure. Hierarchical regression equations allow one to determine the amount of independent variance accounted for by each variable (or, sometimes, sets of variables) in each step, referred to as the change in R^2, or ΔR^2. (This should not be confused with stepwise regression, in which the computer picks the independent variables that significantly relate to the outcome measure and then generates an overall R^2.) If the ΔR^2 for a particular variable is significant, this means that the variable in question accounts for additional variance over and above the amount accounted for by the variables that were entered in earlier steps.

Additional useful statistics generated by the hierarchical regression equations are the b and the beta (β), which are simply the unstandardized and standardized weights, respectively computed for each variable in the model. If the β is positive, that means that there is a positive association between the independent variable and the outcome measure. In other words, the higher the stress, the more symptoms are reported. If the β is negative, there is a negative association between the independent variable in the outcome measure. In other words, when more problem-focused coping is used, fewer symptoms are reported. Betas can be thought of as partial rs. Thus, a hierarchical equation will indicate whether a particular variable is significantly associated with the outcome, as well as the direction of the association.

In hierarchical regression terms, determining whether coping has a direct or buffering effect is entirely dependent on whether the ΔR^2 for the interaction term is statistically significant. If it is not significant, then coping (assuming its ΔR^2 is significant) is said to have a direct effect. In other words, the association between coping and outcome exists regardless of the level of stress that the individual is facing. On the other hand, if the interaction term is significant, the coping variable is said to have a buffering or moderating effect. The relation is dependent upon the degree of stress that an individual is facing.

An example is in order. Let us suppose that a researcher wants to know whether problem-focused and emotion-focused coping have direct or buffering effects on depression in people undergoing a divorce. The researcher would construct a hierarchical regression equation in which the variable indicating the stressfulness of the divorce is entered in the first step, the coping variable in the second step, and the stress × coping interaction term in the third step.

Let us suppose that the outcome of the hierarchical regression for emotion-focused coping shows significant ΔR^2s and positive βs for both the stress and coping variables, but the interaction term is not significant. This means that the more stressful the divorce, the worse the depression, and the more emotion-focused coping used, the worse the depression. Because the interaction term is not significant, emotion-focused coping is said to have a *direct* rather than a buffering effect. In other words, the use of this strategy will increase symptoms regardless of how stressful the divorce is.

Our hypothetical hierarchical regression equation for problem-focused coping, however, yields a different result. Let us suppose that the stress variable accounts for a significant 12% of the variance and has a positive b of .25, the coping variable accounts for an additional 8% and has a negative b of .20, and the interaction term accounts for a significant 5% of the variance and also has a negative b ($-.07$). In this example, problem-focused coping is said to *moderate* the effect of stress on depression.

Note that it is entirely possible that the direct effect of coping will be statistically insignificant, but the interaction term is significant. In other words, the correlation (or partial correlation, controlling for stress) between coping and the outcome measure may appear to be nonsignificant. If researchers do not use a hierarchical regression equation to look for interaction effects, they may erroneously conclude that a particular coping strategy has no effect on the outcome measure.

If the interaction term is significant, before we can say that problem-focused coping buffers, or decreases, the adverse effects of stress on depression, it is necessary to determine *how* problem-focused coping is moderating the effect of stress. This is done by solving the equation in such a manner as to generate three lines (Cohen & Cohen, 1975)—in this instance, the effect of coping under high stress, medium stress, and low stress—and then graphing those lines.

The regression equation is a simple algebraic equation. Let x_1 = stress, x_2 = coping, a = the intercept, and $\hat{Y}$ = the outcome, or depressive symptoms. Remember that the interaction term was generated by multiplying the stress term (x_1) by the coping term (x_2). The researcher then constructs the basic equation:

$$\hat{Y} = b_1x_1 + b_2x_2 + b_3x_1x_2 + a,$$

or, in this instance,

$$\hat{Y} = .25x_1 - .20x_2 - .07x_1x_2 + a.$$

This simply says that depression equals .25 × stress level − .20 × coping level − .07 × the interaction term (plus a, the error term or intercept, which stands for everything else that is not being directly measured but which nonetheless can affect depression).

Then, the researcher calculates what would constitute high, medium, and low stress, generally operationalized as the mean + 1 standard deviation (SD), the mean, and the mean − 1 SD, respectively. The researcher then calculates high, medium, and low levels of problem-focused coping using the same technique. (Sometimes the SD is greater than the mean, resulting in a negative number that is difficult to interpret. I usually just substitute 0 for the low term to simplify things.)

Recollecting high school algebra, three points are needed to generate a straight line. Thus, the regression equation needs to be solved nine times. For the first three solutions, substitute the high stress value for x_1 and then solve the equation for low, medium, and high coping (x_2). Repeat this procedure substituting the medium stress value, and then the low stress value, for x_1. Then graph the three lines. If a buffering effect exists, the graph should look something like Figure 8-2. In other words, if a respondent uses a lot of problem-focused coping, there is no relationship between stress and depression (the bottom line). If, on the other hand, the respondent only uses a little or no problem-focused coping, there is a strong and positive relationship between stress and depression (top line).

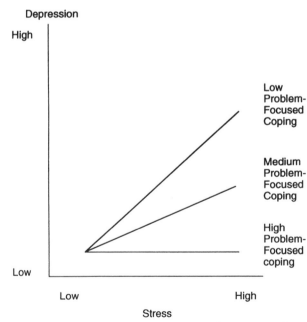

FIGURE 8-2. Buffering model of the effect of coping on depression.

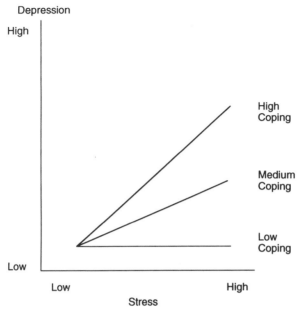

FIGURE 8-3. Enhancing effect of coping on depression.

Note that it is possible to get a moderating effect in which the coping strategy actually enhances the effects of stress. This may happen if the β for the interaction term is positive. In which case, the graph may look something like Figure 8-3. In other words, the more this particular coping strategy is used, the stronger the relationship between stress and depression.

It is also possible to get interaction effects that may look something like Figure 8-4. With this type of interaction effect, a coping strategy may have a very different effect depending upon the seriousness of the problem. For example, ignoring a problem may be a very good strategy if the problem is fairly minor (in common parlance, "not sweating the small stuff"). However, ignoring a serious problem may have disastrous effects. Alternatively, this type of interaction pattern may be common if the coping strategy has a situation-specific effect. In this case, one computes "dummy," or dichotomous, variables indicating the situation(s) and then simply multiplies the dummy variable by the coping strategy. (Note that the dummy variable must be coded as "1, 2" or "−1, 1." Coding a dummy as "0, 1" totally distorts the interaction term by zeroing out three of the four possible cells.)

For comparison purposes, solving an equation in which the in-

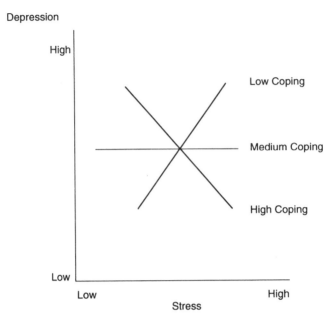

FIGURE 8-4. Situation-specific effects of coping on depresson.

teraction term is not significant will generate three parallel lines. In which case, the graph will look something like Figure 8-5.

There are several things that can go wrong when using a hierarchical regression equation to examine interaction effects. If the lines generated by solving the equation are not straight, but are rather curved, this means that there is a calculation error at some point. First order regression equations by definition generate straight lines, which may or may not accurately depict the relation between stress, coping, and outcomes. It is entirely possible that there is a nonlinear relation between, say, stress and depression. In which case, one can look for nonlinear effects by including squared (or even higher order) terms (in other words, x_1^2) in the regression equation. To my knowledge, no one has tried to examine nonlinear interaction terms in stress research. The other problem is multicollinearity. This results when the variables being multiplied to generate the interaction term are correlated, as stress and coping variables often are. An unfortunate effect of multicollinearity is "bouncing betas," in which the direction of the β term can shift, sometimes dramatically, depending upon which variables are in the equation (Cohen & Cohen, 1975). For example, on the first step of the

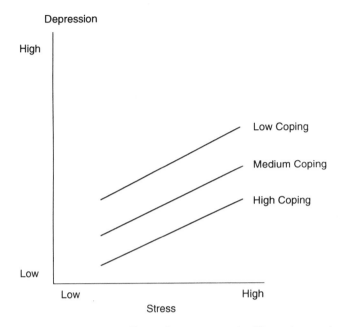

FIGURE 8-5. Direct effects of coping, no significant interaction.

hierarchical regression equation, stress may have a positive β. Once the interaction term is entered, however, stress may have a negative β (hence, the term "bouncing betas"). This does not mean that higher stress levels reduce symptoms. Rather, multicollinearity produces a statistical artifact that can distort the true picture of the results. Multicollinearity may be reduced by "centering" the terms around zero by subtracting the respective means from each of the variables. Centering the terms reduces the magnitude of the correlations between the independent variables, thus reducing multicollinearity. (Note that these are nonlinear transformations, since different values are subtracted for each variable.)

Sometimes researchers will construct a hierarchical equation that includes multiple coping strategies and their interaction terms. In this procedure, the stress variable is entered in step one, the several coping variables in step two, and their several respective stress × coping interaction terms in step three. This procedure has the beneficial effect of parsimony, in that only one regression equation is generated. However, this procedure greatly enhances the problem of multicollinearity. I think this is best avoided by generating separate regression equations for each coping strategy.

Generally, the magnitude of interaction effects are rather small—often about 1% of the variance. Thus, one must have a large enough sample size, or enough statistical power, to ensure that an effect is not erroneously disregarded. * This lack of power is actually very serious. McClelland and Judd (1993) report that interaction effects might be more difficult to find in field (as opposed to experimental) settings, and very large sample sizes may be required to have sufficient power to correctly judge the significance of interaction effects. Thus, we may have been erroneously concluding that coping does not buffer stress, when in actuality we simply do not have enough power (i.e., a sample of sufficient size) in most instances to adequately test for the significance of interaction terms.

Mediating effects are also investigated through regression-based techniques, and structural equation modeling (SEM), including path analysis and latent variable analysis such as LISREL. Path analysis is simply a series of regression equations that trace out the direct and indirect pathways between a predictor variable and an outcome, while latent variable analyses are path models that include factor analyzing the measures to generate the "purified" or latent variable structure. For example, say a researcher has noticed an association between problem-focused coping and quicker recovery from pneumonia. Instead of immediately assuming a direct physiological link, the researcher wonders whether the effects of this coping strategy are mediated through other variables, such as compliance. The two hypothesized models are

Coping → Hospital Stay

versus

Coping → Compliance → Hospital Stay

In order to test these models, two regression equations are computed: one that regresses the variable "length of hospital stay" on both the compliance and the coping measures and one that regresses compliance on coping. This can yield a model looks like this:

---

*Recently, some statisticians have begun to question the wisdom of including interaction terms in a regression equation to test moderating effects (T. Sharf & A. Von Eye, personal communications, 1992). There is some concern that (1) centering may distort the data, (2) the multiplicative terms might actually be examining nonlinear, rather than interaction, effects, and (3) that there has been a lack of theoretically based usage of this technique. However, I have countered that interaction effects are highly effective in demonstrating the situational specificity of coping strategies, and Von Eye has agreed that a theory-driven use of this technique in acceptable.

Coping → Compliance → Hospital Stay

In this model, the coping term no longer is statistically significant once compliance is in the model. If a researcher were to use a standard regression model that only looked at the independent relations between all of the variables in the model and the outcome, he or she might erroneously conclude that coping was unimportant, when in actuality it underlies and facilitates compliance. In other words, all of the effect of coping is mediated through compliance.

It is also possible that coping may have both direct and indirect effects on a given outcome. In this instance, the model would look like that in Figure 8-6. Statistically, entering compliance into the equation does not delete the effect of coping, although it may decrease it.

Of course, in a perfect world (or one with more adequate funding for research), this researcher would also have assessments of immune and pulmonary functioning, as well as levels of serum antibiotics, and so forth. From this simple model, it is not possible to conclude that coping has a direct physiological effect, but it can indicate the degree to which the effect of coping on length of hospital stay is mediated through compliance with the medical regime.

Path modeling can be a rather simple procedure. There are very good programs such as GEMINI (Wolfle & Ethington, 1985), which will compute the standard errors—and therefore, the statistical significance—of the indirect path. Generally, SEM models that examine latent variable effects are somewhat more difficult to interpret but may be more flexible than path models. However, there is also much room for nonsense with SEM procedures. Some researchers simply dump variables into equations, turn the crank, as it were, and let the model run, without a modicum of theory to underlie either the choice of variables or their order in the model, which generally results in uninterpretable models. Garbage in, garbage out, as they say. Nonetheless, judicious use of both moderating and mediating models can force researchers to think carefully about their hypothesized model and can lead to some very exciting research.

FIGURE 8-6. Transactional model of medical compliance.

CHAPTER 9

Coping and Health

In 1979, Norman Cousins wrote a remarkable book entitled *Anatomy of an Illness*. In it, he described his harrowing experience with a very painful, life-threatening illness of no certain cause. Cousins had just returned from a stressful, exhausting trip to Russia when he developed quite terrifying and painful symptoms. What was remarkable about his experience was the way in which he coped with his illness. When the attending physicians could not make an immediate diagnosis, he called in his own experts and began experimenting with alternative treatments, including massive doses of Vitamin C. He decided that hospitals were stressful environments because of their inadequate food, intrusive nursing routines, and restrictive rules and regulations — and, therefore, were no place to recover from illness. Consequently, he checked himself into a hotel, ate gourmet food, and rented funny movies, including comedies by the Marx Brothers and the Three Stooges, having discovered that laughter was about the only thing that eased his pain. As he put it, a good belly laugh kept the pain away for about a half hour. Within a relatively short period of time, he recovered.

A very different approach to illness was taken by former President Jimmy Carter's sister, Ruth Carter Stapleton, who developed breast cancer in midlife. Being deeply religious, rather than fearing death, she welcomed it, since she had a strong belief in the afterlife and heavenly rewards. Refusing all but palliative medical treatment, she died swiftly, within three months.

When I was in graduate school, I became friendly with an 80-year-old woman who also lived in my apartment building. A cultured and often charming woman, she related many delightful tales of growing up in Vienna in a very wealthy and musical family. However, my friend also carried a heavy, lifelong burden that made her very bitter and angry. As a young girl she fled from the Holocaust with only the contents of one suitcase. Despite having exit visas for her parents, she was unable to extract them, and they died in a concentration camp, along with most of her relatives. For reasons that I never fully understood, she blamed her only surviving sister for her parents' death (Vaillant might say that she was projecting her own feelings of guilt onto her sister). My friend developed colon cancer, and, despite exquisite pain, she refused all medications, taking at most a half an aspirin. In the hospital, she refused to speak to a psychiatrist, turning her face to the wall. She was a very difficult patient, complaining bitterly about nearly everything and screaming in pain for hours on end. She suffered terribly for many months, until she was finally medicated against her will, fell into a coma, and died.

All three of these individuals were coping with life-threatening illnesses in very different ways and with very different outcomes. All three were exerting control of a kind. Cousins went to extraordinary lengths to control his environment and his own treatment regimen, which resulted in a cure. Stapleton also exerted control, although in her instance she willingly chose death for religious reasons. My friend also went to extraordinary lengths to exert control over her environment. By doing so, however, she only increased her own suffering — and also that of her sister, who was her primary caregiver. In all of these cases, the way in which these individuals coped with the stress of an illness affected both its course and its outcome.

The study of coping strategies highlights individual differences in how people deal with stress, a process that may moderate the adverse effect of stress on health. Some people "fall apart" under stress, others emerge "sadder but wiser," and yet others seem to thrive in a stressful environment. Ten years ago there were only a handful of studies that linked coping with health outcomes, but in the last few years the number of studies has greatly increased. As of yet, however, there has been little integrative work. To my knowledge, for example, no meta-analyses of general coping strategies and outcomes as yet exist, due in part to the plethora of ways of assessing coping. However, there are some reviews of parts of the literature, including approach–avoidance coping (Roth & Cohen, 1986; Mullen & Suls, 1982), pain management (Jensen, Turner, Romano, & Karoly, 1991), coping and cancer outcomes (Levy, 1991), and coping and arthritis (Manne & Zautra, 1992). The purpose of this chapter is to provide an integrative overview of the general coping and health literature.

Given that our computerized literature searches have yielded several thousand articles on coping published in the last few years, it is not possible to review every single study. This chapter will instead focus on some of the most critical work in this area. Two exclusionary criteria were used. First, the studies used must have actively examined coping strategies; research that simply designated "good" versus "bad" copers on the basis of some outcome measure were excluded, as were those which simply related the psychological "outcomes" of coping (e.g., depression) to some health measure. Second, given the difficulty of reviewing all of these studies, I chose to focus on two major areas of work: (1) coping and mental health and (2) coping related to adaptation to illnesses, such as heart disease, cancer, or rheumatoid arthritis, including some of the underlying physiological processes, such as blood pressure or immune functioning.

Given that there is as yet no consensus as to the best way of measuring coping (see Chapter 7), there is concomitantly no consensus as to the "best" way to cope. Indeed, Pearlin and Schooler in 1978 believed that there were no "magic bullets"—no coping strategies that would work for every individual in every situation—and that observation still holds true today. Nonetheless, there appear to be some interesting patterns in the literature, which suggest that coping strategies mitigate (or sometimes enhance) the effects of stress on health under particular circumstances.

COPING STRATEGIES AND MENTAL HEALTH

How individuals cope with stress is related to their mental health status. Stress and coping variables can account for as much as 50% of the variance in outcomes such as depression or psychological symptoms (Aldwin, 1991; Aldwin & Revenson, 1987; Folkman, Chesney, Pollack, & Coates, 1993). However, there is a paradox in much of the coping literature. The definition of emotion-focused coping is that it regulates or controls the negative affect resulting from stress so that problem-focused efforts can be maintained (Folkman & Lazarus, 1980; White, 1974). *But in nearly every study of coping, emotion-focused coping is associated with increased distress,* and sometimes problem-focused coping is as well (Aldwin & Revenson, 1987). If the function of emotion-focused coping is to decrease stress, why then do our measures almost uniformly show positive relations with symptoms? As we shall see, the relationship between coping strategies and psychological symptoms is highly complex and requires a transactional approach; for several reasons, simplistic, reductionistic methods simply do not work in this area.

First, not only is coping supposed to modify the effects of stress on health, but there are situational modifiers of effects of coping strategies on mental health as well; what "works" in one situation may well increase distress in another. Second, the overall pattern of coping strategies may be more predictive of mental health than the use of any particular strategy. Third, there is a statistical confound between stress, the amount of effort individuals exert, and psychological distress; failure to deal with this confound may well result in a spurious positive relationship between coping and distress. Fourth, there are as yet unresolved issues in causal directionality: Although coping may be linked to psychological symptoms, it is not clear whether coping causes these symptoms or if distressed individuals simply cope differently than nondistressed people. Fifth, there may be individual differences in the effectiveness of coping strategies: Some people may cope in a qualitatively different fashion than others, a difference that may not be readily apparent on our current coping inventories. Finally, we tend to assess a narrow range of outcomes, mainly different forms of psychological distress, and we may be missing whole classes of outcomes for which coping strategies are effective.

Situational Modifiers of Coping Effects

Coping strategies have *situation-specific* effects — that is, a given strategy may have one effect in a particular situation and the opposite effect in another. Enough studies have demonstrated this phenomenon now that researchers ignore this complexifying factor at their peril. For example, some studies have shown that problem-focused coping decreases emotional distress and that emotion-focused coping (paradoxically) increases it (Felton & Revenson, 1984; Mitchell, Cronkite, & Moos, 1983; Mitchell & Hodson, 1983), whereas others have reported the opposite pattern (Baum, Fleming & Singer, 1983; Marrero, 1982).

Several studies have demonstrated that the *controllability* of the stressor affects the ability of coping to reduce stress. In general, problem-focused coping decreases psychological symptoms in situations appraised as controllable, while emotion-focused coping is associated with lower symptom levels in situations appraised as uncontrollable (Mattlin, Wethington, & Kessler, 1990; Vitaliano, DeWolfe, Maiuro, Russo, & Katon, 1990). This might explain the contrary results of the Baum et al. (1983) study cited earlier, which examined people coping with the Three Mile Island nuclear reactor shutdown. In this situation, problem-focused coping, especially trying to do something about the bureaucratic problems that led to the difficulty, probably did result in increased emotional distress, while trying to forget about the problem (about which most people could do little anyway) might well have reduced distress. Deciding to ignore a problem that is eminently solvable, however, will most likely increase psychological distress (Aldwin & Revenson, 1987).

Note that association between coping styles and health outcomes is also affected by the environmental context. An excellent review by Roth and Cohen (1986) identified the controllability of the problem as a key in evaluating the effectiveness of approach–avoidance coping styles. They identified two other factors as well: the *point in time* that the outcome is assessed and the *goodness of fit* between the coping style and situational demands. In their review, Mullen and Suls (1982) found that avoidant strategies were more effective in reducing emotional distress in the short term, while approach strategies were more effective over the long term. In other words, studies may show differing effects of approach–avoidance coping depending upon the time elapsed since the beginning of the particular problem under study.

Similarly, whether or not a coping style will result in increased or decreased distress also depends on the fit between the style and the stressor. A classic study by Miller and Mangan (1983), for example, found that blunters and monitors (another name for approach–avoidance copers) differed in whether they wanted full disclosure by their physicians before an operation. Blunters became more distressed when given additional information, whereas monitors became less distressed.

Finally, the stressfulness of a situation may also affect the relation between a particular coping strategy and mental health. Many problems are minor and self-limiting, and ignoring minor problems is often a reasonable strategy. Similarly, many problems are ambiguous as to their severity, and using threat minimization until more information is obtained may also be sensible. For example, getting a Type 2 result from a Pap smear may indicate incipient cancer—or it may indicate a technical problem, such as the physician assistant's failure to spray the whole slide with the fixative. Taking a "wait and see" attitude until the results of the follow-up pap smear are in is much better than focusing on and obsessing over the problem. Mobilizing a great deal of effort and support for relatively minor problems may end up resulting in greater stress levels—making a mountain out of a molehill, as it were. However, failure to mobilize when faced with an imminent threat to life, such as ignoring a lump in one's breast, could have disastrous consequences for one's physical and mental health. Thus, it is imperative to examine statistical interactions between degree of stress (and/or its controllability) in order to demonstrate that coping buffers stress effects (see Chapter 8). Unfortunately, coping studies that do examine interaction effects are relatively rare.

Studies that examine three-way interactions between stress level, degree of controllability, and coping are nonexistent.

In summary, there are interaction effects between situational characteristics and use of coping strategies or styles that moderate the relation between coping and health outcomes. Thus, one key to successful coping may be the ability to moderate both the type and the degree of effort used in coping with different kinds of stressors. There is an old prayer that sums this up nicely: "Lord, help me to change the things I can change, accept the things I cannot change, and have the wisdom to know the difference."

Patterns of Coping

While most studies examine the individual or joint contributions of coping strategies to mental health, a few researchers have suggested that the pattern, or coping profile, may be more important than the use of any one particular strategy. For example, avoidant coping used in conjunction with problem-focused coping may decrease the adverse effects of stress; however, avoidant coping in the absence of problem-focused coping may increase distress, especially in those situations judged to be controllable (Mattlin et al., 1990).

Vitaliano and his colleagues (1987) have suggested using ratios to calculate the use of coping strategies. In other words, the proportion of problem-focused to emotion-focused coping may be more important than the absolute amount of problem-focused coping per se. Further work has suggested that coping profiles, defined as an individual's pattern of coping strategies— namely, relative reliance on some and de-emphasis of others—may be a more efficacious way of understanding the ways in which individuals cope with stress (Vitaliano et al., 1990).

Coping Effort

Serious problems often result in a great deal of psychological distress and require strenuous coping efforts. This results in an unfortunate statistical confound between stress, coping, and distress; and studies that did not take this confound into account often show that all of the coping strategies used in the study are associated with increased distress (e.g., Spurrell & McFarlane, 1993). This may be especially a problem for studies of traumatic stress (see Aldwin, 1993). Often, such studies use simple correlations or regression equations to associate stress with outcomes that neither control for stress levels nor utilize interaction terms to examine stress buffering. Vitaliano's proportional scoring for coping strategies reviewed in the previous section may be one way of controlling for coping effort.

Another complicating factor is that there may be a nonlinear relation between coping and outcomes. As indicated earlier, sometimes a small amount of avoidant coping is useful, especially if it facilitates problem-focused coping. To my knowledge, however, no one has ever examined nonlinearity in the relation between coping and mental health in a systematic way — namely, by entering second- or even third-order terms into a regression equation.

Alternatively, one could ask the respondent to rate the effectiveness of the coping strategies used, thus distinguishing between *effort* and *efficacy*. Aldwin and Revenson (1987), for example, found that extensive use of negotiation as a coping strategy decreased psychological symptoms only when the respondent thought it was effective; when negotiations were not perceived to be effective, extensive use of this strategy increased distress. Instrumental action also had different effects on mental health, depending upon its perceived efficacy. Individuals who used only a little instrumental action but who perceived that it worked reported the fewest psychological symptoms. Presumably they found the situation easy to handle and were pleased at the outcome of their efforts. On the other hand, individuals who used only a little instrumental action and who did not think they handled the situation very well reported the most psychological symptoms. Perhaps they felt that if they had tried harder, they might have been able to solve their problem.

In addition, emotional discharge and efforts used to control emotions may not be adequately distinguished in most scales (Billings & Moos, 1984). In nearly every study, using alcohol or drugs to regulate emotions is associated with increased distress. Including those strategies in subscales with other items assessing threat minimization, for example, may be mixing apples with oranges.

The Problem of Causal Directionality

An alternative explanation for why coping strategies are often associated with increased distress is that coping strategies are reflecting, rather than causing, psychological distress. Individuals who heavily utilize the type of emotion-focused coping assessed in typical inventories may be doing so because they are in acute distress and are unable to control their emotions. Thus, someone who indicates that he or she "tried not to think about it" very frequently may actually have been obsessing about a problem and unable to stop thinking about it.

Coyne et al. (1981) first examined this problem by assessing the differential use of coping strategies, assessed over a nine-month period, between chronic depressives and putative normals. Coyne and his colleagues found that chronic depressives use more coping in general, but they also used more emotion-focused coping. Rather than being more passive and helpless, as Seligman's (1975) learned helplessness theory of depression would suggest, these depressives were struggling very hard to control both their external environment and their internal milieu. Apparently, however, they were not very successful, despite putting forth massive amounts of effort. This finding was later confirmed in a separate study by Folkman and Lazarus (1986).

Not only is it possible that depressives cope in a manner different from others, but it is also possible that being depressed leads to greater exposure to stressors. Russell and Cutrona (1991), for example, found that depressed older adults were more likely to report both more life events and more hassles in the subsequent months of the study. It is relatively easy to construct a "cascade" model of stress, coping, and depression, in which an individual copes poorly with an initial stressor leading to depression, which in turn leads to a greater likelihood of future stress, and so on (Aldwin & Stokols, 1988; Pearlin, Lieberman, Mullan, & Menaghan, 1981). For example, if an adolescent turns to drugs or alcohol as a means of coping with the death of a father, this drug use in turn may lead to problems with his mother, his school, and perhaps ultimately the authorities. It is equally possible, of course, that positive cascades may happen. Nonetheless, the transactional nature of the relation between coping, stress, and mental health should be acknowledged.

Individual Differences in Coping Effectiveness

A somewhat disturbing possibility, from a methodological viewpoint, is that the same or similar coping strategies may have varying effects in different people. Vitaliano and his colleagues (1990) conducted an intriguing study in which they examined the relation between coping, perceived controllability, and depression in a variety of patient populations. They found that the relation between appraisal, coping, and symptoms were not consistent across samples. Problem-focused coping led to decreased depression in controllable situations only for the nonpsychiatric groups. They concluded that their "goodness of fit" hypothesis did not work in psychiatric samples because of the distortion in their cognitive processes.

Another possible interpretation is the confusion between coping effort and coping efficacy referred to earlier. For the most part, our coping scales are set up to determine whether a person used a particular strategy. However, we do not assess whether that strategy was successfully used by that person. As mentioned earlier, someone who is obsessively ruminating about a problem may "try not to think about the problem" but fail, whereas someone else may use the same strategy but succeed.

There is a methodological conundrum here. On the one hand, Lazarus and his colleagues (Folkman & Lazarus, 1980; Lazarus & Folkman, 1984) have strong arguments in favor of assessing the process of coping as opposed to simply assessing its outcome. For example, only by examining the use of strategy and then relating it to outcome can one scientifically investigate the utility or destructiveness of any particular strategy—a position that I find intuitively and methodologically appealing. However, it is also clear from the numerous interviews that I have done that the *same strategy can be used both effectively and ineffectively by different individuals.*

Another possibility is to redesign our coping inventories to better reflect the qualitative manner in which a strategy is used. For example, two people try negotiating with their work supervisor about a problem. One person becomes arrogant and insulting when discussing the problem, but the other manages to remain relatively politic and arrives at a successful conclusion. As they presently exist, coping scales cannot differentiate between these two very different approaches: They simply ask respondents to indicate whether the problem was discussed. Certainly future work should attempt to include qualitative differentiable strategies, as well as some assessment of coping effectiveness, both with the problem and with the emotions (see Aldwin, 1994).

What Is the Appropriate Outcome of Coping Strategies?

Most studies of coping and mental health utilize symptom checklists, often focusing on depressive symptoms. By restricting our investigation of the outcomes of coping strategies to psychological symptoms, we may be unduly limiting our understanding of why people cope in the manner in which they do. A clinician might hypothesize that for some individuals, maintenance of symptoms has adaptive functions. By maintaining emotional distress about one set of problems, some individuals may be able to exert control over a different area. For example, demonstrated vulnerability may increase dependency upon a loved one, in an attempt to ensure that he or she will not leave. Rather than limit our outcomes to symptomology, we might wish to try to discover what goals the individuals seek to accomplish when they cope with stressful circumstances.

Another interesting possibility lies in the recognition that positive affect and negative affect appear to be orthogonal dimensions (Watson & Clark, 1984). To the extent that we only measure the negative dimension (e.g., symptoms), we could be overlooking the strategies that maintain the positive dimension. A sense of mastery is one of the most positive outcomes of coping with stress. Individuals can feel that they have accomplished something and can develop a new sense of confidence that they have successfully negotiated a difficult work problem, developed new skills, or had new understanding or compassion for others. Both White (1974) and Murphy (1974) have discussed this possibility in early works on coping and adaptation, and Murphy and Moriarty (1976) have pursued this line of inquiry in their longitudinal study of stress and coping in children. Yet, their sample was small, and their study relied upon the interpretation of clinical interviews. It is surprising that there is very little work systematically investigating mastery and other developmental processes as outcomes of coping with stress.

Pearlin and his colleagues (1981), in their classic longitudinal study, found that problem-focused coping was unrelated to current psychological symptoms but did serve two functions. Problem-focused coping was positively related to feelings of mastery. Further, it also helped to decrease the likelihood of future recurrences of stressors. Note, however, that coping with one particular problem may have little effect on generalized mastery. Revenson and Felton (1989), for example, found that the use of problem-focused coping in dealing with rheumatoid arthritis did not generalize one way or the other to overall feelings of mastery.

Summary

In summary, it is clear that there exists highly intricate relations between coping strategies and mental health. The relations may be spefic to the situation, the timing of the strategy, and even individual characteristics. Few studies assess coping and mental health over time, but such studies could yield some interesting data on both positive and negative feedback loops. Further, our definitions of coping outcomes has been very simplistic. There has been an overemphasis on negave outcomes to the detriment of positive ones. We tend to know little about the goals of the individual who is coping with the problem and assume instead that decreased emotionality is the desired outcome. As we shall see in Chapter 11, this is not always the case in all cultures.

ADAPTATION TO ILLNESS

Much of the coping literature is devoted to understanding the strategies used in coping with various illnesses and medical procedures. Chronic illnesses such as heart disease, diabetes, rheumatoid arthritis, cancer, and AIDS have been of particular interest. Given the graying of America, not only have chronic illnesses become more prevalent, but improvements in treatment have resulted in people living longer with chronic illnesses. Indeed, it is important to differentiate between illness and disability. With proper exercise, nutrition, and adherence to medical regimes, people with chronic illnesses, especially if they are diagnosed before much tissue or structural damage has been done, may lead relatively healthy and normal lives for some time. Thus, it is important to understand the process of adaptation to illness.

Moos and Schaefer (1984) identified seven major adaptive tasks in coping with illness. The three illness-related tasks are (1) dealing with the physiological consequences of the illness, including symptoms, pain, and disability; (2) dealing with the treatment and hospital environment; and (3) developing and maintaining good relations with health care workers. The four more general tasks are (1) maintaining some sort of emotional equilibrium; (2) maintaining a sense of self, including competence and mastery; (3) maintaining good relations with family and friends; and (4) preparing for future exigencies.

Unfortunately, only a few of these adaptive tasks have been studied, and most research focuses on at best one or two of these tasks. Most research has focused on coping with pain and medical procedures, and there are also several studies examining mental health outcomes for those with chronic illnesses. However, a qualitative study by Weitz (1989) of 23 men with AIDS does illustrate many of Moos and Schaefer's points very nicely, so I will summarize Weitz's study before reviewing the more quantitative literature.

Weitz pointed out that dealing with uncertainty is a major problem for individuals with chronic illnesses. Generally speaking, before these people with AIDS (they referred to themselves as PWAs) were diagnosed as HIV (human immunodeficiency virus) positive, they used denial and delayed getting tested. Given the variable length of time between being diagnosed as HIV positive and actually coming down with AIDS, testing would not necessarily decrease uncertainty but would increase the stigma and anxiety felt by the PWAs. Thus, the PWAs would attribute their symptoms to a myriad of other causes, such as the flu, drug use, being "run down", and so forth. Even when their symptoms became so bad that they sought the help of physicians, their doctors often refused to test them, either because the doctors were using threat minimization themselves or because they were simply not very knowledgeable about AIDS. Thus, the PWAs not only had to overcome their own defenses but those of the medical staff.

Once diagnosed, most PWAs searched for meaning as a way of reducing anxiety. Two developed "positive" explanations that were probably delusional, although they did undoubtedly serve to reduce anxiety. For example, one man had experienced a series of bad romances that left him suicidal, and "he believed that God had given him AIDS as a way of providing the extra incentive he needed to avoid any further romantic entanglements" (Weitz, 1989, p. 274). Another thought that God had given him AIDS so that he could share his faith with others and show that "even gays can go to heaven." Others blamed themselves for their promiscuity or drug use. The PWAs who had the most distress were those who thought that, while *some* people may deserve to get AIDS, *they themselves* did not.

Four to six months after diagnosis, most of the men were doing better. Uncertainty had been decreased, and the men had learned how to assert some control over a portion of their lives and how to accept not having control over other aspects of their lives. For example, on some days they felt fine, but on other days—often without warning—they were incapacitated. Often, the PWAs chose to avoid making any plans as a way of protecting themselves against disappointment, although at the cost of increased frustration.

Some of the PWAs were very active in their treatment regimens. They maintained hope by participating in experimental treatments, moderating their diet, and exercising when they felt well enough. They also learned to avoid possible sources of infection, not only obvious ones like friends with colds but also nonobvious potential sources of infection like bathroom mold. Some PWAs who did not fit researchers' requirements got their physicians to lie for them so that they would be eligible for experimental treatments. Others cadged the drug AZT by borrowing from friends who were in experimental programs or by using physicians' extras (often left over when an experimental subject died). One young man who was eligible for experimental treatments enrolled in three different programs so that he could get medications for his friends who were not eligible!

Death was one "future exigency" with which the PWAs had to cope. Several of the men had accepted death and had made plans for suicide if their quality of life became too poor. One person hastened death by throwing away his medications: He reasoned that if was going to die anyway, he might as well get it over with.

Thus, coping with illness is a multifaceted process. The strategies that we use (and those used by others around us) make the process more or less painful and may also affect physiological outcomes and hasten or delay death.

Coping with Pain and Medical Procedures

The study of coping strategies within an institutional setting yields some surprising information. We generally think of coping as something that is done by the individual; however, much of the work on coping with pain and medical procedures focuses on institutional practices and on how modifications in these practices can alleviate pain and suffering for the individual patient.

A meta-analysis by Suls and Wan (1989) is a good case in point. They examined two types of coping interventions for painful medical procedures such as surgery: providing sensory information and providing procedural information. Sensory information refers to descriptions about what the patient may feel as a consequence of this information; procedural information refers to descriptions of what will happen (or is happening) during a medical procedure. While the general assumption is that informed consent about procedures and risks is of great benefit to the patient, not all researchers agree. There is some concern that providing information may actually increase pain, discomfort, and perhaps even risk (Langer, Janis, & Wolfer, 1975), especially in people who prefer coping by blunting (Miller & Mangan, 1983).

For example, once I was exhorting a group of senior citizens to become more informed about their health management, and one older man strongly challenged this recommendation. "I don't want to know what's wrong with me," he said, "I just want the doctor to fix it." Individuals who are highly anxious may react adversely to information about risks, or an insensitive manner on the part of the physician may create undue anxiety. Contrast these two statements: "You have a 15% chance of dying during this operation" versus "Eighty-five percent of individuals make it through this operation just fine." (After a move cross-country, I was searching for an immunologist to continue my allergy shots. One physician I consulted said bluntly, "I don't like to give cat allergy shots. There's too much risk of death." Extremely alarmed, I called my previous allergist and asked him about this. "There was such a risk," he admitted, "but it is extremely small. Nonetheless, that is why we had you stay in the office for 20 minutes after the shot." Needless to say, I felt relieved by my previous physician's assurances and searched for a new one with a better "bedside manner.") Thus, it is not surprising that the research on the issue of informed consent and medical procedures has been equivocal.

Suls and Wan (1989) contrasted three types of studies: those with sensory information only; those with procedural information, and those with both types of information. Compared to controls, patients who received sensory preparation had less negative affect and lower levels of self-related pain. Sensory information was also more efficacious in pain reduction than procedural information alone. In general, procedural information in and of itself yielded few benefits. However, providing both types of information was by far the most efficacious in reducing pain and negative affect. Note, however, that there was considerable unexplained variance in outcomes that could not be accounted for by demographic characteristics or study setting (i.e., field vs. laboratory).

Auerbach (1989) identified some key factors that might modify the efficacy of such coping interventions. As with approach–avoidance coping, the controllability of the situation plays an important role: Providing problem-focused interventions may be helpful in controllable situations (e.g., regulating diabetes or asthma), whereas emotion-focused interventions may be helpful in uncontrollable situations (e.g., surgery for a facial tumor). Again, the timing of the intervention may be important. Faust and Melamed (1984), for example, found that children benefited most from a film about their medical procedure when the children were admitted to the hospital the day before the procedure. If they were admitted to the hospital on the day of the procedure and were shown the film, they derived little benefit, presumably because they were too anxious to pay much attention to the film. Auerbach (1989) has also confirmed Miller and Mangan's (1983) original observation of a person-by-situation interaction in the efficacy of coping interventions: Blunters made be made more anxious by the provision of too much information.

Note that interventions can be of two kinds: those that decrease the threat characteristics of the medical procedure (e.g., providing information) and those that attempt to teach the patient coping strategies (e.g., stress management techniques for pain such as hypnosis, imaging, etc.) As Auerbach (1989) has noted, few studies examine how well the individuals actually utilize the coping strategy.

An exception to this trend is a recent study of pain in childbirth by Leventhal, Leventhal, Shacham, and Easterling (1989). In this study, the effect of attendance at Lamaze classes and active monitoring instructions during labor were compared. Women who attended classes and were able to actively monitor their contractions and breathing during labor reported less pain, anger, and fatigue than the controls did. Further examination revealed that women who could monitor were move effective in "pushing" through their contractions and facilitating childbirth.

Gatchel and Baum (1983) reviewed a number of coping interventions designed to reduce pain. They found that a number of different techniques could be used effectively to reduce pain from medical treatments and from acute and chronic injuries. These techniques include biofeedback, hypnosis, and various forms of cognitive imaging. In addition, pain clinics, which teach individuals with chronic illness various techniques for coping with pain, may be very effective. In general, providing patients with control, even over timing and dosage of their medication, can reduce both the perception of pain and the use of analgesics.

The coping resources that individuals can utilize may also affect the level of functional ability in people with chronic pain. In their review, Jensen and his colleagues (1991) reminded us that many individuals with chronic pain rarely seek medical services and continue to work productively. Jensen and his colleagues identified three major psychosocial factors that affect psychosocial adjustment to pain: control beliefs and attributional style, self-efficacy and outcome expectancies, and coping strategies. In general, people who believed they could control the pain, avoided catastrophizing and feelings of helplessness, and those who used active coping strategies were less depressed, reported less pain, and were less likely to take on a sick role that prevented them from fulfilling everyday obligations.

In summary, high anxiety levels are associated with increased pain and poorer outcomes from medical treatments. Coping interventions can be conducted by modifying the behavior of the health care workers, providing procedural and sensory information, and increasing the repertoire of the individual's coping skills. Interventions that are directed at decreasing the threat characteristics of procedures, facilitating control beliefs and active coping strategies, especially in those individuals desiring control, may be extremely effective in reducing pain and suffering.

Coping and Illness Outcomes

The results of studies of coping and illness outcomes are less straightforward. On the one hand, there are many anecdotal instances in the field of medicine about individuals affecting the course of their illness (e.g., Cousins, 1979), and clearly there are differences in how well individuals participate in their health management, comply with medical regimes, and utilize positive health behaviors (e.g., exercising, moderating diet, avoiding smoking and excessive alcohol consumption, etc.), all of which should affect illness outcomes. On the other hand, demonstrating this statistically is more problematic, and there have been some surprising and nonintuitive results in this literature, which will be addressed below. Further, it is a mistake to believe that the course of illness is always under individual control; after all, we will all die of something.

Nonetheless, there have been a number of studies linking coping with outcomes for cancer, heart disease, and diabetes mellitus, among other illnesses (McCabe, Schneiderman, Field, & Skylar, 1991). As I see it, the critical issue in this area is whether active, problem-solving coping, on the one hand, and denial and emotional repression, on the other, have positive or negative effects on the outcome of illness.

A series of British studies on coping and breast cancer, for example, have suggested that active coping styles were prognostic of longer periods of remission, especially in early, nonmetastic cancer (Greer, 1991; Greer & Morris, 1975; Morris et al., 1981). These studies were supported by work by Temoshok and her colleagues (1985) on melanoma. They suggested that women with "Type C personalities," characterized by emotional repression, were much more likely to have poor outcomes. Further, helplessness may also result in poorer prognoses in cervical cancer (Goodkin, Antoni, & Bloom, 1986). In contrast, Dean and Surtees (1989) found that women using denial had better outcomes in breast cancer three months post-surgery.

Cooper and Faragher (1993) reviewed a series of studies they had conducted concerning the interrelationship between, stress, coping, and personality in women with breast cancer. Combining all three of these variables together provided some interesting results. The use of denial was associated with positive outcomes, whereas anger was associated with negative ones. Older women were more likely to have breast cancer, and they were also more likely to have Type C personalities. Interestingly, including age in the regression equations eliminated the effect of Type C personality on breast cancer, and it also eliminated the effects of loss stressors on outcomes. However, age did not eliminate the effects of coping.

A review by Levy (1991) suggests that the relationship between coping, psychological adjustment, and cancer remission may vary over time. Visintainer and Casey (1984) found that melanoma patients who used problem-focused coping also reported more psychological distress at diagnosis, but nine months later they also had higher levels of natural killer (NK) cell activity, an immune system component which attacks tumors. Similarly, Rogentine and his colleagues (1979) found that denial predicts relapse a year post-diagnosis.

Some of the strongest work on the connection between coping and the course of cancer was a series of studies by Fawzy and his colleagues (Fawzy, Cousins, et al. 1990; Fawzy, Kemeny, et al., 1990; Fawzy et al., 1993). In this project, Fawzy and his colleagues conducted a coping intervention with melanoma patients and examined their coping effectiveness, affect, immune function, and survival. The coping intervention consisted of a structured, six-week group intervention that included health education, training in both problem-solving skills and stress management, and psychological support. At the end of the intervention, the experimental subjects had more positive affect and were more likely to use active behavioral coping. At a six-month assessment, the intervention group also had better immune functioning, with a greater percentage of large granular lymphocytes and more NK cells, as well as better NK cell cytotoxic activity. Interestingly, affect was correlated with immune cell changes rather than with coping strategies, suggesting that the effects of coping were mediated through affect, much as the psychoneuroimmunological model presented in Chapter 2 suggests (see Figure 2-1). At a five-year follow-up, nearly one third of the control group had died, but less than 10% of the experimental group had died. Higher distress levels and more active coping at baseline were significantly associated with longer survival, as was an increase in active coping.

On the other hand, an active coping stance may have more deleterious effects with hypertension and heart disease. For example, stronger beliefs in personal mastery or control predicts more severe coronary atherosclerosis (Seeman, 1991), while high monitoring styles may be associated with hypertension (Miller, Leinbach, & Brody, 1989). In contrast, people who use denial during hospitalization for acute coronary disease may have fewer subsequent episodes of angina (Levenson, Mishra, Hamer, & Hastillo, 1989). In his review, Fowers (1992) found that people using denial after cardiac trauma by be less anxious, may have shorter hospitalization periods, and may have lower risks for subsequent morbidity and mortality. However, if denial is used during the trauma, it may be associated with a delay in seeking help. A common observation is that some men have been known to climb stairs during mild heart attacks to convince themselves that they are not having a heart attack!

It would appear that coping strategies have differing effects depending upon their timing and the type of illness. Denial at the beginning of a serious illness may have deleterious effects if it results in a delay in seeking treatment. I know of women who have died of breast cancer because they were too afraid to get a mammogram to see if a suspicious lump were indeed cancer; it was easier to deny until it was too late for efficacious treatment. Postdiagnosis, problem-focused coping may, in the short term, increase distress, whereas denial or repression may decrease it. Some denial may be beneficial in cardiovascular disease, because active coping that may increase emotional distress may also increase blood pressure and general cardiovascular responses (Dolan, Sherwood, & Light, 1992; Light, Dolan, Davis, & Sherwood, 1992; Vogele & Steptoe, 1992), exacerbating cardiovascular disease. However, under certain conditions, stress may actually enhance immune system response (Dienstbier, 1989), although stress is often assumed to have immune-suppressive effects (see O'Leary, 1990, for a review). Thus, problem-focused coping, although it may increase distress, may also aid in fighting cancer.

This is highly speculative, of course, and I know of no study that contrasts cancer and cardiovascular disease outcomes using standard assessments of denial. However, it might explain a puzzling finding by Aikens, Wallander, Bell, and Cole (1992). In a carefully done study, they found that, as expected, stress was associated with poorer metabolic control among Type I diabetics. However, an active form of coping, learned resourcefulness, was also associated with poorer metabolic control, a finding that was unexpected. To the extent that active coping increases psychological distress, at least in the short-term, the side-effects of this coping strategy may harm those physiological processes that are vulnerable to stress.

Finally, how family members cope with a patient's illness may also be important for illness outcomes. For heart patients, how the spouse copes may be critical. Bandura and Waltz (1984), for example, found that the best predictor of a male patient's adherence to a medical regime was the encouragement and support of his spouse. Further, recent work by Coyne and his colleagues (Coyne, Ellard, & Smith, 1990; Coyne & Smith, 1991) presents some troubling data. Cardiac patients did better when their spouses suppressed their own anxiety and allowed the patient more control. However, the psychological and physical cost to the spouse was high. But strategies that improved psychosocial functioning among the spouses had deleterious effects on the cardiac patients. Thus, it may be important to understand not only the way in which an individual is coping with a medical problem, but also the manner in which an individual is interacting with his or her family.

SUMMARY

In 1974, Coelho, Hamburg, and Adams published the papers from the first conferences on coping and adaptation. At that time, coping was seen as a potentially critical intermediary factor moderating the effect of stress on health. Certainly, the research during the ensuing two decades has borne out that assumption. As shown in this review, coping clearly has profound implications for both mental and physical health. However, the picture that has emerged is much more complex than was initially imagined. The two most critical themes that have emerged is that the effect of coping is modified by both the timing and the stressor context. Problem-focused coping, generally perceived as a panacea in most situations, may actually have deleterious effects in uncontrollable situations and in those in which psychological activation may have adverse effects on physiological activation. In contrast, denial, which is generally perceived as antithetical to psychological health, may have positive effects (at least in small doses) if situations are uncontrollable or if it serves to maintain emotional (and perhaps) physiological equilibrium, at least in the short-term. Coping that results in feelings of helplessness and hopelessness, on the other hand, always has adverse effects.

Nonetheless, the potential for clinical intervention is clear. Intervention directed either at medical personnel or at individuals and their families can clearly be efficacious. Interventions that either serve to reduce threat or enhance individual feelings of control (where appropriate) have been unequivocally demonstrated to have positive effects on both mental and physical health. What is needed now is more research on the strategies that serve what Antonovsky (1979) has called a salutogenic effect in situations such as chronic illness (cf. Taylor, Lichtman, & Wood, 1984).

Aldwin and Stokols (1988) have called for the examination of both the positive and negative outcomes of coping on four levels: physiological, psychological, social, and cultural. It may be especially important to determine how individuals trade off effects in these different domains, as well as to study short-term versus long-term effects. A woman undergoing a divorce, for example, may well decide to smoke to alleviate immediate psychological distress, even though she knows that smoking has adverse physical effects and may lead to greater depression in the long run. Or, as in Coyne and Smith's (1991) study, a wife may decide to cope in a way that helps her husband, even though it may increase her own distress. Finally, social activists such as the problem-focused copers in the study of Three Mile Island by Baum et al. (1983) might cope in ways that, in the long run, will do the society as a whole a great deal of good, although it might be associated in the short run with increased psychological and physical distress for themselves (and perhaps their families as well). Thus, in order to understand what constitutes "good" or "bad" coping, we need to know the purpose of a strategy, what its costs and benefits are, and how efficaciously it was used—a far cry from our current technology of correlating strategies with measures of psychological distress or a person's survival time.

Take, for example, the three cases with which we began this chapter, Norman Cousins, Ruth Carter Stapleton, and my 80-year-old friend. If we were correlating coping strategies with survival time, Cousins would clearly be the winner. His extensive use of problem-focused strategies, conceptualization of alternatives, and use of humor clearly contributed to his survival. However, my friend, who used both intro- and extra-punitive strategies that made both her life and that of her sister a living hell, survived longer than did Ms. Stapleton, who had accepted her fate and looked forward to death. Was my friend a "better coper" than Ms. Stapleton? I think not. Did my friend's coping strategies achieve the goals she wanted? Probably—if her goal, as I suspect, was to punish both herself and her sister for surviving the Holocaust while their parents died in Buchenwald.

I do not wish to suggest that we should discontinue doing studies that simply associate coping with the relatively simple outcomes that we have. Certainly Fawzy et al. (1993) showed that coping was a very powerful predictor of survival rates from cancer. However, life is very complicated, much more so than our current technology allows us to model. Lower levels of psychological distress and even survival time are only two possible goals of coping strategies. Quality of life and the achievement of an individual's own goals should also be included in research on coping with illness.

CHAPTER 10

Coping with Traumatic Stress

If it didn't result in death or permanent injury,
I figured it wasn't important.
—*Female POW in Iraq during the Gulf War,
describing how she coped with her brutal
treatment*

In 1956, anthropologist A. F. C. Wallace described the reactions of victims of a deadly tornado in Worcester, Massachusetts. The tornado was especially shocking because it was so unexpected in this New England factory town. Wallace's powerful descriptions emphasized the uniformity of the Worcesterites' reactions: They were stunned, numbed, and alternated between walking around in a daze and crying uncontrollably. The only people who did not seem totally dazed were those engaged in rescue efforts, such as policemen, firemen, and physicians. But even among these people, impairment of cognitive processes was observed. For example, physicians routinely sewed up wounds without noticing that they had not been cleaned, and much of the rescue work had to be redone.

Studies of how people cope with trauma is some of the most fascinating reading in psychology. Classic works include Lindemann's (1943) study on the Coconut Grove Fire, Bettelheim's (1943) and Frankl's (1962) recollections of survival in Nazi concentration camps, Lifton's (1961) study of Chinese thought reform camps, Erikson's

(1976) study of the Buffalo Creek disaster, and Sharanksy's (1988) experiences in a Soviet gulag. Bettelheim's descriptions of the changes in psychological reactions with each phase of the experience, the sources of individual differences in appraisal and coping, and the ways in which coping and defense mechanisms contributed to survival in this extreme environment presaged much of the current literature on coping with trauma.

It is only recently, however, that researchers have conducted more systematic studies. While there has been some overlap with the general literature on stress and coping, for the most part the trauma literature has evolved somewhat independently. The purpose of this chapter is to briefly summarize this trauma literature, drawing upon and extending an earlier review (Aldwin, 1993).

DEFINING TRAUMA

As reviewed in Chapter 4, trauma differs from other stressors in that such events threaten severe injury—up to and including loss of life—usually has a rapid onset, and often occurs to many individuals at once. Admittedly, this is a rather stringent definition of trauma. However, it is similar to that proposed by McCubbin and Figley (1983, p. 220), in which "catastrophic" stress is defined as "sudden and extreme threat to survival which is associated with a sense of helplessness, disruption, destruction, and loss." The *Diagnostic and Statistical Manual of Mental Disorders* (4th ed., DSM-IV; American Psychiatric Association, 1994) takes a similar approach. Traumatic stress is defined as events that involve serious threat to life or physical integrity, either of oneself or significant others, (e.g., the destruction of a home or community that evokes feelings of extreme terror and helplessness).

Others define traumatic events as those that shatter peoples' beliefs that they live in a meaningful, predictable world (Benner, Roskies, & Lazarus, 1980). Epstein (1991) identified four types of cognitive schemata that may be damaged during trauma: beliefs about the benignity of the world, the possibility of justice, the trustworthiness of other people, and self-worth. However, these broader definitions could easily apply to many stressful life events and chronic role strains—for example, being arrested, especially for something one did not do; being stuck in a low-level, poor paying job with little autonomy; being cheated out of due recognition for one's role on a project at work; or even parenting a particularly difficult adolescent, which could easily make one a bit jaundiced about justice, trustworthiness, and self-worth. Indeed, it would be difficult to conceive of any major stressor that did not at least challenge one of these cognitive schema.

Limiting trauma to extreme stressors has a number of advantages. First, defining trauma in this manner identifies the most objective of stressors. Neuroticism may well play a role in the occurrence of life events, hassles, and chronic role strain, but the experience of earthquakes, wars, concentration camps, and so forth, usually has little to do with one's personality characteristics. The distribution of trauma is not completely random—exposure to crime and even combat may reflect socioeconomic status, for example. However, the experience of certain types of trauma, such as war or natural disasters, often occurs fairly randomly or to entire communities—and, thus, personality predispositions to stress may be less of a factor than in other quasi-experimental stress research. Second, such trauma often requires the complete mobilization of resources if one is to survive—and, as such, provides an important picture of the use (and importance) of coping resources and strategies. Third, as mentioned in Chapter 4, trauma has a qualitatively different "feel" than other stressors—even major life events. The hyperreactivity and flashbacks of posttraumatic stress disorder (PTSD) are generally associated with combat or other major trauma, not with chronic role strain.

For example, one PTSD researcher told me of a client who was a Korean war veteran. He showed no war-related problems at all for several decades, until he reached age 50. He was giving a presentation at a board meeting for his business, when all of a sudden everyone sitting at the table "changed" into Asians and seemed to be speaking Chinese, which absolutely terrified him and led him to seek therapy. Similarly, I was once conducting a research project with elderly men regarding the long-term effects of combat exposure. One subject called me and explained that he could not fill out the questionnaire, because every time he tried to he kept seeing blood all over the pages. I assured him that he did not have to fill out the questionnaire and urged him to come in and talk to someone about this experience—which he did. Although he had not even thought about World War II in decades, filling out the questionnaire brought up old, traumatic memories, which were manifested in the form of nightmares and extremely real visions of blood spattering on the questionnaire. I have yet to hear anyone credibly report having flashbacks such as these from stressful life events such as a tenure review, no matter how difficult or distressing. There is something extremely traumatic about nearly dying or seeing others die that evokes a primordial response quite different than that elicited by more common stressors.

One potential problem with limiting trauma to this stringent definition is whether it includes incest. Incest is generally considered to be highly traumatic, although it may not be life threatening per se. However, molesters often use threats of harm, either to the child or his or her family, to ensure compliance and secrecy. Even if the molester is a parent who does not make such threats per se, damage to such a primary bond may evoke basic fears about survival. Children of divorce, for example, may express fears about the availability of food and whether the refrigerator will be empty (Wallerstein & Blakeslee, 1989). Children have fewer resources to cope with stress than adults do; thus, incest may have broad and very negative repercussions (Roth & Lebowitz, 1988), which merits its inclusion in the trauma category.

The purpose of this chapter is to examine how individuals cope with traumatic stress and whether it differs in any way from ordinary, everyday coping. A secondary purpose is to provide a more descriptive, case study approach to coping behavior in order to provide a better sense of coping behaviors than is afforded by more quantitative studies. As we shall see, the qualitative studies of coping with trauma provide a special insight into the adaptation process.

COPING WITH TRAUMA

For a number of reasons, studying how individuals cope with trauma and its aftermath may be particularly crucial for understanding the adaptation process.

First, accounts of coping with trauma are fascinating reading and have a great deal of intrinsic interest. The *Reader's Digest,* for example, routinely includes stories about how people survived airplane crashes, avalanches, sharks, and other assorted disasters, as well as stories about women who fought off serial murderers or rapists, football heroes who recovered from certain quadriplegia, war heroes who survived prisoner of war (POW) camps, and so on. The news media also play up such stories, spending a large proportion of airtime (and column space) on families who survived a blizzard for several days, children who were dug out of wells, puppies who fell down drain pipes, to mention only a few recent stories. There are even television programs that feature rescue workers responding to emergency calls. The stories provide a satisfying (if somewhat illusory) sense of control: You can survive anything, they seem to say, if you just have enough courage, tenacity, faith, a little technical knowledge, and, of course, a lot of luck.

Second, trauma provides a very interesting opportunity for the study of extreme stressors that would never be replicable in a laboratory: Things occur in real life that would never get past human subjects review boards — or animal rights review boards, for that matter. One cannot — and should not — subject humans or other animals to extreme trauma in order to study its psychological consequences (see Ader, 1981 for arguments against using extreme stress in animals). Epstein (1991) has argued that traumatic situations provide an unparalleled opportunity to examine the structure of personality. To study the structure of an atom, he stated, one needs an atom smasher. Trauma functions as an atom smasher for the study of personality—and of adaptive processes in general.

Third, trauma is often unanticipated and may require immediate mobilization of seldom-used resources. Most people are not trained to cope with trauma (with the exception of military or medical personnel) and must thus improvise and develop new strategies very quickly. Unlike many life events or hassles, traumatic events often have long-term effects, which allows one to examine the process of adaptation over time.

Finally, it seems that governments and quasi-governmental agencies continually come up with new ways to inflict torture and other atrocities on people. One need only talk to Guatemalan, Cambodian, or Afghan refugees—and now Bosnian and Somali refugees—to hear of unspeakable acts of brutality. One elderly Afghani I spoke with at a dinner party told me almost gleefully of how he had been tortured by three separate regimes! Some Cambodian refugees that my clinical colleagues treat have hysterical blindness: Having been forced to watch the murder of their children, they can no longer bear to use their eyes. In refugee camps, people may face brutality in some ways even more shocking than that from which they were attempting to flee. In some Thai camps, for example, Cambodian women were routinely raped in front of their husbands and families to ensure that the families would be totally dominated by the thugs that ran the camps (Carolyn Williams, personal communication, 1990). Studying how individuals survive and overcome such traumatic experiences seems to me to be one small way of countering such atrocities.

Phases of Coping with Trauma

Accounts of initial reactions to trauma are often quite remarkable. People sometimes report that time seemed to slow down, so that they could act much more quickly; others froze and seemed paralyzed, unable to respond; yet others dissociated themselves and felt as if they were not a part of what was happening. I remember reading an account of a man who had been mauled by a lion. The lion, he said, had picked him up in his mouth and shaken him, just like a cat does to a mouse. The man said that he now knew what the mouse felt: nothing. While it was happening, his mind went numb. He felt no pain, as if his experience were happening to someone else. Attention may become very focused: it is not uncommon for soldiers who have been wounded in battle to initially feel no pain or even notice that they have been wounded until after the heat of battle.

Many researchers have identified different phases of coping with trauma, which seem to vary by type of trauma. This section will briefly review coping phases for concentration camps, rapes, and natural disasters. Somewhat more attention will be given to accounts of concentration camps, in part because of the richness of the qualitative literature in this area.

Concentration Camps

Bruno Bettelheim (1943), a psychologist who survived Nazi concentration camps, maintained his sanity in part by studying adaptation to the camps in a systematic manner and even enlisting two assistants in his efforts. Bettleheim's efforts were remarkable, not only because of their context, but also because he demonstrated person–environment fit interactions in adaptation even under this extreme stressor. He identified four stages in the concentration camp experience: "initial shock" of being a prisoner, transportation to camp and "initiation" to it, the process of "adapting," and "final adaptation." However, different types of prisoners reacted to these stages differently. Besides Jews, there were political prisoners, Jehovah's witnesses and other conscientious objectors, criminals, homosexuals, people who objected to working conditions, and "personal" prisoners, that is, wealthy people being held for ransom by various Nazi officials.

In the "initial shock" phase, the different types of prisoners manifested very different responses. The criminals and political prisoners were least distressed. Although anxious about the future, the criminals were pleased at seeing people from higher socioeconomic brackets at their own level, whereas the political prisoners took their arrest as indicators of their own importance. Those from the upper classes, on the other hand, maintained the belief that they would be released, that their families would buy them out — and, indeed, many of them did win their freedom. The few who were not rescued maintained a self-imposed isolation as a way of maintaining their sense of superiority.

The middle class inmates were most distressed because they could perceive no justification for their arrests:

> They had no consistent philosophy which would protect their integrity as human beings, which would given them the force to make a stand against the Nazis. . . . They could not question the wisdom of law and

of the police, so they accepted the behavior of the Gestapo as just. What was wrong was that *they* were made objects of a persecution which in itself *must* be right, since it was carried out by the authorities. (Bettelheim, 1943, p. 426; italics in original)

When the middle class prisoners realized their true situation, they seemed to disintegrate, because their worldview was shattered. They were the only ones to commit suicide at this stage; often those that did not kill themselves became very antisocial when they reached the camps—cheating on their fellow inmates, becoming spies for the Nazis, and so on.

The transportation to the camp and the "initiation"—what the Nazis called "welcome"—involved some of the worst torture that the prisoners would experience. At the camp, the guards tortured each prisoner to break down their resistance; the few who did resist were killed. Bettelheim survived this by dissociating—which is about the only possible thing to do under such extreme stress (Figley, 1983; Ursano, Wheatley, Sledge, Rahe, & Carolson, 1986). His goal throughout was to remain alive and internally unchanged. New prisoners in general coped through dissociation and regression. Curiously, minor insults on the part of the guards seemed to be resented more than major ones. While altruism is an important coping strategy during traumas like natural disasters (Smith, 1983), Bettelheim reported that the Nazis quickly suppressed altruistic acts by punishing the whole group if one person tried to protect or help someone else. The prisoners quickly learned that trying to help only resulted in even worse conditions— and, thus, natural leaders were suppressed.

In the "adapting" stage, the prisoners no longer seemed to cope via dissociation. Their focus narrowed to the camp and how to survive in it. They reverted to daydreams about how important, warm, or loved they would be once they got out, even while many were abandoning dreams of ever getting out. In his description of Norwegian concentration camp survivors, Eitinger (1980) also found that the coping strategies of building up an "inner world" and of idealizing the world outside the camps were nearly universal.

In the "final adaptation" stage, the personality of the prisoners changed into what the Gestapo wanted—namely, more useful subjects of the Nazi state. "Old" prisoners—those who had been there at least three years—often identified with the aggressor and incorporated Nazi values. They would zealously enforce the rules among the newer prisoners, even ones that were abandoned by the Nazi guards. For example, one Nazi guard on a whim ordered the prisoners to wash their shoes inside and out with soap. However, the shoes became as hard and heavy as stone, and the order was never repeated. Nonetheless, many of the old prisoners continued washing their shoes, and forced the new prisoners to do so as well. The old prisoners would not admit to accepting Nazi values, but engaged in rationalization to justify their behavior. For example, the newer prisoners often wanted to sabotage their work, but the older prisoners would argue against this, saying that after the war, Germany would need those buildings, or that one should always do one's best, no matter what.

This identification with the aggressor was sometimes taken to an extreme:

> Practically all prisoners who had spent a long time in the camp took over the Gestapo's attitude toward the so-called unfit prisoner. . . . A new-comer who did not stand up well under the strain tended to become a liability for the other prisoners. Moreover, weaklings were those most apt eventually to turn traitor. Weaklings usually died during the first weeks in the camp anyway, so it seemed as well to get rid of them soon-er. So old prisoners were sometimes instrumental in getting rid of the unfit. . . . That this was really a taking-over of Gestapo attitudes can be seen from the treatment of traitors. . . . The way in which they were tortured for days and slowly killed was taken over from the Gestapo. (Bettelheim, 1943, p. 448)

Frankl (1962) was a psychiatrist who also made a scientific study of the various concentration camps that he was in as a way of preserving his sanity. He described three phases to the experience, slightly differ-ent from, although similar to, Bettelheim's: the time directly after ad-mission, the period of entrenchment in camp routine, and release and liberation.

As with Bettelheim, the initial reaction consisted of shock and dis-belief, but Frankl also included the experience of "being overcome" by a grim sense of humor and curiosity. After the first initial selection at Auschwitz, in which 90% of prisoners who arrived on the train were marched to the gas ovens, the remaining 10% were systematically brutalized, stripped of all possessions, denuded of all body hair, sub-jected to torture, and then marched off to showers for their own "cleansing":

> Thus the illusions some of us still held were destroyed one by one, and then, quite unexpectedly, most of us were overcome by a grim sense of humor. We knew that we had nothing to lose except our so ridiculously naked lives. When the showers started to run, we all tried very hard to make fun, both about ourselves and about each other. After all, real water [as opposed to cyanide gas] did flow from the sprays!

> Apart from that strange kind of humor, another sensation seized us: curiosity. . . . Cold curiosity predominated even in Auschwitz, somehow detaching the mind from its surroundings, which came to be regarded with a kind of objectivity. At that time one cultivated this state of mind as a means of protection. . . . In the next few days our curiosity evolved into surprise. (Frankl, 1962, pp. 14–15)

The surprise stemmed from discovering the extent to which they could adapt to such harsh conditions—surprise that they did not develop respiratory disease even after being forced to stand in cold air for several hours after the showers, that they could go without sleep for much longer periods than they imagined, that they could sleep under impossible conditions, or that they did not develop gum disease despite not being able to brush their teeth. (I suspect that in this initial stage, their immune systems were greatly stimulated. See Chapter 4.) Not surprisingly, information seeking was rampant, and most considered suicide at some point.

These reactions began to change after a few days. In the second phase, entrenchment into camp life, the prisoners became apathetic and emotionally deadened. Reality narrowed simply to survival in the camp, which involved the development of various problem-focused strategies, including hoarding bits of food, casually robbing the dead or dying for better clothes, developing elaborate systems to warn of the approach of guards, and humoring the Capos—prisoners who ran the work groups—to gain access to more resources. The prisoners also fantasized a great deal about food and home.

Frankl's account differed markedly from Bettelheim's in his emphasis on the positive strategies that the inmates used. While many did become cruel and did engage in despicable behavior, Frankl documented the use of humor, art, and altruism as coping strategies that were consciously employed:

> Humor was another of the soul's weapons in the fight for self-preservation. . . . I practically trained a friend of mine who worked next to me on the building site to develop a sense of humor. I suggested to him that we would promise each other to invent at least one amusing story daily, about some incident that could happen one day after our liberation. (Frankl, 1962, p. 42)

The prisoners also put on a type of "cabaret" from time to time, trading jokes, singing songs, and reciting poetry, even though it meant missing their evening portion of soup.

The altruism of the prisoners (and sometimes even the guards) made life possible in the camps. According to Frankl, the prisoners often looked out for each other. While they tried to protect themselves, they also tried to protect their closest friends and sometimes people who were simply fellow countrymen. More experienced inmates would give advice about survival strategies to newcomers, often risking terrible retribution from the Nazis. While it was strictly forbidden to rescue anyone who was committing suicide, the prisoners tried to watch other inmates who were judged to be suicide risks in order to prevent these inmates from making any attempts to kill themselves. Frankl recounted one episode in which a starving man was being sought for stealing a few pounds of rotten potatoes. The Nazis threatened to withhold food from everyone for 24 hours unless the inmates produced the man. While there was much grumbling, not one of the 2,500 men in the camp gave up the name of the culprit, even though the Nazis did carry out their threat. Frankl himself provided both individual and sometimes collective psychotherapy for other inmates, in addition to his occasional official duties in taking care of typhoid victims—which usually amounted only to the distribution of half an aspirin to a few of his patients.*

For Frankl, the maintenance of a sense of meaning or purpose in life was critical to survival. If an inmate lost that, he or she also lost the will to live—and often died. Most important of all was spiritual growth and development.

> In spite of all the enforced physical and mental primitiveness of the life in a concentration camp, it was possible for spiritual life to deepen. Sensitive people who were used to a rich intellectual life may have suffered much pain (they were often of a delicate constitution), but the damage to their inner selves was less. They were able to retreat from their terrible surroundings to a life of inner riches and spiritual freedom. (Frankl, 1962, p. 35)

Frankl related several instances of what can only be called transcendent states that he experienced in the midst of this terrible suffering. He felt that these experiences allowed him to maintain his sense of dignity and self-worth, to not become "worse than an animal."

> In the final analysis it becomes clear that the sort of person the prisoner became was the result of an inner decision, and not the result of camp influences alone. Fundamentally, therefore, any man can, even under such circumstances, decide what shall become of him. . . . The way they

---

*When I read Frankl's account of only being able to distribute half an aspirin at a time to his patients, I understood why the elderly Jewish woman who was dying of colon cancer (see Chapter 8) would accept only half an aspirin as a pain killer.

bore their suffering was a genuine inner achievement. It is this spiritual freedom—which cannot be taken away—that makes life meaningful and purposeful. (Frankl, 1962, p. 66)

Frankl is not the only person to note the link between spirituality, maintenance of meaning and the preservation of dignity even under intolerable circumstances. Lifton (1961) detailed a similar process in a Catholic priest held in a Chinese Communist concentration camp, and Sharansky (1988) provided a similar account in his experiences in a Soviet gulag.

In some ways, Frankl's account of the third stage—postliberation—was the saddest. Having deadened their emotions for so long, the inmates could not immediately experience joy at their new freedom. It took a while for everyday emotions to return, which was sometimes aided by the recounting of their experiences. The former prisoners ate prodigious amounts, which is hardly surprising. Bettleheim's "identification with the aggressor" emerged anew in some of the inmates. Some became ruthless oppressors, justifying their behavior by their own terrible experience. Many also became bitter and disillusioned. Persons who had kept themselves alive with the thought of reunion with a loved one had a particularly difficult time when they discovered the extent of their losses. However, Frankl believed that most of the survivors eventually recovered.

Lomranz (1990) reviewed the literature on the long-term adaptation of the Holocaust survivors and identified two further stages: laying foundations and maintenance. During the "laying foundations" period, survivors built a new life: finding a country in which to live, learning the language and the customs of that country, finding a way to make a living, and building a new family. This period often lasted for several years.

During the maintenance period, the survivors had developed a reasonably stable mode of adaptation. Lomranz identified three different patterns. In keeping with McCubbin, Olson, and Larsen's (1982) caution that adaptation to traumatic stress is not just an individual affair but involves the entire family, Lomranz based his three modes on different types of "family culture":

> Different kinds of family cultures were created, depending on the survivors' personalities, histories, perceptions of the Holocaust, assumptive worlds, and resources. . . . Some families exhibited a somewhat forced happy atmosphere, emphasizing the importance of external appearance. Others were pervaded by a more solemn mood, and the atmosphere at times resembled continuous mourning. Boundaries and privacy were discouraged, and it was often a complicated matter to develop intimacy. Nutrition, body care, and material support often sub-

stituted for emotional closeness. . . . Many of the families . . . develop[ed] a traditional, authoritarian, constricted atmosphere. There was little delegation of authority. (Lomranz, 1990, pp. 110–111)

The families also differed in both the degree and manner in which the Holocaust was discussed. Some people were open about their experiences and "bore witness" publicly, writing their memoirs and engaging in various Holocaust-related projects. However, if the survivors complained and exhibited trauma-related symptoms, family members often retreated from them. Thus, it is not surprising that in many families, especially the authoritarian ones (and, presumably, the "forced happy" ones), the Holocaust was a taboo subject. Some did not discuss their experiences even with their spouses; others hid their feelings so well that extended family members did not even realize they had been in the camps. For many people, denial and suppression worked well for decades.

Lomranz believed that the maintenance period lasted only until old age, because the developmental tasks in late life would force the survivors to change their mode of adaptation, especially among those who used denial and repression to control their emotions. In late life, the inevitable losses of loved ones would remind the survivors of the many other loved ones that were lost. Life review is also a developmental task in late life and underlies ego integration or despair; but Lomranz questions whether the Eriksonian requirement to accept one's life as necessary, unique, and inevitable in order to achieve ego integration is realistic, given the totally unacceptable experience in the death camps.

The Kahanas and their colleagues have also been studying late life adaptation to the Holocaust (for a review see Kahana, 1992). These studies have been more rigorous than most, in that they have used standard indicators of mental and physical health, as well as stress and coping measures. Whereas many studies had utilized clinical or treatment seeking populations, the Kahanas and their colleagues have studied nonclinical populations. Further, they have carefully compared Holocaust survivors who emigrated to the United States and Israel with ethnically similar groups of people who emigrated before the war.

According to research done by the Kahanas and their colleagues, survivors were generally in worse physical and mental health than the comparison group. The survivors reported more physical symptoms, primarily "psychogenic ones" such as ulcers, but often did not report differences in more serious illness such as cancer or arthritis. Survivors also experienced intrusive thoughts regarding their trauma (75% experienced this at least once a week) and reported slightly more psychological distress and lower morale. However, their social functioning was often higher than that of the comparison group. Despite less education, their income was considerably higher. They were more likely to be employed and had "superior job histories." They also had more stable marriages (75% were married to other Holocaust survivors) and fewer residential moves. Survivors were also more likely to participate in community activities and evinced greater feelings of responsibility toward their communities.

When asked whether experiencing the Holocaust affected coping with problems in late life, some (45%) confirmed Lomranz' hypothesis that it made coping more difficult, but 26% said it made it easier ("Once you survive the Holocaust, you can survive anything") (Kahana, 1992, p. 164). Nearly all said they were "different" as a result of their experiences. Nearly half (46%) saw themselves as negatively affected, but 34% reported strengths and positive features. Of those who reported positive sequelae, nearly half (46%) reported better coping resources and strength of character, 36% were more appreciative of life, and 27% saw themselves as more humane, empathetic, and compassionate toward others.

Personality, coping, and social support variables were correlated with positive affect. These included Holocaust experiences with family and friends, having an altruistic attitude toward the world and an internal locus of control, and having a spouse who was also a survivor (Kahana, 1992). Additional analyses on the Israeli samples (Harel, Kahana, & Kahana, 1988) found that a combination of variables predicted 52% of the variance in the psychological well-being among survivors: better physical health, higher instrumental coping, lower use of emotional coping, and less use of social concern, as well as marriage to a Holocaust survivor, fewer life crises, communication with coworkers, and not being resigned to fate. Thus, physical health, stress and coping, the utilization of social resources, and attitudes toward life accounted for a large proportion of the variance in psychological well-being in later life among Holocaust survivors.

A number of observations can be made from these often remarkable accounts of this trauma. First, one would think that the overwhelming "environmental press" of a Nazi concentration camp would obviate any individual attempts at coping and adaptation. However, there were clear differences in how individuals responded to the camps: Bettelheim saw only bestiality, whereas Frankl also saw courage, altruism, and even transcendence.

Second, coping strategies changed over time in response to the changing demands of this traumatic experience: Initial dissociative reactions gave way to emotional numbing, which facilitated problem-focused attempts at survival. Third, the inmates consciously developed a number of problem-focused strategies for survival, which included information seeking, analysis of the ways of avoiding the worst of the punishments and gaining access to more resources, and sharing resources and developing innovative ways of using them. Emotion-focused strategies included emotional numbing, the use of fantasy to provide a respite from camp life, the conscious use of humor, and spiritual growth. Fourth, Frankl noted that the goal of coping behaviors was not necessarily survival: many felt that maintaining personal integrity was a higher goal and would engage in altruistic acts that they knew would shorten their own lifespans, or they would refuse to perform what they perceived to be immoral acts even if it meant not surviving. As Frankl put it, "the best of us did not survive."

Coping after the traumatic events is also critical to adaptation. Lomranz and the Kahanas documented individual differences in adaptive strategies after the Holocaust that had various costs and benefits. Coping strategies, the utilization of social resources, and attitudes toward life accounted for over 50% of the variance in psychological well-being in late life, which suggested that adaptive strategies were critical for recovery from this trauma. Finally, many if not most of the Holocaust victims carried lifelong physical and emotional scars; however, nearly a third reported having developed in positive ways from this most onerous of experiences, such as developing more coping resources, greater strength of character, and more humaneness.

Rape and Incest

In an early study of rape victims, Burgess and Holstrom (1976) suggested that in a traumatic experience there are three different phases which elicit different types of coping strategies. In the first or threat phase, the three types of strategies included cognitive assessment concerning the nature and severity of the threat, verbal tactics, and physical action. While one third of the women whom Burgess and Holstrom interviewed used multiple strategies, an equal number used none, due to physical or psychological paralysis.

During the second phase—the attack itself—a greater range of strategies was identified. Problem-focused coping included physical action (fight or flight), as well as cognitive and verbal strategies. Emotion-focused strategies included affective responses (crying or screaming), psychological defenses (mainly emotional numbing and dissociation), and physiological reactions, including vomiting, passing out, and urinating. (One could also argue that these physiological reactions could be viewed as problem-focused strategies, if they were used purpose-fully to deter the attacker.)

In the third phase, immediately after the attack, the strategies uti-lized included bargaining for freedom, freeing oneself, and alerting others (seeking social assistance and/or reporting the rape to author-ities).

Others have studied longer term reactions to rape. Ward (1988) argued that most victims use defense mechanisms, including repression-suppression, rationalization, intellectualization, denial, undoing, regres-sion, minimization, dramatization, and displacement of anger. Cohen and Roth (1987) studied 72 rape victims who were contacted via newspaper advertisements. These women reported higher levels of psy-chological distress than normative samples, but lower than women as-sessed immediately after a rape. The more force used in the rape, the greater the distress. Surprisingly, the length of time since the rape oc-curred was negatively related only to intrusive thoughts; Cohen and Roth argued that other symptoms decline only in the first three months after a rape and then remain relatively stable. In general, women who reported the rape to the police and confided in someone relatively quick-ly (or sought professional help) did better than women who only tried to repress the problem. Harvey, Orbuch, Chalisz, and Garwood (1991) confirmed that rape victims who confided in someone quickly had better outcomes than those women who confided later. However, the response of the confidant was also important: Women whose confidants respond-ed negatively had poorer outcomes than women with supportive con-fidants.

Although the tendency is to assume that trauma has long-term negative outcomes, this might not be the self-perception of the victims. Burt and Katz (1987) found that over 50% of the rape victims in their sample felt that they had changed in a positive direction, and fewer than 15% felt that they had changed in a negative direction. Burt and Katz factor analyzed these women's responses and found four growth factors: improved self-concept, self-directed activity, less passivity, and less stereotyped attitudes.

In general, incest victims tend to be worse off than adult women who were raped (Harvey et al., 1991), in part because children have fewer psychological resources to cope with stress than adults do (Roth & Lebowitz, 1988). Silver, Boon, and Stones (1983) interviewed 77 women (identified through a newspaper advertisement) who had ex-perienced incest. In contrast to Burt and Katz's (1987) study, only 20% of the incest victims reported positive outcomes. These women were primarily those who did have confidants and who were able to "make sense" out of the event, mainly through the victims' understanding their father's behavior as a function of family dynamics (e.g., due to the mother's illness or unavailability) or as a result of the father's mental illness or character disorder.

Unlike Cohen and Roth's (1987) study, in which characteristics of the rape were related to later distress, Draucker (1989) did not find that various qualities of the incestuous experience were related to psychological distress in adulthood (although the 103 women ranged in age from 18 to 64, which may have blurred these effects). However, how the women coped with the problem (by searching for meaning, developing a sense a mastery, and enhancing self-esteem through downward comparisons) did relate to depression, self-esteem, and social role functioning in the expected manner.

Incestuous experiences may not necessarily interfere with coping abilities. Reis and Heppner (1993) compared stress and coping measures in a small sample of mother–daughter pairs from incestuous families (in which males were the perpetrators) with a nonclinical sample. Not surprisingly, both mothers and daughters from incestuous families perceived their families as significantly more stressful than the comparison sample. Although the mothers from incestuous families perceived themselves as worse copers, there were no differences between the two groups of mothers on the family coping scale. Further, abused daughters did not differ on any of the coping or distress measures from the comparison daughters. Reis and Heppner (1993) argued that there is a role reversal in incestuous families, with girls having a great deal of responsibility. They may become relatively resourceful because they have to take on the mother's role to compensate for her ineffectiveness. However, inspection of the items on the coping scale used in this study revealed few negative or harmful coping strategies. The mothers' perception of themselves as ineffective (with which, apparently, the authors concurred) was not reflected in the family coping scale, suggesting that the latter did not include a full range of coping strategies. Thus, the harm that these girls experienced may not have been reflected in the measures used.

Nonetheless, the pattern of results from these rape and incest studies is similar to that found in the Holocaust studies. How one copes with the events, especially after the fact, may be more important to mental health over the long run than the existence of the trauma itself.

Natural Disasters

According to Smith (1983), the effects of natural disasters are most significant if they are sudden, unexpected, or prolonged, and, if they occur at night. While much research attention has been focused on the most devastating disasters, most are not that traumatic. "In fact, disasters may have some 'therapeutic' features. It is not uncommon for victims to express positive feelings from participating in the community recovery process. A sense of adequacy, mastery, increased community solidarity, and general optimism often comes from collectively responding to the challenges of a crisis" (Smith, 1983, p. 124). Smith (1983) identified four phases of adaptation to a natural disaster. The first, or heroic, phase occurs during the event and immediately afterward. This phase is often characterized by altruism. The second, or honeymoon, phase is characterized by social solidarity and cleanup efforts. In the third stage, disillusionment can set it. People might withdraw from community effort and express negative feelings toward governmental agencies, especially if there is less than expected aid. Finally, in the reconstruction phase, individuals assume responsibility for their own recovery and rebuild their community.

To a certain extent, this somewhat rosy picture of the effects of a natural disaster may be limited to countries like the United States that have a great deal of resources, rather stringent building codes that limit the devastation that occurs in other countries, and reasonably efficient governmental responses to crises. In other countries, the effects of natural disasters can be more devastating and recovery much more difficult. An earthquake of a 5.0 magnitude on the Richter scale that often causes only minor damage in California could result in thousands of deaths in countries such as Iran, Mexico, or China, which do not have stringent earthquake building codes. In Bangladesh or rural India, there may be few, if any, adequate roads, which often delays rescue efforts for days, resulting in widespread deaths due to secondary causes such as typhoid. If there is widespread destruction and loss of life, the consequences of a natural disaster may last for years.

Some of the most moving descriptions of psychological reactions to a disaster is provided by Lifton (1968), who conducted first-hand interviews with survivors of Hiroshima. While it was not a "natural" disaster, most residents had no idea that they had been bombed, and responded as if it were some sort of natural disaster. Many thought that the whole world was simply dying. As one Protestant minister said: "The feeling I had was that everyone was dead. The whole city was destroyed. . . . I thought all of my family must be dead—it doesn't matter if I die. . . . I thought this was the end of Hiroshima—of Japan—of humankind" (quoted in Lifton, 1968, p. 22). One young boy was pinned down under debris: "There were roof tiles and walls—everything black—entirely covering me. So I screamed for help. . . .

And from all around I heard moans and screaming. . . . I thought that I too was going to die" (quoted in Lifton, 1968, p. 21).

The few people who survived were often stunned and behaved like automatons, wandering around in a daze. Many were so badly burned and disfigured that even their closest relatives could not recognize them. One sociologist described the unreality of the scene:

> Everything I saw made a deep impression—a park nearby covered with dead bodies waiting to be cremated. . . . Very badly injured people evacuated in my direction. . . . The most impressive thing I saw was some girls, very young girls, not only with their clothes torn off but with their skin peeled off as well. . . . My immediate thought was that this was like the hell I had always read about. . . . I had never seen anything which resembled it before, but I thought that [if] there should be a hell, this was it—the Buddhist hell, where we were taught that people who could not attain salvation always went. (quoted in Lifton, 1968, p. 29)

As with the concentration camps, many people described themselves as emotionally numbed. One noncommissioned officer who was in charge of mass cremations found that he could do his job with little difficulty: "After a while they became just like objects or goods that we handled in a very businesslike way. . . . Of course I didn't regard them simply as pieces of wood—they were dead bodies—but if we had been sentimental we couldn't have done the work. . . . We had no emotions. . . . I was temporarily without feeling" (quoted in Lifton, 1969, p. 31). This emotional numbing often lasted for months. Others were racked with survivor guilt—why had they survived, when most of their loved ones had not?

Thus, it is not surprising that even within the United States exposure to disasters has been associated with chronic stress and symptoms of PTSD. This may be especially true when the disaster is technological than when it is natural (for a review, see Baum & Fleming, 1993). Technological disasters are those disasters that result from the use (or often misuse) of technologies such as nuclear power or from inadequate industrial safety measures, for example, at chemical or petroleum processing plants or in mine shafts. For reasons that are not hard to understand, disasters are more distressing when they are thought to involve human carelessness, greed, or indifference to the fate of others.

Reactions to natural disasters are very similar to other sources of trauma, such as concentration camps and rapes. We will next examine whether coping with trauma is different than coping with regular stressors.

Differences and Similarities between Coping with Trauma and Everyday Coping

There are certain similarities between coping with trauma and everyday coping. As we have seen, people undergoing trauma utilize analysis and problem-focused action, social support, negotiation skills, humor, altruism and prayer. However, there are also marked differences.

First of all, people in traumatic situations may have much less conscious control over their coping strategies. Emotional numbing is a hallmark of emotion-focused coping during trauma. Further, the use of defense mechanisms such as denial and distortion may be much more marked. Even among people trained to deal with trauma, such as soldiers, paralysis may occur. Solomon (1993) recounted the experience of a crack paratrooper during the Yom Kippur war:

> I saw dying men, soldiers of mine, who'd been training for several months, call me to help them. I want to go over, but I can't! My legs won't carry me. Even if it might have been possible to reach them, I couldn't have gone. I wanted to walk, but I found myself crying. I was sweating, crying, and trembling. I was shaking, shaking like a leaf. A madness of fear. . . . I was rooted in one spot. I was lying there and couldn't get up. (p. 43)

Second, confiding in someone may play a more central role in coping with trauma. Although social support is widely recognized as important in adapting to stress, surprisingly, in the coping literature this strategy is generally associated with negative outcomes (Monroe & Steiner, 1986). However, most trauma studies show that confiding in others is associated with better outcomes (Pennebaker, Barger, & Tiebout, 1989; Pennebaker & O'Heeron, 1984; Silver et al., 1983), especially if confiding receives a positive response (Harvey et al., 1991). In both literatures, having a supportive family is seen as crucial to adaptive coping (Coyne & Downey, 1991; McCubbin & Patterson, 1983), while involvement in community efforts is much more important in trauma literature, especially natural disasters (Smith, 1983).

Third, the process of coping with trauma may last for a much longer time than coping with everyday problems. Horowitz (1986) showed that a traumatic event may initially lead to outcry, then denial, which in turn may be followed by intrusive memories, flashbacks, and obsessive review. Individuals may oscillate between denial and obsession until they begin the process of working through—namely, acceptance and the development of adequate coping skills. It is also not unusual for such reactions to be delayed, sometimes for months or even years (cf. Solomon, 1993). Further, how one copes with problems after the trauma may be more important to recovery than the initial exposure to trauma (Wolfe, Keane, Kaloupek, Mora, & Winde, 1993).

Interestingly, Baum and his colleagues are developing a model of long-term adaptation to trauma (Baum, Cohen, & Hall, 1993; Davidson & Baum, 1993). They argue that trauma has long-term negative effects primarily through the intrusiveness of flashbacks, which can result in a state of chronic stress, the hyperarousal and catecholamine disturbances seen in PTSD. Further, certain personality types may be associated with the propensity to have intrusive thoughts, since it appears to be related to the propensity to have vivid daydreams (Derry, Deal, & Baum, 1993).

Finally, trauma researchers highlight the development of meaning and transformation of the self to a much greater extent than is common in the general coping literature (Epstein, 1991; Roth & Newman, 1991; Silver et al., 1983). Indeed, meaning may be an important factor in the greater stressfulness of technological in contrast to natural disasters. An earthquake or tornado is not, after all, personal. However, in a technological disaster, as well as with other traumas such as rape, incarceration in a concentration camp, or even war, other individuals may be seen as having perpetrated the harm in such a way as to dehumanize their victims. When the gratification of the perpetrator is more important than harm to others, or when corporate profits are seen as more important than human life, one's fundamental sense of self may be called into question.

Thus, it is not surprising that the outcome of coping with trauma may be a fundamental change in identity (Horowitz, 1986; Roth & Newman, 1991). To a certain extent, change in self-identity may be the outcome of coping with all major stressors. If nothing else, people learn that they can cope with and overcome adversity—or, unfortunately, that they cannot. However, if Epstein (1991) is correct, and trauma smashes one's fundamental identity, then the ability to create a new, positive identity may be a *sine qua non* of successful coping with trauma. Roth and Newman (1991) suggested that the best way of coping with trauma is to gradually dose oneself with manageable amounts of emotional material, come to an understanding of its meaning, and recalibrate conceptions of the self and the world until some sort of reasonable fit is found.

This creation of a new identity may explain why so many people report positive outcomes of coping with trauma. In general, it is not unusual for people to report positive outcomes of coping with stress (see Chapter 13). Researchers have shown positive outcomes in coping with divorce (DiGiulio, 1989), widowhood (Lieberman, 1992), and rape (Burt & Katz, 1987). Ebersole and Flores (1989) found that 66% of a sample of undergraduates reported positive outcomes from their most sorrowful or painful experience, while Chiriboga (1984) found that negative events were equally as likely to predict positive change as negative change on a variety of indicators of well-being in a longitudinal study of community residents. In short, coping with stress is not simply an expenditure of resources but can result in the development of new coping resources as well.

SUMMARY

Studies of how individuals cope with trauma provide an unparalleled opportunity for studying human adaptation. These studies emphasize that the coping process changes over time, as a result not only of the changing demands of the stressor, but also of the changing needs of the self. Further, the function of coping is not only to regulate the situation and the emotions, but also the maintenance of ego integrity and human dignity under overwhelming conditions. Further, the ultimate outcome of coping can be seen as transformational—both of the self and of the larger community.

CHAPTER 11

Culture, Stress, and Coping

T here is unequivocal evidence that the situational context affects coping (see Chapter 7; see also Eckenrode, 1991; Moos, 1984). Not only do situational characteristics influence the choice of coping strategies but they also affect the outcome of coping. What is less well understood is the process through which the sociocultural context affects the stress and coping process (cf. Dressler, 1986). As the old saying goes, a fish is the worst person to ask about water. Likewise, the influence of culture on the stress and coping process is so pervasive that it is little noticed — except when one is in a different cultural context and the contrast between how one expects others to react and how they actually behave becomes striking, often uncomfortably so.

One of the best anecdotal studies was presented by Bateson (1968), who described her experience of losing a premature infant when doing fieldwork in the Philippines:

> On the afternoon of that day I was able to describe, so that my husband and I would be prepared, the way in which Filipinos would express sympathy. They show concern, in this as in many other contexts, by asking specific factual questions and the primary assumption about those who have suffered a loss is that they should not be left alone. Rather than a euphemistic handling of the event and a denial of the ordinary course of life, one should expect the opposite. Whereas an American will shake hands and nod his head sadly, perhaps murmuring, "We were so sorry to hear," and beat a swift retreat, a Filipino will say, "We were so sorry to hear that your baby died. How much did it weigh? How long was labor?" Etc., etc.

Had I not been in a position to make these generalizations and predictions the most loving behavior on the part of the Filipinos, genuinely trying to express concern and affection, would have seemed like a terrible violation and intrusion. In order to handle the affront and to control myself against breaking down in the face of sudden reminders of grief, I would have had to impose a rigid self-control that would have reinforced in the Filipinos the belief that many hold, that Americans don't really grieve. . . . Some societies organize their recognitions of bereavement around an effort to help the bereaved control himself and forget, while other societies are geared to help him express and live out his grief. (quoted in Levine, 1973, pp. 17–18)

Not surprisingly, psychologists tend to see coping as a function of an individual's personality or social context, while anthropologists view coping as primarily a function of the individual's (sub)culture — two diametrically opposed views. As a postdoctoral scholar, I tried to publish a paper entitled "Culture as a Determinant of Coping Behavior" in an interdisciplinary journal. The editor sent me two reviews. The review by the anthropologist was essentially, "This is so obvious. Why bother to publish it." By contrast, the gist of the review by the psychologist held that this was the most outrageous thing he had heard, and he considered it too ridiculous to publish. As a relative novice, I was crushed. I did not know how to reconcile these two opposing reviews, so did not pursue publication at that time. However, I still believe that culture is crucial to our understanding of the stress and coping process. Luckily, more empirical research has been published in this area in the past decade, a synthesis of which will be the focus of this chapter.

On the surface, it would appear that the psychological and anthropological viewpoints are diametrically opposed. After all, the very definition of coping is the study of individual differences in response to stress. If there is a strong cultural component to the process, then would this not by definition negate the emphasis on individual differences? This contradiction is apparent only if one holds a monolithic viewpoint of culture — namely, that it affects every individual in the culture in the same way. However, several decades ago, the cultural anthropologist A. F. C. Wallace (1966) defined cultures in terms of "mazeways." A mazeway consists of patterns of beliefs, values, and commitments, as well as expected behaviors, resources, and so forth, that shape individual behavior. There may be different pathways inside the mazeway for different subcultural groups, such as males and females, or for different socioeconomic or ethnic subgroups. Thus, a culture does not affect individuals within it in a uniform manner, and different groups adhere to different parts of the mazeway. In our culture, for example, it is more acceptable for a woman to cry than it is for a man. At different historical times and in different modern subcultures, violence as a means of conflict resolution has been more or less acceptable. Duels were once an acceptable means of resolving insults or competing social claims; historians tell us that fisticuffs and even duels were common among congressmen in the 19th century. Thus, the types of stressors that an individual encounters, and the range of acceptable coping strategies, are determined in part by an individual's position in the mazeway.

Culture can affect the stress and coping process in four ways. First, the cultural context shapes the types of stressors that an individual is likely to experience. Second, culture may also affect the appraisal of the stressfulness of a given event. Third, cultures affect the choice of coping strategies that an individual utilizes in any given situation. Finally, the culture provides different institutional mechanisms by which an individual can cope with stress.

This model is presented in Figure 11-1. Cultural demands and resources affect both situational demands and individual resources, both of which in turn affect the appraisal of stress. In addition, cul-

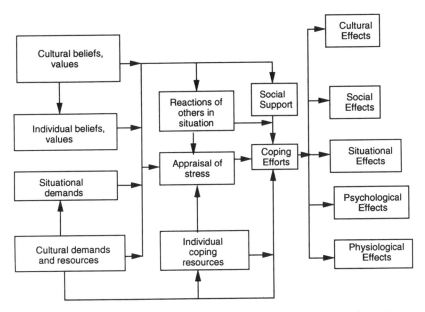

FIGURE 11-1. A sociocultural model of stress, coping, and adaptation.

tural beliefs and values influence not only individual beliefs and values, but also the reactions of others in the situation, which also affect the appraisal of stress. How an individual copes is affected by four factors: the appraisal of stress, the individual's coping resources, the resources provided by the culture, and the reactions of others.

Further, the outcome of coping not only has psychological and physical outcomes, but also social and cultural outcomes (see Aldwin & Stokols, 1988). As we have seen in the previous chapter, how an individual copes affects not only that person but also others in the immediate social environment. Further, to the extent to which an individual (or groups of individuals) modify or create cultural institutions in the process of coping with a problem, they also affect the culture, providing a means of coping for others facing similar problems. Grassroots movements such as Mothers Against Drunk Driving and the development of support groups for different illnesses or bereavement are good examples of this phenomenon. Thus, the sociocultural viewpoint of coping emphasizes that coping behavior nearly always occurs in a social context and is both affected by that context and contributes to its change (Gross, 1970).

CULTURE AND STRESS

As mentioned earlier, the patterns of stressors that individuals are likely to face is profoundly affected by their (sub)cultural context. This section will discuss two ways in which culture can affect the experience of stress. First, certain stressful life events can be seen as normative—that is, most individuals in a given culture or cultural subgroup will experience a particular event at specified times in their lives. Adolescent puberty rituals are one example of a normative life event, retirement is another.

Second, by differentially allocating social resources, cultures pattern the types and levels of stress that individuals are likely to experience. For example, contrast the types of stressors faced by inner-city children versus those in an affluent suburb. While the latter may face achievement-related problems such as the fierce academic competition in top-ranked schools and the anguish of whether they can live up to the achievement expectations of the parents, get into an ivy league college, and so forth, the former may face more fundamental problems, such as problems in housing, nutrition, and family stability, as well as inadequate schools, which impair the possibility of learning. Further, the inner-city child often faces violence on the way to, or even inside, the schools.

Cultural Patterning of Normative Stress

While life events can be considered as events that occur somewhat randomly to individuals, closer inspection reveals that whether a particular event occurs and the manner in which it occurs often reflect cultural beliefs and practices. As we shall see, the sanctioning of the occurrence of stressful events for individuals may also be a means for cultures to solve larger problems. Since it is often easier to understand such processes in foreign cultures, we will first discuss adolescent puberty rituals, then retirement in American culture, as examples of normative stressful life events.

Puberty Rituals

Victor Turner (1969) provided some of the most interesting insights into the nature of rituals in general and puberty rituals in particular. In some cultures, there is a relatively abrupt transition from childhood to adulthood that is demarcated by a ritual. This may be done on an individual basis, as when a Navajo youth spends several days in isolation in the wilderness awaiting a dream that will reveal his adult role, or it may be performed in a group setting, perhaps for a cohort of young girls who have started menses in the previous year.

While the actual form of puberty rituals varies from culture to culture, Turner (1969) identified several key elements common to many. First, the youth is required to revoke or eschew the child identity. This is achieved through the giving away of childhood toys and other property, the renunciation of a childhood name, and changes in the physical appearance, such as shaving the head or wearing ritual clothes. Second, the youth enters a *liminal* stage, in which he or she is neither child nor adult and which may be typified by social isolation, sequestering of the group in special quarters, and certain ritual foods, clothing, or baths. Third, the youth faces an extremely stressful ordeal, often involving public scarification or mutilation of the body. How the youth endures the pain may often be a key feature in determining adult roles and status. Fourth, the youth is given a new adult identity, characterized by a new name, adult clothing, secret knowledge, and the like.

In Euro-American culture, there are very few normative puberty rituals. Bar mitzvahs (and now bat mitzvahs for girls) are practiced in the Jewish subculture. However, these occasions are not very stressful, other than the relatively minor stress of public speaking. Few would concede that these 13-year-olds are now adults. Clearly, puberty rituals are not a necessary or unavoidable stressor. So why would some cultures choose to subject their youth to such extreme stress?

According to Turner (1969), the severity or arduousness of puberty rituals is in part a function of early childhood rearing practices. In some cultures, children, especially male children, are allowed nearly continuous access to the mother. Nursing may last for several years, and the child may sleep with his mother or other female relatives for many years. In order to enforce incest taboos, it becomes necessary to forcefully separate youths from their mother and other female relatives and to completely change identities and customary practices.

Alternatively, one could argue that in subsistence cultures, in which there is an abbreviated lifespan, it is necessary to accelerate the acquisition of adult roles and functions in order to ensure the reproductive survival of the group. A ritual abruptly demarcating the transition from childhood to adulthood may serve this function. In modern industrial cultures, with their longer lifespans and prolonged period of dependent adolescence, such rituals are no longer necessary — and, indeed, would be counterproductive.

Whatever the explanation, it is clear that cultures may sanction the occurrence of certain stressful life events. Retirement provides a good example of such an event in this culture.

Retirement

Prior to World War II, retirement was not a widespread phenomenon. In agrarian cultures, relatively few individuals lived to an advanced age, and most worked until death or disability forced them to stop. Women typically had children until menopause, extending the period of child rearing. While certain cultures may have provided different roles for the elderly, mandated withdrawal from economic activity is a relatively new phenomenon.

Sociologists have argued that the creation of the retirement status was primarily a governmental response to an economic crisis: the Great Depression (Quinn & Burkhauser, 1990). At that time, there were simply too few jobs. Older workers needed to be encouraged to leave the work force so that younger workers could gain employment. Obviously, economic safeguards were needed to provide sustenance for the newly retired (and for those elderly who could not find employment), so the Social Security Administration was created to soften the blow of mandatory retirement. (This was also a way of cycling more money into the economy, by transferring income from workers to older people to be spent on maintenance requirements, such as housing, food, and health care.)

This institutional solution to a social problem, though, had adverse consequences for some individuals, who now experienced a new stressful life event: retirement. Indeed, early work on retirement (Rosow, 1974) described this as an anomic, highly stressful state, with few social norms or functions to provide structure to everyday life. Retirement was thought to have adverse effects on physical and psychological health.

However, the widespread creation of pension plans decreased the economic stresses associated with retirement and allowed retirees to pursue leisure activities. New roles have been created for the elderly. Many engage in what Ivan Illich (1981) has called "shadow work": noneconomically compensated activity that is nonetheless vital for the maintenance of society. These activities include providing child care for grandchildren so that adult daughters can reenter the labor market, providing care for disabled spouses or parents, and volunteering in soup kitchens, literacy programs, and the like (see also Antonucci & Jackson, 1990). Thus, retirement is no longer perceived as a highly stressful life event. Less than one third of retiring males in one middle-class sample found retirement to be more than "a little" stressful (Bossé, Aldwin, Levenson, & Workman-Daniels, 1991), and health problems may be more of a cause than a consequence of retirement (Ekerdt, Baden, Bossé, & Dibbs, 1983).

Thus, one way in which cultures can influence the stress process is by mandating the experience of particular life events by certain subgroups within a culture. These events often denote changes in social status, such as puberty rituals, retirement, or O level examinations. They are often highly stressful, but the distress may be mitigated through other social institutions (e.g., pensions). The mandating of such events is often a response to other social problems, that is, certain social goals are achieved, consciously or unconsciously, through subjecting certain populations to stress at specific points in the life cycle.

Though often normative, culturally mandated stressful life events may also occur at irregular intervals, as when the federal government constricts the monetary supply to combat inflation, knowing that such a restriction will inevitably lead to unemployment, temporary or otherwise, on the part of vulnerable populations (see Aldwin & Revenson, 1986, for a discussion of this issue). This leads us to a discussion of the second way in which cultures can influence the experience of stress: through the allocation of resources.

Resource Allocation

Arsenian and Arsenian (1948) proposed that cultures can be characterized as "tough" or as "easy". Their basic premise was that individuals can be characterized in terms of goal-driven behavior. Cultures vary in the number and quality of goals aspired to by individuals. Further, resources and access to the paths through which one achieves socially sanctioned goals are not distributed equally among individuals or subgroups within the culture. A tough culture is one that provides few valued goals and that severely restricts access to the pathways through which an individual may achieve that goal. In contrast, an easy culture is one that provides multiple valued goals and relatively easy access to at least one of these goals. In one Pacific Island culture, for example, there were three basic goals: material wealth, political power, and spiritual leadership. These three goals were mutually exclusive; one could aspire to one and not the others. By virtue of the kinship structure, nearly every adult male in the culture could expect to achieve one of the three goals. This would be considered an "easy" culture.

Another example of culturally patterned stressors is that all cultures have mechanisms for educating the young. The difficulty of those systems, the importance attributed to them, and the means by which success is documented vary across cultures. In many British-style systems, elementary and secondary education is very difficult, and achievement is documented primarily through a rigid and universal examination system (O level examinations). Access to higher education is determined solely through performance on those examinations. In Asian cultures, such as Japan and Korea, which follow the British model, success on O level examinations is valued very highly, and the amount of stress that elementary and secondary school students experience is very high.

By contrast, in American school systems, elementary and secondary education is somewhat less rigorous, and there are multiple pathways to higher education (e.g., later attaining a graduate equivalency diploma or making up skills in community colleges). However, higher education is generally much more rigorous, and the stress experienced by college students is consequently higher. (See Aldwin & Greenberger, 1987, for a discussion of these issues.)

Arsenian and Arsenian hypothesized that tough cultures would take their toll on both the mental health of individuals and the social health of the community. In cultures with severely restricted goals and unequal access to paths, individuals are expected to exhibit psychological problems, such as alcoholism, drug abuse, and suicides. Similarly, in tough cultures, crime is expected to flourish, as people pursue goals through illegitimate means.

While industrialized countries are thought to provide a greater range of goals than those found in traditional agrarian societies, in reality there may be óne overarching goal—such as material wealth—access to which may be severely restricted for some people. From this perspective, it is not surprising that inner-city youths' aspirations to material wealth may be just as strong as that of relatively affluent suburban youths. However, for inner-city youths the legitimate means of gaining such wealth are very limited, and thus it should come as no surprise to cultural anthropologists that robbery, prostitution, and drug dealing would be prevalent within this group. The stress of inadequate access to resources is compounded by the undue stress resulting from the violence accompanying such illegal activities as robbery, prostitution, and drug dealing; and severe mental and physical health problems may be very prevalent. (For a more modern perspective on this theory, see Colby, 1987).

As tempting as it may be to derive a unidimensional scheme on which to array cultures—from "easy" to "tough"—Wallace's (1966) conception of mazeways argues for a more complex perspective. Obviously, cultures in which famine and war are prevalent are objectively more stressful than more prosperous and peaceful societies. However, from a mazeway perspective, the types of stressors faced by individuals within a culture vary according to gender, socioeconomic status, and ethnicity. American culture may be considered a relatively easy culture for affluent white Americans, but a very tough one for inner-city youths or Native Americans.

Further, the importance of the subjectivity of appraisals of stress cannot be overlooked. Thus, even in very prosperous societies by worldwide standards, such as the United States and Japan, the death rate among youths has been increasing. Stress within a culture may be expressed differently. As the old sociological maxim goes, white youths kill themselves, while African-American youths kill each other. Rather than rank cultures by their degree of stressfulness, it might be useful to examine the cultural patterns in the distribution and appraisal of stressors.

Cultural Influences on the Appraisal of Stress

While some stressors, such as bereavement, may be universal, cultures vary considerably in both their definitions of what is considered to be a stressor and in the degree to which a given event is appraised as stressful. For example, some cultures emphasize individual achievement, whereas in others being special in any way may be considered a threat (see, e.g., Heider's [1958] distinction between individualistic and collectivistic cultures). A classic example of this is provided by Rubel (1969). In Mexican-American culture, it was thought that children could become ill if someone outside the immediate family praised or admired them (*mal ojo*). Once ill, the child could only become well if the outsider patted the child in such a way as to remove the *mal ojo*.

Thus, in close-knit Mexican-American families (at least of a generation ago), praise for a child from an outsider constituted a stressful
event, in marked contrast with the pride that an Anglo-American
mother may feel when her child is praised.

For someone within a culture, this difference between cultures in
the appraisal of stress may be difficult to fathom. In giving a talk in
Mexico on this subject one time, I tried to dramatize this difference
by using the example of premarital sexual activity on the part of adolescents (Aldwin, 1985). In some cultures, such as Mexico, premarital
sexual activity, especially on the part of daughters, is perceived to be
a terrible problem that can bring dishonor to the whole family, and
in some cultures such sexual activity can even be used to justify the
killing of the daughter, as in Egypt. In other cultures, such as Tahiti,
premarital sexual activity on the part of adolescents is considered normative and even desirable. Some members of the audience became very
upset, and one person argued that in "higher" cultures, such behavior
was very properly viewed as disgraceful. My reply that the Swedes considered such behavior as normative evoked even more distress!

While anecdotal instances of cultural differences in the perception of what is stressful abound in the anthropological literature, there
are very few systematic studies of social differences in the appraisal
of stress. However, a few studies are suggestive. One study tried to
measure stress by using Holmes and Rahe's (1967) stressful life event
measure in South Africa, and found that it correlated very little with
standard distress measures (Swartz, Elk, & Teggin, 1983). This suggests that a stress measure standardized in one culture may not be very
useful in another, if that other culture has radically different views of
what is considered stressful.

Again, many anecdotes can be provided. In one African culture,
for example, multiple wives are expected. If a husband fails to marry
additional women, a solitary wife may experience a great deal of stress,
since she will not have sister–wives to help in child rearing, farming,
and so forth. Contrast this with attitudes toward bigamy in our culture.

A little closer to home, my mother-in-law, Liz, related a very funny
episode. A Southern Methodist, she married into a kosher Jewish family during World War II. Liz and her infant son lived with this family in New York while her husband was in the service. Trying to help
out in whatever way she could, she cooked a large, elaborate meal.
Throughout the meal, her mother-in-law cried silently, with tears
streaming down her cheeks. Unknowingly, Liz had essentially destroyed
the kitchen equipment by failing to observe the ritual separation of
utensils used for meat and dairy products required in kosher kitchens!
While funny in retrospect, at this time this was an extremely stressful
problem for all concerned.

Ethnic differences in the appraisal of stress may have more serious consequences. Recently in Stockton, a motorist blinked her lights at another car to indicate to the driver that his lights were off. The driver misinterpreted her action as having hostile or disrespectful intent ("dissing him") and coped with this perceived threat in a way deemed appropriate by his particular subculture: He pulled out a gun and killed her. What may be a relatively innocuous action to one individual may be appraised in a very different way by another, especially if there is little overlap or contact between their respective subcultural groups.

Although there is a large amount of literature on acculturation stress (Coelho & Ahmed, 1980), there have been few systematic studies of cross-cultural differences in what is appraised as stressful. Gibson and her colleagues (1991) are currently conducting a 17-nation study of problems and coping. Some 7,000 respondents were asked to describe a problem that caused them to feel worried or pressured, and then subsequent questions were asked concerning coping strategies. One hundred different categories of problems were identified, subsequently grouped into 13 classes, ranging from extreme poverty, war, and catastrophe to problems with courtship and dating. In contrast, only 37 different coping strategies were identified, grouped into standard Western-style classes: problem-solving, stress management, interpersonal interactions, providing and seeking social support, and so forth. In this preliminary report, only data from 3,870 adolescents were examined. In addition, the focus was on socioeconomic rather than cross-cultural differences. Thus, within each culture, respondents were classified as advantaged, disadvantaged, and disadvantaged–poverty (except for the then Soviet Union, the representative of which refused to categorize its citizens along class lines). Not surprisingly, schooling problems were the most commonly cited problems for most groups, although the disadvantaged–poverty groups most frequently cited family issues. Looking at types of problems within the overarching classes yielded more differences among the socioeconomic groups. For example, among the schooling issues, academic failure was most frequently cited problem among the advantaged and disadvantaged groups, while mental disability was most commonly cited problems among the disadvantaged–poverty adolescents. Interestingly, domestic quarreling was most often cited by the advantaged and disadvantaged–poverty group among the family issues, while "growing up" was most problematic for the two disadvantaged groups, in contrast to self-confidence, in the class of problems concerning personal identity and self-concept.

From a cultural perspective, this preliminary report left much to be desired. The data cited above were simply rank ordered, with no attempt to examine whether the differences were statistically significant. No information was provided on how respondents were obtained, which might have affected the types of problems reported. For example, if adolescent respondents were recruited primarily through schools, it is not surprising that school problems would most immediately come to mind. Further, no cross-cultural comparisons were done, although the authors hinted that the perception of stress does vary across cultures in this massive data archive: "The samples from countries making up the four disadvantaged–poverty groups vary considerably in their reporting of poverty as a problem. Examination of the data by country shows that responses ranged from 0% (Brazil) and 2.0% (India) to 10.7% (Venezuela) and 14.9% (Philippines)" (Gibson et al., 1991, p. 211). Nonetheless, this study could provide important insights into the cultural differences in the appraisal of stress in future reports.

The Gibson study is a good example of an etic approach to culture and stress. In an etic approach, a framework is developed in one culture and applied to others. Very different findings may result when an emic method is applied—that is, when indigenous models are allowed to develop within cultures. For example, Ingstad (1988) examined a similar stressful situation in two different cultures. She interviewed Norwegian and Botswana parents who had a disabled child. The Norwegian parents were more likely to appraise this incident as a disastrous problem. They felt guilty for this occurrence and had vague thoughts that it was a punishment from God. In contrast, the Botswana parents were more likely to attribute the problem to a breaking of a taboo or to an ancestor's anger. As one woman who had given birth to a brain damaged child put it, "I know it was caused by the difficult delivery, but I think it happened because I did not take good enough care of my mother when she was dying from cancer" (Ingstad, 1988, p. 357). The Botswanans tended not to feel guilty, because the majority of conditions were attributed to witchcraft, or sorcery, caused by a (sometimes unknown) enemy. The Botswanans also tended to feel that the child's disability was not a terrible tragedy, in part because of the general difficulty of their lives. Rather than a punishment from God, they were more likely to believe that the disability was a positive sign of God's trust in the ability of the parents to care for a disabled child. Thus, a similar problem may be appraised (and presumably coped with) very differently depending upon indigenous belief systems.

SOCIAL AND CULTURAL INFLUENCES ON COPING

Chapter 9 provided examples of how coping by family members affects individual coping and outcomes, but coping is also influenced by broader social and cultural factors. In order to understand the larger question of how a culture affects coping behaviors, it may be instructive to first examine how a social context influences the use of coping strategies.

In an early study of the ways in which graduate students coped with doctoral examinations, Mechanic (1978) emphasized the role that interpersonal interactions and modeling played in determining strategies used by individuals to study for their exams. The graduate students developed belief systems about the best ways in which to cope with this stressful situation on the basis of their own prior experience with tests as well as their observations of the concomitant efforts of other graduate students preparing for exams. Students consulted others in their attempts to appraise the situations, wishing to know how important the exams were, whether they were likely to be difficult or easy, and so forth. Further, whom they consulted also affected how they coped with the problem. One group of students whose offices were somewhat isolated developed a very characteristic way of coping: they decided that the examinations did not require that much preparation and did not make the effort to study as much as was required. Not surprisingly, as a group they also did less well on the examinations than the more centrally located students, who developed a more realistic appraisal of the importance of the examination and of the degree of effort required to study for it. Thus, Mechanic described coping as a *consensual* process because of the collective beliefs that developed about the exam and that guided individual efforts in preparation.

Janis and Mann's (1977) study of group think also provides a good example of how consensual appraisals and coping strategies develop in crisis situations. As in Mechanic's study, consensual appraisals developed by an in-bred group without sufficient input by others with different viewpoints can result in inappropriate beliefs leading to sometimes disastrous coping actions. Janis and Mann analyzed the Bay of Pigs disaster and found that the decision-making process became distorted by an inappropriate consensus developed by President John F. Kennedy and his group of advisors. In an effort to maintain secrecy, only a small group of decision makers considered the possible courses of action. There was a tendency to suppress differing viewpoints, and the group developed an unrealistic appraisal of the situation. Due to their beliefs in the invincibility of the United States armed forces and the inadequacy of Castro's, the advisors failed to take appropriate safeguards in their invasion attempt, which thus lead to the defeat of the invading forces. Subsequently, President Kennedy appointed his brother, Robert Kennedy, who was attorney general, as the official "devil's advocate," to ensure more appropriate input into decision-making processes.

In more ordinary circumstances, Thoits (1986) examined the role that social support plays in the coping process. Not only do individuals provide concrete and emotional aid in coping with problems, but they also provide feedback about the appropriateness of the appraisal process and emotional regulation. As in Mechanic's study, friends and relatives may tell an individual that he or she is "making a mountain out of a mole hill," as it were, or not taking a problem seriously enough. They may also suggest certain coping strategies or discourage the use of others.

Given that the choice of coping strategies may be an inherently social process, it should not be surprising that cultures may influence how individuals cope with stress. While there is an extensive literature on how culture affects adaptational processes (Bateson, 1972; Colby, 1987; Dubos, 1965), much of the anthropological literature has focused on the ways in which psychological disorders vary by cultures, with much debate about whether there are culture-specific mental illnesses (such as *amok* in Indonesia, *susto* in South America, or *ataque* among Puerto Ricans in New York) or whether the structure of psychological disorder (e.g., depression, schizophrenia) is universal, with only the symptom content varying. (For a review of these issues, see Kleinman, 1980). Nonetheless, it is clear that cultures may differ in the ways in which emotion is expressed.

Less attention has been paid to the more general ways in which culture can influence the use of coping strategies. Mechanic (1974) argued that the ability of individuals to acquire coping skills and their success depends upon the efficacy of the solutions that the culture provides and the adequacy of the institutions that teach them. Further, Antonovsky (1979) stated that "Culture . . . give[s] us an extraordinarily wide range of answers to demands. The demands and answers are routinized: from the psychological point of view, they are internalized; from the sociological point of view, they are institutionalized. . . . A culture provides . . . ready answers . . . with keening for a death, an explanation for pain, a ceremony for crop failure, and a form for disposition and accession of leaders" (pp. 117–118).

More specifically, it is necessary to examine studies that document differences in coping behavior by (sub)cultural groups. As I see it, cultures may differ in both their preferred means of emotion-focused coping as well as problem-focused coping. Differences in emotion-focused coping center around issues of emotional control versus emotional expression, as well as the patterning of emotional expression. Cultures may also differ in generalized attitudes toward control and instrumental activity—preferences for external or internal control and direct versus indirect approaches to mastery.

Culture and Emotion-Focused Coping

Control versus expression of emotional responses to stress is a major dimension along which cultures may vary. The Bateson anecdote cited at the beginning of this chapter is a good example of this. Americans tend to perceive grief as an emotion that should be controlled in public and expressed only in private, while Filipinos (and many other cultures) permit the public expression of grief. In general, Northern European cultures tend to prefer emotional control—the proverbial British "stiff upper lip." Many other cultures, however, sanction emotional expression, often in stereotypical ways. In the coping literature, this has been studied primarily in (sub)cultural differences in response to pain.

Zborowski (1952) provided one of the first studies of ethnic differences in coping with pain. Among hospitalized patients, individuals from Italian and Jewish ethnic groups exhibited the most expressive behavior in response to pain (including groaning and moaning). In contrast, both Irish-American and what Zborowski termed "Old American" patients tried to minimize their pain and to effect a kind of stoicism. Withdrawal from other people when in pain was most characteristic of Old American patients, whereas Jewish patients expressed more anxiety and worry about their pain. These behavioral differences clearly reflect cultural beliefs about the best ways to manage pain and differences in the acceptability of emotional expression.

Since the Zborowski study, a number of researchers have investigated cultural and ethnic differences in coping with pain in both clinical and laboratory settings (for reviews see Moore, 1990; Zatzick & Dimsdale, 1990). Several studies have confirmed Zborowski's original findings (Koopman, Eisenthal, & Stoeckle, 1984; Lipton & Marbach, 1984; Zola, 1966). Interestingly, Chinese respondents in Moore's (1990) study had a category of pain, called *suantong,* which is apparently unique to their culture. *Suantong* pain can be best described as an itchy, dull, or stabbing pain caused by inflammation. Interestingly, they described tooth drilling in a dental context as *suantong,* or a dull pain, not requiring chemical anesthesia, in contrast to Americans who characterized drilling as a sharp pain requiring pain relievers. However, not all studies have demonstrated cultural differences in the perception and expression of pain, depending in part upon the racial–ethnic grouping utilized in the research.

Zatzick and Dimsdale (1990) offered two generalizations in their review of this literature. First, various studies have shown that there are no cross-cultural differences in the perception of pain threshold, that is, the ability to discriminate painful stimuli. This argues that any differences in pain tolerance are not neurophysiological in origin but rather are cultural. Second, studies that utilized racial groupings (e.g., white vs. black) were less likely to find differences in coping with pain than studies that utilized ethnic groupings. That is, there may be ethnic differences within racial groups, such as Zborowski's initial findings of differences between Italian-Americans and Irish-Americans. Zatzick and Dimsdale emphasized that members of an ethnic group by definition share cultural beliefs about the most appropriate manner in which to cope with and express pain.

An even more intriguing possibility is that there may be cultural patternings in the expression of emotion up to and including the manifestation of mental illness. For example, some conceptions of culture-specific mental illness view these as temporary states and culturally sanctioned reactions to stress, which are not necessarily inherently pathological as long as they remain short-term reactions (Garrison, 1977; Maduro, 1975; Weidman, 1979). These syndromes are often manifested under quite specific and usually highly stressful situations. For example, *ataque* among Puerto Ricans in New York is used to describe a particular syndrome characterized by extreme emotional expression, fainting spells, and fuguelike behavior, often self-destructive, which the person may or may not remember later. For example, one woman, when informed that her son had an accident, started screaming, fainted, and then leaped up and tried to jump out a window (Garrison, 1977). According to Garrison, *ataque* is the expected behavior under certain circumstances, including a death in the family or witnessing acts of aggression that the individual is powerless to stop (e.g., a husband beating a child).

Similarly, "falling out," a quasi-epileptoid state found among American, Haitian, and Cuban blacks, occurs in situations in which an individual feels extreme fear or rage, under stressful conditions at school or in sports competitions, or in highly crowded situations. Falling out serves to remove individuals temporarily from these stressful conditions, thus functioning to regulate emotions (Weidman, 1979).

Current psychological theories of stress and coping assume that emotions should be controlled and their expression minimized. For example, Pearlin and Schooler (1978) defined coping as "any response to external life strain that serves to prevent, avoid, or control emotional responses". This viewpoint reflects the attitude of Northern Europeans and Anglo-Americans toward emotional control. In other cultures, however, less emphasis may be placed on emotional control, and displays of emotion may be deemed appropriate and desirable. Indeed, among Puerto Ricans in New York, failure to have an *ataque* under culturally specified situations may be seen as a sign of being cold or hard-hearted (Garrison, 1977).

In studies of coping effectiveness, contemporary psychological work operationalizes "successful coping" as that which is associated with the fewest psychological symptoms under stress (Folkman & Lazarus, 1980). However, this may reflect only the attitudes of some cultures regarding appropriate coping behavior and outcomes. If emotional expression, or even specific psychological symptoms, are mandated coping responses to stress in certain cultures, then it would be misleading to characterize only those strategies associated with a few symptoms as effective coping strategies. Rather, it is important to understand what is perceived to be effective coping in any given culture.

Emotional expression may have important problem-focused functions in particular social situations. In the example noted above, a Puerto Rican woman may have an *ataque* in order to attract her husband's attention and distract him from beating his child. The expression of psychological symptoms can be seen as an indirect attempt to control a social situation (see Szasz's [1961] discussion of psychological symptoms as oblique attempts at communication). Paradoxically, emotional expression may actually be viewed as a form of instrumental activity, albeit an indirect one. Saunders (1977) described *zar* possession states among Egyptian women primarily as an indirect means of influencing husbands in a culture in which direct influence is prohibited. Thus, a woman may only be able to escape from intolerable demands by becoming seriously ill or may impose demands upon her family by using the *zar* spirit that possesses her to insist upon certain goods or services (including a sewing machine!).

Thus, cultures clearly vary in the type of emotion-focused coping sanctioned in different situations. Some cultures focus on the suppression of emotions while others demand the display of emotions in culturally appropriate patterns. Earlier in this century, for example, it was considered appropriate in America for a woman to slap the face of a man who made an "indecent" suggestion. This coping strategy served as a means of anger expression, as an interpersonal confrontation to set limits on unacceptable behavior, and as a validation of the honor of the woman. Note that the woman may not have "consciously" chosen this strategy, it was simply the "acceptable" means of coping with inappropriate behavior, extensively modeled in literature and the movies. Nowadays, inappropriate suggestions are labeled as "sexual harassment", and slapping is no longer considered an acceptable means of coping (perhaps due to a weakening of the taboos against hitting women—which means that slapping may invite retaliation). Women are struggling to develop other means of coping—up to and including the filing of lawsuits. Clearly, however, emotion-focused coping is to a large extent based upon cultural norms and expectations. To my knowledge, however, there has been no attempt to develop a scale to systematically document cultural differences in emotion-focused coping per se. More work, however, has been done on cultural differences in a type of problem-focused coping, namely, the preferred manner of exerting control.

Culture and Problem-Focused Coping

In general, problem-focused coping is defined as an attempt to control or manage a stressful situation. Since Rotter's (1966) seminal work on locus of control, there have been literally hundreds of studies examining control and psychological adaptation. Not surprisingly, many of the cross-cultural studies of coping behavior have focused on control or mastery.

In a review of studies using the Hoffman Inkblot Test to determine coping styles, Diaz-Guerrero (1979) concluded that Mexican children exhibit more passive or self-modifying coping styles than American children, who are more likely to receive high ratings for active coping styles. In a multinational study that administered a self-image questionnaire, Offer and his colleagues (1981) also concluded that American adolescents were more likely to use active coping style, compared to their Irish or Australian peers. Interestingly, Israeli teenagers were seen as the most active and mastery oriented of all the groups. These studies, however, only inferred coping behavior from personality measures, and did not directly assess the use of coping strategies in specific stressful situations.

A more recent study specifically examining the use of coping strategies in a stressful situation confirmed the greater Israeli prevalence of active coping, as compared to Americans. Etzion and Pines (1986) examined coping and burnout among Israeli and American human services professionals. They concluded that the greater use of active coping strategies among Israelis contributed to the generally lower prevalence of burnout in this highly stressed profession.

Western conceptions of control generally dichotomize into active versus passive, internal versus external, and so forth. Reynolds (1976) argued that an active versus passive dichotomy may be too simplistic, and suggested a more complex view:

Instead of an active-struggling versus a passive-acceptance dichotomy, I would suggest that a more useful contrast between Oriental and Western approaches to problem solving lies in the locus of preferred activity. One's phenomenological reality is a product of one's inner state and objective reality. By manipulating either factor it is possible to change phenomenological reality. It seems that, in very general terms, the West is more accepting of activity directed toward changing objective· reality. . . . But I must reemphasize that the Japanese value is not passive resignation. It is simply tactical. Certain sorts of problems are held to be best handled by indirection and internal change. (pp. 110–111)

A good example of indirect coping is provided by Sue (personal communication, 1982), a clinician specializing in Asian cultures. He was consulted by a woman who had difficulties with her in-laws. Given cultural strictures concerning the relations between in-laws, this woman could not directly confront her in-laws with the problems they were causing her, nor would her husband confront his parents — certainly the advice that a Western clinician not sensitive to cultural differences would suggest. Instead, Sue suggested that the woman enlist the aid of a sympathetic uncle who could intercede on her behalf. The uncle, who was the mother-in-law's older brother and who, therefore, was in a position of authority over her, was invited to dinner. While not directly addressing the problem, the uncle's remarks concerning how tired the daughter-in-law looked was sufficient warning to convince the mother-in-law to move out, thereby solving the problem. This woman could not use the type of direct action sanctioned by Western values but could exert control through indirect action. Thus, preference for indirect action should not be confused with passivity.

Nor should locus of preferred activity be confused with current conceptions of locus of control, which simply refers to beliefs concerning whether an individual can directly affect the external environment. Locus of preferred activity, on the other hand, refers to the realm in which an individual chooses to exercise control, for example, controlling internal reactions to a problem.

Nor should acceptance of a problem be confused with a passive stance. Brickman and his colleagues (1982) have argued for a distinction between responsibility for the occurrence of an event versus responsibility for its solution, or outcome. Individuals may not have much control over the occurrence of a particular event, but the recognition of that lack of control does not necessarily preclude instrumental activity. Aldwin (1991), for example, found that older individuals may deny responsibility for the occurrence of an event and even its management but yet use just as much problem-focused coping as younger people. (This topic will be discussed in greater detail in Chapter 12.)

Acceptance may prove to be a buffer against stress and may mitigate against stress and excessive self-blame. In a test of the learned helplessness theory of depression, Coyne, Aldwin, and Lazarus (1981) found that chronic depressives were no less likely to try to exert control over their environment than nondepressives were. On the contrary, depressives were *less* likely to accept that some situations are not amenable to control and *more* likely to try to exert control over ungovernable situations. The depressives were apparently less able to perceive which situations were amenable to control and to adjust their activities accordingly; consequently, they were more likely to blame themselves for things going wrong. This finding was subsequently confirmed by Folkman and Lazarus (1986). Cultural beliefs in fate (sometimes known as *karma* or *joss* in Asian cultures), where they do not lead to passivity, may aid in absolving an individual of an undue sense of failure or incompetence or in warding off depression.

Coping in a nonculturally prescribed manner may result in greater stress. Hwang (1979) examined how men cope with residential crowding in Taiwan. Lower socioeconomic groups coped in ways characterized by lower self-confidence and fatalism. Regardless of social class, men who used coping styles that emphasized traditional cultural values and interpersonal cooperation experienced less interpersonal stress and lower symptom levels. Coping styles that emphasized self-assertion and achievement enhancement, however, were associated with more interpersonal stress, psychosomatic disorders, and depression. Shek and Cheung (1990) have argued that cultures may be divided into those that place greater reliance on the self (internal locus of coping) and those that rely more on others (external locus of coping). The example provided above by Sue (1982) is a good instance of the latter.

Kashima and Triandis (1986) applied Heider's classic (1958) distinction between individualistic and collectivistic cultures to one type of coping behavior: self-serving bias. According to attribution theory, people tend to credit themselves for success and to attribute failure to external circumstances (for a review see Zuckerman, 1979). Kashima and Triandis hypothesized that self-serving bias was more important for individualistic cultures, as a consequence of their emphasis on self-reliance and the implied greater threat of failure. In a controlled experiment contrasting the attributions of Japanese and American students, Kashima and Triandis found that their hypotheses were only partially supported. American students used self-serving biases only in relatively ambiguous circumstances; when the task was less ambiguous, the two groups of students tended to use similar attributions.

Thus, the situational context can modify cultural influences on coping strategies.

Interestingly, bicultural individuals may develop two separate coping repertoires, depending upon the cultural context. Kiefer (1974), for example, found that Nissei, second-generation Japanese-Americans, appeared to have different rules of behavior depending upon whether the problematic situations involved other Japanese-Americans or individuals outside their cultural group. Aboriginal adolescents in Australia also appear to use different strategies in coping with conflicts arising from demands made by parents and/or the traditional culture and those made by Western-style teachers in the mission school (Davidson, Nurcombe, Kearney, & Davis, 1978).

Even among individuals using active, problem-focused coping, there may be ethnic differences in preferences for types of direct action. Caplovitz (1979) studied differences in preferences for coping with inflation among various American ethnic groups. Controlling for income level and impact of inflation, there was considerable overlap in the types of strategies used. However, Anglo-Americans were most likely to try to curtail expenditures by decreasing their standard of living, African-Americans were most likely to spend time hunting for bargains, while Spanish-speaking groups were most likely to share with family members or neighbors.

In summary, sociocultural groups appear to generate not only consensual belief systems concerning the origin and meaning of stressors but also beliefs concerning the most appropriate means of both emotion- and problem-focused coping. These beliefs may be situation specific. Further, trying to cope in ways that run contrary to the general cultural ethos may increase stress, even though those same strategies used by members of a different culture may be efficacious in reducing emotional distress. Even more rarely examined, however, are the more generalized institutions that cultures provide to individuals in order to help them cope with problems.

INSTITUTIONS AS COPING MECHANISMS

Mechanic (1974) argued that, to a large extent, the efficacy of an individual's coping is dependent upon how well the culture provides a range of coping resources and transmits coping skills. Thus, coping strategies are influenced not only by cultural beliefs concerning the most appropriate means of handling specific types of problems, but also by social and cultural institutions for problem-solving and tension reduction (Mechanic, 1978).

Some examples of institutionalized assistance in coping are obvious. The legal system is the formal means of conflict resolution, and a cross-cultural comparison of legal systems might provide interesting insights into the cultural beliefs that govern those processes. For example, it is interesting that in Euro-American cultures that emphasize personal control, relatively little individual control can be exercised in the court system, where decisions are made primarily by lawyers and judges. In other cultures such as Mexico and Saudi Arabia where seemingly less emphasis is placed on personal control, plaintiffs may have much more influence over the amount and type of punishment meted out to the perpetrator (Nader, 1985).

In addition to formal systems for conflict resolution, all cultures provide some form of ritualized advice that may consist of religious counselors, professional ones (e.g., psychiatrists, psychologists, social workers, etc.) or quasi-formal support groups such as Alcoholics Anonymous. Tseng (1978) argued strongly that fortune-telling may be a sort of folk-counseling service. Clients typically present a wide variety of problems concerning health, business, academic examinations, marriage, and so forth, and receive not only interpretations as to the causes of their problems, but also specific suggestions as to how to cope. This is so prevalent in some Asian cultures that Shek and Cheung (1990) included an item assessing the consultation of fortune-tellers on the Chinese Coping Inventory.

Hsu (1976) found that advice provided by Taiwanese diviners was usually culturally conservative—that is, individuals were advised not to be too aggressive or ambitious and to behave in ways that were appropriate for their social role and status. Certainly this is reminiscent of the advice that newspaper columnists in the United States provide. It may also be that turning to astrologers and fortune-tellers for advice may be more prevalent in this culture than is usually thought, as recent examples of President and Nancy Reagan suggest. Nonetheless, cultures usually provide a variety of institutions that give advice to individuals. What type of advice is sought, and the source of that advice, may depend in part upon the ethnic group or social class to which an individual belongs (Neighbors, Jackson, Bowman, & Gurin, 1983).

Finally, rituals of various sorts may also be viewed as cultural mechanisms that aid individuals in both emotion- and problem-focused coping. Wallace (1966) described a number of goals, categories, and functions of rituals:

> All ritual is directed toward the problem of transformations of state in human beings and nature. Sometimes the goal is to ensure the quickest and most thorough transformation into an end state desired by the ritual

actor; sometimes the goal is to prevent an undesired transformation from occurring. Sometimes the target is an individual; sometimes it is a group. Sometimes the transformation is a minor one, a correction which will restore equilibrium and status quo . . . sometimes it is a question of radical transformation of the system, the attainment of a new level of equilibrium or even of a new quality of organization. (pp. 106–107)

Through their symbolic ability to transform personal and situational states, rituals provide an opportunity for individuals and social networks to cope with various stresses. Funeral rituals help to serve these functions for the bereaved, marriage rituals for newlyweds, and rites of passage for individuals undergoing status transitions. Among other things, rituals focus social support on individuals who are undergoing a transition, and in general they provide a sense of closure for one part of an individual's life, that allowing him or her to make the transition to a new life (Constantinides, 1977). Obviously, some rituals are better at this than others are (the retirement luncheon, for example, is a ritual that at best may provide a sense of closure, but which may do little toward helping the retiree cope with his or her change in status). Further, healing rituals, which often take place in a quasi-ritual context, provide a significant source of both advice and social support for individuals who are undergoing a crisis or who may have problems of adaptation in general (Good, 1977; Obeyesekere, 1977; Spiro, 1978).

Wallace (1966) hypothesized that there exists a dynamic balance between the types of stressors typically faced by individuals in a culture and culturally-sanctioned means of coping with them. Thus, having a child out of wedlock may not be very stressful in Tahitian or Swedish cultures because it is common for kin to adopt babies from young girls with little or no shame involved. However, Wallace hypothesized that undue stress arises when there is a mismatch between culturally patterned stressors and coping responses. If the pattern of stressors changes to cross-cultural contact, technological or social change, natural disasters, famine, war, and so forth, then the typical means of coping with problems may no longer "work," and there may be an increase in social problems such as alcoholism, divorce, child abuse, and psychiatric problems. At that point, it is incumbent upon individuals within a culture to derive new patterns of problem solving. This often occurs through what Wallace termed "revitalization movements," usually religious in nature, which establish new patterns of beliefs, values, and adaptive behaviors. Revitalization movements are often characterized by a desire to return to traditional values or, conversely, to develop a new utopian society. Through a series of case studies, Wallace cautioned that failure on the part of revitalization movements (usually through inflexibility or an inability to accommodate to the powers that be), or an inability to invent new adaptational patterns, can ultimately result in the death of the culture.

It is tempting to apply Wallace's theory to the urban crisis that exists not only in America but throughout the world today. The change from an agrarian to a technological society displaces thousands of agricultural families. In England's industrial revolution, these displaced workers migrated to America, displacing Native Americans. Currently, however, most displaced agricultural workers flee from the countryside to the city, as typified by the migration patterns of African-Americans from the rural South to the northern industrial cities or of Mexican workers to the United States. Old cultural patterns, which may have been adaptive in an agrarian culture, are no longer appropriate to an urban situation. This, compounded with a systematic denial of access to resources, has resulted in extreme stress on African-American culture, resulting in typical patterns of social pathology (such as crime, drug and alcohol abuse, child abuse and other forms of violence). From Wallace's perspective, the Nation of Islam movement is a fairly typical revitalization movement that offers new beliefs, values, and adaptive patterns (e.g., emphasis on self-reliance, avoidance of drug and alcohol use, adherence to a work ethic, emphasis on family integrity, etc.). Unfortunately, it also increases in-group solidarity by the demonization of other ethnic groups, which brings it into direct conflict with the dominant culture. Thus, whether or not this (or some other revitalization) movement will be successful, remains to be seen.

The point to be emphasized, however, is that the relation between culture and individual coping is not unidirectional — rather, individual behaviors can reinforce or change existing patterns of coping. Grass roots movements are often examples of individuals banding together to develop and provide alternative means of coping with some social problems. As Good (1970) pointed out, the coping techniques described by psychologists

> refer to what the individual may do *in those situations in which he must act alone or on his own resources* . . . . it is a major characteristic of man as distinguished from other organisms, however, that one of his major management techniques is that of developing an *organization* that will handle the threat, or of creating an environment in which the threat does not occur. Of course individuals act, as always, but they are manipulating some type of organization or structure that has been set up. (p. 59)

Thus, individuals manipulate existing organizations or structures, but they may also create them through the development of new organizations, legislation, or the development of new procedures and services. Therefore, it is important to understand not only that cultures affect individuals' coping behaviors, but also that individuals' coping behaviors can affect their culture. Indeed, recognition of the fact that individuals can and do change cultures provides the only ray of hope for overturning the culture of violence that is fast developing in America's urban areas.

SUMMARY

Psychological research has neglected sociocultural influences on the stress and coping process. As we have seen, cultures influence the types of stressors that individuals experience, through the sanctioning of normative life changes or through patterns of resource allocation. They also influence the appraisal process, either through beliefs and values prevalent within a wider cultural setting or developed through consensual processes in more specific social situations. Further, cultures may define certain coping behaviors as more appropriate than others; and what is deemed appropriate is not uniform within a culture but, rather, varies as a function of the individual's position in the cultural mazeway. Finally, the relationship between the individual and the culture is bidirectional. Not only do people cope in ways that affect other individuals, but through the modification or development of new organizations, structures, and attitudes, an individual or group of individuals may affect social change.

CHAPTER 12

Developmental Studies of Coping

As mentioned earlier, perhaps the most important aspect of coping for adaptation is that it is flexible: Rather than a person's "adaptational style" being "set in stone" due to genetics or fixation at early stages of personality development, coping strategies are thought to be plastic, to develop in the course of dealing with the ever-changing stress in the environment. This assumption leads naturally to questions of how (and when) the various coping abilities develop and how (and whether) they change over the life course.

Ten years ago it would not have been possible to adequately address these questions, but the last decade has seen a tremendous increase in coping studies in both young and old populations. Although many gaps still exist, understanding the development of coping strategies, and what is "normal" and "abnormal" coping at different ages can greatly expand our understanding of the development of psychopathology and mental health throughout the life course.

This chapter will address these questions, first surveying the literature on coping in infancy and childhood and then examining the rather scanty literature on adult developmental processes.

COPING IN INFANCY AND CHILDHOOD

At first blush, the idea that infants "cope with stress" seems odd. They appear primarily to eat, sleep, eliminate, and, of course, cry. However, to the extent that coping strategies can be seen as basic attempts to regulate both the external and the internal environment, humans clearly engage in regulatory actions starting at a very early age—perhaps even prenatally. William James thought that infants experienced the world as a "blooming, buzzing confusion," an inherently meaningless (and by implication) stressful place. Early psychoanalysts rhapsodized about the "oceanic" blissfulness of the womb and the stress of emerging into the harsh, cruel world. Folk wisdom held that infants were blind, deaf, and dumb, as it were, little more than a crudely functioning alimentary canal. However, we know that all of these views are incorrect (Bower, 1977).

Fetal Coping?

Rather than a timeless, quiet void, the womb is actually a very noisy place. Not only is the fetus privy to the heart beat and digestive noises of the mother, but environmental noises can also be clearly perceived inside the uterus, which is known by any mother who has had to leave a concert because her fetus was kicking at the noise. (Indeed, it is rather incredible that the myth of this supposedly serene intrauterine environment ever had any credence.)

The fetus responds not only to environmental noise and light, but also to the mother's movement, nutritional intake, and even her stress hormones (Field, 1991). Pregnant women will often tell of having to modify their behaviors so as not to upset the fetus—avoiding spicy foods, loud concerts, arguments, certain sitting or lying positions, and so forth—especially in the last trimester, when the fetus can express its displeasure by kicking. (One pregnant friend of mine complained bitterly of her fetus's uncanny ability to aim its kick at her bladder when displeased!)

To the extent that coping is defined as intentional behavior, however, it is difficult to credit a fetus with exhibiting coping strategies per se. Certainly kicking, hiccupping, arm waving and the like can be seen as automatic responses of the nervous system, a sort of startle reflex in response to sudden environmental change or stimulation. It is interesting, though, that fetuses have been observed to suck their thumbs in utero. Again, while sucking is primarily an instinctual response, it is also undoubtedly soothing—perhaps a primitive first attempt at emotion-focused coping. Indeed, in premature neonates, nonnutritive sucking reduces physiological stress responses to invasive procedures, decreases fussiness and crying, and may even promote weight gain (for a review see Field, 1991).

Coping in Infancy

Similarly, it would be a mistake to credit infants with sophisticated, cognitively based coping strategies. However, longitudinal studies done at the Menninger Clinic by Lois Murphy and her colleagues have clearly shown that even very young infants attempt to regulate both their external and internal environments (for a review see Murphy & Moriarty, 1976). This was one of the first studies to make detailed observations of a group of infants both in the laboratory and in their home environment and to follow these children into late adolescence.

Infants are not passive recipients of parental care. Close observation by Murphy and her colleagues revealed a number of strategies that infants use to try to regulate the external and internal environment. Even young infants will try to manipulate their physical environment. They will bat at encroaching blankets, wriggle to obtain a more comfortable position, and make motor efforts to retrieve a lost nipple. Infants are also very sensitive to social stimulation, requiring some, but becoming quickly overloaded. Murphy not only observed individual differences in the amount or type of stimulation desired, but also found that even very young infants will try to regulate the amount of incoming stimulation by closing their eyes, turning their heads, falling asleep, or, if all else fails, crying loudly when they are overstimulated. An infant even a few weeks old will solicit social stimulation through eye contact, smiles, and gurgling, but will turn away if too much stimulation is proffered. Certainly infants are also able to modulate their cries in order to signal the type of distress they are experiencing (e.g., hunger, wetness, fright, etc.). Further, Bell and Harper (1977) clearly demonstrated that infants modify and regulate their parents' behavior as well.

When upset, nearly all babies will suck their own thumb for comfort. Other such early behavioral forms of emotion-focused coping include rocking, distracting oneself by playing with toes, or, if nothing else works, fussing and crying (Karraker & Lake, 1991).

One of Murphy's most important discoveries concerned the infant's ability to regulate stress by alternating periods of effort with rest: "Ronald at twenty-eight weeks was seen to struggle for thirty-five minutes in his effort to master getting up on all fours. During this period he pushed strenuously until he was tired, then flopped down on the floor, sucking his thumb until he was rested enough to try again. This alternation of effort and rest went on until he finally succeeded" (Murphy & Moriarty, 1976, p. 91). It would seem that even infants use both problem-focused and emotion-focused coping in stressful situations, concurring with Folkman and Lazarus's (1980) observation of a similar phenomenon in adulthood. However, the pattern of approach–avoidance alternation did vary among infants. Some children recovered easily, others took much longer periods. Nonetheless, an important task of infancy appears to be to learn how to regulate the internal environment sufficiently to engage in more or less sustained problem-focused efforts. Some babies seem to find this an easier task than others, and difficulty in self-regulation in infancy correlated with similar problems in later childhood. Murphy and Moriarty (1976) observed that the "best outcomes" were among those children whose parents recognized and encouraged their infants' attempts to cope with problems and who were sensitive to their infants' needs and rhythms. Perhaps sensitivity as well as consistency is necessary to instill what Erikson (1950) called a basic sense of trust.*

Coping among Toddlers

Certainly toddlers have a much greater range of coping resources than infants. Their greater physical coordination and mobility and the development of language makes manipulating the physical and social environment much easier. However, they are still highly dependent upon their parents or other caretakers for solutions to many problems, although many infants show an almost distressingly strong desire for autonomy. The "terrible twos," protestations of " Me do it!" and toddlers' almost insatiable curiosity and tendency to get into everything can be seen as their active attempts to increase their coping repertoire and their ability to manipulate both the physical and the social environment. This increase in coping repertoire could underlie the sense of autonomy that may develop during this period (Erikson, 1950).

Further, toddlers are able to solicit social support under stress with strategies other than crying. A parent is often used as a security object, with the child running toward, touching, clinging, or sometimes simply making eye contact with the parent when frustrated, angry, or frightened.

While toddlers' emotional responses to stressors in the environment are still fairly undifferentiated (Cummings, 1987), they may nonetheless take a more active role in trying to regulate their emotions. While thumb sucking and rocking are still prevalent, many toddlers emotionally invest in a transitional object, such as a favorite blanket or stuffed animal, which seems to provide an important source of com-

---

*I am indebted to Professor Brenda Bryant for pointing out the similarity between the development of coping strategies and Erikson's (1950) theory of psychosocial development in adulthood.

fort when stressed. Toddlers may also develop less endearing habits, such as masturbation. The same sort of alternating effort and rest, or problem- and emotion-focused coping, occurs in toddlers as well. Note, however, that the emotion-focused coping efforts still appear to be primarily behavioral rather than cognitive.

Coping among Preschoolers

Preschoolers are much more aware of their social environment than are younger children (Cummings, 1987), and they have a larger coping repertoire that allows for much more differentiated response to the environment. They are better able to balance the need for autonomy with the need for cooperation (Murphy & Moriarty, 1976), and they recognize that different coping strategies "work" better with some people or situations than others. Wheedling may work best as a strategy with Daddy, naked aggression can be directed against siblings and friends, while crying and fussing may work best with Mom. (Bryant, [personal communication, 1993] has observed children of this age practice "making faces" in the mirror so that they will be better able to convey their feelings.) Indeed, Band and Weisz (1988) claim to be able to differentiate between emotion-focused crying and problem-focused crying. According to Compas, Worsham, and Ey (1992), the ability to generate multiple solutions to interpersonal problems emerges around ages 4–5, but more sophisticated means-end thinking does not appear until ages 6–8.

Defense mechanisms such as repression, denial, and displacement can be observed in preschoolers (Murphy & Moriarty, 1976; Wallerstein & Kelly, 1980). For example, Cummings (1987) found that preschoolers who appeared unresponsive to a social stressor (adults arguing in the next room in an experimental setting) were nonetheless more likely to report feeling "mad" and were subsequently more verbally aggressive toward a playmate. Wallerstein and Kelly (1980) observed that preschoolers whose parents were divorcing would often flat out deny that their father was no longer living in their house (one even insisted that he was sleeping in her bed) but would express fears that some monster might come and eat them up. Further, Murphy and Moriarty (1976) observed that, under duress, nearly all preschoolers would "regress in the service of the ego," that is, they would loose recently acquired skills, such as bladder control. Alternatively, they might take up earlier, abandoned behaviors, such as thumb sucking or reattaching to a transitional object. Acting in a more infantile manner often gets the parents to focus more attention on them, a reassurance that preschoolers desperately need.

Parents are still the primary source of social support for preschoolers. The presence of older siblings and grandparents can provide an alternative source of support, albeit one used less frequently. However, preschoolers' limited ability to conceptualize and verbalize their problems means that friends are not generally a source of social support, as far as this construct is typically understood.

Coping in Middle Childhood

One of the most consistent findings in the child coping literature is the dramatic increase in emotion-focused coping between the ages of 6 and 9 (Altschuler & Ruble, 1989; Band & Weisz, 1988; Brown, O'Keefe, Sanders, & Baker, 1986; Compas et al., 1992; Wertleib, Weigel, & Feldstein, 1987). During this age period, children become more able to verbalize and differentiate their feelings. They also become much more adept in calming themselves, although they still tend to become overwhelmed when they cannot manage their feelings.

Wallerstein and Kelly (1980) relate the rather touching anecdote of a 6-year-old whose parents were divorcing and who could not go to sleep at night. The child's strategy for calming himself was to pin a note at the foot of his bed, telling himself that it was alright and that he should go to sleep now. Older children are better able to use cognitive distraction and self-reassuring statements (Altschuler & Ruble, 1989).

Further, children become much more differentiated in the types of emotion-focused coping they use. Spirito, Stark, Grace, and Stamoulis (1991) found that the situation greatly affects which strategies children use. With academic problems children were more likely to use cognitive restructuring and self-criticism, but the children blamed others when dealing with friends and siblings. Not surprisingly, they were also more likely to yell at siblings and peers than at parents or teachers.

Children in middle childhood are also more able to seek social support outside their immediate family (Bryant, 1985). Interestingly, it is between ages 6 and 9 that gender differences in seeking social support emerge, with girls seeking more support than boys (Wertlieb, et al., 1987; Frydenberg & Lewis, 1990), a pattern that continues into adulthood.

Developmental shifts in problem-focused coping, however, show a more complex pattern. On the one hand, children in grammar school develop more sophisticated cognitive skills. More complex means–end thinking comes into play between 6 and 8 (Compas et al., 1992). In addition, at this age beliefs concerning the controllability of the environment become more realistic, judgments of control become more differentiated, and control may be associated with more problem-focused coping. Indeed, Weisz (1986) suggested that a key developmental task in childhood involves learning to distinguish between those situations in which persistence pays off and those in which it does not. This ability may also underlie Erikson's (1950) stage of industry.

However, the few studies that have directly examined the relation between age and problem-focused strategies have variously found increases, decreases, and stability (Compas et al., 1992). Closer examination of this literature suggests a number of possible reasons for this inconsistency. Again, the situational context may play an important role. While overall there appears to be no change, problem-focused coping may increase in interpersonal situations but may decrease in less controllable situations such as medical or dental examinations (Compas et al., 1992), thus canceling each other out in the aggregate. Further, age effects may vary by type of problem-focused coping. The one study that found a decrease in overall problem-focused coping with age also conducted a closer examination of this issue by identifying four different subtypes (Band & Weisz, 1988). Only one subtype decreased with age: a strategy called "problem-focused avoidance" (e.g., hiding under the bed to avoid going to the dentist). As children gain in coping resources and are better able to discriminate between controllable and uncontrollable problems, it makes sense that this type of problem-focused strategy decreases. While children of all ages overwhelmingly use avoidant strategies, these tend to shift from escapism or behavioral strategies to cognitive distraction (Altschuler & Ruble, 1989; Elwood, 1987), although there are undoubted individual differences in the rates at which this occurs.

Most studies of coping in school-aged children rely on semi-structured interviews, with either self-generated problems or common vignettes. These are then coded for the presence or absence of certain coping strategies, resulting in simple dichotomous variables. While the change in emotion-focused coping from behavioral avoidance and calming to more cognitive strategies is powerful enough to be revealed using this technique, problem-focused changes may be subtler and more difficult to assess. The quality of problem-focused thoughts and actions are generally not examined, although they may be more likely to exhibit developmental shifts paralleling the increases in cognitive complexity seen during these years. In general, it would be safe to assume that coping repertoires increase and become more differentiated in middle childhood.

Coping in Adolescence

Somewhat less is known about coping among "normal" adolescents (Stark, Spirito, Williams, & Guevremont, 1989), as much of the existing literature deals with various adolescent clinical populations (e.g., de Anda, Javidi, Jefford, Komorowski, & Yanez, 1991; Spirito, Overholswer, & Stark, 1989). However, a few generalizations can be made: On the positive side, problem-focused coping in adolescents should become more sophisticated with the onset of formal operations (Greene & Larson, 1991). Further, a decrease in egocentrism should allow for better interpersonal negotiation skills. For example, arguments among children in grammar school often consist of little other than competing assertions ("Is too! Is not!") or, at best, appeals to authority ("Says who?" "My Daddy, that's who!"). In contrast, adolescents are more capable of reasoned arguments (although the reasoning often appears rather self-serving). Good problem-focused coping skills in adolescence have been associated with a measure of "optimal adjustment" based on Erikson's first six stages (Jorgensen & Dusek, 1990).

Adolescents may turn more to their friends and siblings for social support than to their parents (Murphy & Moriarty, 1976), especially if there is family discord (Wallerstein & Kelly, 1980). Note, however, that McCubbin, Needle, and Wilson (1985) found that adolescents who had good family problem solving skills were less likely to engage in the use of alcohol, drugs, or cigarettes to cope with stress. Further, adolescents from families who can express emotions in a healthy manner and resolve conflicts demonstrate better coping and less use of avoidance and substance abuse (Perosa & Perosa, 1993).

However, it is in adolescence that some types of maladaptive coping strategies are adopted—namely, using drugs, alcohol, or cigarettes to reduce distress (although, sadly, even younger children have started imitating their elders in this regard, with undoubtedly even more devastating consequences, given their neurological immaturity). One strategy that may be particularly dangerous for a teenager is social withdrawal. Spirito et al. (1989) examined stress and coping processes among three groups of adolescents: suicide attempters, distressed teens, and nondistressed teens. Suicide attempters were mainly distinguished by having more problems with their parents than did the other two groups and by withdrawing more from others under stress. Distressed teens who did not attempt suicide were actually higher in wishful thinking and resignation than those who did attempt suicide.

It is also in adolescence that gender differences in depression appear, with women reporting more depressive symptoms than men

(Peterson et al., 1993). Compas, Oroson, and Grant (1993) hypothesized that this is because there may be gender differences in types of emotion-focused coping that also emerge in adolescence. According to Nolen-Hoeksema (1991), men are socialized to use distraction in response to depressive moods, while women are socialized to be attentive to emotional reactions, which may lead them to ruminate about their problems, thus maintaining or enhancing depressive feelings.

Thus, adolescence may constitute a critical stage in the development of coping skills. Very young children use primarily behavioral forms of emotion-focused coping: sucking thumbs, rocking themselves, hugging transitional objects, and so forth. In grammar school, this gradually shifts to verbal reassurances and then to purely cognitive strategies, as children learn how to calm themselves down, cheer themselves up, and generally, learn to manage their emotions in a culturally appropriate manner. It is possible, however, that some individuals never really master these internal techniques but continue to rely more on behavioral emotion-focused strategies. Perhaps they have "difficult" or "sensitive" temperaments that are more difficult to control, or it may be that their early environment was too chaotic or stressful to permit acquisition of these skills. Once they reach adolescence and have more access to licit and illicit substances, they may turn to these external ways of modifying internal states. When used to excess, however, alcohol, nicotine, and various other pharmaceutical agents may actually intensify negative affect in the long run, thus creating more problems than they solve. If true, then this suggests that a more effective drug abuse prevention program would concentrate on improving cognitive emotion-focused coping strategies in preteens and adolescents to provide more adaptive alternatives.

Children and Extreme Stress

A large part of the children's literature has been devoted to children's coping under extremely stressful circumstances. At least two areas have generated enough studies to merit reviewing: children of divorce and children coping with illness and medical procedures.

Children of Divorce

One of the most dramatic shifts in American culture in the past 50 years has been the increase in divorce rates. Various estimates have suggested that at least half of the present generation of children and youths have experienced the divorce of their parents. It is thus critical to understand the short- and long-term effects of what has become practically a normative childhood stressor.

Judith Wallerstein and her colleagues (Wallerstein & Blakeslee, 1989; Wallerstein & Kelly, 1980) and Mavis Hetherington and her colleagues (Hetherington, Cox, & Cox, 1985; Hetherington, 1993) have conducted longitudinal studies of children of divorce. For the past 15 years, Wallerstein and her colleagues have followed over 100 children, initially ranging in age from toddlers to adolescents. Their data leave no doubt that for children divorce is highly stressful. Children become emotionally distraught, often showing great anger at the parent whom they perceive (rightly or wrongly) to have caused the divorce, and their school work and peer relationships may suffer, at least temporarily. Further, the effects of divorce on adaptation appear to vary by age. Very young children may regress, throw wild tantrums, blame themselves for "causing" the divorce, and become very fearful about where they will live and whether they will have enough to eat. Adolescents may take advantage of their relative independent status and withdraw from the family, spending more time with friends. Those in middle childhood are more likely to "take sides" and become used as allies in parental battles.

One particularly valuable aspect of Wallerstein's study is the long-term follow-up. While some children appear to emerge relatively unscathed, other children appear to experience long-term adverse effects. In general, a key variable affecting children's outcome following divorce is sufficient contact with both parents. If the parents and children managed to work out some sort of reasonable modus operandi and the children enjoyed the support of both parents and were sheltered from their strife, the long-term effects of divorce can be minimal. However, all too often the noncustodial parent (usually the father) had only intermittent contact with his children or sometimes disappeared completely. In this instance, the children suffered greatly, unless, of course, the father was highly abusive or mentally ill, in which case cessation of contact was preferable. In Wallerstein's study the extent to which the children clutched at any vague glimmer of a demonstration of love or caring from their mostly absent fathers was very poignant.

The long-term effects of divorce also appeared to vary by the age of the child. The younger and the older children in general did best. If the mother remarried, very young children were generally able to establish good ties with their new stepfather. Adolescents, on the other hand, were better able to physically escape and establish independent lives, especially if their fathers helped with college (which was surprisingly rare, even in this relatively affluent, Marin County sample).

Although the parents tended to shelter very young children and adolescents could protect themselves, those children who were in their middle years when their parents divorced appeared to experience the worst long-term effects. If their parents remarried and started new families, the children often felt left out and isolated. Boys especially had a difficult time accepting new stepfathers and suffered acutely from lack of contact with their own fathers. After many years of child support, fathers were generally reluctant to help with college, severely limiting the economic future of their children.

Hetherington's studies confirm that preadolescents are more vulnerable to the effects of parental divorce (Hetherington, 1993). However, Hetherington reported some interesting sex differences that partially contradict Wallerstein's findings. Younger boys appear to have had more problems than girls in households headed by a single mother. If their mothers remarried, they did initially have a difficult time adapting to their stepfathers; however, over time, even preadolescent boys eventually adapted to and benefited from the new arrangement. Preadolescent girls, however, continued to have a difficult time (Hetherington, 1991).

Wallerstein and Blakeslee (1989) provided several sad case studies of these children of divorce as young adults. Some young women were highly promiscuous, maintaining several lovers at any given time and quickly rejecting them before they themselves were rejected. A few young men appeared to drift aimlessly through low-paying jobs, drugs, and petty theft, in the best "Generation X" manner. Wallerstein concluded that the price children pay for their parents' divorce is too high.

While widely cited in the popular press, there are some limitations to Wallerstein's study. The setting was a clinic, and at least some of the families were referred by the courts as being particularly troubled. Thus, the sample may have been experiencing more problems than the norm. Further, the lack of a comparison group renders generalization problematic. Although some of these children clearly do not have very good outcomes, one cannot tell from this study whether the number of these children is significantly greater than would be expected in children coming from intact families. In her longitudinal research, Hetherington (1989) also reported that boys in divorced families and children in remarried families did show more problems in adjustment than did children from nondivorced families. However, she stressed that the child's temperament, quality of family relations, and extrafamilial factors contributed to individual differences in adaptation to divorce.

Nonetheless, several studies with control groups have called into question to what extent children from divorced families are more troubled than those from intact ones (Enos & Handel, 1986; Kurdeck & Sinclair, 1988). For example, Compas and William (1990) examined stress, coping, and psychological adjustment in single- and two-parent families for both the mothers and their children. Not surprisingly, single mothers reported lower incomes and more stress than did married mothers. They were also more anxious and depressed, which was partially due to their lower incomes. Interestingly, single mothers also used more problem-solving coping and positive reappraisal, supporting the "growth spurt" Wallerstein and Blakeslee (1989) reported among some of their divorced mothers. However, no significant differences emerged between the children from these two types of families in either stress levels, problem behavior (using both standardized self-ratings and parental reports), or coping strategies.

Compas and William further examined the relationship between parental distress and child distress separately for the two types of families. In two-parent families, a mother's psychological symptoms were clearly correlated with her child's hassles and behavior problems. However, the children in the single-parent families seemed unaffected by their mother's psychological distress. The only significant correlation was between mother's hassles and her assessment of her child's behavior problems, and obviously the behavior problems may be a source of the mother's hassles rather than being caused by them. It would seem that the single mothers in this study went to great pains to protect their children from the former's psychological distress. Thus, there appear to be inconsistencies in the literature concerning the degree of long-term adverse effects of parental divorce among children.

No one would argue that divorce has highly adverse short-term effects on children. Most children would prefer to remain in intact families and, according to Wallerstein and Kelly (1980), appear fairly oblivious to marital difficulties that their parents might be experiencing (except in cases of manifest physical abuse). However, to what extent long-term harm is done is unclear. Like many clinical studies, Wallerstein may have overestimated the adverse long-term effects by her sample selection and lack of a comparison group. However, community surveys such as that of Compas and Williams (1990) often underestimate problems, given their greater reliance on standardized scales, which are not as sensitive as clinical interviews in detecting problems, and the fact that the most troubled people in the community tend not to respond to surveys.

Perhaps Rutter's (1981) admonition on children and stress is apropos here. In his longitudinal studies of children's reaction to stress, Rutter found that most children were fairly resilient and could readily rebound from experiencing a major adverse life event. However, with multiple adverse events, or when a life event was coupled with other adverse circumstances such as poverty, poorer long-term outcomes were more likely (see also Hetherington, 1984; Werner & Smith, 1992). Thus, children of divorce who enjoy the emotional and financial support of both parents and who are protected from postmarital strife, may be able to adapt quite well to the divorce. However, emotional and financial rejection by one parent, being drawn into post-marital conflict, or being subjected to the caretaker parent's mental illness or alcohol problems may compound the stressful effects of parental divorce. Further, Hetherington et al. (1985) warned that children of divorce are at risk for experiencing additional adverse life events, which may increase their vulnerability. Parents need to be aware that how they cope with divorce will strongly affect their children's ability to cope, and parents should be especially vigilant for the possible effects of additional adverse life events.

Pediatric Coping Studies

An area of great interest in the child coping literature concerns how children who are caught up in medical procedures cope with either fairly routine medical examines (e.g., vaccinations or dental work) or with chronic and/or life-threatening illnesses. Certainly children find medical procedures very threatening, since they have limited ability to understand either the purpose or the consequences of the procedures. As Peterson (1989) remarked, a common fear among children who undergo venipuncture is that all of their blood may leak out! Children with leukemia, heart disease, or other serious, chronic illnesses are of special interest. They are often subjected to medical procedures that are especially terrifying. Steward (1993) has videotaped dozens of children who were undergoing stressful medical examinations. One particularly poignant example involved a 5-year-old girl who was screaming in terror as the nurses held her down for a spinal tap. She made it very clear that she was convinced that they were going to kill her. Obviously, understanding the ways in which children cope with such procedures can help medical staff facilitate the most adaptive coping. Further, many children need to be active collaborators in the management of chronic illnesses such as diabetes. Thus we need to understand and facilitate the coping strategies in such children.

Many of the pediatric coping studies focus on simple approach–avoidance coping strategies. In her review of eight studies which used various means of identifying approach–avoidance coping, Peterson

(1989) found that most studies demonstrate positive consequences of approach coping in children, regardless of how this coping is assessed. Further, distress was reduced for children by preparing them for medical procedures with information via films or by role-playing with dolls. However, a minority of children prefer exclusively avoidant coping strategies, which unfortunately has been sufficient justification for hospital administrators to discontinue such efforts.

Other approaches to pediatric coping take a more ecological point of view. For example, Kazak (1989) argued that a social ecological perspective must be taken when studying stress and coping among chronically ill children. In this model, the family is viewed as a relatively homeostatic system, and a change in behavior of one family member elicits homeostatic responses from the others. Thus, behaviors that might normally be viewed as "maladaptive" may actually be very adaptive under these extremely demanding conditions. For example, rigidity is seen as a negative trait, but may be adaptive when rigid adherence to a medical regime is absolutely necessary for survival (Kazak, Reber, & Snitzer, 1988).

Further, the social context may modify the relation between a particular coping strategy and outcomes. For example, Lumley, Abeles, Melamed, Pistone, and Johnson (1990) examined the interaction between a mother's coping behaviors and her child's temperament during a stressful medical procedure. Regardless of whether approach-avoidance coping was used, it was the asynchrony of the coping behaviors in the parent–child dyad that was related to distress. Thus, when both members of the dyad used either avoidant or approach coping, the child exhibited less distress. However, approach coping in children was related to greater distress if the parent used avoidant coping and vice versa.

Two rather surprising observations can be made about the pediatric coping literature. The first is how well children and their families appear to cope with chronic illness. Differences in coping behaviors among children with cancer and those without are relatively few (Bull & Drotar, 1991), and the few that exist appear to be due more to the severity of the problem than to the illness per se (Ritchie, Caty, & Ellerton, 1988). Indeed, Wells and Schwebel (1987) found no differences in psychological disturbance or family dysfunction between chronically ill and normal children.

The other surprise is that nearly all of the studies of children's coping used only psychological outcomes. In marked contrast to the adult literature, very few relations between physiological outcomes and children's coping have been drawn (but see Marrero, 1982).

Summary

The study of the normal development of the coping process in children is still in its infancy, as it were. However, a great deal of effort has gone into the development of techniques to study this issue, and a number of interesting observations (or perhaps hypotheses) can be drawn. From a very young age, children attempt to modify their internal and external environment. Obviously, in infancy, the tools with which to do this are very few and fairly primitive. However, as children develop, their coping repertoire increases and may shift from primarily behavioral actions to more cognitive ones. Developmental changes in emotion-focus coping have emerged fairly clearly in the literature; these changes can perhaps best be described as a shift from simple self-calming behaviors, such as thumb sucking and rocking, to verbal reassurances and more cognitive control over emotions. Developmental shifts in the utilization of social support are also obvious; infants and toddlers depend primarily on their parents for support, which later gradually shifts more to peers in middle childhood and adolescence.

Unfortunately, developmental changes in problem-focused coping have not emerged as clearly from the literature. In examining this issue, it is a little surprising that stress and coping researchers have not drawn more on the cognitive development literature (but see Band, 1990; Greene & Larson, 1991). Certainly, both adequate appraisal processes and problem-focused coping must of necessity rest upon cognitive skills for comprehending the physical and social environment, as well as problem-solving skills and the ability for abstract reasoning. It is also surprising that stress and coping researchers have not drawn more upon Kohlberg's (1984) moral reasoning paradigm, which would seem to be highly applicable in coping with stress in everyday life. It may be that our conceptualization of problem-focused coping is as yet too simplistic to permit examination of developmental issues. Nonetheless, it is true that very simple means must be used to examine coping in children, but both child and adult coping studies could benefit from a closer examination of the problem-solving literature.

A recurring theme is the resiliency of children, which will be addressed in greater depth in Chapter 13. Given the proper support, children can bounce back from even extremely stressful situations, such as divorce or a chronic illness. What is less clear, however, is how children learn to cope with problems. Obviously a great deal of experimentation occurs. However, while it is generally assumed that children follow a general social learning model in that they learn coping skills from their parents, surprisingly, no study has actively examined this issue (Luthar & Ziegler, 1991). Adolescence may be a particularly crucial time, since adolescents have access to external means of emotion-focused coping, such as alcohol and drugs, which may prove harmful if used in excess. Thus, it is not enough to document developmental trends in coping strategies. A crucial next step should be how these strategies develop and what interventions can be used to promote adaptive coping and coping skills training in children.

DEVELOPMENTAL CHANGES IN COPING STRATEGIES IN ADULTHOOD

A few studies have begun to examine how coping strategies change in adulthood. In general, these studies can be divided into two types, those which examine defensive mechanisms, and those which examine coping strategies. As we shall see, the former are more likely to describe systematic changes with age, while definitive developmental patterns are more difficult to ascertain in the latter.

Depending upon how the term "age" is defined, the effects of age on coping strategies can be roughly divided into three categories. First, if aging is understood as biological aging, then age may have an indirect effect on coping strategies through the increase in health problems associated with aging. As one ages, there are changes in types of problems experienced (Aldwin, 1990). The elderly are more likely to be coping with both their own health problems and those of significant others, especially spouses. They are more likely than younger adults to experience bereavement or to suffer the loss of close friends and relatives.

As Folkman and Lazarus (1980) have pointed out, both health and loss problems are more likely to evoke palliative or emotion-focused coping than instrumental action. McCrae (1982) suggested that differences in coping strategies among younger and older adults is primarily a result of differences in the types of problems that they face. Therefore, any study of aging and coping strategies needs to determine whether the older respondents are coping with health problems.

Second, age effects can also be understood in terms of cohort differences. There may be historical characteristics in the present population of older adults that affect their choice of coping strategies. To my knowledge, this has not been examined in the literature, but one could hypothesize that the lower levels of education in the present aged cohort, compared to younger groups, may predispose them to less active forms of mastery, given the positive association between education and internal locus of control (Lefcourt, 1976).

Third, age can also be understood in terms of intrinsic developmental processes. These have been examined in greater detail with defensive processes.

Changes in Defense Mechanisms with Age

Gutmann (1974) presented the first study of how adaptive strategies change in adulthood. Using TAT (Thematic Apperception Test) cards, he observed a shift in mastery styles that appears to occur across the lifespan. In young adults, responses to TAT cards reflected active mastery — that is, they were more likely to describe active patterns that were directed toward confronting and resolving problems. In contrast, the themes emerging from the stories told in response to TAT stimuli by middle-aged adults reflected what Gutmann termed "passive" mastery techniques — that is, these adults tended to tell stories involving the acceptance of problems and resignation to them. In contrast, the stories of older adults reflected what Gutmann termed "magical mastery" — that is, the stories seemed to resolve themselves, or they would focus on what Gutmann thought of as irrelevant aspects of the picture. Gutman attempted to show that this decremental developmental shift occurred cross-culturally when he compared various Israeli ethnic groupings with patterns seen in the United States.

However, there are a number of problems with this study. Responses on TATs do not necessarily reflect the actual use of coping strategies in everyday problems. Further, alternative explanations for the phenomenon that Gutmann observed are possible, including age differences in education and socialization to Western norms. To the extent that younger members of other cultures are more exposed to Western culture and education patterns, it is to be expected that a more active stance might be seen.

Surprisingly, there have been no published attempts of which I am aware to replicate this pattern. In part, this may be because the use of projective techniques has fallen into disfavor in contemporary psychology. However, as a graduate student, I attempted to replicate Gutmann's study by applying his coding scheme to the TATs gathered as part of the Transitions Study (Lowenthal, Thurnher, & Chiriboga, 1975), a 10-year longitudinal study of adolescents, young adults, empty nesters, and preretirees. While the sample size was very small, and insufficient for publication, the pattern of results that I found was interesting. When I coded for mastery content, I was unable to replicate Gutmann's observations. However, when I coded for the amount of energy that the respondents put into their stories, I was able to find age-related patterns. Thus, although there is little evidence for a clear decrement in defensive styles with age, Gutmann's schema is useful because it can lead to an examination of how acceptance of problems change with age and how coping effort might change — observations to which we will return later.

In contrast, Vaillant (1977) suggested that there is an incremental developmental process occurring across the lifespan, characterized by a shift from neurotic or immature defensive styles in early adulthood to more mature defensive styles among the middle-aged (see Chapter 7). Immature adaptive mechanisms are characterized by fantasy, projection, hypochondriasis, passive–aggressive behavior, and acting out, while neurotic mechanisms are characterized by intellectualization, repression, reaction formation and displacement. Mature mechanisms, on the other hand, include sublimation, altruism, anticipation, and humor. Using longitudinal, open-ended data from a sample of high-functioning Harvard men, Vaillant found that, as men age, most (but not all) use more mature defensive mechanisms. More importantly, the use of mature mechanisms was associated with greater social competence, as indexed by length of marriage, upward mobility, number of children, and so forth.

A standard criticism of this study is that it was done on Ivy League college alumni, and the degree of generalizability to the larger population is unknown. Further, the study relied exclusively on ratings of defense mechanisms from open-ended material. Thus, Vaillant, Bond, and Vaillant (1986) sought to replicate this study using a longitudinal sample that initially consisted of older children who were at high risk, having been labeled as juvenile delinquents (or predelinquents). Although ratings were used in this study, a more standardized index of defense mechanisms (Bond, Gardner, & Sigel, 1983) was also used. The same pattern of relations between mature defense mechanisms and social competence was observed, but unfortunately no relations with age were presented. While Vaillant (1993) also applied his rating scheme for defenses to a sample of Terman women and the severely disadvantaged controls of the juvenile delinquent study, no developmental trends were presented, although, using a variety of indicators, he did show that those who achieved mature defenses tended to be more adjusted.

A study by Costa, Zonderman, and McCrae (1991) provided a more systematic study of cross-sectional correlations between age and three different defense mechanism inventories, using relatively equal samples of both men and women. Unfortunately, these inventories (some of which have rather idiosyncratic scale labels) were administered to varying numbers of respondents over an 8-year period, rendering interpretation difficult. Further, only correlations with age were presented, so it is difficult to draw any definitive conclusions from this study, given the well-known confound between age, period, and cohort effects. However, it would seem that the more problematic mechanisms, such as projection and "maladaptive action pattern", were negatively correlated with age, whereas repression–denial mechanisms were positively correlated.

It makes a certain amount of intuitive sense that, with age, people become more adept at dealing with life's problems. These intrinsic developmental processes may be better understood in terms of experience. As people age, they are exposed to a greater variety of problems, and hopefully through this process have learned which types of coping strategies are generally ineffective and which types can achieve their goals in various situations. Some individuals may develop self-limiting lifestyles through which they manage to avoid many problems by severely restricting their range of activities, or they may cling to ineffective means of coping with problems (Lowenthal et al., 1975). But, in general, through experience, people may increase their coping repertoires and become more able to successfully cope with difficulties. Further, a certain amount of repression or denial may be useful at older ages. Certainly it is a truism that 80% of the elderly rated their health as better than average, and some problems may be best ignored rather than confronted. Unfortunately, as we shall see, this optimistic portrayal of increased adaptability in adulthood is somewhat more difficult to show using standard coping strategy measures.

Do Coping Strategies Change with Age?

In one of the earliest studies on coping strategies and age, McCrae (1982) found that older adults used fewer escapist and hostile strategies, but few differences in problem-focused coping emerge from this study once controlling for the type of problem. Studies using a more standardized assessment of coping, the WOCS (Folkman & Lazarus, 1980, 1986), have generally confirmed these findings. Several studies have found that older adults used less escapism or avoidant coping but used similar levels of problem-focused coping (Aldwin & Revenson, 1985; Felton & Revenson, 1987; Irion & Blanchard-Fields, 1987).

In a follow-up to his earlier study, McCrae (1989) was able to replicate his previous findings cross-sectionally, but not longitudinally. That is, he was unable to show that over time there is a decrease in escapist strategies. However, the follow-up period was relatively short (less than 10 years) and the age of the sample was extremely heterogeneous. It is not likely that individuals changing from 20 to 28 will show the sample developmental shift as someone changing from 80 to 88. Thus, no definitive conclusions can be drawn from this study.

The exception to this general trend was a study by Folkman, Lazarus, Pimley, and Novacek (1987), which found that older people used less planful problem solving and more escape avoidance. However, Folkman and her colleagues examined the *relative* use of those coping strategies, or ratio of the strategy to the overall number of strategies used. Only then did age differences emerge on the coping strategies. Nonetheless, Aldwin (1991) was unable to replicate this finding, even when relative ratios scoring on the revised WOCS was used. Rather, age was once again unrelated to problem-focused coping but was negatively related to escapism.

This study examined a conundrum in the aging literature. On the one hand, the literature on locus of control suggests that older individuals may be more external in their orientation, at least on some dimensions (Lachman, 1986). If this were so, however, one would expect that older individuals would use less problem-focused coping—which, as we have seen, is not supported by the stress and coping literature. Using a community sample ranging in age from 20 to 70, Aldwin (1991) examined both the appraisals of responsibility for the occurrence and management of problems, as well as coping strategies used in a recent stressful problem. The first path model showed that the appraisals of responsibility were related to coping strategies in the expected directions: People who thought they were not responsible for the problem or its management were less likely to use instrumental action and more likely to use escapism. However, when age was added to the path model, something very interesting happened. Even controlling for health problems as the stressor, older people were less likely to disclaim responsibility for both the occurrence and the management of problems, thus supporting the literature on locus of control. Nonetheless, the older people reported just as much problem-focused coping and less escapism than younger groups. Further, there were no age differences in perceived efficacy. In other words, older people disclaimed responsibility for their problems, but nonetheless went ahead and handled them.

One interpretation of this data is that older adults have learned that, in reality, problems happen and that blaming themselves is a waste of time (and energy). Indeed, older adults did rate their problems as less stressful. This discrepancy between appraisals and coping may be explainable in terms of Baltes's (1987) theory of energy conservation. Adolescents, who have a lot of energy, often waste of lot of it in inappropriate self-blame and guilt feelings—the classic Sturm und Drang of adolescents. Older adults, on the other hand, may avoid the energy costs of such emotional upheaval by refusing to accept responsibility, thereby avoiding self-blame and guilt, but nonetheless going ahead and doing what is necessary to manage a problem.

These changes in adaptive strategies appear to be very important for mental health in later life. In Aldwin's (1991) study, age was negatively correlated with depression—a result often found in community samples. However, the path model demonstrated that age was only indirectly related to depression through its effect on stress appraisal, coping, and perceived efficacy variables. In other words, the older adults reported better mental health than did the younger ones, but only because they had changed the way in which they appraised and coped with stress. Interestingly, older abusers of drugs and alcohol may not show the same age-related decreases in stress appraisals, and they are more dissatisfied with their coping efforts than elders who are not substance abusers (Folkman, Bernstein, & Lazarus, 1987).

Although it is commonly thought that older individuals are faced with seemingly insoluble problems such as those concerning health problems and losses—and, thus, are more passive (Rodin, 1986)—Aldwin (1991) found that having a health problem to cope with was positively associated with perceived efficacy. In other words, health problems were something that older individuals felt they could handle—and handle well. Zautra and Wrabetz (1991) also found that older adults appraised as efficacious their coping with both chronic health problems and loss, and that perceived efficacy was associated with less distress, even in the face of health downturns.

Labouvie-Vief has argued that both cognitive and emotional complexity increase with age and that this increase affects the way in which older individuals both appraise and cope with stress (Labouvie-Vief, DeVoe, & Bulka, 1989; Labouvie-Vief, Hakim-Larson, DeVoe, & Schoeberlein, 1989; Labouvie-Vief, Hakim-Larson, & Hobart, 1987). Further, standard coping inventories may not be sensitive to these developmental changes. Even if older and younger people endorse the same strategy on a checklist, they may have very different motives and goals for that behavior. For example, Labouvie-Vief and her colleagues (1987) showed that younger people sought social support primarily for self-validation, while older individuals were trying to get feedback as to the appropriateness of their coping strategies. Labouvie-Vief argued that qualitative interviews may be necessary to understand the ways in which coping strategies change with age.

I am currently examining this issue using 1,000 interviews from the Normative Aging Study (NAS) on men ranging from ages 45 to 90. The men reported on a problem that had occurred in the past week, ranging from relatively minor problems with home repair to extremely serious legal and health problems. Many NAS men mentioned spontaneously that they no longer got as upset as they did when they were younger; and, indeed, the older men report fewer problems, appraised them as less stressful, and reported fewer negative emotions than did the middle-aged men (Aldwin, Chiara, & Sutton, 1993). Many were more accepting of the fact that problems can and will happen, and seemed to be better able to take things in stride. The older men were less likely to use interpersonal confrontation and escapism as strategies. While they reported fewer strategies, there were no differences in their perceived coping efficacy, again suggesting that they may be more effective copers.

I suspect that most (but not all) men and women learn to weed out the ineffective strategies as they grow older, and ceteris paribus, avoid strategies such as escapism. Further, I also suspect that the nature of control changes, shifting more from an external focus to an internal one, similar to Reynolds's (1976) construct of preferred locus of activity (see Chapter 11). As Altschuler and Ruble (1989) remarked, learning to differentiate between controllable and uncontrollable stressors is an important developmental task in childhood, and this learning process may continue in adulthood as we confront more and more complex problems. Perhaps the acceptance that Gutmann (1974) observed in older adults is not passivity per se, but the recognition that some problems resolve themselves and others are not resolvable. Being able to be more selective about which problems to actively pursue may be a very adaptive strategy, especially in a time of decreasing resources (e.g., energy).

Baltes (1987) has argued that successful adaptation in late life consists of compensation with selective optimization. In other words, older adults learn to compensate for health limitations and optimize those capacities that they do retain. This was supported by anthropologists Johnson and Barrer (1993), who observed adaptive strategies used by the very old—those over 80 years of age:

> First, to make their lives more manageable, they organize objects in their environment to enhance their functioning on the activities of daily living. They are able to increase their mobility through the use of canes and walkers. Hand railings are often installed in bathrooms and on stairs. Hearing aids and amplifiers on telephones improve their hearing, and magnifying glasses permit them to read. The living surroundings also are often narrowed and simplified. Some homes have been stripped of all extraneous objects to make housekeeping easier. Other environmental changes concern rearranging furniture so that there is always something to grasp onto or to break a fall.
>
> Second, coping with limitations on their mobility outside the home is more challenging. When walking outdoors, some respondents use a grocery cart filled with bags of cement to stabilize themselves. Other individuals who are still able to walk independently exercise caution. One

woman shops at a distant grocery store, because it is at the end of a bus line and seats are available on her return trip. . . . One respondent who still drives plots out the streets and plans his exact route in order to avoid getting lost, while another drives around the block rather than making a left turn at a busy intersection.

Third, to enhance their control over the environment, routinization of daily activities is a common strategy. In attempts to create a predictable environment, days are scheduled so there is neither too much nor too little to do. . . . This highly structured routinization of daily activities results in the ritualization of the routine aspects of daily life, a process by which the mundane aspects of their lives take on more significance. (pp. 73–74)

Johnson and Barrer (1993) also provided clues as to why older individuals may appraise their problems as less stressful:

First, respondents commonly de-emphasize their health problems by the use of positive comparisons. Namely they use their age peers as a reference point to define their own health as superior. No matter how frail and debilitated these respondents are, they point to many others who are in worse shape. . . . One woman who was unable to stand up unassisted described her health as better than others because she didn't have "breathing or heart problems." . . .

A second type of appraisal results in the dissociation of one's body from an illness episode or disease state. For example, one 89-year-old woman had been hospitalized twice in the previous year. A bout with pneumonia was passed off, "It was nothing. Look at me, you can tell nothing happened." Some months later she had a serious allergic reaction to seafood. "It was not my body that had anything to do with it. It was the clam chowder." . . .

A third type of appraisal constricts their sense of personal control over their health. Often a sense of inevitability, fate, or luck dominate their discussions. "I'm like an old car—the parts are wearing down." Such a fate is often viewed as natural. . . . These positive views are expressed even among those with high impairment. "What can I say, I've had bypass surgery, I now have shingles, I'm isolated and lonely, I'm losing my strength and my confidence in myself. But glory to God, I'm feeling well". (p. 75)

These are good illustrations of Costa, Zonderman, and McCrae's (1991) findings of a correlation between repression–denial defense mechanisms and age. Further, as indicated in Chapter 11, beliefs in fate, when they do not lead to passivity, may aid in absolving an individual of an undue sense of failure or incompetence or in warding off depression.

These examples also nicely illustrate Baltes's (1987) "compensation with selective optimization"; however, statistically demonstrating increases in this strategy as people grow older is more difficult. Most coping inventories do not have items that actively tap these strategies. It is also not clear that this is learned at any one point in life. Rather than a "hard" stage model with universal stages that everyone goes through at specified time periods, developmental changes in coping in adulthood may not occur to everyone, or on a set schedule, and thus "softer" developmental models may be necessary (Kohlberg & Ryncarz, 1990). The creative use of reality-distorting mechanisms is also apparent in extreme old age.

Nonetheless, the importance of stress and coping strategies in later life may be a key to good adaptation, even in the face of illness and disability. To the extent that we have learned to understand our limited role in stress, are able to detach from situations as appropriate, and decrease maladaptive strategies, we may be able to maintain good mental health in later life.

SUMMARY

Not surprisingly, developmental shifts in coping strategies are easier to document in childhood than in adulthood. In childhood, emotion-focused coping appears to shift from external, behaviorally oriented strategies to internal, cognitively based ones. Problem-focused coping becomes more differentiated and context-specific as coping repertoires increase with age. As adults, hopefully we learn how to differentiate between problems that are essentially uncontrollable, those which will probably resolve themselves, and those for which effort is fruitful. We may become less easily upset (although certainly not always), and may actually engage in less coping, if we have learned which strategies "work" in a given situation.

Clearly, though, not everyone learns to cope efficaciously. Some people rely more and more on drugs and alcohol or continue to cope in ways that are damaging either to the problem, oneself, or others in the situation. What is less well understood is that coping is not simply a homeostatic mechanism but can be intrinsically developmental, or transformational, which is the topic of the next chapter.

CHAPTER 13

Transformational Coping

Sweet are the uses of adversity,
which, like the toad, ugly and venomous,
wears yet a precious jewel in his head.
— SHAKESPEARE, *As You Like It,* Act I, Scene II.

My years in the military were the most painful years
of my life. They were also the most useful.
— NORMAN MAILER, *National Public Radio,* Fall 1992

Pain and suffering can have a steeling—a hardening—
effect on some children, rendering them capable
of mastering life with all its obstacles
— MANFRED E. BLEULER (cited in Anthony, 1987a)

The impetus for early studies of adaptation under stress was the general observation that some people "broke" under stress while others seemed to flourish (Stouffer, 1949; Menninger, 1963). However, formal theories have generally abandoned the bifurcated model suggested by the early studies and have adopted a linear, homeostatic model of adaptation to stress. That is, stress is by definition harmful to well-being (whether physical, mental, or social) and that the greater the stress, the worse the effect. Coping serves a homeostatic function whereby emotions are managed, problems are solved, and life returns to "normal."

The more I study stress and coping processes, the more I am convinced that adaptation simply does not work that way, and that it is time to examine the evidence for nonlinear, nonhomeostatic models in order to better understand why some people "break" and others flourish. In the first place, the relation between stress and well-being is not necessarily linear. As Rutter (1981) pointed out, the effect of stress may be multiplicative rather than additive, or a variety of other nonlinear models may be posited (Aldwin, Levenson, & Spiro, 1994). Further, there is copious evidence, which will be reviewed in greater detail below, that both positive and negative effects can result from undergoing a stressful experience (Aldwin & Stokols, 1988; Antonovsky, 1979, 1987; Dienstbier, 1989; Moos & Schaefer, 1986; Zautra & Sandler, 1983). Rutter (1987) has even gone so far as to suggest that the absence of experience with stressors may constitute a vulnerability factor, reminiscent of Epstein's (1982) and Meichenbaum's (1985) assertion of an inoculation effect of coping with stress.

Stress is so ubiquitous that it seems intuitively unlikely that its effects on adaptation are solely negative. Indeed, much of the clinical, anecdotal literature has suggested that people may perceive benefit in undergoing extreme stress, such as breast cancer (Rollin, 1986) or near-death experiences (Ring, 1982). People have gone so far as to say things like, "Having cancer is the best thing that has ever happened to me" (Weisman, 1979). Now, it is quite likely that much of this involves some element of self-deception, a cognitive reframing that occurs so as to make an unbearable situation more bearable (Taylor & Brown, 1988). And certainly the term "Pollyanna" is often applicable, in that some people will use acute denial to reject any element of the negative. However, this perception of benefit happens so often, in so many types of situations, that it seems prudent to at least examine the phenomenon as a *Ding an Sich*—namely, that there is at least a possibility that people do derive benefit. If this is possible, then understanding how this occurs has obvious practical and clinical benefits.

It is by now a truism that stressors do not have uniform effects on all people at every time. Vulnerability and resilience to stress is clearly affected by factors such as age, sex, social class, family dynamics, social support, temperament, self-efficacy, and coping skills (Elder, 1974; Garmezy & Masten, 1986; Rutter, 1987; Werner & Smith, 1992). However, even the most recent work on resilience has emphasized primarily the ability to maintain competence under adverse conditions and has shied away from the potential benefit of having undergone stressors (but see Anthony, 1987a; Beardslee, 1989; Elder & Clipp, 1989; Lyons, 1991; Werner & Smith, 1992).

Thus, coping does have homeostatic functions, especially in the short-term, but it may also have transformational functions, particularly when one takes a long-term viewpoint. In part, whether the effect of coping is homeostatic or transformational depends upon the type of outcome being examined. If, as is usually the case in stress and coping research, the outcome is some sort of negative affect or symptom increase, then, yes, some coping strategies may have a homeostatic function—although some strategies seem to increase distress (Aldwin & Revenson, 1987). However, if the outcome is something like skill acquisition, relational status, or self-knowledge, the effect of coping can be seen as transformational—that is, encountering and coping with a stressful situation has resulted in a change of some sort. This change may be minor or major, positive or negative, transient or permanent.

Admittedly, the notion that stress can have positive effects is a highly controversial one within the scientific community. When I present these ideas at scientific conferences, the reactions range from flat-out disbelief and active hostility to puzzled reactions as to why I would think this was a new idea (I don't). However, the dominant mode within the stress and coping field has focused for so long on the negative effects of stress, that the notion of positive effects may seem improbable to many researchers and clinicians. However, the Chinese character for crisis is a combination of the symbols for danger and opportunity, reminiscent of Kobasa's (1979) challenge component of hardiness. Opportunity implies the opportunity for gain, whether tangible or intangible. Thus, it seems appropriate to pull together and synthesize the existing literature from several different areas that documents the positive aspects of stress.

The purpose of this chapter is to explore the idea of the stress and coping process as a transformational and developmental phenomenon. Indeed, it can be argued that stress may be a necessary condition in order for individuals to grow as human beings. First, philosophical and psychoanalytic literature supporting this viewpoint will be reviewed. Second, the physiological literature on the positive aspects of stress on neuroendocrine and immune function will be reviewed, followed by studies of positive psychosocial effects in children and adults. Third, we will examine theoretical models that may account for these "anomalous" outcomes of stress, drawing heavily on deviation amplification models. Finally, we will explore the utility of a relatively new construct, chaos theory, in understanding the long-term developmental outcomes of stress.

ARGUMENTS FOR THE DEVELOPMENTAL IMPLICATIONS OF STRESS

This section will only briefly touch upon some of the major philosophical, religious, and psychoanalytic perspectives on the developmental role of pain and suffering. For more in-depth treatments of this subject, interested readers should consult this very extensive literature. This review is meant to be only a brief introduction to this topic, and is presented primarily for heuristic reasons, on the assumption that most stress and coping researchers, myself included, may be relatively unfamiliar with these notions.

Philosophical Perspectives

From time immemorial, philosophers have attempted to understand the reason for the existence of pain and struggle. For example, Plato argued that pleasure and pain form one dimension and that one could not exist without the other. That is, the experience of pleasure exists only relative to the existence of pain. Tragedy played a central role in Greek thinking, with heroes pursuing their *daimon,* or inner sense of destiny, in the face of fate or gods (see Norton, 1974). Rather than tragedy being an outgrowth of heroes pursuing their *daimon,* however, it is possible that tragedy is the means through which heroes uncover their *daimon.*

According to Norton (1974), Silenus held that people are like clay figurines that have an inner figure of gold. The *daimon* is that golden inner figure. How that inner figure is uncovered, however, is unclear. Perhaps tragedy, or stressful episodes, provides a means by which individuals can "knock off" the outer clay covering and thereby discover (or develop) the golden inner figure.

Kierkegaard (1985) believed that despair was an absolutely essential precondition for development in adulthood. He posited three stages of adult development: the aesthetic, the ethical, and the stage of faith. He believed that despair was necessary in order for humans to progress through the stages of adult development. Only by facing and fulfilling the demands of each stage can one achieve the "despair" necessary to "leap" to the next stage. Using modern terminology, substituting the more mundane term of "stress" for the more poetical term "despair", one can conjecture that stress is a necessary prerequisite for advancing through the stages of adult development, an assumption, as will be seen, that is echoed in the writings of Erikson (1950).

Religious Perspectives

From a stress and coping perspective, religious beliefs and practices can be seen as a cultural means of providing people with ways of appraising and coping with stress (see Chapter 10). Certainly, religious frameworks provide a meaning for the occurrence of stress, and spiritual figures such as priests and ministers spend a great deal of their time providing support for people in transitions, whether these are marriages, births, or deaths.

The presentation here is meant to provide only a simplistic guide to some religious beliefs as they might apply to stress and coping processes. Space and time limitations do not permit all of the religious belief systems to be covered, nor the differences of belief systems associated with different sects of any given religion. For example, Christian sects may vary markedly in their attitude toward pain and suffering (to say nothing of the different branches of Judaism, Buddhism, Hinduism, and Islam). In addition, with a given religious tract, there may be markedly contradictory advice that can be viewed as recognizing the necessity for a contextualist approach: Different problems call for different strategies. For example, Christ's admonishment to "turn the other cheek" is balanced by his angry eviction of the merchants from the temple. Further, religions present idealistic goals that may or may not be followed in everyday life: Christians "turn the other cheek" probably as often as Buddhists practice detachment. Thus, one cannot make overarching statements about Christian, Buddhist, or atheistic coping styles. Nonetheless, comparison of the overarching beliefs of different religions provide interesting cross-cultural perspectives on beliefs relevant to the stress and coping process.

Vedantic Indian religions are sometimes collectively (but somewhat erroneously) referred to as Hinduism. From this perspective, suffering is part of *maya,* or illusion. The only way to transcend suffering is to free oneself from the cycle of birth and rebirth. This cycle is necessary for people to "work off," as it were, bad *karma,* or fate, resulting from incorrect action in previous lives. One's progress on this task is indexed by the station to which one is born, whether as an animal or in a particular caste. Thus, the extent to which one suffers in life is due in part to the *karma* accrued in previous lives. From this perspective, one has little control over the occurrence of stressors. However, the extent to which one copes with these stressors in an ethical or appropriate way may affect one's future life. The cycle is only broken once one achieves *samadhi,* and is no longer required to undergo the cycle of birth and rebirth.

The Hindu classic, the *Bhagavad Gita* (translated by Mascaro,

1986), presents an interesting twist on this process. In this rather radical presentation, all action is predetermined. If people cannot and do not have free will—if they have no control over problems or how they cope with them, then the process through which one progresses through the cycle to avoid pain and suffering is unclear. Yet, even within the *Bhagavad Gita* there are calls for the necessity of making an effort to behave in a righteous manner. As mentioned in previous chapters, the ability to attribute to fate things that go wrong can markedly reduce anxiety and may be an efficacious coping strategy, especially if it does not get in the way of making appropriate coping efforts.

The Buddhist framework is rather similar, but the Buddhists more clearly distinguish between pain and suffering. In this framework, pain is unavoidable, but peoples' attitudes and behaviors can affect the degree to which they suffer. (This attitude is reminiscent of current distinctions in the psychological literature on pain. See Chapter 9.) The key is to learn to detach from the world, particularly from desires, which are seen as the source of suffering. If one is indifferent to worldly success, for example, one will not suffer if worldly success is not achieved. Suffering flows only from attachment to material, psychological, or social needs. Some Buddhist sects go so far as to encourage meditation on oneself as a putrefying corpse, to extinguish one's attachment to one's self. From this standpoint, the existence of stressors is far less important than one's appraisal of them, and the detached stance, or the avoidance of commitments, is the only way to avoid suffering.

Suffering and pain also play a central role in the Judeo-Christian perspective. In this framework, suffering stems from the original sin, the fall of Adam and Eve from paradise, and, as such, is an inherent part of the human condition. As a result of eating the forbidden fruit from the Tree of Knowledge at the urging of Satan, Adam and Eve were banished from Eden and were then subject to work stress (having to earn their bread by the sweat of their brow), illness, and labor pains, among other difficulties. The metaphysical importance of Christ's suffering was to make possible human salvation: the chance to avoid suffering, not in this life, but in the next. To the extent that individuals have sufficient humility and fortitude to endure suffering and to avoid the pleasures of sin, they may attain the unending joy of heaven. In contrast to the Buddhist view of the centrality of appraisal, how one copes with temptations and stressors is paramount: Rather than avoiding suffering, one should embrace it as a way of identifying with the suffering of Christ (see John Paul II, 1984).

Both the Bible, in the Book of Job, and the Koran explicitly state that suffering is a means by which God tests people: "Be sure we shall test you with something of fear and hunger, some loss in goods or lives or the fruits (of your toil)" (II:155–157, translated by Ali, 1946). However, in keeping with an emphasis on a merciful God, the Koran is somewhat more explicit in its suggestion that stress is tempered with mercy: "God does not compel a soul to do what is beyond its capacity" (II:285; translated by Cleary, 1993, p. 18). In Islam, suffering is one of encouraging remembrance of God. For example, a *hadith,* or saying of the Prophet Mohammed, suggests that illness is a way of God's drawing people closer to him — a belief that some Christians also share (see Lewis, 1962, pp. 96–97). However, Rabbi Harold Kushner (1981) explicitly rejected the notion that God causes suffering as a means of testing or encouraging remembrance. Kushner argued that stress is simply a part of life and God is primarily a source of comfort and strength under duress, rather than being a causal agent.

Some Sufic writers take a more explicitly developmental perspective. Rumi, in the *Masnavi* (translated by Whinfield, 1973) remarks that evolution progressed from an inanimate stage (rocks), through plants, to animals and then people. Humans alone have the capacity to "soar higher than the angels." ibn Arabi, in his *Bezels of Wisdom* (translated by Austin, 1980) believes that stress plays an important role in this developmental process. From his perspective (an admittedly heretical one from the point of view of orthodox Islam), Adam and Eve's eating fruit from the Tree of Knowledge, with its attendant suffering, was absolutely critical to be able to soar "higher than the angels." Through the exercise of free will, humans can fall lower than animals (i.e., further away from God) or can soar "higher than angels" (i.e. can become closer to God than the angels, who cannot exercise free will, which is an attribute of God). Thus, seen in a long-term view, the Fall of Man was not the source of original sin but, rather, was indicative of the human possibility of development, through knowledge and the development of the capacity of free will. Suffering, then, is a means, not of salvation, but of the development of specific capacities.

In some ways, Taoism is the most explicit of the major religions in suggesting the best way to appraise stress and develop both coping and management skills. In this system, stressful events arise from within the individual: "Good and bad thoughts are the cause of events, receiving blessings and bringing on misfortune are the effect of events" (Liu, translated by Cleary, 1988, p. 10). Like the Buddhists, the Taoists also emphasize detachment, but are more explicit about the importance of preserving equilibrium in order to increase vitality and not disperse energy by becoming unduly worried about events. The construct of yin and yang is used to emphasize contextualist approaches to coping and the importance of maintaining flexibility when handling problems. Taoists advocate the development of virtues by associating with good people and by practicing humility, patience, perseverance, and perspicacity. Once having achieved harmony with oneself and with nature, then "your nature and destiny are up to you, not up to Heaven" (Liu, translated by Cleary, 1988, p. 14).

Nearly all of these religions have practices that utilize stress in one form or another, mainly through abstinence and deprivation.* Most religious traditions, for example, utilize some form of fasting as a way of increasing concentration, especially during meditation. Many traditions also utilize procedures that involve detachment from pain, including the yogic practice of walking across burning coals, the Shiite practice of self-flagellation, and the Native American Sundance ritual. Some Christian mystics also utilized pain and humiliation as a way of achieving ecstatic states (Underhill, 1961) in a manner reminiscent of Solomon's (1980) opponent process, which will be described in greater detail below. While it is easy to dismiss these practices as a form of masochism, their widespread use in religious practices suggests that they have some sort of utility.

Thus, all religions have characteristic attitudes toward human pain and suffering. In all of these frameworks, pain and suffering is an inescapable aspect of being human—another way of saying that stress is ubiquitous. However, in Buddhism and Hinduism, suffering is an indication that one is caught up in *maya*—and, therefore, suffering is to be eliminated, not by changing the environment, but by altering one's appraisal of stress and by developing detachment. In Judeo–Christian–Islamic perspectives, one could argue that coping is more central—how one deals with the inevitable "slings and arrows of outrageous fortune." Stress, whether fortuitous or self-inflicted, is seen as an opportunity to develop the virtues of patience and fortitude or to develop more fully as human beings. Taoism seems to combine both perspectives, advocating appraisal, specific coping processes, and the development of wisdom.

Psychoanalytic Perspectives

Psychoanalytic perspectives can be seen as supporting the developmental notions of stress. According to Freud (1927), the ego develops through the necessity of mediating between the demands of the id, the environment, and the superego. Thus, the stress generated by unfulfilled (or unfulfillable) demands requires the development of new and more adaptive psychic structures.

---

*I am indebted to Dr. Michael R. Levenson for insight.

This theme was expanded upon by ego psychologists such as Adler (1956), who held that individuals' achievements often stemmed from a compensation for defects. Thus, oratorical skills can develop from an initial speech defect, athletic competence from physical limitations. Clearly, this is not the only mechanism through which individuals can develop outstanding skills and achievements, but the stress associated with limitations may provide an impetus for such skills to develop.

Erikson (1950) described development as consisting of eight stages through which individuals progressed by resolving developmental crises peculiar to each stage, such as ego integrity versus despair in later life. Implicit in his theory is that development occurs only through facing and resolving the problems inherent in each stage. Although the evidence for the sequencing and timing of Erikson's adult stages is as yet slim (see Aldwin & Levenson, in press), he has identified major developmental problems that individuals can face in adulthood.

For example, Erikson claimed that the central problem for youths is intimacy versus isolation, which is resolved through either a successful marriage or through the inability to fundamentally relate to others. Yet, careful reading of the original indicates that not only intimacy or isolation issues but all of the developmental crises can arise at many different times in the life course, a point also reiterated by Gilligan (1982).

Intimacy versus isolation may be especially relevant during times of major stress upon families, as when a child becomes chronically or terminally ill. Many clinicians have remarked that under such stress, marriages can fall apart. Yet, other families report an increased closeness, a drawing together that sustains them through the ordeal (Coyne & DeLongis, 1986). Once again, stress can be seen as a catalyst that brings to the forefront important developmental issues, which can be coped with more or less "successfully" if "success" can be defined as increasing capacity to cope with future stress and to develop characteristics important to adult development, such as the capacity for intimacy.

In many ways, Jung (1966) was the most explicit of the dynamic theorists in stating the importance of stress for development in adulthood. For Jung, individuation consists of making conscious hitherto unconscious needs and agendas. One way in which this is done is through the generation of crisis situations, which forces individuals to take stock of their lives, allowing the expression of needs and the development of capacities which had lain dormant. Mental illness, then, is perceived as a way in which the unconscious generates a crisis, which occurs to individuals who have very strong potential for growth and individuation. This theme was echoed by some of the ego psychologists, such as Hartman (1950), who were fascinated with the relation between schizophrenia and creativity, especially among children of schizophrenic parents (for a review see Anthony, 1987a).

Thus, the psychodynamic literature can be interpreted as indicating that struggles with either stage-related crises or with individual stressors are ways in which the ego develops. Indeed, one could argue that without stressors and crises of various sorts, ego development could not occur. If these theorists are correct, it should be possible to discover in the more recent scientific literature examples of positive outcomes of stressful events. The next section will review these findings.

STRESS AS AN IMPETUS FOR PHYSIOLOGICAL DEVELOPMENT

There is actually a growing literature on the positive outcomes of undergoing stress, which covers both physiological outcomes (primarily neuroendocrine and immune functioning) and psychosocial outcomes. The following sections will briefly review this literature, drawing upon and updating an earlier review by Aldwin and Stokols (1988).

Neuroendocrine System

Some of the earliest literature on the anomalous or positive outcomes of stress examined the effects of stressing young mice or rats, sometimes referred to as "infant-handled" rats. Subjecting infant rats in the first ten days of life to environmental stressors such as handling or mild electric shock can have certain beneficial effects on later behavior and neuroendocrine functioning (Denenberg, 1964; Levine, 1966; Levine, Haltmeyer, Karas, & Denenberg, 1967). According to Gray (1971), these rats mature at a more rapid rate, including earlier appearance of body hair, opening of the eyes, myelinization, locomotion, and puberty. In adulthood, infant-handled rats may also exhibit more exploratory behavior and may show characteristic neuroendocrine responses to stress. Generally, this consists of greater and more rapid neuroendocrine responses, accompanied by a more rapid return to baseline levels. Interestingly, this same pattern of neuroendocrine response is also exhibited by alpha or dominant males in baboon colonies (for a review see Sapolsky, 1993).

Intrigued by the findings on the effects of infant handling in rats, anthropologist J. Whiting and his colleagues utilized cross-cultural data to examine whether there are parallel effects of exposure to environmental stress in human infants (for a review see Landauer & Whiting, 1981). In a variety of samples, mean adult physical stature was shown to be significantly greater in cultures with stressful procedures in infancy (e.g., circumcision, scarification, sleeping apart from parents) than in those cultures that carefully protect infants from stressful stimulation. Interestingly, early vaccination (before age 2) also appears to enhance physical growth, apart from any effect on morbidity and mortality.

Dienstbier (1989) has recently developed a neuroendocrine model of "physiological toughness" that can result from stress, drawing in part on earlier work by Miller (1980). Rather than viewing physiological arousal as exclusively negative, Dienstbier marshaled an impressive array of evidence demonstrating positive effects. For example, increases in catecholamines were shown in numerous studies to be positively correlated with better performance on a variety of tasks, and increases in adrenaline also correlated with lower levels of neuroticism and hassles.

Dienstbier (1989) distinguished between SNS (sympathetic nervous system)–adrenal–medullary arousal, mediated by catecholamines, and pituitary–adrenal–cortical arousal, mediated by corticosteroids. Exposure to stressors can result in what Dienstbier termed the "ideal pattern" of SNS arousal: low catecholamine base rates, rapid increases in response to stress, and then a quick return to baseline. "When energy-generating catecholamine responses are elicited in the context of potential control, for which effective instrumental coping responses are likely to lead to success, then positive emotional attributions and responses are likely" (Dienstbier, 1989, p. 87). In contrast, chronically elevated catecholamine base rates are correlated with poorer psychological adjustment and health problems, and "the pattern for cortisol arousal is for low base rates and delayed cortisol responses with challenge or stress" (Dienstbier, 1989, p. 87).

Toughening is divided into passive and active types. "Passive toughening" occurs via exposure to shock or cold, and does not require action on the part of the organism. "Active toughening," in contrast, requires regular activity such as swimming in cold water or aerobic exercise. Successful coping with a challenge is also seen as a mode of "active toughening."

Note, however, that the temporal patterning of stressors is important. Intermittent stress, which allows for recovery between episodes, is associated with better catecholamine and cortisol arousal patterns. However, with continuous stress, the organism does not have a chance for recovery, resulting in both catecholamine and cortisol depletion, similar to Selye's (1956) third stage in the General Adaptation Syndrome, exhaustion.

Thus, exposure to stress, whether in young or adult organisms, can result in future physiological responses that are more adaptive and less harmful to the organism if such exposure allows for adequate recovery time and does not result in catecholamine and cortisol depletion. Interestingly, Dienstbier (1989) noted that ingesting stress-reducing chemicals may complicate this process. Gray (1981, 1983) found that a single dose of tranquilizers given to animals had positive effects similar to toughening manipulations — perhaps by allowing a respite. However, tranquilizers given continuously during toughening procedures prevented physiological toughening. Similar effects have also been noted for beta blockers (Dimsdale, Alpert, & Schneiderman, 1986).

If true, this research has profound clinical implications. For example, let us hypothesize that alcohol has similar effects, resulting in short-term toughening but long-term weakening of neuroendocrine responses. Therefore, adolescents who utilize alcohol to cope with stress may seriously impair their ability to handle future stress. This hypothesis is corroborated by Vaillant (1983), who suggested that chronic alcohol consumption leads to the "alcoholic personality" rather than vice versa (see also Levenson, Aldwin, Spiro, & Bossé, 1992). Further, if successful coping has been seen (at least in animal models) to result in physiological toughening, it would be interesting to speculate that ineffective coping strategies such as escapism may result in future physiological weakening.

In summary, Dienstbier (1989) has developed a very intriguing model of the positive aspects of stress on neuroendocrine and catecholamine functioning. He has marshaled an impressive array of evidence to suggest that intermittent stress, especially that which is coped with successfully, can result in more adaptive physiological responses to future stressors.

Immune System

Infant-handled rats also develop more robust immune systems in later life, as assessed by strength of response to immune challenges (Solomon & Amkraut, 1981). In adulthood, exposure to environmental stressors such as noise and spatial disorientation can enhance immune system functioning and retard tumor growth rates in mice and rats (for reviews see Monjan, 1981; Riley, Fitzmaurice, & Spachman, 1981). The critical factors in immunoenhancement appear to be the duration and timing of stress. Counterintuitively, chronic stress may enhance immune system functioning, if it occurs prior to exposure to chemical carcinogens and viral or bacterial agents. However, if stress occurs after the exposure to the noxious agent, it may decrease immune capacity (Joasoo & McKenzie, 1976; Monjan & Collector, 1977;

Newberry, 1976; Newberry & Songbush, 1979; Rashkis, 1952; Solomon, 1969; Solomon & Amkraut, 1981). Dienstbier (1989) also reviewed evidence suggesting that the physiological toughening effects of stress can also be seen with the immune system. Thus, although common wisdom believes that stress impairs the immune function, under certain conditions stress can actually enhance immune capacity.

Summary

Although the hypothesis that stress can have positive effects on physical functioning in both animals and humans is somewhat radical, at this point there is a fair amount of evidence to support such a proposition. Indeed, it makes a certain amount of evolutionary sense that adaptive organisms developed ways of withstanding and even profiting from stress. However, it should be emphasized that not every type of stress shows such positive effects. These studies focused on aversive stimulation, as opposed to deprivation. Stress resulting from the absence of stimulation or nutritional deprivation, clearly has deleterious effects. Thus, great caution should be used in generalizing from these results to the general effects of stress on development. Nonetheless, Evans (1974, p. 376), in a footnote to the Shakespearean quote on the "sweetness of adversity," notes that the jewel on the toad was supposed to have great curative power against disease, suggesting that Shakespeare observed that adversity might also mitigate against disease. Again, a transactional or contextualist model rather than a simplistic determinist one would seem to be most probable.

STRESS AS AN IMPETUS FOR PSYCHOSOCIAL DEVELOPMENT

For heuristic purposes, the studies of the positive effects of stress can be divided into those studies examining children under stress and those that focus on adults.

Positive Aspects of Stress in Children

At first glance, the suggestion that stress may have positive effects in children is practically heretical in the current climate of concern about child abuse, pederasty, and the dramatic increase in violence in urban neighborhoods and schools, to say nothing of the millions of children currently exposed to war, famine, and poverty around the world. No one in their right minds would wish such problems on any child. But the current thinking that it is best to try to protect children from all harm (cf. Miller, 1990)—and, some cynics would say, even from the consequences of their own actions—may be an example of the pendulum swinging too far in the other direction. (Some schools have even stopped flunking students on the grounds that it may hurt their self-esteem!)

However, as has been often noted, stress is ubiquitous, and it is simply not possible (and not even desirable) to protect children from all of life's problems. Which is not to say that, by stating that stress may have positive effects, I am advocating child abuse, as some of my esteemed colleagues have suggested. Rather, given that stress is a fact of life, how is it that some, or even most children, are able to use what can be termed transformational coping strategies?

Children themselves seem to be able to recognize the positive effects of stress. As one 14-year-old boy put it:

> As you encounter one stressful experience, it strengthens you like a vaccine for a future crisis. One acquires a callousness and builds up a sort of reserve. When you are young, there is a natural ability to survive a crisis; you aren't as deeply involved; even though a minor crisis may seem great, or is exaggerated, it disappears quickly. As one grows older, the natural ability to live ahead and forget, diminishes, but experience in living gives you a maturity that takes the place of your natural ability to survive—you have to bounce back or you couldn't go on. (quoted in Murphy & Moriarty, 1976, p. 263)

It is true the overwhelming majority of studies of children under stress find negative effects (for reviews see Furman, 1974; Rutter, 1981; Berlinsky & Biller, 1982). However, children can be remarkably resilient to stress, and the vast majority of children tend to "bounce back" (Felsman & Vaillant, 1987; Garmezy, 1983; Murphy & Moriarty, 1976; Werner & Smith, 1982, 1992) and in some cases may demonstrate enhanced psychosocial functioning in later life (Anthony, 1987a, 1987b).

Probably one of the most stressful experiences that a child can have is growing up with a mentally ill parent. It is well known that such children may suffer terribly, especially if the parent is severely disturbed or psychotic. Such children are themselves at high risk for problems in later life, including juvenile delinquency, alcohol and drug abuse, and even psychosis. Yet for years, clinicians who have studied families in which one parent is psychotic have recognized that even within one family the children may vary markedly in their vulnerability or resilience. The following quotation illustrates this range in impact very nicely:

A woman, suffering from schizophrenia of the paranoid type . . . insisted on eating at restaurants because she thought someone was poisoning the food at home. Her 12-year-old daughter adopted the same phobic attitude. Another daughter, 10 years old, would eat at home when the father was there; he was normal. Otherwise, she would go along to a restaurant. But a 7-year-old son always ate at home, and when the psychiatrist asked how he could do so, the boy simply shrugged and said, "Well, I'm not dead yet." The older girl eventually developed an illness like her mother's. The younger went to college and did reasonably well. The boy—the invulnerable—performed brilliantly all through school and afterward. His mother's illness apparently had given him both a tremendous need and a tremendous ability to overcome all sorts of problems. (Anthony, 1987b, p. 152)

In recent years there has been a tremendous increase in studies of resilience in children who are, by all accounts, highly vulnerable. These include children of schizophrenic parents (Garmezy & Masten, 1986; Masten, Best, & Garmezy, 1990; Worland, Janes, Anthony, McGinnis, & Cass, 1984); poverty-stricken youths at high risk for juvenile delinquency in Boston during the 1940s (Felsman & Vaillant, 1987; Long & Vaillant, 1984); lower-class children in Britain (Rutter, 1987); multi-ethnic poverty-stricken children growing up in Kuaui during the 1960s (Werner & Smith, 1982, 1992); and highly stressed inner-city children (Cowen, Wyman, Work & Parker, 1990; Wyman, Cowen, Work, & Parker, 1991). What is remarkable is that nearly all of these studies have found not only that a large percentage of such markedly stressed children do remarkably well, but also that similar factors appear to buffer the effects of stress, regardless of cohort, social class, or ethnicity. The three basic factors include cognitive skills, temperament, and social integration (Garmezy & Masten, 1986).

A nearly universal finding is that children with a higher level of intelligence, generally assessed through IQs, are more likely to be resilient. This makes a great deal of sense. More intelligent children are more likely to develop better and more realistic coping strategies, as in Anthony's (1987b) example of the young boy who figured out that eating at home had yet to kill him, contrary to his mother's paranoid fantasy. Further, more intelligent children may function well at school, which provides them with a source of achievement and self-esteem that can buffer other stressors. The one exception to this general rule is a study by Luthar (1991). However, her sample consisted of female adolescents; the cultural bias against intelligence in pubescent girls is well known (Gilligan, Lyons, & Hamner, 1990), and in the case of adolescent girls, intelligence may actually constitute an additional stressor.

Second, resilient children are often deemed to have "sunny" dispositions (Garmezy, 1983) or are perceived by their parents to be "easy babies" (Wyman et al., 1991). Such children may be temperamentally protected from depression or neuroticism, which may allow them to face stress with great equanimity. Others have commented on higher levels of self-esteem and self-efficacy in these children (Cowen et al., 1990). Sunny dispositions may also contribute to resilience by increasing the likelihood of positive interactions with adults and other children.

Third, social interactions also play an important role in the development of resilience. The presence of at least one supportive adult, either within or outside the immediate family, is absolutely crucial (Werner & Smith, 1982). Consistent and supportive discipline from at least one parent is also important (Wyman et al., 1991). Further, in those families with a mentally ill parent, identification with the healthy parent is also critical (Garmezy, 1983; Mosher, Pollin, & Stabenau, 1971). In adolescence and young adulthood, finding a mate who is both stable and supportive may be one way out of a troubled past (Vaillant, 1993; Werner & Smith, 1992).

However, Wolin and Wolin (1993) are critical of the idea that vulnerable children are "rescued" by a supportive adult. As clinicians who have intensively studied resilience in adult children from troubled families, the Wolins believe that resilient children actually seek out social support, sometimes in quite innovative ways. They presented a case study in which a young girl with a totally dysfunctional family carefully cultivated a relationship with a somewhat depressed and isolated older man who lived next door. The older man would often sit on the porch, not doing much of anything. The young girl spent some months working up to a relationship with this man. First, she played where he could see her for a few weeks, jumping rope on the sidewalk in front of his house. Then she initiated contact gradually, first by shy smiles and then hellos. The older man would go for short walks around the neighborhood, and she began asking if she could join him. Eventually, they developed a very close relationship, much to the benefit of both parties. Thus, having a supportive relationship requires effort from both parties.

The Wolins identified a number of coping strategies that they believe lead to vulnerability and resilience. Strategies to be avoided include dwelling on the past; blaming parents for own's own failures; and seeing oneself as a helpless, hopeless victim. Resilient children and adults found and built on their own strengths; improved deliberately and methodically on their parents' lifestyles; married consciously into strong, healthy families; and worked hard at building a cohesive family.

The Wolins systematized their clinical observations into seven categories of resiliency:

1. *Insight*—understanding that the parent is troubled, not "normal," and that the parent's behavior is not the child's fault;
2. *Independence*—separating from troubled families and carefully regulating contact so as not to be drawn into the parent's problems;
3. *Relationships*—cultivating positive interactions with others and marrying well;
4. *Initiative*—finding ways of managing stressful environment, through trial and error, perseverance, and "chunking" of tasks into manageable bits;
5. *Creativity*—finding creative solutions to problems and actively trying to transform negative things into positive ones;
6. *Humor*—using humor to mitigate negative situations and transform them;
7. *Morality*—differentiating right from wrong and adhering to moral action as the source of greatest strength.

While there is a general consensus on the factors leading to reliance in children, many researchers are quick to point out that there is no such thing as a child who is completely invulnerable to stress (Anthony, 1987a); rather, such children show a "checkerboard" of competence and vulnerabilities that may change over time (Murphy & Moriarty, 1976). Further, Luthar and Zigler (1991) point out that highly stressed children who are behaviorally or academically competent may nonetheless show symptoms of anxiety and depression. Indeed, Cowen et al. (1990) found no differences in anxiety or depression between stress-resilient and stress-affected children. Thus, Rutter (1987) emphasized that resilience to stress should be viewed as a *process*, a person–environment interaction, rather than as a characteristic of the individual per se.

A central theme of this chapter, however, is not only that people can withstand stress, but that they may also benefit in some fashion from having undergone stressful experiences. Within the child literature, evidence for this supposition is as yet weak, but nonetheless intriguing. While studies of parental loss generally show increased vulnerability to psychiatric disorder (for a review see Laajus, 1984), others have found scientific and artistic genius to be associated with bereavement in childhood (Albert, 1983; Eisenstadt, 1978; Simonton, 1984). Perhaps the isolation that such children may experience allows them to explore and develop their creative abilities. However, it is also possible that there is a confound with parental age. Older parents often have children who excel in various endeavors; however, the parents' age puts their children at greater risk for bereavement. To my knowledge, no studies of bereavement and genius have attempted to control for parental age.

Nonetheless, this observation of early childhood stress and genius is supported by Goertzel and Goertzel's (1962) study of over 400 famous men and women in the 20th century. They found that over 75% of these exemplars were highly stressed in childhood by physical handicaps or defects, difficult parenting, broken homes, or poverty. Of course, in the absence of a control group, no definitive conclusion can be drawn from this observation, but the finding is still intriguing.

Why would growing up with psychosocial and physical stressors result in high achievement? Obviously, Adler's (1956) compensation mechanisms can be seen to play a role. In addition, highly intelligent children may flee into creative or scientific endeavors to escape from an intolerable home life. Anthony (1987b) drew upon Piaget's biography for a case study:

> One of the direct consequences of my mother's poor mental health was that I started to forego playing for serious work very early in childhood; this I did as much to imitate my father (a scholar of painstaking and critical mind who taught me the value of systematic work) as to take refuge in a private and nonfictitious world. *I have always detested any departure from reality,* an attitude which I related to this important influential factor of my early life, namely my mother's poor mental state. (Piaget, 1952, p. 237; italics in original)

While scientifically oriented children may "flee into reality," artistically oriented children may "flee into fantasy." Interestingly, Anthony (1987a) suggested that the somewhat schizoid ability to go off into flights of fancy, or to have thin ego boundaries, may actually be a buffer against stress rather than a result of stress. As Hartmann (1950) pointed out, the ability to see things differently from other people, to fantasize and regress in the service of the ego is practically a sine qua non for scientific and creative achievement. In keeping with the transactional model, the process probably goes both ways. Creativity and fantasy may provide a useful coping resource and, in some cases, may be facilitated by a highly stressful environment.

In other instances achievement may simply be necessary for survival. Work by Glen Elder (1974) provided the clearest example of how stress can promote positive adaptation in children. Elder found that the effects of economic deprivation during the Depression had differential effects on middle- and working-class children. During the

Depression, deprived children were more emotionally sensitive and generally more psychologically distressed than nondeprived children. The economically deprived working-class children were less adaptive on most measures than their nondeprived peers and continued to experience difficulties into adulthood. Over time, however, the middle-class children appeared to profit from their experience: They matured more quickly; were more likely to be responsible, industrious and achievement-motivated; and set clearer goals for themselves than their nondeprived peers. This trend continued into adulthood. Surprisingly, Kahana (1992) found a similar pattern of high achievement, stable marriages, and close relations with children among survivors of the Holocaust.

Werner and Smith (1992) cautioned that resilient children may pay a price for their good adaptation. As adults, those who had been classified as resilient children reported higher rates of physical illness. Further, Elder (1992, personal communication), in informal observations of the mortality rates among the Berkeley and Oakland samples, suspected that his adaptive children of the Depression may have had somewhat shorter lifespans than their nonstressed peers. Thus, one may adapt to stress and even derive some strengths from the experience, but there may be losses nonetheless.

Summary

As mentioned earlier, no one in their right mind would want to unduly stress children. However, given life's reality, this is going to happen. Children will become ill, parents may become disabled or die, and economic hardship will occur. Understanding the ways in which resilience and even growth can derive from undergoing such stressful experiences is crucial to developing a good model of positive mental health.

Positive Aspects of Stress in Adulthood

Anecdotal evidence for the positive aspects of stress in adulthood is very common. I maintain a file of newspaper clippings of various people, including the rich and the famous, who attribute positive outcomes to highly negative events. I will quote from an article by Linda Ellerbee that appeared in the Sunday *San Francisco Chronicle–Examiner* (March 23, 1993):

> A year and a month ago I was diagnosed with breast cancer. What do I know now? I know that trying to figure out this last year is a lot like trying to bite a basketball. You see, there's been so much good that has happened.
>
> I remember back in the beginning, right after I'd found out the terrible news, a friend who's HIV positive told me that there would be positive things that would come to me because I had a life-threatening illness. I remember laughing at him. Better living through cancer? Puleeze.
>
> Today I begin to understand how right he is. . . . I am . . . happier than I've ever been in my life.

Ellerbee attributed her happiness not only because she had survived a bout with cancer (at the time that the article was written), but also because she had learned to appreciate her family and her work, had quit smoking, and had started exercising—so that she felt very healthy and energetic. She stated that "everyday life seems to me now to be a great good gift" and continued: "You think I sound like Pollyanna? You think maybe I'm making this up, trying to put a good face on a bad deal? I'd like you to meet 300 friends of mine who feel pretty much as I do [referring to a meeting of breast cancer survivors]. . . . Now, we can't all be lying, can we?" I could quote as liberally from many other biographical and literary sources. The fact is, the positive effects of stress do not appear to be anomalous in the general community, and it is time that this fact received more systematic attention in the scientific community.

As we have seen in previous chapters, there is a great deal of evidence for the negative aspects of stress. More than 10,000 studies of the negative effects of stress have been conducted in both laboratory and field conditions (Vingerhoets & Marcelissen, 1988). While the effects of stressful life events on mental health are generally modest and disappear after six months to one year (Depue & Monroe, 1986), they may contribute to the development and exacerbation of chronic physical illness. The effects of hassles on mental health are even briefer, generally abating within a day or two (DeLongis, Folkman, & Lazarus, 1988). Major trauma, however, may have prolonged negative effects on both mental and physical health (see Chapter 9).

Although most research on stress in adulthood has focused on identifying negative sequelae, a growing number of studies have found evidence for positive outcomes of stressful experiences in adulthood. Some researchers have even reported a significant correlation between stress and positive affect (DeLongis et al., 1988; Zautra, Reich, & Guarnaccio, 1990), while Chiriboga (1984) reported that life events were equally likely to result in positive and negative outcomes.

There are at least four ways in which stress can result in positive effects. These include stress inoculation, increases in mastery and self-confidence, changes in perspectives and values, and strengthening of social ties. These will be highlighted by drawing upon the combat exposure literature. Finally, it will be argued that stressful experiences may be a crucible in which wisdom is developed.

The Inoculation Effect

The inoculation effect has been much discussed in the clinical literature and, indeed, underlies many behavioral clinical treatments, including desensitization (Epstein, 1982; Meichenbaum, 1985). That is, undergoing stressful experiences may render future similar experiences less distressing, in part through an increase in an individual's coping repertoire. Certainly, we all remember the first time we entered a classroom, went on a first date, or drove on the freeway. Indeed, sometimes our mastery becomes so complete that we can scarcely remember why we were afraid in the first place.

My favorite cinematic example of this comes from the movie 9 to 5. There is a very funny scene in which the character portrayed by Jane Fonda timidly confronts a huge copying machine for the first time. Fonda's character punches the confusing array of buttons nearly at random, and the copier spews forth multicolored paper all over the room, nearly burying her. The scene suddenly shifts to the next time that she is copying something, and the machine obediently churns out the correct numbers of copies, all neatly collated and stapled.

However, the inoculation effect may not necessarily be limited to similar experiences. For example, Ruch, Chandler, and Harter (1980) found that women who had experienced a moderate amount of stress in the past year showed better recovery from rape than those who had experienced either many or no stressful events. Indeed, as mentioned earlier, Rutter (1987) has suggested that the lack of experience with stressors may be a vulnerability factor.

Increase in Mastery

Second, successfully coping with a stressful experience may increase desirable personality characteristics such as self-confidence or an internal locus of control, especially for individuals who were lacking in these characteristics. For example, Cook, Novaco, and Sarason (1982) investigated the effects of boot camp on recruits' locus of control. They found a significant interaction effect between locus of control and the supportiveness of the drill sergeant. Recruits with external loci of control who developed good relations with the drill sergeant acquired more internal loci of control—that is, they felt they were more able to control themselves and their environment. Similar recruits whose drill sergeants believed in strict discipline and used training procedures to unnecessarily increase stress did not show such gains. Pearlin, Lieberman, Menaghan, and Mullan (1981) also documented increases in mastery in adults who underwent stressful experiences.

Increases in positive capacities are not limited to individuals, but can also be seen in collective circumstances. Scudder and Colson (1982) described the effects of forced relocation (due to the construction of a dam) on tribes in Africa. The initial effects of forced relocation were clearly deleterious. Lives were extremely disrupted, and mortality rates increased, especially among the very young and the very old. Yet, in the long run, tribes that had experienced relocation often developed more diverse economies and creative solutions to cultural problems than did tribes that were not forced to relocate.

Change in Perspectives and Values

Undergoing stressful experiences, especially extremely threatening ones, may change both an individual's perspective on problems and his or her value hierarchy. For example, collective trauma may reduce in magnitude the effects of merely personal problems. Thus, suicide rates and admissions to mental hospitals decrease during times of war (Antonovsky, 1979; Keegan, 1984). After nearly dying, individuals often report a change in perspective, a decreased interest in material wellbeing and petty hassles, and an increase in focus on family and/or spirituality (Ring, 1974). (Note that these changes can occur regardless of whether a respondent had a "near-death experience.") Indeed, it is not at all unusual for cancer and heart disease patients, to remark, like Linda Ellerbee in the above example, that they find renewed appreciation of family and work.

The men in the Normative Aging Study whom I interviewed about the types of resources that they drew upon when coping with problems often mentioned experiences such as combat trauma or the death of a child. After having undergone extreme stressors, everyday hassles no longer seemed important to them. One man explained that he had been shot down in the Pacific and spent the night bobbing about in the water with a fierce battle ranging around him. He promised himself that if he managed somehow to survive that night, nothing was ever going to bother him again—and, he said, nothing has. Perhaps the well-documented decrease in stress ratings with age reflects a lifetime accumulation of experiences with which to make a comparison regarding the relative importance of individual stressors.

Strengthening of Social Ties

Another well-documented positive effect of stress is a strengthening of social ties. After every natural trauma, television reporters invariably use clips of people talking about how great it was that everyone pulled together and pitched in. Indeed, Quarantelli (1985) statistically documented a decrease in psychiatric hospitalizations, drug use, liquor sales, and even crimes following a devastating tornado in one community. Obviously, this does not always occur, especially for individual stressful events. Indeed, the existence of negative social interactions for people undergoing problems such as cancer is also well documented (Dunkel-Schetter, 1981; Rook, 1984). Nonetheless, the possibility of strengthened social ties clearly exists.

Combat Exposure as an Exemplar

Studying the long-term consequences of exposure to combat constitutes a stringent test of the hypothesis that stress can have positive, developmental effects, since the horrors of war are well known and documented. Not only does war wreak physical havoc, but it also creates mental health problems: Twenty-three percent of the battlefield casualties in World War II were psychiatric (Friedman, 1981). These problems may continue after the war, as indicated by the marked increase in suicides and accidents among veterans in the first five years after a war (Centers for Disease Control, 1987). However, soldiers often recount positive aspects of their experience, including heroism, the close friendships, and the development of leadership and coping skills.

Elder and Clipp (1989) suggested that exposure to combat stress could result in either pathogenic or positive developmental effects. Drawing upon the experiences of members of the Berkeley and Oakland Growth and Guidance Studies, Elder and Clipp identified 18 positive and negative outcomes of military experience. The positive outcomes included learning to cope with adversity, self-discipline, a broader perspective, development of lifelong friends, and valuing life more, whereas negative effects included separation from loved ones, combat anxiety, and loss of friends. The undesirable experiences generally referred to losses and negative affective states, whereas positive experiences were more likely to refer to skills or resource acquisition. Men who had been in heavy combat were most likely to list coping, self-discipline, and valuing life as positive outcomes, but they were also more likely to have emotional problems at service exit and later in life.

Ursano, Wheatley, Sledge, Rahe, and Carlson (1986) also found that men who had been heavily exposed to combat identified similar positive resources stemming from their experience. However, Ursano and his colleagues cautioned that the men who identified such resources did not necessarily differ in tests of positive mental health.

Aldwin and colleagues (1994) systematically tested these observations using a more standardized measure of combat exposure, Elder and Clipp's (1989) scale of positive and negative military experiences and a commonly used measure of PTSD. They found that the men in the Normative Aging Study overwhelming endorsed the positive consequences of military experience, with most items receiving over 90% endorsement rates. Surprisingly, the higher the combat exposure, the more men were likely to report positive effects. Further, men who were able to derive positive benefits from combat exposure were less likely to report PTSD symptoms in later life, even controlling for current depressive symptoms and response styles. This finding is supported by Casella and Motta (1990), who found that the men who did not develop PTSD after exposure to combat were characterized by an ability to derive positive meaning from their combat experiences.

Thus, standard theories of stress and coping would not predict that undergoing traumatic circumstances such as combat would result in positive effects. Indeed, the negative effects of combat trauma are well known. However, most studies have been done in clinical populations and, thus, may have overemphasized the negative sequelae of trauma. However, studies that investigate positive aspects in "normal" populations have found strong evidence for the positive aspects of stress and even trauma (see Chapter 10).

The Development of Wisdom

Beardslee (1989) reviewed a series of in-depth, qualitative studies that he conducted on civil rights workers, survivors of childhood cancer, and adolescents with emotionally disturbed parents. Surprisingly, the most striking finding was an increase in self-understanding, which was defined as

> an internal psychological process through which an individual makes causal connections between experiences in the world at large and inner feelings. The process of self-understanding leads to an explanatory and organizing framework for the individual. This organizing framework develops over time and eventually becomes a stable part of the individual's experience. Self-understanding requires not only the presence of thought and reflection about oneself and events, but also action congruent with such reflection. In mature self-understanding there is an emotional importance tied to the organizing framework that has evolved: the in-

dividual believes that self-knowledge is valuable, takes the process of self-understanding seriously, and devotes time and effort to it. (p. 54)

Other aspects of self-understanding include a realistic appraisal of both situational demands and the individual's personal capacities for action, a willingness to change and develop new skills when necessary, and a problem-focused orientation towards the world. In addition, the individuals in Beardslee's studies also evidenced increases in empathy, altruism, and generativity and had a strong sense of ego integrity. In short, these characteristics described by Beardslee are what lifespan developmental psychologists have described as wisdom (Baltes & Smith, 1990; Clayton & Birren, 1980; Kramer, 1990; & Sternberg, 1990).

Thus, not only moderate stress, but also extreme stress, may provide a catalyst for growth. How this occurs is not at all clear. Even less well understood are the factors that may lead to negative or positive long-term outcomes of stress.

MODELS OF POSITIVE AND NEGATIVE STRESS OUTCOMES

Maslow is reputed to have said that if your only tool is a hammer, then you will tend to treat everything like a nail. The seduction of psychological thought by simplistic, deterministic models has lead to the often unexamined assumption that $a \rightarrow b$ and only b. It appears somewhat heretical to suppose that not only can $a \rightarrow b$, but $a \rightarrow not\ b$ as well. In other words, within standard models, how can the same stimulus (i.e., stress) lead to one outcome (negative effects) but also its opposite (positive effects)? After all, we tend to interpret our statistics in rather unidirectional ways. Interpreting a correlation of, for example, .3, we are apt to say that there is a modest relationship between, say, stress and physical symptoms—implying, of course, that stress leads to an increase of physical symptoms, and, for the time being, ignoring all those instances of stress that led to decreases in symptoms but got masked in aggregate by the greater preponderance of negative effects (DeLongis et al., 1988). Similarly, when we conduct an experiment, find our F test significant, examine the cells, and discover that our manipulation worked in the expected direction, we conclude that X causes Y. All of the people who ended up in the unexpected cells are conveniently ignored, due, it is supposed, to "error"—unless, of course, we remember to look for interaction effects and include the types of (usually contextual) data that may help to account for seemingly anomalous effects.

Thus, it seems odd to propose that opposite effects can derive from the same stimulus, whether in different people or contexts, or within the same people but at different times, or even simultaneously. Yet, it would appear that a comprehensive model of adaptation must of necessity be able to account for both the negative and the positive sequelae of stress. Luckily, there are several models existent in the psychological literature that might serve the purpose: independence of positive and negative affect, opponent process, deviation amplification, and chaos. Again, this section will expand upon a review initially conducted by Aldwin and Stokols (1988).

Independence of Positive and Negative Affect

Bradburn and Caplovitz (1965) first discovered the surprising fact that positive and negative affect appear to be relatively orthogonal or independent dimensions. That is, one would expect that the two dimensions would be inversely related (i.e., negatively correlated), but the bulk of the subsequent research has confirmed the orthogonality of positive and negative affect (Watson & Clark, 1984). Given that these dimensions are independent, it is not surprising that stress might have different effects on them. Indeed, in an early model delineating the positive and negative aspects of stress, Zautra and Sandler (1983) proposed two different models of stress and outcomes, one of which would lead to positive outcomes, and the other to negative ones. Thus, stress could have positive or negative outcomes, presumably in different people.

Although in many ways this model is plausible and rather tempting, it is likely that positive and negative effects may coexist in the same person, either simultaneously but in different contexts, or within the same context but in some sort of temporal pattern (McGrath & Beehr, 1990). For example, a move across country to take a new job might be great for one's career, but very bad for one's relationship with spouse or children. Or an initially difficult career move could end up working out very well. Note that both of the contextual or temporal models could theoretically result in a low or nonexistent correlation between positive and negative outcomes. Thus, others have posited models that include both positive and negative affects or other outcomes within the same framework.

Opponent Process Model

Solomon (1980) developed the opponent process model as a counter to classical conditioning models of drug addiction. He hypothesized that a strong affective state, whether positive or negative, is followed by its opposite—hence opponent—process. At the onset of a stimulus, state *a* is greater than state *b*. However, over time, the organism overcompensates, and state *b* becomes stronger than state *a*.

For example, the first few times that opiates are used, the experience is usually pleasurable, with only mild negative aftereffects. But with more frequent opiate use, the initial doses are no longer adequate to produce the same level of euphoria (state *a*), but the negative aftereffects (state *b*) become stronger and stronger. However, increasing the dosage of the opiate in an attempt to recapture the initial euphoria only succeeds in increasing the dysphoria, until the unfortunate addict needs the drug simply to escape from its negative effects.

Note that the opponent process can also work in the opposite direction. Epstein (1982) has researched the effects of parachute jumping rather extensively. He demonstrated that the initial terror of the jump is followed by euphoria. Eventually, with enough jumps, the terror (state *a*) decreases, and the euphoria (state *b*) increases. As mentioned earlier, this sort of opponent process might be involved in the various aversive practices used by religionists to achieve ecstatic states.

The opponent process is readily applicable to stress research (Craig & Siegel, 1980). Certainly, rebound effects can be seen in affective, neuroendocrine, and immune functioning. The correlation between hassles and positive affect (DeLongis et al., 1988) might be an example of an opponent process. In the words of Charlie Brown, banging your head against a wall is useful because it feels so good when it stops! Interestingly, long-term trauma outcomes are associated with severity of initial reaction. Traumatized individuals who reacted strongly were more likely to recover and exhibit fewer signs of PTSD than were individuals with initially weaker reactions (Lyons, 1991). Certainly, an opponent process would also explain why organisms that exhibit sharp increases in neuroendocrines following stressors return more quickly to a homeostatic state: The stronger the *a* process, the stronger the *b* process.

However, there may be limits to the applicability of opponent processes, especially to situations involving chronic or multiple stressors. From an opponent process standpoint, one would expect that environmental change resulting in depression should always be followed by euphoria or mania. While this may occur with bipolar depressions, it clearly does not account for unipolar depressions (Ranieri & Weiss, 1984). Further, multiple stressors may overwhelm the usual opponent processes and create chronic, negative conditions (Rutter, 1981), which may fruitlessly cycle in a negative manner (Horowitz, 1976).

It is interesting to speculate that an opponent process is the norm for stressful events and that mental illness reflects a disruption in that process. Individuals who do not have a quick, strong initial reaction to a stressful event may be unable to bounce back but, instead, may linger in a negative state for a long period. Perhaps abreactive therapies for PTSD (Keane, Fairbank, Caddell, Zimering, & Bender, 1985) are sometimes successful because they can break into this negative spiral and reestablish an opponent process. However, this is often difficult to do successfully.

Many years ago, a friend once spoke to me at great length about his experience with a troubling set of symptoms. (My friend likes to think of himself as the "strong, silent" type, and his initial reaction to any problem is to isolate himself from family and friends; he only discusses problems long after the fact.) At first the problem was diagnosed as cancer; but right before the operation, the physicians discovered that they had misdiagnosed the problem and that the problem was in reality a simple infection that was treatable with antibiotics. Rather than being relieved and even euphoric that he did not have cancer, my friend plunged into a deep depression that lasted for several months over what he had thought was his close brush with death. Perhaps if he had allowed himself to react more emotionally at the first diagnosis, he could have garnered social support and allowed himself to feel relief once he learned of the misdiagnosis.

However, there are other limitations to a simple opponent process model. As mentioned earlier, many life changes have both positive and negative components, and it is not clear how an opponent process model would handle mixed affect. Further, while it might apply to immediate affective processes, its applicability to long-term outcomes such as changes in skill levels or self-esteem is less certain.

Deviation Amplification and Chaos Theory

Systems theory (von Bertalanffy, 1950) offers a broad theoretical framework for understanding how multiple factors interact in a complex process. However, the initial presentations of this theory posited a homeostatic model in which multiple feedback loops would regulate change in any system and eventually return it to its initial state. However, Maruyama (1963) proposed a modification of systems theory that can at least theoretically account for both homeostasis and long-term change. He hypothesized that there are two types of feedback systems: deviation countering and deviation amplification systems. Deviation countering systems are more commonly studied, and involve self-regulation mechanisms with a single feedback loop with which to establish equilibration. Common examples include the regulation of blood pressure and the maintenance of body weight. Deviation countering processes can result in either homeostasis or stable cycling around a central point.

In contrast, deviation amplification processes promote change, whether positive or negative. According to Maruyama (1963), deviation amplifying processes can account for dissimilar products of similar conditions: "A small initial deviation, which is within the range of high probability, may develop into a deviation of low probability" (p. 167). Examples of deviation amplification processes include Myrdal's (1962) "vicious circle" model of economics and poverty or the tendency of emotionally troubled individuals to cope in ways that will intensify their problems (Coyne, Aldwin, & Lazarus, 1981; Folkman & Lazarus, 1986; Aldwin & Revenson, 1987). Interestingly, Sellers and Peterson (1993) found that pessimists, who attribute causality to internal sources, were more likely to use both problem- and emotion-focused coping—an overuse of coping efforts that could well lead to more depression, in turn reinforcing pessimism. A deviation amplification model could also nicely account for Elder's (1974) research on children of the Depression cited earlier, in which he showed that the same type of event, economic deprivation, could have very different long-term effects depending upon whether the children were middle class or working class.

In Maruyama's model, deviation countering and amplification are not seen as conflicting models but rather as alternative possibilities. However, it is not clear what factors predict whether a countering or amplification process will occur. In theory, an odd number of feedback loops will result in deviation countering while an even number would result in deviation amplifying. However, in living, open systems, it is very difficult to determine the exact number of feedback loops—and, thus, for stress research a better model must be developed.

Aldwin & Stokols (1988) identified some characteristics of the stressor that affect this process. By definition, some environmental changes are self-limiting (e.g., relatively minor), while others have the potential to function as catalysts for change, including the timing, speed, and scope of the change, as well as its meaning to the individual. Environmental changes that occur at a particularly inopportune time, that are rapid, that disrupt several life domains, and that are highly meaningful are hypothesized to result in change. Whether this change is positive or negative, however, may depend upon personal resources, social support, and chance.

Based in part on the resilience studies reviewed earlier, one can hypothesize that these personal resources include intelligence, ability to elicit positive responses from the environment, flexibility in attitudes, determination, and perhaps the willingness to take personal risks.

In many ways, this is very similar to Kobasa's (1979) construct of hardiness, which includes commitment, coping abilities, and the tendency to appraise problems as challenges. Clearly, the existence of supportive others to provide both instrumental and emotional support is mentioned time and again in both scientific studies and in autobiographies of highly successful individuals.

Antonovsky (1979, 1987) has argued persuasively for a sense of coherence (SOC) as an important way of overcoming and growing through stress. Antonovsky (1987) defined SOC as

> A global orientation that expresses the extent to which one has a pervasive, enduring though dynamic feeling of confidence that (1) the stimuli deriving from one's internal and external environments in the course of living are structured, predictable, and explicable; (2) the resources are available to one to meet the demands posed by these stimuli; and (3) these demands are challenges, worthy of investment and engagement. (p. 19)

While similar to Kobasa's (1979) construct of hardiness, Antonovsky takes a much more explicitly sociocultural stance, by arguing that a sense of coherence may derive largely from the configuration of the sociocultural context. However Anson, Carmel, Levenson, Bonneh, and Moaz (1993) found that having a strong personal SOC was more important than collective resources (i.e., living in a religious vs. nonreligious kibbutz). However, there was a statistical interaction between the two, so that those persons with high personal and collective resources were especially resilient to stress.

Finally, one cannot ignore the element of chance, or luck, in determining the positive or negative outcomes of stress. However, the ability to capitalize on chance may be a function of personality. For example, optimists tend to use more problem-focused coping (Friedman et al., 1992; Long & Sangster, 1993), which could conceivably allow one to take advantage of any fortuitous circumstances.

In many ways, chaos theory (cf. Gleick, 1987; Pendick, 1993) is a more sophisticated offshoot of deviation–amplification theory. Chaos theory is a way of understanding temporal relations that change over time and that use nonlinear differential equations. Chaos theory also posits that initially very small changes may result in very different patterns of long-term change. It further suggests that such change may not be relatively predictable, but that in some limited circumstances it may be possible to model chaotic processes. The application of chaos theory to lifespan development is clear (Lewis, 1990), although it may be a better model of rhythmic processes such as heart rate. To my knowledge, though, no one has applied chaos theory to stress-related changes in neuroendocrine function over time.

SUMMARY

In summary, there is a fair amount of evidence from a wide variety of sources that stress can have positive effects. Not only has this hypothesis been posited from philosophical, literary, and anecdotal sources, but there is solid evidence from both the child and adult developmental literature, as well as studies of neuroendocrine and immune function.

In part, the key to understanding the positive aspects of stress lies in how the individual (or individuals within a culture) copes with a given stressor. Rather than simply a homeostatic function, the more important role of coping may be transformation. Unfortunately, the transformational aspects of coping have received little attention in the stress and coping literature. Clearly, we need more information on how individuals can transform themselves through the process of coping with stress, including increased mastery and self-knowledge, and the ability to take a different perspective on stress. The ability to transform a situation is also of extreme importance — to be able to perceive and act upon opportunity in crises. Thus, transformational coping may be the key to positive mental health.

CHAPTER 14

Toward a New Theory of Adaptation

I began this book with the statement that a paradigm shift is currently underway in science—a shift from reductionism to transactionism. I argued that a transactionist viewpoint is necessary for understanding highly complex phenomenona such as stress, coping, and adaptation, in all their myriad facets—hence, the "elephant in the dark" metaphor.

The Persian poet Rumi included this story of the elephant in his *Mathwani*. In Farsi, the word for elephant is "fil." However, the ancient Persians also borrowed the Greek word for philosophy, "filsofi." Thus, the play on words so beloved by the Persian poets suggests that the elephant in the story stands for knowledge.* Only by taking multiple perspectives can we truly know any complex phenomenon, and, as the old joke goes, the only thing more complex than the weather is human behavior.

I have tried to bring together physiological, psychological, developmental, social, and cultural perspectives on the process of how individuals cope with stress, as well as delineate methodological issues involved in both the measurement of stress and coping and in understanding their implications for health. The danger in any such endeavor is, of course, indigestion. When faced with overwhelming masses of information, how can one make sense of any huge corpus? Given the often

---

*I am indebted to my friend Robert Darr for this observation.

conflicting theoretical and methodological stances, wherein lies the truth?

TRANSACTIONISM AND COPING

The complexity of the subject matter notwithstanding, a number of conclusions about the process of coping with stress can be made, drawing upon a transactionist perspective.

First of all, it is eminently clear that simply categorizing coping as "approach" or "avoidance" is inadequate. The subtleties of different types of approach or avoidant coping militate against this. Depending upon the type of strategy and extent of its use, avoidant strategies may facilitate or inhibit problem-focused efforts. Avoidant strategies can facilitate problem-focused strategies if they serve as a "time-out" that enables individuals to regroup their resources. Further, qualitative differences in the types of approach coping may lead to their being effective or ineffective.

The literature is absolutely clear that both the source and the effect of coping strategies are *contextual*. That is, people use different strategies at varying phases of the problem, often shifting back and forth between approach and avoidant coping. Moreover, these strategies have different effects, depending upon the circumstances. Using avoidant coping in controllable circumstances may increase psychological distress and the seriousness of the problem, but such strategies may be useful in uncontrollable circumstances. Approach coping, while generally useful, may have detrimental effects if used in uncontrollable situations.

Second, variations in the use of coping strategies are in part a function of individual predilections. However, the evidence is overwhelming that situational demands modify coping responses, as do the behaviors of others in the social context. Further, there are cultural and class differences in what are considered to be appropriate responses to stress, to say nothing of differences in its appraisal. Thus, approaches that exclusively examine personality processes may be methodologically "cleaner" in that such scales may have more reliable factor structures and better internal validity, but their external validity is limited, on both a theoretical and a practical level.

Third, standard approaches to coping may overemphasize control over the environment and the emotions. While instrumental action may often be the best approach, sometimes deferring action, or simply letting events play themselves out, may be a better strategy. Many minor stressors are by nature self-limiting and ignoring them may be the best strategy. Given that so many coping strategies show negative statistical associations with outcomes, many of the strategies seem only to make a problem worse. Further, there are dangers in suppressing legitimate emotions; indeed, some cultures encourage the expression of emotions and feel that suppression is unhealthy.

Fourth, researchers must differentiate between coping effort and coping efficacy. Simply put, more coping is not necessarily better coping. The level of effort made should be appropriate to the demands and importance of the stressor. The most efficacious coping may well be that which expends the least effort, whereas expending great effort in relatively trivial circumstances may be ineffectual and associated with negative outcomes. To complicate an already overly complex situation, highly stressful situations may activate both great coping effort and distressing emotions. Thus, statistically examining the relation between coping and outcome may be extremely tricky and may require more sophisticated methods. The use of simple correlations or regression equations will most likely yield equivocal results: In the literature one can find examples of problem-focused coping alternately bearing positive, negative, or no relation to outcomes. One must control for the degree of stressfulness of the problem or the level of coping effort, or one must utilize interaction terms with coping efficacy for a more accurate picture of the effect of any given coping strategy.

Fifth, the effects of coping strategies must be examined on a variety of levels, including physiological, psychological, social, and cultural. Strategies that may have benefits on one level may entail undue costs on others. Coping with work problems in a way that maximizes career success, for example, may create health or family problems. The challenge is to come up with "mini–max" strategies—those that minimize costs and maximize benefits, both within and across domains—which is not an easy thing to do.

Further, coping strategies not only affect the immediate situation, but may also affect the larger sociocultural environment. Individual or collective coping strategies can affect on cultural mores and/or institutional structures, either through changing perceptions about what constitutes appropriate coping strategies or through changing the availability of coping resources for a given problem.

For example, I was surprised to learn that my mother's efforts to cope with the financial problems of widowhood had led directly to a change in congressional laws. My father, a career military officer, had died unexpectedly, and it took several months for survivor benefits to begin. My mother argued that the family should receive his accrued vacation pay in the interim, but at that time the laws forbade it. She went to her congressman, who got an amendment through Congress to allow my mother and future military widows access to their spouses' vacation pay.

Sixth, the effect of coping strategies must also be examined over time. Most models of adaptation are homeostatic: They assume that coping serves primarily as a deviation-countering device. Indeed, many problems are relatively minor or self-limiting, and coping serves primarily homeostatic functions. However, coping strategies may also set in motion deviation–amplification processes, which in the long run may result in quite different outcomes. On the one hand, it is all too easy to utilize ways of coping that are expedient in the immediate circumstances but that have adverse long-term consequences. Conversely, being able to tolerate immediate stress may be beneficial in the long run.

For example, many students find preparing for an exam very stressful. Decreasing this stress in the short run by using avoidant strategies — going to a movie, playing video games, or watching television — may make the student feel better temporarily but has negative consequences for future achievement if such distractions result in a lack of preparation for the exam. However, learning to tolerate the stress associated with studying may decrease distress during the actual exam and may facilitate achievement.

Differentiating between short- and long-term outcomes may be especially important for traumatic stressors. Given that the traumatic experiences may result in a fundamental change in identity that unfolds over a long period of time, delineating the long-term effects of traumatic stress may require a chaos model approach, in which initially small differences in coping may lead to dramatically different outcomes over time.

Seventh, examining only the negative aspects of stress yields a partial picture of the effects of coping strategies. Both common knowledge and, to an increasing extent, the scientific literature have shown unequivocally that psychosocial stress can have positive effects, whether this is in terms of "physiological toughening," the development of mastery and self-esteem, enhanced perspectives on life, or a larger coping repertoire for use in future stressful situations. Indeed, it makes good evolutionary sense that successful organisms benefit from adversity in ways that make future adaptation easier, or at least more probable. However, some minimum level of resources is required to prevent maladaptive spirals from occurring, and sometimes overwhelming "environmental press" or simple bad luck can prevent any benefits from being derived from a stressful circumstance. But rather than view coping as merely the expenditure of resources (Hobfoll, 1989), the literature suggests that coping can involve the development of resources as well — which brings us to the last issue.

Eight, there is very little literature on the process by which coping strategies develop, either in childhood or adulthood. While common sense would suggest that children learn by imitating their parents, only a handful of studies in the pediatric coping literature have examined this issue—but only from the perspective of synchronicity of parent–child coping styles rather than tracking the development of strategies. In addition to social modeling, trial and error is another reasonable hypothesis. Yet theorists such as Vaillant (1977, 1993) have argued that adaptation is not a process primarily subject to rational control. Defense mechanisms are largely unconscious and, thus, are not amenable to either choice or volitional development but change only as a result of some sort of neurological development or unconscious introjection of significant others. This debate reflects but a larger problem in psychology today: the issue of free will versus determinism.

FREE WILL VERSUS DETERMINISTIC MODELS OF ADAPTATION

In addition to a tension between reductionism and transactionism, there is a related paradigmatic crisis occurring in psychology: the problem of determinism versus free will (Bandura, 1989; Sappington, 1990; Sperry, 1988). In its effort to become a bona fide "science," psychology has sought to develop deterministic models of human behavior. In psychoanalytic models, behavior was determined by largely unconscious forces, the interplay between the id and the ego, shaped by early child rearing practices. This model was next replaced by environmental conditioning: Behavior was a result of rewards and punishments, either in the current environment or in an individual's past history. Currently, psychology appears entranced with deterministic models driven by biology, in terms of either genetic endowment or neurological structure. A transactional approach obviates these relatively simplistic models, showing that behavior is a complex and dynamic composite of a variety of sources. Yet, a transactional model is incomplete if it does not address the other central conundrum within the field. Does human behavior simply reflect the confluence of a mass of influences, or does its understanding require the inclusion of volition as a construct?

As reviewed in Chapter 13, the various great religions have also entertained an apparently paradoxical relationship between determinism and free will. To a certain extent, our behavior is driven by fate, karma, predestination, or other inexorable forces, and yet we are required to go to great efforts to achieve salvation or enlightenment. How is this possible if our behavior is determined?

Vaillant (1976, 1993) struggled with this issue in the context of stress and coping research. He noted, quite correctly, that it is impossible simply to "will" ourselves to cope in another manner. He explicitly uses the "mature" coping strategy of humor as an example. Forced humor falls flat and does not "work." Yet, such deterministic models cannot account for the development of coping strategies, which an examination of any qualitative study reveals is at least partly a function of conscious effort. Frankl (1962), for example, documented the way in which he and his friends developed a sense of humor as a way of coping with the horrors of life in a concentration camp. He invented a simple exercise: Each day, he and his fellow prisoners were to come up with a scenario in their future life in which their experiences and adaptive modes in the concentration camp could be seen to be humorously inappropriate.

I was once arguing with a clinical colleague about the disease model of alcoholism, to which he was a firm adherent. People, he said, do not choose to become addicted—it is a function of a genetic predisposition to respond pathologically to alcohol. Yet, he was also complaining that it was impossible to treat addicts or get them to change unless they first made a commitment to changing themselves. If alcoholism is determined by our biological makeup, how is it that a conscious choice is a prerequisite to change? (cf. Peele, 1985).

At another time, I was arguing with yet a different colleague who adhered strongly to a genetic model of schizophrenia. When I suggested that symptoms are meaningful and reflect choices made by people, however ill advised, he recounted a horrendous episode of a client who was found in a bathtub amidst his own fecal matter. How could this be a matter of choice? Behavior, as we all know, is a result of personal predispositions and environmental contingencies. When I suggested a third possibility—that individuals make conscious choices—my colleague literally could not hear the word "choice" and decided that I must be a radical environmentalist.

On the other hand, refusal to recognize influences—whether genetic or environmental—on human behavior is also foolhardy. I remember yet another argument I had with a theoretical psychologist who felt very strongly that conditioning procedures simply did not apply to human beings. For him, all human behavior was rational and choice driven. Yet, ignoring such influences flies in the face of copious evidence to the contrary.

Sappington (1990) reviewed a number of approaches toward the free will versus determinism debate. He would describe this last example of the theoretical psychologist as the "libertarian" stance: Although humans are faced with both internal and external constraints on their behavior, people are always free to make choices that are not determined by outside factors. An intermediate position between libertarianism and the "hard" determinism of psychoanalysis, behaviorism, behavior genetics, and cognitive neuroscience, is "soft" determinism, which holds that people make choices but that the choices are determined by other factors. In other words, if a person has a choice between working and playing and chooses to play, that choice is strongly influenced by both external factors and personal history.

Psychologists from several different fields have argued for the inclusion of volition and free will in the scientific study of psychology. Contrary to Skinner's (1971) assertion that free will makes a scientific study of psychology impossible, Bandura (1989) and Howard and Conway (1986) have argued persuasively that including volitional constructs in research designs increases the amount of variance that can be accounted for in statistical models of human behavior. However, Sappington (1990) noted that

> data suggesting that conscious choices can account for the bulk of variance in human behavior do not alter the basic issue of whether the choices themselves are ultimately determined by factors outside the person. If conscious choices can ultimately be explained in terms of factors such as environmental stimuli, genetic structures, or past learning history, then this would support the soft determinist position. Because the data on conscious choice do not address the issue of the origin of choice, they do not allow one to decide between the libertarian or the soft determinist position. (p. 26)

Tageson (1982) suggested that free will is not a given but can develop as a result of cognitive maturation, environmental options, and becoming aware of the unconscious influences on behavior. To the extent that an individual can become aware of these influences, he or she can learn to compensate for them. While Sappington (1990) admitted the intuitive appeal of Tageson's model, he argued that this model is still limited in that it cannot account for *how* an individual becomes aware of unconscious influences or learns to choose among options.

Combining a transactionist viewpoint with a developmental one suggests a possible resolution to this conundrum. To a large extent, our behavior is determined—by our biology, our culture, the immediate situation, our developmental level (whether cognitive or socioemotional), and our past history. We respond automatically and often quite unconsciously to various stimuli. Depending largely upon our cultural backgrounds, we respond with shock and horror to the loss of virginity in our daughters, to sexual activity between adults and children, or to Serbian marksmen targetting Moslem children at play. Such shock is only "natural"—until, of course, one finds a culture that has completely different assumption system as to what is "natural."

However, it is within a stressful situation that uncertainty arises. By definition, stress arises when our coping resources—our usual way of doing things—are inadequate to the demands of the situation. As Acredolo and O'Connor (1991) have suggested, uncertainty may be a prerequisite for development. Uncertainty—and all its attendant uncomfortable emotions—is the impetus for a reexamination of our current schemata. According to Acredolo, uncertainty marks the beginning of change in Piaget's schemata of cognitive development. A very young child will be absolutely certain that the tall, thin glass holds more than the short, wide glass. With a slightly older child, one can watch the uncertainty on his face when confronted with two seemingly inexorable "facts": The amount of liquid being poured back and forth is constant, but the tall, thin glass apparently holds more than the short, wide one. This uncertainty allows the child to reexamine his old schemata, and develop new, more sophisticated levels of cognition. Indeed, one could argue that uncertainty is a prerequisite for change.

Similarly, choice and the exercise of free will is impossible unless one recognizes how decisions are made and what influences them. Uncertainty in stressful situations in adulthood may lead one to reexamine one's behavior, thoughts, feelings, and motivation, and learn to recognize unconscious influences on behavior, whether situational, cultural, or personal. The recognition of influences, then, allows for the development of choice.

Elsewhere (Aldwin, 1992), I have argued that stress provides the impetus for development in adulthood. As Baltes (1987) noted, one of the central conundrums for the field of adult development is whether development in adulthood exists. While psychologists such as Erikson (1950), Kohlberg (1984), and Loevinger (1977) have described developmental patterns in adulthood that they held to be universal, sociologists such as Dannefer (1984) and Featherman and Lerner (1985) have argued that there is no universal developmental sequence in adulthood, because roles and cultures vary so widely that there is no one sequence of stages that describes the adult life course in different demographic groups. However, stressful experiences can be seen as providing a universal context for development in adulthood. While the *content* of a stressful experience varies across social roles or cultures, the *experience* of stress is universal. The process of coping with stress provides a means through which development can occur. When coping with stress, people are provided an opportunity to develop the capacities and skills that are deemed admirable by a particular culture. However, there is no universal sequence that all adults go through, largely because such development is volitional (cf. Brandstädter, Krampen, & Heil, 1986).

One can extend this hypothosis concerning stress and adult development to the problem of determinism versus free will. When stress occurs, the old and largely determined way of doing things is shown to be inadequate or limited. Stress, then, provides the opportunity for the exercise of choice. We can, of course, choose to adhere to the old, comfortable way of doing things, but that choice may entail unacceptable costs, which may include failure, social isolation, or even insanity. However, a stressful event may force us to develop new ways of perceiving situations and modes of behavior. *Thus, free will is a characteristic that can develop through the process of coping with stress, to the extent that uncertainty leads to greater reflection.*

The development of free will is undoubtedly a gradual process. Vaillant was correct to talk about the impossibility of simply "willing" something to happen. Someone can no more "will" a sense of humor than I can "will" myself to suddenly be able to run a marathon. However, this is too simplistic a notion of what the exercise of free will entails. It is not a magical wand that suddenly makes everything different. Rather, one can set into motion and sustain a process through which one's goals can gradually be achieved—whether that involves a sense of humor, athletic prowess, or something else entirely.

Note that in this model, stress does not "cause" this development, but rather provides an opportunity. Negative adaptive models may be equally or perhaps more likely. In some ways it is easier to envision the negative process, using chaos and deviation amplification models. In most circumstances, initially small deviations can be easily countered and behavior returned to "normal." However, factors may intervene that set off a deviation amplification process, resulting in a maladaptive spiral. Using the language of Markov chain analysis, a statistically improbable behavior can result from a chain of relatively minor events. Each small event increases the probability of the next one, and the improbable behavior becomes greater with each step.

Runyan (1978) described the process through which a person becomes a heroin addict. No one wakes up one day and says, "Oh, I think I'll become a heroin addict today," nor does anyone specifically formulate a goal to become an addict. Rather, the process involves a series of small, incremental decisions that gradually lead to a serious constraint on behavior. According to Runyan, the process begins by living in a neighborhood in which there are addicts. One gradually gets to know them and may befriend some. Being a friend, one might start doing favors that may involve helping the addicts obtain drugs. Then one might start being a drug user oneself. People typically begin by snorting heroin or smoking it in cigarettes or with marijuana, believing themselves to be stronger than others or less vulnerable to its effects. The use of the drug may increase, until the person needs to directly inject it into veins to get the required effect. The person is finally addicted, and his or her whole life may narrow to serving that addiction, to the detriment of work, family, health, and self-respect.

Similarly, no one "decides" to become a schizophrenic. But an adolescent under stress (and who perhaps has a biological propensity for neurotransmitter imbalances) may act in ways that alienate others. He or she may become more and more withdrawn. Social isolation cuts one off from social regulation of cognition and affect, and one's thought processes and emotional states may become more and more bizarre, which in turn increases the isolation. Self-neglect can lead to inadequate nutrition, exercise, and sleep, which in turn further increases the neurotransmitter imbalance, often abetted by the utilization of alcohol and drugs. At some point the neurochemical imbalance may become so bad (or even permanent) that antipsychotic medications are essential to reduce symptoms. In a transactional model, intervention can (and should) be done at multiple levels. Interestingly, Bradshaw (1993) recently described a coping skills training approach with schizophrenics that substantially reduced recidivism.

Thus, stress can set into motion deviation amplification processes that can easily be seen to result in poor mental and physical outcomes and loss of the ability to exercise control. However, as reviewed in Chapters 10 and 13, there is ample evidence that this deviation can be positive as well. Take, for example, Piaget's response to his schizophrenic mother. He fled into scientific endeavors, which brought him into more contact with his father. One can easily imagine a positive feedback cycle, in which approval from his father caused Piaget to pursue his scientific studies, which in combination with his high intelligence led him to start publishing scientific papers in early adolescence, which led to more societal approval, and so on. The point is that stress can create deviance and deviance can be either positive or negative (or, most likely, some combination thereof).

However, as Sappington (1990) pointed out, chaos models are themselves deterministic. In chaos models, behavior may not be predictable, but it is still determined—the complexity of the interaction between multiple forces simply makes the eventual path unpredictable. A "soft" deterministic model is also congruent with chaos theory. Thus, the ability to demonstrate both negative and positive adaptive spirals is not conclusive proof that stress provides a context for the development of free will per se.

Sappington's critique of Tageson's model of free will as a developmental process is based upon a missing link: How do people become aware of unconscious influences on their behavior? As indicated earlier, stress can create an uncertainty that leads people to more closely observe and examine their behavior. Stated in stronger terms, stress and especially trauma can challenge or even destroy one's whole assumption system about personal safety, justice, the nature of interpersonal relations, and one's role in the world. This destruction of the self must be dealt with in some way; a new self must be constructed. In the vernacular, people often speak of "picking up the pieces." As reviewed in Chapter 10, the end result of the process of coping with the aftermath of trauma is the creation of a new identity—which is why such coping behavior is often a better predictor of outcomes than the original exposure was.

Let us assume that negative spirals have a higher probability of occurrence than do positive ones. After all, it is relatively easy to blame others for failures—my boss had it in for me, my ex-husband was a louse, and so forth—or to internalize victimization as the justification for pathological, self-destructive, or even criminal behavior. Negative spirals generally require the expenditure of less energy and, therefore, are easier to set into motion. Positive adaptive spirals may be much more difficult to set into motion, since they require a fair amount of energy expenditure. For example, if one is an inner-city adolescent, it is probably easier to become pregnant and go on welfare than overcome the barriers to achievement in ghetto schools and go to college. One must develop and coordinate sufficient cognitive, social, financial, and institutional resources to achieve this goal. The further along one is on a negative spiral, the more resources one must expend to reverse this process.

In order to overcome adverse influences, one must become aware of them, determine their source, and how such influences work. Conscious decisions are often required to set into motion and to maintain positive spirals. Note that such consciousness is not an "either/or" phenomenon; rather, it develops gradually and can be instigated and/or supported by others in the environment, until one learns how to recognize possible options, estimate what the likely outcome of different coping strategies may be, and learns how to instigate and sustain courses of action by marshaling both internal and external resources. In short, coping can become what Langer (1989) might describe as mindful.

MINDFUL COPING

The development of judgment is central to the field of "post-formal" operations. In the field of human development, there is a growing recognition of the importance of what can be called "meta-cognition", the ability to think about thinking. The development of logical, formal methods of thought such as that found in scientific thinking is crucial to adequate adult functioning. Yet, there is an increasing acknowledgement of the limits to that thinking, and of the necessity of developing dialectic, situational, and flexible thought processes, sometimes referred to as "post-formal" operations (cf. Alexander, Druker, & Langer, 1990).

Langer's (1989) concept of mindfulness is one of the best examples of this new trend in the human development literature. Mindlessness involves premature cognitive commitment, as typified by the adherence to stereotypical thoughts and actions. Langer provided a charming example of this. A friend of hers always cut off the end of a roast before baking it. When queried as to why she did this, she looked puzzled, and said, "That's how my mother always did it." She called her mother for an explanation, who replied, "That's how my mother always did it." The friend then called her grandmother, who explained that the pot in which she baked roasts was too short, so she always had to cut the ends off of them! Mindless actions and thoughts are perpetuated not only in ourselves, but can persist for generations.

Mindfulness, on the other hand, involves being able to step outside of our categories. We set limitations on our cognitions and our actions, by assuming "that's the way things are" or "that's as much as I can do." In experiment after experiment, Langer showed that altering those cognitions can lead to increased performance. Students generated more creative solutions to problems when the teacher simply said, "X *may* be something," implying that it actually can be something else. Telling students that others had solved a seemingly insoluble problem led to solutions, even if others actually had not solved the problem. Conversely, professional women who were able to solve complex math problems became unable to solve them when asked to assume a subordinate role, that is, when one person was designated as the "supervisor" and the other as the "assistant."

Recognizing that explanations are conditional may be a critical factor in the development of creativity and genius. A recent "Nova" program on Nobel Prize winning physicist Richard Feynman demonstrated this nicely. Feynman's salesman father was a frustrated scientist, and he tried to impart his love of knowledge and scientific curiosity to his son. For example, when Feynman was quite small, he asked his father why the ball in his wagon rolled to the back whenever he started to pull the wagon forward. His father thought for a moment, and said, "Son, nobody really knows. We have a name for it—it's called inertia—but nobody really knows why it happens." This sort of conditional explanation—recognizing that naming something does *not* mean that one understands it—precludes premature cognitive commitment and encourages greater reflection. In contrast, Feynman also played intellectual games with his children but it was always clear that he knew the answers, that the world was concretely defined. This may encourage intelligence, but not creativity and originality.

Stressful events such as a major illness or the death of a parent in childhood may also lead to uncertainty, which could lead to a better capacity for reflection. This capacity may account for some of the association between parental death and genius noted in Chapter 13. In addition, such children are by definition deviant. I recently attended a talk by Isabel Allende, who was reflecting on why she became a writer. "I never fit in," she said. "I always saw things a little differently from other people." One could also hypothesize a chain of possible events leading from parental bereavement to genius. Such children may feel a little different. Lacking two parents, they may not be socialized in the usual manner or they may be uncertain of themselves, and their social skills may be a little awkward. Such children may tend to spend more time alone. If artistically inclined, they may spend a lot of time fantasizing or drawing; if scientifically inclined, they may spend a lot of time reading or thinking. In many ways, "seeing things differently" from others may be very stressful, but it may also be very useful. It is also easy to see how "not fitting in" could lead to negative spirals; hence, the dual outcomes of juvenile delinquency and genius due to bereavement.

The relevance of the mindfulness construct to creative and effective coping is obvious. When confronted with stressors, we may make automatic assumptions that limit our options. We fall into stereotypical roles and reactions that often are not necessary and may create additional stress. Getting upset over trivia is a good example of this. The trick is not to fall into stereotypical roles or exhibit an expected reaction.

I once was on a trolley in San Francisco when a hostile, belligerent (and rather intoxicated) man came aboard. When the bus driver asked him for his fare, he pulled a knife and threatened to kill him. Not surprisingly, the driver simply waived his fare. Much to my dismay, the man then stood next to me, continuing to mumble angry imprecations against the bus driver and fiddle with the knife in his pocket. He stood in such a way that there was no chance of moving. Instead, I looked at him and said, "Why bother?" A surprised expression crossed his face, and he said, "Why bother? You're right!" He immediately stopped being angry, but unfortunately became rather amorous! If I had acted afraid and like a potential victim, this would only have fed the man's anger. *Ceteris paribus,* not acting like a victim (nor like a belligerent antagonist) may be the best way of surviving in our difficult urban environments.

Another mindful technique is the ability to see alternative possibilities in everyday tools. In the explosion in New York's World Trade Center, there were many newspaper accounts of people acting in heroic and unexpected ways to rescue themselves and others. One group of people were stuck in an elevator in between floors. After waiting awhile, they figured out that no one was coming to rescue them. They used their keys to scratch through plaster so that they could escape and then used the lights on their beepers to provide illumination so that they could find their way in the dark.

The ability to perceive opportunities in problems is an example of mindfulness par excellence. We all know of people who were fired and who went on to create their own successful businesses, diabetics who learned how to become healthier through moderating their diet and exercise, or amputees who learned how to ski or compete in the wheelchair olympics. Obviously, some problems are not amenable to this sort of literal transformation, as when a loved one develops inoperable cancer. Yet one may be able to use the time remaining to develop a special closeness.

A woman who runs the local hospice once told me how her trainees changed their thoughts about death. At the start of the training, most of the volunteers expressed the preference for a sudden, unexpected death—presumably one with little suffering, such as an instantly fatal car accident or a massive coronary. After the training period, however, most of the volunteers felt that having the time to prepare for death and say goodbye to loved ones was far preferable, even if it involved suffering with cancer.

Most of Langer's work has been done in experimental settings in which mindfulness was induced. However, my colleagues Michael Levenson and Ron Spiro and I have been working with Ellen Langer in developing a questionnaire to assess mindfulness using more or less standard techniques current in personality instruments. However, our various attempts have not worked very well. Upon due reflection, we determined that our lack of success was due to the fact that mindfulness is not a personality trait, but rather reflects a process that individuals may or may not bring to bear upon a given situation. As such, it parallels the problems that researchers have faced in developing coping inventories. Indeed, mindfulness can be seen as an attribute of some types of coping strategies. Levenson (personal communication, 1994) noted that mindfulness is an example of development that is neither ontogenetic, sociogenic, nor hierarchical and, thus, may be very difficult to assess or track.

Nonetheless, it is interesting to speculate on the process by which people develop mindful coping strategies. Sometimes such strategies arise out of despair—as when the individuals trapped in the World Trade Center knew that they had to do something fairly unusual to escape death. Necessity is the mother of invention, as the saying goes. But in more ordinary circumstances, mindfulness develops through a process of self-observation and self-questioning. First, one must be able to take perspective on the problem: How important is this problem *really*? The religious traditions that recommend keeping death in mind may not be as masochistic as they first seem, if reminders of death are used as a perspective-gaining device. Second, one must be able to observe one's own cognitions, emotions, and behaviors. The proverbial construct of the point of view of a person from Mars is relevant here: How could I have felt, thought, or behaved differently?

Third, to the extent possible, one must learn to develop the ability to perceive different options in situations. We all have thought of the perfect "comeback" five minutes after someone has insulted us. Some people, however, are blessed with the ability to think of snappy replies in the immediate situation. My favorite example of that is the interchange that took place over a hundred years ago in Britain's House of Lords. One member was haranguing another, saying something like, "My lord, you will die either of the pox or on the gallows." The snappy reply was, "That, sir, depends upon whether I embrace your mistress or your morals." I believe that negative emotions, whether anxiety, anger, or embarrassment, prevent the free flow of thought upon which such smooth reactions depend. The ability to take perspective and detach from negative emotions may free up this cognitive process.

Above all, however, one must develop the ability to be honest with oneself. Denying or suppressing negative emotions, even through intellectualizing, is not the same as detachment. As has been noted earlier, under certain circumstances, some denial or suppression is efficacious (cf. Lazarus, 1983). However, habitual denial or self-deception can only interfere with growth, as does intellectual obsession over the "truth," I must hasten to add. As Vaillant (1977) noted, the use of humor may be a mature coping strategy, not when humor is used in a cruel manner to make fun of others, but when it is used as a means of seeing the "funny edge" to a situation or as a way of making the truth about our own selves more palatable. As Beardslee (1989) pointed out, self-knowledge can be one benefit of having to cope with serious, chronic stressors.

Clinicians may be quick to point out that this process of developing mindful ways of coping is very reminiscent of what they seek to achieve with their clients in therapy. Self-observation, development of new perspectives, liberation from crippling negative emotions, enhancement of self-knowledge, and the establishment of new modes of coping are often therapeutic goals. Obviously, different clinical traditions may emphasize one or another of these processes.

However, most people are not in therapy, and studies need to be conducted that address how (and, indeed, even whether) putatively "normal" individuals achieve these goals. At this point, our conceptualization of this process, to say nothing of its assessment, is as yet in its infancy. Apart from the intrinsic interest in understanding positive adaptation, studies such as these may help to inform the therapeutic process.

SUMMARY

The study of coping with stress has for too long focused on the negative. As mentioned earlier, it has been all to easy to identify the ways in which people mishandle stress, ways that lead to increased difficulties or heightened emotional distress. The challenge facing the field is to understand the ways in which individuals cope to creatively solve problems, or better yet, to prevent problems from occurring in the first place (the much-lauded but little understood construct of anticipatory coping). Above all, coping must be seen as a means for human development, whether that development is viewed in terms of mastery, ego integrity, individuation, wisdom, or free will. In order to accomplish this, we must facilitate communication and mutual respect between researchers, clinicians, and, especially, our respondents, who so painfully disclose to us their struggles to cope with problems.

References

Acredolo, C., & O'Connor, J. (1991). On the difficulty of detecting cognitive uncertainty. Special Issue: Cognitive uncertainty and cognitive development. *Human Development, 34,* 204–223.

Ader, R., & Cohen, N. (1982). Behaviorally conditioned immunosuppression and murine systemic lupus erythematosus. *Science, 215,* 1534–1536.

Ader, R. (Ed.). (1981). *Psychoneuroimmunology.* New York: Academic Press.

Ader, R., Felten, D. L., & Cohen, N. (1991). *Psychoneuroimmunology* (2nd ed.). San Diego: Academic Press.

Adler, A. (1956). *The individual psychology of Alfred Adler.* New York: Harper & Row.

Aikens, J. E., Wallander, J. L., Bell, D. S. H., & Cole, J. A. (1992). Daily stress variability, learned resourcefulness, regimen adherence, and metabolic control in Type I diabetes mellitus: Evaluation of a path model. *Journal of Consulting and Clinical Psychology, 60,* 113–118.

Albert, R. S. (Ed.). (1983). *Genius and eminence.* New York: Pergamon Press.

Aldwin, C. (1982). *The role of values in stress and coping processes: A study in person–situation interactions.* Unpublished doctoral dissertation University of California, San Francisco.

Aldwin, C. (1985, May). *Cultural influences on the stress and coping process.* Paper presented at the international symposium entitled "Manejo del stress: Implicaciones biológicas, psicosociales y clínicas," Ensenada, Mexico.

Aldwin, C. (1990). The Elders Life Stress Inventory (ELSI): Egocentric and nonegocentric stress. In M. A. P. Stephens, S. E. Hobfall, J. H. Crowther, & D. L. Tennenbaum (Eds.), *Stress and coping in late life families* (pp. 49–69). New York: Hemisphere.

Aldwin, C. (1991). Does age affect the stress and coping process? Implications of age differences in perceived control. *Journal of Gerontology, 46,* 174–180.

Aldwin, C. (1992). Age, coping, and efficacy: Theoretical framework for examining coping in life-span developmental context. In M. L. Wykle, E. Kana, & J. Kowal (Eds.), *Stress and health among the elderly* (pp. 96–114). New York: Springer.

Aldwin, C. (1994, August). *The California Coping Inventory.* Paper presented at the annual meeting of the American Psychological Association, Los Angeles, CA.

Aldwin, C. (1993). Coping with traumatic stress. *PTSD Research Quarterly, 4,* 1–3.

Aldwin, C. M., Chiara, G., & Sutton, K. J. (1993). Stress and coping in older men: Findings from the Normative Aging Study. *The Gerontologist, 33,* 248.

Aldwin, C., Folkman, S., Coyne, J., Schaefer, C., & Lazarus, R. S. (1980, August). *The Ways of Coping Scale: A process approach.* Paper presented at the annual meeting of the American Psychological Association, Montreal, Quebec, Canada.

Aldwin, C., & Greenberger, E. (1987). Cultural differences in the predictors of depression. *American Journal of Community Psychology, 15,* 789–813.

Aldwin, C. M., & Levenson, M. R. (in press). Aging and personality assessment. In M. P. Lawton & J. Teresi (Eds.), *Annual review of gerontology/geriatrics.* New York: Springer.

Aldwin, C. M., Levenson, M. R., & Spiro, A. (1994). Vulnerability and resilience to combat exposure: Can stress have lifelong effects? *Psychology and Aging, 9,* 34–44.

Aldwin, C., Levenson, M. R., Spiro, A. III, & Bossé, R. (1989). Does emotionality predict stress? Findings from the Normative Aging Study. *Journal of Personality and Social Psychology, 56,* 618–624.

Aldwin, C., & Revenson, T. (1985, August). *Age differences in stress, coping, and perceived efficacy.* Paper presented at the annual meeting of the American Psychological Association, Anaheim, CA.

Aldwin, C., & Revenson, T. (1986). Vulnerability to economic stress. *American Journal of Community Psychology, 14,* 161–175.

Aldwin, C. & Revenson, T.A. (1987). Does coping help? A reexamination of the relationship between coping and mental health. *Journal of Personality and Social Psychology, 53,* 337–348.

Aldwin, C., Spiro, A. III, Clark, G., & Hall, N. (1991). Thymic peptides, stress, and psychological symptoms in older men: Findings from the Normative Aging Study. *Brain, Behavior, and Immunity, 5,* 206–218.

Aldwin, C., & Stokols, D. (1988). The effects of environmental change on individuals and groups: Some neglected issues in stress research. *Journal of Environmental Psychology, 8,* 57–75.

Alexander, C., Druker, S. M., & Langer, E. (1990). Introduction: Major issues in the exploration of adult growth. In C. Alexander & E. Langer (Eds.), *Beyond formal operations: Alternative endpoints in human development* (pp. 3–34). New York: Oxford University Press.

Alexander, F. (1950). *Psychosomatic medicine: Its principles and applications.* New York: Norton.

Ali, A. Y. (Trans.). (1946). *The Koran.* New York: McGregor & Werner.

Altschuler, J. A., & Ruble, D. N. (1989). Developmental changes in children's awareness of strategies for coping with uncontrollable stress. *Child Development, 60,* 1337–1349.

American Psychiatric Association. (1987). *Diagnostic and statistical manual of mental disorders* (3rd ed., rev.) (DSM-III-R). Washington, DC: Author.

American Psychiatric Association. (1994). *Diagnostic and statistical manual of mental disorders* (4th ed.) (DSM-IV). Washington, DC: Author.

Amirkhian, J. H. (1990). A factor analytically derived measure of coping: The Coping Strategy Indicator. *Journal of Personality and Social Psychology, 59,* 1066–1074.

Anson, O., Carmel, S., Levenson, A., Bonneh, D. Y., & Moaz, B. (1993). Coping with recent life events: The interplay of personal and collective resources. *Behavioral Medicine, 18,* 159–166.

Anthony, E. J. (1987a). Risk, vulnerability, and resilience: An overview. In E. J. Anthony & B. J. Cohler (Eds.), *The invulnerable child* (pp. 3–48). New York: Guilford Press.

Anthony, E. J. (1987b). Children at high risk for psychosis growing up successfully. In E. J. Anthony & B. J. Cohler (Eds.), *The invulnerable child* (pp. 147–184). New York: Guilford Press.

Antonovsky, A. (1979). *Health, stress and coping.* San Francisco: Jossey-Bass.

Antonovsky, A. (1987). *Unravelling the mystery of health: How people manage stress and stay well.* San Francisco: Jossey-Bass.

Antonucci, T. C., & Jackson, J. S. (1990). The role of reciprocity in social support. In B. R. Sarason, I. G. Sarason, & G. R. Pierce (Eds.), *Social support: An interactional view* (pp. 173–198). New York: Wiley.

Appley, M. H., & Turnbull, R. (1986). A conceptual model for the examination of stress dynamics. In M. H. Appley & R. Trumbull (Eds.), *Dynamics of stress: Physiological, psychological, and social perspectives* (pp. 21–45). New York: Plenum.

Aronson, E. (1980). *The social animal.* San Francisco: Freeman.

Arsenian, J., & Arsenian, J. M. (1948). Tough and easy cultures: A conceptual analysis. *Psychiatry, 11,* 377–385.

Auerbach, S. M. (1989). Stress management and coping research in the health care setting: An overview and methodological commentary. *Journal of Consulting and Clinical Psychology, 57,* 388–395.

Averill, J. R., & Rosenn, M. (1972). Vigilant and nonvigilant coping strategies and psychophysiological stress reactions during anticipation of electric shock. *Journal of Personality and Social Psychology, 23,* 128–141.

Baltes, P. B. (1987). Theoretical propositions of life-span developmental psychology: On the dynamics between growth and decline. *Developmental Psychology, 24,* 611–626.

Baltes, P. B., & Smith, J. (1990). Toward a psychology of wisdom. In R. J. Sternberg (Ed.), *Wisdom: Its nature, origins, and development* (pp. 87–120). New York: Cambridge University Press.

Band, E. B. (1990). Children's coping with diabetes: Understanding the role of cognitive development. *Journal of Pediatric Psychology, 15,* 27–41.

Band, E. B., & Weisz, J. R. (1988). How to feel better when it feels bad:

Children's perspectives on coping with everyday stress. *Developmental Psychology, 24,* 247–253.

Bandura, A. (1989). Human agency in social cognitive theory. *American Psychologist, 44,* 1175–1184.

Bandura, B., & Waltz, M. (1984). Social support and the quality of life following myocardial infarction. *Social Indicators Research, 14,* 295–311.

Barker, R. G. (1968). *Ecological psychology: Concepts and methods for studying the environment of human behavior.* Stanford, CA: Stanford University Press.

Barron, R. M., & Kenny, D. A. (1986). The mediator–moderator variable distinction in social psychological research: Conceptual, strategic, and statistical considerations. *Journal of Personality and Social Psychology, 51,* 1173–1182.

Bateson, G. (1972). *Steps to an ecology of mind.* New York: Ballantine Books.

Bateson, M. C. (1968). Insight in a bicultural context. *Philippines Studies, 16,* 605–621.

Baum, A., Cohen, L., & Hall, M. (1993). Control and instrusive memories as possible determinants of chronic stress. *Psychosomatic Medicine, 55,* 274–286.

Baum, A., & Fleming, I. (1993). Implications of psychological research on stress and technological accidents. *American Psychologist, 48,* 665–672.

Baum, A., Fleming, R., & Singer, J. (1983). Coping with victimization by technological disaster. *Journal of Social Issues, 39,* 117–138.

Baum, A., & Singer, J. (Eds.). (1987). *Handbook of psychology and health: Vol. 5. Stress.* Hillsdale, NJ: Erlbaum.

Beardslee, W. R. (1989). The role of self-understanding in resilient individuals: The development of a perspective. *American Journal of Orthopsychiatry, 59,* 266–278.

Bell, R. Q., & Harper, L. V. (1977). *Child effects on adults.* Hillsdale, NJ: Erlbaum.

Benner, P., Roskies, E., & Lazarus, R. S. (1980). Stress and coping under extreme circumstances. In J. E. Dimsdale (Ed.), *Survivors, victims, and perpetrators: Essays on the Nazi holocaust* (pp. 219–258). Washington, DC: Hemisphere.

Berg, I., & Hughes, M. (1979). Economic circumstances and the entangling web of pathologies: An esquisse. In L. A. Ferman & J. P. Gordus (Eds.), *Mental health and the economy* (pp. 15–62). Kalamazoo, MI: Upjohn Institute for Employment Research.

Berlinsky, E. B., & Biller, H. B. (1982). *Parental death and psychological development.* Lexington, MA: Heath.

Bettelheim, B. (1943). Individual and mass behavior in extreme situations. *Journal of Abnormal Social Psychology, 38,* 417–452.

Billings, A. G., & Moos, R. H. (1984). Coping, stress, and social resources among adults with unipolar depression. *Journal of Personality and Social Psychology, 46,* 877–891.

Bleuler, M. (1984). Different forms of childhood stress and patterns of adult psychiatric outcome. In N. F. Watt, E. J. Anthony, L. C. Wynne, &

J. Rolf (Eds.), *Children at risk for schizophrenia: A longitudinal perspective* (pp. 547–542). Cambridge, England: Cambridge University Press.

Bolger, N. (1990). Coping as a personality process: A prospective study. *Journal of Personality and Social Psychology, 59,* 525–537.

Bond, M., Gardiner, S. T., & Sigel, J. J. (1983). An empirical examination of defense mechanisms. *Archives of General Psychiatry, 40,* 333–338.

Bossé, R., Aldwin, C., Levenson, M. R., & Workman-Daniels, K. (1991). How stressful is retirement? Findings from the Normative Aging Study. *Journal of Gerontology, 46,* 9–14.

Bower, T. G. R. (1977). *A primer of infant development.* San Francisco: Freeman.

Bradburn, N. M., & Caplovitz, D. (1965). *Reports on happiness: A pilot study of behavior related to mental health.* Chicago: Aldine.

Bradshaw, W. H. (1993). Coping-skills training versus a problem-solving approach with schizophrenic patients. *Hospital and Community Psychiatry, 44,* 1102–1104.

Brandstädter, J., Krampen, G., & Heil, F. (1986). Personal control and emotional evaluation of development in partnership relations during adulthood. In M. Baltes & P. Baltes (Eds.), *The psychology of control and age* (pp. 265–296). Hillsdale, NJ: Erlbaum.

Brenner, M. H. (1973). *Mental illness and the economy.* Cambridge, MA: Harvard University Press.

Brenner, M. H. (1979). Influence of the social environment on psychopathology: The historic perspective. In J. E. Barrett (Ed.), *Stress and mental disorder* (pp. 161–200). New York: Raven Press.

Brickman, P., Rabinowitz, V. C., Karuza, J., Jr., Coates, D., Cohn, E., & Kidder, L. (1982). Model of helping and coping. *American Psychologist, 37,* 368–384.

Brown, G. W. (1989). Life events and measurement. In G. W. Brown & T. O. Harris (Eds.), *Life events and illness* (pp. 3–45). New York: Guilford Press.

Brown, G. W., & Harris, T. O. (1978). *Social origins of depression: A study of psychiatric disorder in women.* New York: Free Press.

Brown, G. W., & Harris, T. O. (Eds.). (1989a). *Life events and illness.* New York: Guilford Press.

Brown, G. W., & Harris, T. O. (1989b). Depression. In G. W. Brown & T. O. Harris (Eds.), *Life events and illness* (pp. 49–93). New York: Guilford Press.

Brown, J. M., O'Keefe, J., Sanders, S. H., & Baker, B. (1986). Developmental changes in children's cognition to stressful and painful situations. *Journal of Pediatric Psychology, 11,* 343–357.

Bryant, B. K. (1985). The neighborhood walk: Sources of support in middle childhood. *Monographs of the Society for Research in Child Development, 50*(3, Serial No. 210).

Bull, B. A., & Drotar, D. (1991). Coping with cancer in remission: Stressors and strategies reported by children and adolescents. *Journal of Pediatric Psychology, 16,* 767–782.

Burgess, A. W., & Holmstrom, L. L. (1976). Coping behavior of the rape victim. *American Journal of Psychiatry, 133,* 413–418.

Burt, M. R., & Katz, B. L. (1987). Dimensions of recovery from rape: Focus on growth outcomes. *Journal of Interpersonal Violence, 2,* 57–82.

Bush, J. P., Melamed, B. G., Sheras, P. L., & Greenbaum, P. E. (1986). Mother–child patterns of coping with anticipatory medical stress. *Health Psychology, 5,* 137–157.

Byrne, D. (1964). Repression–sensitization as a dimension of personality. In B. A. Maher (Ed.), *Progress in experimental personality research* (Vol. 1, pp. 169–220). New York: Academic Press.

Calhoun, J. B. (1962). Population density and social pathology. *Scientific American, 206,* 139–150.

Cannon, W. B. (1915). *Bodily changes in pain, hunger, fear, and rage: An account of recent researches into the function of emotional excitement.* New York: Appleton.

Cannon, W. B. (1929). *Bodily changes in pain, hunger, fear and rage: An account of recent researches into the function of emotional excitement* (2nd ed.). New York: Appleton.

Cannon, W. B. (1939). *The wisdom of the body.* New York: Norton.

Caplovitz, D. (1979). *Making ends meet: How families cope with inflation and recession.* Beverly Hills, CA: Sage.

Carrere, S., Evans, G. W., Palsane, M. N., Rivas, M. (1991). Job strain and occupational stress among urban transit operators. *Journal of Occupational Psychology, 64,* 305–316.

Carver, C. S., & Scheier, M. F. (1994). Situational coping and coping dispositions in a stressful transaction. *Journal of Personality and Social Psychology, 66,* 184–199.

Carver, C. S., & Scheier, M. F., & Weintraub, J. K. (1989). Assessing coping strategies: A theoretically-based approach. *Journal of Personality and Social Psychology, 56,* 267–283.

Casella, L., & Motta, R. W. (1990). Comparison of characteristics of Vietnam veterans with and without posttraumatic stress disorder. *Psychological Reports, 67,* 595–605.

Catalano, R., & Dooley, D. (1979). Does economic change provoke or uncover behavioral disorder: A preliminary test. In L. A. Ferman & J. P. Gordus (Eds.), *Mental health and the economy* (pp. 321–346). Kalamazoo, MI: Upjohn Institute for Employment Research.

Centers for Disease Control. (1987). Postservice mortality among Vietnam Veterans. *Journal of the American Medical Association, 257,* 790–795.

Cervantes, R. C., Padilla, A. M., & Salgado de Snyder, N. (1990). Reliability and validity of the Hispanic Stress Inventory. *Hispanic Journal of Behavioral Sciences, 12,* 79–82.

Chiriboga, D. (1984). Social stressors as antecedents of change. *Journal of Gerontology, 39,* 468–477.

Chiriboga, D. (1992). Paradise lost: Stress in the modern age. In M. Wykle, E. Kahana, & J. Kowal (Eds.), *Stress and health among the elderly* (pp. 35–71). New York: Springer.

Clayton, V. P., & Birren, J. E. (1980). The development of wisdom across the life span: A reexamination of an ancient topic. In P. B. Baltes & O. G. Brim (Eds.), *Life-span development and behavior* (Vol. 3, pp. 103–135). New York: Academic Press.

Cleary, T. (Ed. & Trans.) (1993). *The essential Koran: The heart of Islam.* New York: Harper Collins.

Coddington, R. (1972). The significance of life events as etiological factors in the diseases of children. *Journal of Psychosomatic Research, 16,* 7–18.

Coelho, G. V., & Ahmed, P. I. (1980). *Uprooting and development: Dilemmas of coping with modernization.* New York: Plenum.

Coelho, G. V., Hamburg, D. A., Adams, J. E. (Eds.). (1974). *Coping and adaptation.* New York: Basic Books.

Cohen, J., & Cohen, P. (1975). *Applied multiple regression/correlation analysis for the behavioral sciences.* Hillsdale, NJ: Erlbaum.

Cohen, F., & Lazarus, R. S. (1973). Active coping processes, coping dispositions, and recovery from surgery. *Psychosomatic Medicine, 35,* 375–389.

Cohen, L. J., & Roth, S. (1987). The psychological aftermath of rape: Long-term effects and individual differences in recovery. *Journal of Social and Clinical Psychology, 5,* 525–534.

Cohen, S., Tyrell, D., & Smith, A. (1991). Psychological stress and susceptibility to the common cold. *New England Journal of Medicine, 325,* 606–612.

Cohen, S., Tyrrell, D. A., & Smith, A. P. (1993). Negative life events, perceived stress, negative affect, and susceptibility to the common cold. *Journal of Personality and Social Psychology, 64,* 241–256.

Colby, B. N. (1987). Well-being: A theoretical program. *American Anthroplogist, 89,* 879–895.

Coles, R. (1977). *The children of crisis: Vol. 6. Privileged ones: The well-off and the rich in America.* Boston: Little, Brown.

Compas, B. E., Orosan, P. G., & Grant, K. E. (1993). Adolescent stress and coping: Implications for psychopathology during adolescence. *Journal of Adolescence, 16,* 33–39.

Compas, B. E., & Williams, R. A. (1990). Stress, coping, and adjustment in mothers and young adolescents in single- and two-parent families. *American Journal of Community Psychology, 18,* 525–545.

Compas, B. E., Worsham, N. L., & Ey, S. (1992). Conceptual and developmental issues in children's coping with stress. In A. M. La Greca, L. J. Siegel, J. L. Wallander, & C. E. Walker (Eds.), *Stress and coping in child health* (pp. 7–24). New York: Guilford Press.

Constantinides, P. (1977). Ill at ease and sick at heart: Symbolic behaviour in a Sudanese healing cult. In Lewis, I. (Ed.), *Symbols and sentiments* (pp. 61–84). New York: Academic Press.

Cook, T. M., Novaco, R. W., & Sarason, I. G. (1982). Military recruitment training as an environmental context affecting expectancies for control of reinforcement. *Cognitive Therapy and Research, 6,* 409–428.

Cooper, C., & Faragher, E. (1992). Coping strategies and breast disorders/cancer. *Psychological Medicine, 22,* 447–455.

Costa, P. T., Zonderman, A. B., & McCrae, R. R. (1991). Personality, defense, coping, and adaptation in older adulthood. In E. M. Cummings,

A. L. Greene, & K. H. Karraker (Eds.), *Life-span developmental psychology: Perspectives of stress and coping* (pp. 277–293). Hillsdale, NJ: Erlbaum.

Cottington, E., & House, J. (1987). Occupational stress and health: A multivariate relationship. In A. Baum & J. Singer (Eds.), *Handbook of psychology and health* (pp. 41–62). Hillsdale, NJ: Erlbaum.

Cousins, N. (1979). *Anatomy of an illness as perceived by the patient.* New York: Bantam Books.

Cowen, E. L., Wyman, P. A., Work, W. C., & Parker, G. R. (1990). The Rochester Child Resilience Project: Overview and summary of first year findings. *Development and Psychopathology, 2,* 193–212.

Coyne, J. (1992, August). *But life is not a controlled experiment: Problems in the assessment of coping.* Paper presented at the annual meeting of the American Psychological Association, Washington, DC.

Coyne, J., Aldwin, C., & Lazarus, R. S. (1981). Depression and coping in stressful episodes. *Journal of Abnormal Psychology, 90,* 439–447.

Coyne, J., & DeLongis, A. (1986). Going beyond social support: The role of social relationships in adaptation. *Journal of Consulting and Clinical Psychology, 54,* 454–460.

Coyne, J., & Downey, G. (1991). Social factors and psychopathology: Stress, social support, and coping processes. *Annual Review of Psychology, 42,* 401–426.

Coyne, J., Ellard, J. H., & Smith, A. F. (1990). Social support, interdependence, and the dilemmas of helping. In B. Sarason, I. Sarason, & G. Pierce (Eds.), *Social support: An interactional view* (pp. 129–149). New York: Wiley.

Coyne, J., & Smith, D. A. F. (1991). Couples coping with a myocardial infarction: A contextual perspective on wives' distress. *Journal of Personality and Social Psychology, 61,* 404–412.

Craig, R. L., & Siegel, P. S. (1980). Does negative affect beget positive affect? A test of the opponent-process theory. *Bulletin of the Psychonomic Society, 14,* 404–406.

Cronbach, L. J., & Snow, R. E. (1977). *Aptitudes and instructional methods: A handbook for research on interactions.* New York: Irvington.

Cummings, E. M. (1987). Coping with background anger in early childhood. *Child Development, 58,* 976–984.

Dannefer, D. (1984). Adult development and social theory: A paradigmatic reappraisal. *American Sociological Review, 49,* 100–116.

Davidson, G. R., Nurcombe, B., Kearney, G. E., & Davis, K. (1978). Culture, conflict and coping in a group of Aboriginal adolescents. *Culture, Medicine and Psychiatry, 2,* 359–372.

Davidson, L. M. & Baum, A. (1993). Predictors of chronic stress among Vietnam veterans: Stress exposure and intrusive recall. *Journal of Traumatic Stress, 6,* 195–212.

De Anda, D., Javidi, M., Jefford, S., Komorowski, R., & Yanez, R. (1991). Stress and coping in adolescence: A comparative study of pregnant adolescents and substance abusing adolescents. *Children and Youth Services Review, 13,* 171–182.

Dean, C., & Surtees, P. G. (1989). Do psychological factors predict survival in breast cancer? *Journal of Psychosomatic Research, 33,* 561–569.

DeLongis, A., Bolger, N., & Kessler, R. C. (1987, August). *Coping with marital conflict.* Paper presented at the annual meeting of the American Psychological Association, New York.

DeLongis, A., Bolger, N., Kessler, R., & Wethington, E. (1989). The contagion of stress across multiple roles. *Journal of Marriage and the Family, 51,* 175–183.

DeLongis, A., Coyne, J. C., Dakof, G., Folkman, S., & Lazarus, R. S. (1982). Relationship of daily hassles, uplifts, and major life events to health status. *Health Psychology, 1,* 119–136.

DeLongis, A., Folkman, S., & Lazarus, R.S. (1988). The impact of daily stress on health and mood: Psychology and social resources as mediators. *Journal of Personality and Social Psychology, 54,* 486–495.

Denenberg, V. H. (1964). Critical periods, stimulus input, and emotional reactivity: A theory of infantile stimulation. *Psychological Review, 71,* 335–357.

Depue, R. A., & Monroe, S. M. (1986). Conceptualization and measurement of human disorder in life stress research: The problem of chronic disturbance. *Psychological Bulletin, 99,* 36–51.

Derry, P., Deal, M., & Baum, A. (1993). The relationship of intrusive and avoidant thoughts about a stressor to daydreaming styles. *Journal of Nervous and Mental Disease, 181,* 456–457.

Diaz-Guerrero, R. (1979). The development of coping style. *Human Development, 22,* 320–331.

Dienstbier, R. A. (1989). Arousal and physiological toughness: Implications for mental and physical health. *Psychological Bulletin, 96,* 84–100.

DiGiulio, R. C. (1989). *Beyond widowhood: From bereavement to emergence and hope.* New York: Free Press.

Dimsdale, J. E., Alpert, B. S., & Schneiderman, N. (1986). Exercise as a modulator of cardiovascular reactivity. In K. A. Matthews, S. M. Weiss, T. Detre, T. M. Dembroski, B. Falkner, S. B. Manuck, & R. B. Williams, Jr. (Eds.), *Handbook of stress, reactivity, and cardiovascular disease* (pp. 365–384). New York: Wiley.

Dohrenwend, B. S., Dohrenwend, B. P., Dodson, M., & Shrout, P. E. (1984). Symptoms, hassles, social supports, and life events: Problem of confounded measures. *Journal of Abnormal Psychology, 93,* 222–230.

Dohrenwend, B. S., Krasnoff, L., Askenasy, A., & Dohrenwend, B. P. (1978). Exemplification of a method for scaling life events: The PERI life events scale. *Journal of Health and Social Behavior, 19,* 205–229.

Dolan, C. A., Sherwood, A., & Light, K. C. (1992). Cognitive coping strategies and blood pressure responses to real-life stress in healthy young men. *Health Psychology, 11,* 233–242.

Dooley, D. (1985). Causal inference in the study of social support. In S. Cohen & S. L. Syme (Eds.), *Social support and health* (pp. 109–120). San Diego, CA: Academic Press.

Draucker, C. B. (1989). Cognitive adaptation of female incest survivors. *Journal of Consulting and Clinical Psychology, 57,* 668–670.

Dressler, W. W. (1986). The social and cultural context of coping: Action, gender and symptoms in a southern Black community. *Social Science and Medicine, 21,* 449–506.

Dubos, R. (1965). *Man adapting.* New Haven: Yale University Press.

Dunkel-Schetter, C. (1981). *Social support and coping with cancer.* Unpublished doctoral dissertation, Northwestern University.

Dunkel-Schetter, C., Feinstein, L. G., Taylor, S. E., & Falke, R. L. (1992). Patterns of coping with cancer. *Health Psychology, 11,* 79–87.

Dunn, A. J. (1989). Psychoneuroimmunology for the psychoneuroendocrinologist: A review of animal studies of the nervous-immune system interactions. *Psychoneuroimmunology, 14,* 251–274.

Durkheim, E. (1933). *The division of labor in society.* New York: Free Press.

Ebersole, P., & Flores, J. (1989). Positive impact of life crises. *Journal of Social Behavior and Personality, 4,* 463–469.

Eccles, J., & Robinson, D. N. (1984). *The wonder of being human: Our brain and our mind.* New York: The Free Press.

Eckenrode, J. (Ed.). (1991). *The social context of coping.* New York: Plenum.

Eisenstadt, J. M. (1978). Parental loss and genius. *American Psychologist, 33,* 211–223.

Eitinger, L. (1980). The concentration camp syndrome and its late sequelae. In J. Dimsdale (Ed.), *Survivors, victims, and perpetrators* (pp. 127–161). Washington, DC: Hemisphere.

Ekerdt, D., Baden, L., Bossé, R., & Dibbs, E. (1983). The effect of retirement on physical health. *American Journal of Public Health, 73,* 779–783.

Elder, G. H. (1974). *Children of the Great Depression.* Chicago: University of Chicago Press.

Elder, G. H. & Caspi, A. (1988). Economic stress in lives: Developmental perspectives. *Journal of Social Issues, 44,* 24–45.

Elder, G., & Clipp, E. (1989). Combat experience and emotional health: Impairment and resilience in later life. *Journal of Personality, 57,* 311–341.

Elwood, S. W. (1987). Stressor and coping response inventories for children. *Psychological Reports, 60,* 931–947.

Endler, N., & Parker, J. D. A. (1990). Multidimensional assessment of coping: A critical evaluation. *Journal of Personality and Social Psychology, 58,* 844–854.

Enos, D. M., & Handal, P. J. (1986). The relation of parental marital status and perceived family conflict to adjustment in white adolescents. *Journal of Consulting and Clinical Psychology, 54,* 820–824.

Epstein, S. (1982). Conflict and stress. In L. Goldberger & S. Bresnitz (Eds.), *Handbook of stress: Theoretical and clinical aspects* (pp. 49–60). New York: Free Press.

Epstein, S. (1991). The self-concept, the traumatic neurosis, and the structure of personality. In D. Ozer, J. H. Healy, & A. J. Stewart (Eds.), *Perspectives in personality* (Vol. 3, pp. 63–98). London: Kingsley.

Erikson, E. (1950). *Childhood and society.* New York: Norton.

Erikson, K. T. (1976). *Everything in its path.* New York: Simon & Schuster.

Etzion, D., & Pines, A. (1986). Sex and culture in burnout and coping among human service professionals: A social psychological perspective. *Journal of Cross-Cultural Psychology, 17,* 191–209.

Evans, G. (1974). *The Riverside Shakespeare.* Boston: Houghton Mifflin.

Evans, G. W. (Ed.). (1982). *Environmental stress.* New York: Cambridge University Press.

Evans, G. W., & Jacobs, S. V. (1982). Air pollution and human behavior. In G. W. Evans (Ed.), *Environmental stress* (pp. 105–132). New York: Cambridge University Press.

Everly, G. S., Jr. (1989). *A clinical guide to the treatment of the human stress response.* New York: Plenum.

Faust, J., & Melamed, B. G. (1984). The influence of arousal, previous experience, and age on surgery preparation of same-day and in-hospital pediatric patients. *Journal of Consulting and Clinical Psychology, 52,* 359–365.

Fawzy, F. I., Cousins, N., Fawzy, N. W., Kemeny, M., & Morton, D. L. (1990). A structured psychiatric intervention for cancer patients: I. Changes over time in methods of coping and affective disturbance. *Archives of General Psychiatry, 47,* 720–725.

Fawzy, F. I., Fawzy, N. W., Hyun, C., Elashoff, R., Guthrie, D., Fahey, J. L., & Morton, D. L. (1993). Malignant melanoma: Effects on an early structured psychiatric intervention, coping, and affective state on recurrence and survival six years later. *Archives of General Psychiatry, 50,* 681–689.

Fawzy, F. I., Kemeny, M., Fawzy, N. W., Elashoff, R., Morton, D., Cousins, N., & Fahey, J. L. (1990). A structured psychiatric intervention for cancer patients: II. Changes over time in immunological measures. *Archives of General Psychiatry, 47,* 729–735.

Featherman, D. L., & Lerner, R. M. (1985). Ontogenesis and sociogenesis: Problematics for theory and research about development and socialization across the lifespan. *American Sociological Review, 50,* 659–676.

Felitti, V. J. (1991). Long-term medical consequences of incest, rape, and molestation. *Southern Medical Journal, 84,* 328–331.

Felsman, J. K., & Vaillant, G. E. (1987). Resilient children as adults: A forty year study. In E. J. Anthony & B. J. Cohler (Eds.), *The invulnerable child* (pp. 289–314). New York: Guilford Press.

Felton, B. J., & Revenson, T. A. (1984). Coping with chronic illness: A study of illness controllability and the influence of coping strategies on psychological adjustment. *Journal of Consulting and Clinical Psychology, 52,* 343–353.

Felton, B. J., & Revenson, T. A. (1987). Age differences in coping with chronic illness. *Psychology and Aging, 2,* 164–170.

Field, T. (1991). Stress and coping from pregnancy through the postnatal period. In E. M. Cummings, A. L. Greene, & K. H. Karraker (Eds.), *Lifespan developmental psychology: Perspectives on stress and coping* (pp. 45–59). Hillsdale, NJ: Erlbaum.

Figley, C. R. (1983). Catastrophes: An overview of family reactions. In C. R. Figley & H. I. McCubbin (Eds.), *Stress and the family: Vol. II. Coping with catastrophe* (pp. 3–20). New York: Brunner/Mazel.

Finney, J. W., Mitchell, R. E., Cronkite, R. C., & Moos, R. H. (1984). Methodological issues in estimating main and interactive effects: Examples from coping/social support and stress field. *Journal of Health and Social Behavior, 25,* 85–98.

Folkman, S., Berstein, L., & Lazarus, R. S. (1987). Stress processes and the misuse of drugs in older adults. *Psychology and Aging, 2,* 366–374.

Folkman, S., Chesney, M., Pollack, L., & Coates, T. (1993). Stress, control, coping and depressive mood in human immunodeficiency virus-positive and -negative gay men in San Francisco. *Journal of Nervous and Mental Disease, 181,* 409–416.

Folkman, S., & Lazarus, R. S. (1980). An analysis of coping in a middle-aged community sample. *Journal of Health and Social Behavior, 21,* 219–239.

Folkman, S., & Lazarus, R. (1985). If it changes it must be a process: Study of emotion and coping during three stages of a college examination. *Journal of Personality and Social Psychology, 48,* 150–170.

Folkman, S., & Lazarus, R. (1986). Stress processes and depressive symptomatology. *Journal of Abnormal Psychology, 95,* 107–113.

Folkman, S., Lazarus, R. S., Dunkel-Schetter, C., Delongis, A., & Gruen, R. (1986). The dynamics of a stressful encounter: Cognitive appraisal, coping, and encounter outcomes. *Journal of Personality and Social Psychology, 50,* 992–1003.

Folkman, S., Lazarus, R., Gruen, R., & Delongis, A. (1986). Appraisal, coping, health status, and psychological symptoms. *Journal of Personality and Social Psychology, 50,* 571–579.

Folkman, S., Lazarus, R. S., Pimley, S., & Novacek, J. (1987). Age differences in stress and coping processes. *Psychology and Aging, 2,* 171–184.

Fondacaro, M. R., & Moos, R. H. (1987). Social support and coping: A longitudinal analysis. *American Journal of Community Psychology, 15,* 653–673.

Fowers, B. J. (1992). The Cardiac Denial of Impact Scale: A brief, self-report research measure. *Journal of Psychosomatic Research, 36,* 469–475.

Frankenhauser, M. (1980). Psychobiological aspects of life stress. In S. Levine & H. Ursin (Eds.), *Coping and health* (pp. 203–223). New York: Plenum.

Frankl, V. E. (1962). *Man's search for meaning: An introduction to logotherapy.* Boston: Beacon Press.

Freud, A. (1966). *The ego and the mechanisms of defense* (rev. ed.). New York: International Universities Press.

Freud, S. (1927). *The ego and the id* (J. Strachey Ed. & Trans.). New York: Norton. (Orignal work published 1923.)

Friedman, M. J. (1981). Post-Vietnam syndrome: Recognition and management. *Psychosomatics, 22,* 931–943.

Friedman, L. C., Nelson, D. V., Baer, P. E., Lane, M., Smith, F. E., & Dworkin, R. J. (1992). The relationship of dispositional optimism, daily life stress, and domestic environment to coping methods used by cancer patients. *Journal of Behavioral Medicine, 15,* 127–141.

Frydenberg, E., & Lewis, R. (1990). How adolescents cope with different concerns: The development of the Adolescent Coping Checklist (ACC). *Psychological Test Bulletin, 3,* 63–73.

Furman, E. (1974). *A child's parent dies: Studies in childhood bereavement.* New Haven: Yale University Press.

Garmezy, N. (1983). Stressors of childhood. In N. Garmezy & M. Rutter (Eds.), *Stress, coping, and development in children* (pp. 43–84). New York: McGraw-Hill.

Garmezy, N., & Masten, A. S. (1986). Stress, competence, and resilience: Common frontiers for therapist and psychopathologist. *Behavior Therapy, 17,* 500–521.

Garrison, V. (1977). The Puerto Rican syndrome in psychiatry and *Espiritismo.* In V. Crapanzano & V. Garrison (Eds.), *Case studies in spirit possession* (pp. 383–449). New York: Wiley.

Gatchel, R. J., & Baum, A. (1983). *An introduction to health psychology.* Reading, MA: Addison-Wesley.

Gazzaniga, M. S., (1989). Organization of the human brain. *Science, 245,* 947–952.

Gibson, J. T., Westwood, M. J., Ishiyama, F. I., Borgen, W. A., Showalter, W. M., Al-Sarrat, Q., et al. (1991). Youth and culture: A seventeen nation study of perceived problems and coping strategies. *International Journal for the Advancement of Counseling, 14,* 204–216.

Giel, R. (1991). The psychosocial aftermath of two major disasters in the Soviet Union. *Journal of Traumatic Stress, 4,* 381–392.

Gilligan, C. (1982). *In a different voice: Psychological theory and women's development.* Cambridge, MA: Harvard University Press.

Gilligan, C., Lyons, N. P., & Hanmer, T. J. (Eds.). (1990). *Making connections: The relational worlds of adolescent girls at Emma Willard School.* Cambridge, MA: Harvard University Press.

Gleick, J. (1987). *Chaos: Making a new science.* New York: Viking Press.

Goertzel, V., & Goertzel, M. G. (1962). *Cradles of eminence.* Boston: Little, Brown.

Good, B. (1977). The heart of what's the matter: The semantics of illness in Iran. *Culture, Medicine, and Psychiatry, 1,* 25–58.

Goodkin, K., Antoni, M., & Bloom, P. (1986). Stress and hopelessness in the promotion of cervical intrepithelial neoplasm to invasive squamous cell carcinoma of the cervix. *Journal of Psychosomatic Research, 30,* 67–76.

Gray, J. A. (1971). *The psychology of fear and stress.* New York: McGraw-Hill.

Gray, J. A. (1981). *The physiopsychology of anxiety.* Oxford: Oxford University Press.

Gray, J. A. (1983). Anxiety, personality and the brain. In A. Gale & J. A. Edwards (Eds.), *Physiological correlates of human behavior: Vol. III. Individual differences and psychopathology* (pp. 31–43). London: Academic Press.

Greene, A. L., & Larson, R. W. (1991). Variation in stress reactivity during adolescence. In E. M. Cummings, A. L. Greene, & K. H. Karraker (Eds.) *Life-span developmental psychology: Perspectives on stress and coping* (pp. 195–209). Hillsdale, NJ: Erlbaum.

Greer, S., & Morris, T. (1975). Psychological attributes of women who develop breast cancer. *Journal of Psychosomatic Research, 19,* 147–153.

Gross, E. (1970). Work, organization and stress. In S. Levine & N. A. Scotch (Eds.), *Social stress* (pp. 54–110). Chicago: Aldine.

Gutmann, D. L. (1974). Alternatives to disengagement: The old men of the Highland Druze. In R. A. LeVine (Ed.), *Culture and personality: Contemporary readings* (pp. 232–245). Chicago: Aldine.

Guttman, R., Bach, F. H., Bach, M. K., Claman, H. N., David, J. R., Jeannet, M., Lindquist, R. R., McKhann, C. F., Papermaster, D., & Schwartz, R. S. (1981). *Immunology.* Kalamazoo, MI: Upjohn.

Haan, N. (Ed.). (1977). *Coping and defending.* New York: Academic Press.

Hallstrom, T., Lapidus, L., Bengston, C., & Edstrom, K. (1986). Psychological factors and risk of ischaemic heart disease and death in women: A twelve-year follow-up of participants in the population study of women in Gothenburg, Sweden. *Journal of Psychosomatic Research, 30,* 451–459.

Hardy, D. D., & Smith, T. W. (1988). Cynical hostility and vulnerability to disease: Social support, life stress, and physiological response to conflict. *Health Psychology, 7,* 447–459.

Harel, Z., Kahana, B., & Kahana, E. (1988). Psychological well-being among Holocaust survivors and immigrants in Israel. *Journal of Traumatic Stress, 1,* 413–429.

Hartman, H. (1950). Comments on the psychoanalytic theory of the ego. In *Essays on ego psychology.* New York: International Universities Press.

Harvey, J. H., Orbuch, T. L., Chalisz, K. D., & Garwood, G. (1991). Coping with sexual assault: The roles of account-making and confiding. *Journal of Traumatic Stress, 4,* 515–531.

Heim, E., Augustiny, K., Schaffner, L., & Valach, L. (1993). Coping with breast cancer over time and situation. *Journal of Psychosomatic Research, 37,* 523–542

Hetherington, E. M. (1984). Stress and coping in children and families. *New Directions for Child Development, 24,* 7–33.

Hetherington, E. M. (1991). Presidential address: Families, lies, and videotapes. *Journal of Research on Adolescence, 1,* 323–348.

Hetherington, E. M. (1993). An overview of the Virginia Longitudinal Study of Divorce and Remarriage with a focus on early adolescence. Special Section: Families in transition. *Journal of Family Psychology, 7,* 39–56.

Hetherington, E. M., Cox, M., & Cox, R. (1985). Long-term effects of divorce and remarriage on the adjustment of children. *Journal of the American Academy of Child Psychiatry, 24,* 518–530.

Heider, F. (1958). *The psychology of interpersonal relations.* New York: Wiley.

Hobfall, S. (1989). Conservation of resources: A new attempt at conceptualizing stress. *American Psychologist, 44,* 513–524.

Hobfall, S., & Dunahoo, C. (1992, August). *Are we studying coping strategies or piecemeal behavior?* Paper presented at the annual meeting of the American Psychological Association, Washington, DC.

Holahan, G. K., Holahan, C. J., & Belk, S. S. (1984). Adjusting in aging: The role of life stress, hassles, and self-efficacy. *Health Psychology, 3,* 315–328.

Holahan, C., & Moos, R. (1985). Life stress and health: Personality, coping and family support in stress resistance. *Journal of Personality and Social Psychology, 49,* 739–747.

Holmes, D., & Rahe, R. (1967). The Social Readjustment Rating Scale. *Journal of Psychosomatic Research, 11,* 213–218.

Horowitz, M. J. (1976). *Stress response syndromes.* New York: Aronson.

Horowitz, M. J. (1986). *Stress response syndromes* (2nd ed.). Northvale, NJ: Aronson.

House, J. S., Landis, K. R., & Umberson, D. (1988). Social relationships and health. *Science, 241,* 540–545.

Howard, G. S., & Conway, C. G. (1986). Can there be an empirical science of volition? *American Psychologist, 41,* 1241–1251.

Howell, J. T. (1973). *Hard living on Clay Street: Portraits of blue collar families.* Garden City, NY: Anchor Press.

Hsu, J. (1976). Counseling in the Chinese temple: A psychological study of divination by "Chien" drawing. In W. Lebra (Ed.), *Culture-bound syndromes, ethnopsychiatry, and alternate therapies* (pp. 210–221). Honolulu: University of Hawaii Press.

Hwang, K. K. (1979). Coping with residential crowding in a Chinese urban society: The interplay of high-density dwelling and interpersonal values. *Acta Psychological Taiwanica, 21,* 117–133.

ibn Arabi, M. (1980). *Bezels of wisdom* (R. W. J. Austin, Trans.). Ramsey, NJ: Paulist Press.

Illich, I. (1981). *Shadow work.* Boston: Boyars.

Ingstad, B. (1988). Coping behavior of disabled persons and their families: Cross-cultural perspectives from Norway and Botswana. *Rehabilitation Research, 11,* 351–359.

Irion, J. C., & Blanchard-Fields, F. (1987). A cross-sectional comparison of adaptive coping in adulthood. *Journal of Gerontology, 42,* 502–504.

James, W. (1890). *Principles of psychology.* New York: Holt.

Janis, I., & Mann, L. (1977). *Decision-making: A psychological analysis of conflict, choice, and commitment.* New York: Free Press.

Jenkins, C., Hurst, M., & Rose, R. (1979). Life changes: Do people really remember? *Archives of General Psychiatry, 36,* 379–384.

Jensen, M. P., Turner, J. A., Romano, J. M, & Karoly, P. (1991). Coping with chronic pain: A critical review of the literature. *Pain, 47,* 249–283.

Joasoo, A., & McKenzie, J. M. (1976). Stress and immune response in rats. *International Archives of Allergy and Applied Immunology, 50,* 659–663.

Joffe, P., & Naditch, M. P. (1977). Paper and pencil measures of coping and defense processes. In N. Haan (Ed.), *Coping and defending* (pp. 280–298). New York: Academic Press.

John Paul II. (1984). *On the Christian meaning of human suffering: Salvifi Dolores.* Boston: St. Paul Books & Media.

Johnson, C. I., & Barer, B. M. (1993). Coping and a sense of control among the oldest old. *Journal of Aging Studies, 7,* 67–80.

Jorgensen, R. S., & Dusek, J. B. (1990). Adolescent adjustment and coping strategies. *Journal of Personality, 58,* 503–513.

Jung, C. G. (1966). *Two essays on analytical psychology.* Princeton: Princeton University Press.

Kahana, B. (1992). Late-life adaptation in the aftermath of extreme stress. In M. Wykel, E. Kahana, & J. Kowal (Eds.), *Stress and health among the elderly* (pp. 5–34). New York: Springer.

Kanner, A. D., Coyne, J. C., Schaefer, C., & Lazarus, R. S. (1981). Comparison of two modes of stress measurement: Daily hassles and uplifts vs. major life events. *Journal of Behavioral Medicine, 4,* 1–39.

Kaplan, H. B. (1991). Social psychology of the immune system: A conceptual framework and review of the literature. *Social Science and Medicine, 33,* 909–923.

Karasek, R., & Theorell, T. (1990). *Healthy work: Stress, productivity, and the reconstruction of working life.* New York: Basic Books.

Karraker, K. H., & Lake, M. (1991). Normative stress and coping processes in infancy. In E. M. Cummings, A. L. Greene, & K. H. Karraker (Eds.), *Life-span developmental psychology: Perspectives on stress and coping* (pp. 85–108). Hillsdale, NJ: Erlbaum.

Kashima, Y., & Triandis, H. C. (1986). The self-serving bias in attributions as a coping strategy: A cross-cultural study. *Journal of Cross-Cultural Psychology, 17,* 83–97.

Kasl, S. (1983). Pursuing the link between stressful life experiences and disease: A time for reappraisal. In C. I. Cooper (Ed.), *Stress research* (pp. 79–102). New York: Mentor Books.

Kazak, A. E. (1989). Families of chronically ill children: A systems and social-ecological model of adaptation and challenge. *Journal of Consulting and Clinical Psychology, 57,* 25–30.

Kazak, A., Reber, M., & Snitzer, L. (1988). Childhood chronic disease and family fuctioning: A study of phenylketonuria. *Pediatrics, 81,* 224–230.

Keane, T. M., Fairbank, J. A., Caddell, J. M., Zimering, R. T., & Bender, M. E. (1985). A behavioral approach to assessing and treating posttraumatic stress disorder in Vietnam veterans. In C. R. Figley (Ed.), *Trauma and its wake: The assessment and treatment of posttraumatic stress disorders* (pp. 257–294). New York: Brunner/Mazel.

Keane, T. M., Fairbank, J. A., Caddell, J. M., Zimering, R. T., Taylor, K. L., & Mora, C. A. (1989). Clinical evaluation of a measure to assess combat exposure. *Psychological Journal of Consulting and Clinical Psychology, 1,* 53–55.

Keegan, J. (1984). Shedding light in Lebanon. *Atlantic, 253,* 4–55.

Kemeny, M. E., Cohen, F., Zegans, L. S., & Conant, M. A. (1989). Psychological and immunological predictors of genital herpes recurrence. *Psychosomatic Medicine, 51,* 195–208.

Kenny, D., & Judd, C. (1984). Estimating the nonlinear and interactive effects of latent variables. *Psychological Bulletin, 99,* 422–431.

Kessler, R., & Wethington, E. (1986). *Some strategies of improving recall of life events in a general population survey.* Ann Arbor: Survey Research Center, University of Michigan.

Kiecolt-Glaser, J. K., & Glaser, R. (1989). Psychoneuroimmunology: Past, present, and future. *Health Psychology, 8,* 677–682.

Kiefer, C. (1974). *Changing cultures, changing lives.* San Francisco: Jossey-Bass.

Kierkegaard, S. (1985). *Fear and trembling.* New York: Viking Penguin.

Kinney, J. M., & Stephens, M. A. P. (1989). Hassles and uplifts of giving care to a family member with dementia. *Psychology and Aging, 4,* 402–408.

Kleinman, A. (1980). *Patients and healers in the context of culture: An exploration of the borderland between anthropology, medicine, and psychiatry.* Berkeley: University of California Press.

Kobasa, S. (1979). Stressful life events, personality and health: An inquiry into hardiness. *Journal of Personality and Social Psychology, 37,* 1–11.

Kohlberg, L. (1984). *Essays on moral development: Vol. 2. The psychology of moral development.* San Francisco: Harper & Row.

Kohlberg, L., & Ryncarz, R. A. (1990). Beyond justice reasoning: Moral development and consideration of a seventh stage. In C. Alexander & E. Langer (Eds.), *Beyond formal operations: Alternative endpoints in human development* (pp. 191–207). New York: Oxford University Press.

Koopman, C., Eisenthal, S., & Stoeckle, J. D. (1984). Ethnicity in the reported pain, emotional distress, and requests of medical outpatients. *Social Science and Medicine, 18,* 487–490.

Kramer, D. A. (1990). Conceptualizing wisdom: The primacy of affect-cognition relations. In R. J. Sternberg (Ed.), *Wisdom: Its nature, origins, and development* (pp. 279–313). Cambridge, England: Cambridge University Press.

Krause, N. (1986). Stress and sex differences in depressive symptoms among older adults. *Journal of Gerontology, 6,* 727–731.

Kuhn, T. (1970). *The structure of scientific revolutions.* Chicago: University of Chicago Press.

Kurdek, L. A., & Sinclair, R. J. (1988). Adjustment of young adolescents in two-parent nuclear, stepfather, and mother-custody families. *Journal of Consulting and Clinical Psychology, 56,* 91–96.

Kushner, H. S. (1981). *When bad things happen to good people.* New York: Avon.

Laajus, S. (1984). Parental losses. *Acta Psychiatrica Scandinavia, 60,* 1–12.

Labouvie-Vief, G., DeVoe, M., & Bulka, D. (1989). Speaking about feelings: Conceptions of emotion across the life span. *Psychology and Aging, 4,* 425–437.

Labouvie-Vief, G., Hakim-Larson, J., DeVoe, M., & Schoeberlein, S. (1989). Emotions and self-regulation: A life span view. *Human Development, 32,* 279–299.

Labouvie-Vief, G., Hakim-Larson, J., Hobart, C. (1987). Age, ego level, and the life-span development of coping and defense processes. *Psychology and Aging, 2,* 286–293.

Lachman, M. E. (1986). Locus of control in aging research: A case for multidimensional and domain-specific assessment. *Psychology and Aging, 1,* 34–40.

Landauer, R. K., & Whiting, J. W. M. (1981). Correlates and consequences of stress in infancy. In R. H. Munroe, R. L. Munroe, & B. B. Whiting (Eds.), *Handbook of cross-cultural human development* (pp. 355–375). New York: Garland.

Lange, C., & James, W. (1922). *The emotions.* Baltimore: Williams & Wilkins.

Langer, E. J. (1989). *Mindfulness.* New York: Addison-Wesley.

Langer, E. J., Janis, I. L., & Wolfer, J. A. (1975). Reduction of psychological stress in surgical patients. *Journal of Experimental Social Psychology, 11,* 155–165.

Lazarus, R. S. (1966). *Psychological stress and the coping process.* New York: McGraw-Hill.

Lazarus, R. S. (1982). Thoughts on the relations between emotion and cognition. *American Psychologist, 37,* 1019–1024.

Lazarus, R. S. (1983). The costs and benefits of denial. In S. Breznitz (Ed.), *The denial of stress* (pp. 1–30). New York: International Universities Press.

Lazarus, R. S. (1984). On the primacy of cognition. *American Psychologist, 39,* 124–129.

Lazarus, R. S. (1990). Theory-based stress measurement. *Psychological Inquiry, 1,* 3–13.

Lazarus, R. S. (1991). *Emotion and adaptation.* New York: Oxford University Press.

Lazarus, R. S., & Alfert, E. (1964). The short-circuiting of threat. *Journal of Abnormal and Social Psychology, 69,* 195–205.

Lazarus, R. S., Averill, J. R., & Opton, E. M., Jr. (1974). The psychology of coping: Issues of research and assessment. In G. V. Coelho, D. A. Hamburg, & J. E. Adams (Eds.), *Coping and adaptation* (pp. 249–315). New York: Basic Books.

Lazarus, R. S., DeLongis, A., Folkman, S., & Gruen, R. (1985). Stress and adaptational outcomes: The problem of confounded measures. *American Psychologist, 40,* 730–777.

Lazarus, R. S., & Folkman, S. (1984). *Stress, appraisal, and coping.* New York: Springer.

Lazarus, R. S., Speisman, J. C., Markoff, A. M., & Davison, L. A. (1962). A lab study of psychological stress produced by a motion picture film. *Psychological Monographs, 76*(34, Whole No. 553).

Lefcourt, H. M. (1976). *Locus of control: Current trends in theory and research.* Hillsdale, NJ: Erlbaum.

Leigh, H., & Reiser, M. F. (1980). *The patient: Biological, psychological, and social dimensions of medical practice.* New York: Plenum.

Levenson, J. L., Mishra, A., Hamer, R. M., & Hastillo, A. (1989). Denial and medical outcome in unstable angina. *Psychosomatic Medicine, 51,* 27–35.

Levenson, M. R., Aldwin, C., Spiro, A. III, & Bossé, R. (1992). Personality, alcohol problems and heavy drinking in older men. *The Gerontologist, 32,* 259.

Leventhal, E. A., Leventhal, H., Shacham, S., & Easterling, D. V. (1989). Active coping reduces reports of pain from childbirth. *Journal of Consulting and Clinical Psychology, 57,* 365–371.

Levine, R. (1973). *Culture, behavior, and personality.* Chicago: Aldine.

Levine, S. (1966). Sex differences in the brain. *Scientific American, 498,* 84–91.

Levine, S., Haltmeyer, G. G., Karas, C. G., & Denenberg, V. H. (1967). Physiological and behavioral effects of infant stimulation. *Physiology and Behavior, 2,* 55–59.

Levy, S. M. (1991). Behavioral and immunological host factors in cancer risk. In P. M. McCabe, N. Schneiderman, T. M. Field, & J. S. Skyler (Eds.), *Stress, coping and disease* (pp. 237–252). Hillsdale, NJ: Erlbaum.

Lewis, C. S. (1962). *The problem of pain: How human suffering raises almost intolerable intellectual problems.* New York: Macmillan.

Lewis, M. (1990). Development, time, and catastrophe: An alternate view of discontinuity. In P. B. Baltes, D. L. Featherman, & R. M. Lerner (Eds.), *Life-span development and behavior* (Vol. 1, pp. 325–350). Hillsdale, NJ: Erlbaum.

Lieberman, M. A. (1992). Limitations of psychological stress model: Studies of widowhood. In M. L. Wykle, E. Kahan, & J. Kowal (Eds), *Stress and health among the elderly* (pp. 133–150). New York: Springer.

Lifton, R. J. (1961). *Thought reform and the psychology of totalism: A study of "brainwashing" in China.* New York: Norton.

Lifton, R. (1968). *Death in life: Survivors of Hiroshima.* New York: Random House.

Light, K. C., Dolan, C. A., Davis, M. R., & Sherwood, A. (1992). Cardiovascular responses to an active coping challenge as predictors of blood pressure patterns 10 to 15 years later. *Psychosomatic Medicine, 54,* 217–230.

Lindemann, E. (1944). Symptomatology and management of acute grief. *American Journal of Psychiatry, 101,* 141–148.

Linsky, A., & Straus, M. (1986). *Social stress in the United States: Links to regional patterns in crime and illness.* Dover, MA: Auburn House.

Lipowski, Z. J. (1970). Physical illness, the individual, and the coping process. *Psychiatry in Medicine, 1,* 91–102.

Lipton, J. A., & Marbach, J. J. (1984). Ethnicity and the pain experience. *Social Science and Medicine, 19,* 1279–1298.

Liu, I-Ming. *Awakening to the Tao* (T. Cleary, Trans.). Boston: Shambala.

Locke, S. E., Kraus, L., Leserman, J., Hurst, M. W., Heisel, J. S., & Williams, R. M. (1984). Life change stress, psychiatric symptoms, and natural killer cell activity. *Psychosomatic Medicine, 46,* 441–453.

Loevinger, J. (1977). *Ego development: Conceptions and theories.* San Francisco: Jossey-Bass.

Lomranz, J. (1990). Long-term adaptation to traumatic stress in light of adult development and aging perspectives. In M. A. P. Stephens, J. H. Crowther, S. E. Hobfall, & D. L. Tennenbaum (Eds.), *Stress and coping in later-life families* (pp. 99–124). New York: Hemisphere.

Long, B. C., & Sangster, J. I. (1993). Dispositional optimism/pessimism and coping strategies: Predictors of psychosocial adjustment of rheumatoid and osteoarthritis patients. *Journal of Applied Social Psychology, 23,* 1069–1091.

Long, J. V. F., & Vaillant, G. E. (1984). Natural history of male psychological health, XI: Escape from the underclass. *American Journal of Psychiatry, 141,* 341–346.

Lowenthal, M. F., Thurnher, M., & Chiriboga, D. (1975). *Four stages of life.* San Francisco: Jossey-Bass.

Lumley, M. A., Abeles, L. A., Melamed, B. G., Pistone, L. M., & Johnson, J. H. (1990). Coping outcomes in children undergoing stressful medical procedures: The role of child-environment variables. *Behavioral Assessment, 12,* 223–238.

Luthar, S. (1991). Vulnerability and resilience: A study of high risk adolescence. *Child Development, 62,* 600–616.

Luthar, S. S., & Zigler, E. (1991). Vulnerability and competence: A review of research on resilience in childhood. *American Journal of Orthopsychiatry, 61,* 6–22.

Lynch, J. (1979). *The broken heart: The medical consequences of loneliness.* New York: Basic Books.

Lyons, J. A. (1991). Strategies for assessing the potential for positive adjustment following trauma. *Journal of Traumatic Stress, 4,* 93–111.

Maddi, S. R., Bartone, P. T., & Pucetti, M. C. (1987). Stressful events are indeed a factor in physical illness: Reply to Schroeder and Costa. *Journal of Personality and Social Psychology, 33,* 833–843.

Maduro, R. (1975). Voodoo possession in San Francisco: Notes on therapeutic regression. *Ethos, 3,* 425–447.

Manne, S. L., & Zautra, A. J. (1992). Coping with arthritis: Current status and review. *Arthritis and Rheumatism, 35,* 1273–1280.

Marrero, D. (1982). *Adjustment to misfortune: The process of coping with diabetes mellitus in children and their parents.* Unpublished doctoral dissertation, University of California, Irvine.

Marshall, G. D., & Zimbardo, P. G. (1979). Affective consequences of inadequately explained physiological arousal. *Journal of Personality and Social Psychology, 37,* 970–988.

Maruyama, M. (1963). The second cybernetics: Deviation-amplifying mutual causal processes. *American Scientist, 51,* 164–179.

Mascaro, J. (Trans.). (1986). *The Bhagavad Gita.* Middlesex, England: Penguin.

Mason, J. W. (1971). A re-evaluation of the concept of "non-specificity" in stress theory. *Journal of Psychiatric Research, 8,* 323–333.

Mason, J. W. (1975). A historical view of the stress field. *Journal of Human Stress, 1,* 6–27.

Masten, A. S., Best, K. M., & Garmezy, N. (1990). Resilience and development: Contributions form the study of children who overcome adversity. *Development and Psychopathology, 2,* 425–444.

Mattlin, J., Wethington, E., & Kessler, R. C. (1990). Situational determinants of coping and coping effectiveness. *Journal of Health and Social Behavior, 31,* 103–122.

McCabe, P. M., Schneiderman, N., Field, T. M., & Skyler, J. S. (Eds). (1991). *Stress, coping and disease.* Hillsdale, NJ: Erlbaum.

McClelland, G., & Judd, C. (1993). Statistical difficulties of detecting interactions and moderator effects. *Psychological Bulletin, 114,* 376–390.

McCrae, R. R. (1982). Age differences in the use of coping mechanisms. *Journal of Gerontology, 37,* 454–460.

McCrae, R. R. (1984). Situational determinants of coping responses: Loss, threat, and challenge. *Journal of Personality and Social Psychology, 46,* 919–928.

McCrae, R. R. (1989). Age differences and changes in the use of coping mechanisms. *Journals of Gerontology: Psychological Sciences, 44,* 161–169.

McCrae, R. R., & Costa, P. T. (1986). Personality, coping, and coping effectiveness in an adult sample. *Journal of Personality, 54,* 385–405.

McCubbin, H. I., & Figley, C. R. (1983). Bridging normative and catastrophic family stress. In H. I. McCubbin & C. R. Figley (Eds.), *Stress and the family: Vol. I. Coping with normative transitions* (pp. 218–228). New York: Brunner/Mazel.

McCubbin, H. I., Needle, R. H., & Wilson, M. (1985). Adolescent health risk behaviors: Family stress and adolescent coping as critical factors. *Family Relations: Journal of Applied Family and Child Studies, 34,* 51–62.

McCubbin, H. I., Olson, D. H., & Larsen, A. S. (1982). Family Crisis Oriented Personal Scales. In D. Olson, H. I. McCubbin, H. Banes, A. Larsen, M. Muxen, & M. Wilson (Eds.), *Family inventories* (pp. 101–120). St. Paul, MN: University of Minnesota, Family Social Science.

McCubbin, H. I., & Patterson, J. M. (1983). Family transitions: Adaptation to stress. In H. I. McCubbin & C. R. Figley (Eds.), *Stress and the family: Vol. I. Coping with normative transitions* (pp. 5–25). New York: Brunner/Mazel.

McGaugh, J. L. (1985). Peripheral and central adrenergic influences on brain systems involved in the modulation of memory storage. *Annals of the New York Academy of Sciences, 444,* 150–161.

McGrath, J. E., & Beehr, T. A. (1990). Time and the stress process: Some temporal issues in the conceptualization and measurement of stress. Special Issue: Advances in measuring life stress. *Stress Medicine, 6,* 93–104.

Mead, M. (1928). *Coming of age in Samoa.* New York: Mentor Books.

Mechanic, D. (1974). Social structure and personal adaptation: Some neglected dimensions. In G. V. Coelho, D. Hamburg, & J. E. Adams (Eds.), *Coping and adaptation* (pp. 32–44). New York: Basic Books.

Mechanic, D. (1978). *Students under stress: A study in the social psychology of adaptation.* Madison: University of Wisconsin Press.

Meichenbaum, D. (1985). *Stress inoculation training.* New York: Pergamon Press.

Meichenbaum, D., & Cameron, R. (1983). Stress inoculation training: Toward a general paradigm for training coping skills. In D. Meichenbaum & M. E. Jaremko (Eds.), *Stress reduction and prevention* (pp. 115–145). New York: Plenum.

Menninger, K. (1963). *The vital balance: The life processes in mental health and illness.* New York: Macmillan.

Miller, A. (1990). *The untouched key: Tracing childhood trauma in creativity and destructiveness.* New York: Doubleday.

Miller, N. E. (1980). A perspective on the effects of stress and coping on disease and health. In S. Levine & H. Ursin (Eds.), *Coping and health* (pp. 323–354). New York: Plenum.

Miller, S. (1980). When is a little information a dangerous thing? Coping with stressful events by monitoring vs. blunting. In S. Levine & H. Ursin (Eds.), *Coping and health* (pp. 145–170). New York: Plenum.

Miller, S. M., Leinbach, A., & Brody, D. S. (1989). Coping style in hypertensive patients: Nature and consequences. *Journal of Consulting and Clinical Psychology, 57,* 333–337.

Miller, S., & Mangan, C. E. (1983). Interacting effects of information and coping style in adapting to gynecological stress: When should the doctor tell all? *Journal of Personality and Social Psychology, 45,* 223–236.

Millon, T. (1982). On the nature of clinical health psychology. In T. Millon, C. Green, & R. Meagher (Eds.), *Handbook of clinical health psychology* (pp. 1–28). New York: Plenum.

Minuchin, S. (1974). *Families and family therapy.* Cambridge, MA: Harvard University Press.

Mitchell, E. R., Cronkite, R. C., & Moos, R. H. (1983). Stress, coping and depression among married couples. *Journal of Abnormal Psychology, 92,* 433–448.

Mitchell, E. R., & Hodson, C. A. (1983). Coping with domestic violence: Social support and psychological health among battered women. *American Journal of Community Psychology, 11,* 629–654.

Monjan, A. A., & Collector, M. T. (1977). Stress-induced modulation of the immune response. *Science, 196,* 307–308.

Monjan, A. A. (1981). Stress and immunological competence: Studies in animals. In R. Ader (Ed.), *Psychoneuroimmunology* (pp. 185–228). New York: Academic Press.

Monroe, S. M., & Steiner, S. C. (1986). Social support and psychopathology: Interrelations with preexisting disorder, stress, and personality. *Journal of Abnormal Psychology, 95,* 29–39.

Moore, R. (1990). Ethnographic assessment of pain coping perceptions. *Psychosomatic Medicine, 52,* 171–181.

Moos, R. H. (1984). Context and coping: Toward a unifying conceptual framework. *American Journal of Community Psychology, 12,* 5–25.

Moos, R. (1990). Conceptual and empirical approaches to developing family-based assessment procedures: Resolving the case of the Family Environment Scale. *Family Process, 29,* 199–208.

Moos, R. H., Brennan, P. L., Fondacaro, M. R., & Moos, B. S. (1990). Approach and avoidance coping responses among older problem and non-problem drinkers. *Psychology and Aging, 5,* 31–40.

Moos, R. H., & Moos, B. S. (1983). Adaptation and the quality of life in work and family settings. *Journal of Community Psychology, 11,* 158–170.

Moos, R. H., & Schaefer, J. A. (1984). The crisis of physical illness. In R. Moos (Ed.), *Coping with physical illness* (pp. 3–26). New York: Plenum.

Moos, R. H., & Schaefer, J. A. (1986). Life transitions and crises: A conceptual overview. In R. H. Moos (Ed.), *Coping with life crises: An integrated approach* (pp. 28–33). New York: Plenum.

Morris, T., Greer, S., Pettingale, K. W., & Watson, M. (1981). Patterns of expression of anger and their psychological correlates in women with breast cancer. *Journal of Psychosomatic Research, 25,* 111–117.

Morrissey, R. F. (1977). The Haan model of ego functioning: An assessment of empirical research. In N. Haan (Ed.), *Coping and defending* (pp. 250–279). New York: Academic Press.

Mosher, L., Pollin, W., & Stabenau, J. (1971). Families with identical twins discordant for schizophrenia. *British Journal of Psychiatry, 118,* 29–42.

Mullen, B., & Suls, J. (1982). The effectiveness of attention and rejection as coping styles: A meta-analysis of temporal differences. *Journal of Psychosomatic Research, 26,* 43–49.

Murphy, L. (1974). Coping, vulnerability, and resilience in childhood. In G. V. Coelho, D. A. Hamburg, & J. E. Adams (Eds.), *Coping and adaptation* (pp. 69–100). New York: Basic Books.

Murphy, L., & Moriarty, A. (1976). *Vulnerability, coping, and growth: From infancy to adolescence.* New Haven: Yale University Press.

Murrell, S., & Norris, F. H. (1984). Resources, life events, and changes in positive affect and depression in older adults. *American Journal of Community Psychology, 12,* 445–464.

Murrell, S., Norris, F. H., & Hutchins, G. L. (1984). Distribution and desirability of life events in older adults: Population and policy implications. *Journal of Community Psychology, 12,* 301–311.

Myrdal, G. (1962). *An American dilemma: The Negro problem and modern democracy.* New York: Harper & Row.

Nader, L. (1985). A user theory of legal change as applied to gender. *Nebraska Symposium on Motivation, 33,* 1–33.

Neighbors, H. W., Jackson, J. S., Bowman, P. J., & Gurin, G. (1983). Stress, coping and Black mental health: Preliminary findings from a national survey. In R. Hess & J. Hermalin (Eds.), *Innovations in prevention* (pp. 5–29). New York: Haworth.

Newberry, B. H. (1976). Inhibitory effects of stress on experimental mammary tumors. *Abstracts of the International Symposium on Detection and Prevention of Cancer, 314,* 35.

Newberry, B. H., & Songbush, L. (1979). Inhibitory effects of stress on experimental mammary tumors. *Cancer Detection and Prevention, 2,* 222–223.

Nolen-Hoeksema, S. (1991). Responses to depression and their effects on the duration of depressive episodes. *Journal of Abnormal Psychology, 100,* 569–582.

Nolen-Hoeksema, S., & Morrow, J. (1991). A prospective study of depression and posttraumatic stress symptoms after a natural disaster: The 1989 Loma Prieta earthquake. *Journal of Personality and Social Psychology, 61,* 115–121.

Norris, F. H. (1992). Epidemiology of trauma: Frequency and impact of different potentially traumatic events on different demographic groups. *Journal of Consulting and Clinical Psychology, 60,* 409–418.

Norris, F. H., & Murrell, S. A. (1987). Transitory impact of life-event stress on psychological symptoms in older adults. *Journal of Health and Social Behavior, 28,* 197–211.

Norton, D. L. (1974). *Personal destinies: A philosophy of ethical individualism.* Princeton: Princeton University Press.

O'Leary, A. (1990). Stress, emotion, and human immune function. *Psychological Bulletin, 108,* 363–382.

Obeyesekere, G. (1977). Psychocultural exegesis of a case of spirit possession in Sri Lanka. In V. Crapanzano & V. Garrison (Eds.), *Case studies in spirit possession* (pp 235–294). New York: Wiley.

Offer, D., Ostrov, E., & Howard, K. (1981). *The adolescent: A psychological self-portrait.* New York: Basic Books.

Ogrocki, P. K., Stephens, M. A. P., & Kinney, J. (1990, November). Assessing caregiver coping: State vs. trait approaches. *The Gerontologist, 30,* 135A.

Ornstein, R., & Thompson, R. F. (1984). *The amazing brain.* Boston: Houghton Mifflin.

Page, W. F., Engdahl, B. F., & Eberly, R. E. (1991). Prevalence and correlates of depressive symptoms among former prisoners of war. *Journal of Nervous and Mental Disease, 179,* 670–677.

Parkes, C. M., & Weiss, R. S. (1983). *Recovery from bereavement.* New York: Basic Books.

Paykel, E. S. (1983). Methodological aspects of life events research. *Journal of Psychosomatic Research, 27,* 341–352.

Pearlin, L. I. (1989). The sociological study of stress. *Journal of Health and Social Behavior, 30,* 241–256.

Pearlin, L. I., Lieberman, M. A., Menaghan, E. G., & Mullan, J. T. (1981). The stress process. *Journal of Health and Social Behavior, 22,* 337–356.

Pearlin, L., & Schooler, C. (1978). The structure of coping. *Journal of Health and Social Behavior, 19,* 2–21.

Peele, S. (1985). *The meaning of addiction: Compulsive experience and its interpretation.* Lexington, MA: Lexington Books.

Pendick, D. (1993). Chaos of the mind. *Science News, 143,* 138–139.

Pennebaker, J. W., Barger, S. D., & Tiebout, J. (1989). Disclosure of traumas and health among Holocaust survivors. *Psychosomatic Medicine, 51,* 577–589.

Pennebaker, J. W., Colder, M., & Sharp, L. K. (1990). Accelerating the coping process. *Journal of Personality and Social Psychology, 58,* 528–527.

Pennebaker, J. W., & O'Heeron, R. C. (1984). Confiding in others and illness rate among spouses of suicide and accidental-death victims. *Journal of Abnormal Psychology, 93,* 473–476.

Perosa, S. L., & Perosa, L. M. (1993). Relationships among Minuchin's Structural Family Model, identity achievement, and coping style. *Journal of Consulting Psychology, 40,* 479–489.

Peterson, A. C., Compas, B. E., Brooks-Gunn, J., Stemmler, M., Ey, S., & Grant, K. E. (1993). Depression in adolescence. *American Psychologist, 48,* 155–168.

Peterson, L. (1989). Coping by children undergoing stressful medical procedures: Some conceptual, methodological, and therapeutic issues. *Journal of Consulting and Clinical Psychology, 57,* 380–387.

Petrie, A. (1978). *Individuality in pain and suffering.* Chicago: University of Chicago Press.

Piaget, J. (1952). Autobiography. In E. Boring, H. Langfeld, H. Werner, & R. Yerkes (Eds.), *A history of psychology in autobiography* (Vol. 4, pp. 237–256). Worcester, MA: Clark University Press.

Popper, K. R., & Eccles, J. C. (1977). *The self and its brain.* New York: Springer.

Quarantelli, E. L. (1985). An assessment of conflicting views on mental health: The consequences of traumatic events. In C. R. Figley (Ed.), *Trauma and its wake* (pp. 173–215). New York: Brunner/Mazel.

Quinn, J. F., & Burkhauser, R. V. (1990). Work and retirement. In J. E. Birren & K. W. Schaie (Eds.), *Handbook of the psychology of aging* (3rd ed., pp. 300–327). New York: Van Nostrand Reinhold.

Rabkin, J., & Streuning, E. (1976). Life events, stress, and illness. *Science, 194,* 1013–1020.

Ranieri, D. J., & Weiss, A. M. (1984). Induction of depressed mood: A test of the opponent process theory. *Journal of Personality and Social Psychology, 47,* 1413–1422.

Raphael, K. G., Cloitre, M., & Dohrenend, B. P. (1991). Problems of recall and misclassification with checklist methods of measuring stressful life events. *Health Psychology, 10,* 62–74.

Rashkis, H. A. (1952). Systemic stress as an inhibitor of experimental tumors in Swiss mice. *Science, 116,* 169–171.

Reich, J. W., & Zautra, A. (1981). Life events and personal causation: Some relationships with satisfaction and distress. *Journal of Personality and Social Psychology, 41,* 1002–1112.

Reichard, S., Livson, F., & Peterson, P. G. (1962). *Aging and personality.* New York: Wiley.

Reis, S. D., & Heppner, P. P. (1993). Examination of coping resources and family adaptation in mothers and daughters of incestuous versus nonclinical families. *Journal of Consulting Psychology, 40,* 100–108.

Revenson, T. A., & Felton, B. J. (1989). Disability and coping as predictors of psychological adjustment to rheumatoid arthritis. *Journal of Consulting and Clinical Psychology, 57,* 344–348.

Reynolds, D. K. (1976). *Morita psychotherapy.* Berkeley: University of California Press.

Riesman, D. (1961). *The lonely crowd: A study of the changing American character.* New Haven: Yale University Press.

Riley, V., Fitzmaurice, M., & Spackman, D. (1981). Psychoneuroimmuno-logic factors in neoplasia: Studies in animals. In R. Ader (Ed.), *Psychoneuroimmunology* (pp. 31–102). New York: Academic Press.

Ring, K. (1982). *Life at death: An investigation of the near-death experience.* New York: Coward, McCann, & Geoghegan.

Ritchie, J. A., Caty, S., & Elleron, M. L. (1988). Coping behaviors of hospitalized preschool children. *Maternal–Child Nursing Journal, 17,* 153–171.

Rodin, J. (1986). Health, control, and aging. In M. M. Baltes & P. B. Baltes (Eds.), *The psychology of control and aging* (pp. 139–165). Hillsdale, NJ: Erlbaum.

Rogentine, G., Van Kammen, D., Fox, B., Docherty, J., Rosenblatt, J., Boyhd, S., & Bunney, W. (1979). Psychological factors in the prognosis of malignant melanoma: A prospective study. *Psychosomatic Medicine, 41,* 647–655.

Rollin, B. (1986). *First, you cry.* Philadelphia: Lippencott.

Rook, K. (1984). The negative side of social interaction: Impact on psychological well-being. *Journal of Personality and Social Psychology, 46,* 1097–1108.

Rose, R. M. (1978). *Air traffic controller health change study: A prospective investigation of physical, psychological and work-related changes.* Springfield, VA: National Technical Information Service.

Rosow, I. (1974). *Socialization to old age.* Berkeley: University of California Press.

Roth, S., & Cohen, L. J. (1986). Approach, avoidance, and coping with stress. *American Psychologist, 41,* 813–819.

Roth, S., & Lebowitz, L. (1988). The experience of sexual trauma. *Journal of Traumatic Stress, 1,* 79–107.

Roth, S., & Newman, E. (1991). The process of coping with sexual trauma. *Journal of Traumatic Stress, 4,* 279–297.

Rotter, J. B. (1966). Generalized expectancies for internal versus external control of reinforcement. *Psychological Monographs, 80* (Whole No. 609).

Rowlison, R., & Felner, R. (1989). Major life events, hassles, and adaptation in adolescence: Confounding in the conceptualization and measurement of life events revisited. *Journal of Personality and Social Psychology, 55,* 432–444.

Rubel, A. J. (1969). Concepts of disease in Mexican-American culture. In L. R. Lynch (Ed.), *The cross-cultural approach to health behavior* (pp. 174–205). Rutherford, NJ: Fairleigh Dickinson University Press.

Ruch, L. O., Chandler, S. M., & Harter, R. A. (1980). Life change and rape impact. *Journal of Health and Social Behavior, 21,* 248–260.

Rumi, J. (1973). *The Mathwani* (E. H. Whinfield, Trans.). London: Octagon Press.

Runyan, W. M. (1978). The life course as a theoretical orientation: Sequences of person-situation interactions. *Journal of Personality, 46,* 552–558.

Russell, D. W., & Cutrona, C. E. (1991). Social support, stress, and depressive symptoms among the elderly: Test of a process model. *Psychology and Aging, 6,* 190–201.

Rutter, M. (1981). Stress, coping, and development: Some issues and questions. *Journal of Child Psychology, Psychiatry, and Allied Disciplines, 22,* 323–356.

Rutter, M. (1987). Psychosocial resilience and protective mechanisms. *American Journal of Orthopsychiatry, 57,* 316–331.

Sapolsky, R. M. (1993). Endocrinology alfresco: Psychoendocrine studies of wild baboons. *Recent Progress in Hormone Research, 48,* 437–468.

Sappington, A. A. (1990). Recent psychological approaches to the free will versus determinism issue. *Psychological Bulletin, 108,* 19–29.

Sarason, I., Johnson, J. H., & Siegel, J. M. (1978). Assessing the impact of life changes: Development of the Life Experiences Survey. *Journal of Consulting and Clinical Psychology, 46,* 932–946.

Saunders, L. W. (1977). Variants in zar experience in an Egyptian village. In V. Crapanzano & V. Garrison (Eds.), *Case studies in spirit possession* (pp. 177–191). New York: Wiley.

Schachter, S., & Singer, J. (1962). Cognitive, social, and physiological determinants of emotional state. *Psychological Review, 69,* 379–399.

Scheier, L. M., & Kleban, M. H. (1992, August). *Multidimensional structure of psychological distress in the aged.* Paper presented at the annual meeting of the American Psychological Association, Washington, DC.

Scherg, H., & Blohmke, M. (1988). Associations between selected life events and cancer. *Behavioral Medicine, 14,* 119–124.

Schnurr, P., Rosenberg, S., & Friedman, M. (1993). Change in MMPI scores from college to adulthood as a function of military service. *Journal of Abnormal Psychology, 102,* 288–296.

Schönpflug, W. (1985). Goal directed behavior as a source of stress: Psychological origins and consequences of inefficiency. In M. Frese & J. Sabini (Eds.), *The concept of action in psychology* (pp. 172–188). Hillsdale, NJ: Erlbaum.

Schroeder, F. H., & Costa, P. (1984). Influence of life event stress on physical illness: Substantive effects or methodological flaws. *Journal of Personality and Social Psychology, 46,* 853–863.

Scudder, T., & Colson, E. (1982). From welfare to development: A conceptual framework for the analysis of dislocated people. In A. Hansen & A. Oiler-Smith (Eds.), *Involuntary migration and resettlement: The problems and responses of dislocated people* (pp. 267–287). Boulder, CO: Westview Press.

Seeman, T. (1991). Personal control and coronary artery disease: How generalized expectancies about control may influence disease risk. *Journal of Psychosomatic Medicine, 35,* 661–669.

Seligman, M. (1975). *Helplessness: On depression, development and death.* San Francisco: Freeman.

Sellers, R. M., & Peterson, C. (1993). Explanatory style and coping with controllable events by student-athletes. *Cognition and Emotion, 7,* 431–441.

Selye, H. (1956). *The stress of life.* New York: McGraw-Hill.

Shapiro, D. (1965). *Neurotic styles.* New York: Basic Books.

Sharansky, N. (1988). *Fear no evil.* New York: Random House.

Shek, D. T. L., & Cheung, C. K. (1990). Locus of coping in a sample of Chinese working parents: Reliance on self or seeking help from others. *Social Behavior and Personality, 18,* 327–346.

Silver, R. L., Boon, C., & Stones, M. H. (1983). Searching for meaning in misfortune: Making sense of incest. *Journal of Social Issues, 39,* 81–102.

Simonton, D. K. (1984). *Genius, creativity, and leadership: Histriometric inquiries.* Cambridge, MA: Harvard University Press.

Skinner, B. F. (1971). *Beyond freedom and dignity.* New York: Knopf.

Smith, R. S. (1991). The immune system is a key factor in the etiology of psychosocial disease. *Medical Hypotheses, 34,* 49–57.

Smith, S. M. (1983). Disaster: Family disruption in the wake of natural disasters. In C. R. Figley & H. I. McCubbin (Eds.), *Stress and the family: Vol. II. Coping with catastrophe* (pp. 120–147). New York: Brunner/Mazel.

Solomon, G. F. (1969). Stress and antibody in rats. *International Archives of Allergy and Applied Immunology, 35,* 97–104.

Solomon, G. F., & Amkraut, A. A. (1981). Psychoneuroendocrinological effects on the immune response. *Annual Review of Microbiology, 35,* 155–184.

Solomon, R. L. (1980). The opponent-process theory of acquired motivation: The costs of pleasure and the benefits of pain. *American Psychologist, 35,* 691–712.

Solomon, Z. (1993). *Combat stress reaction: The enduring toll of war.* New York: Plenum.

Spanier, G. B., & Glick, P. C. (1981). Marital instability in the U.S.: Some correlates and recent changes. *Family Relations, 31,* 329–338.

Sperry, R. W. (1988). Psychology's mentalist paradigm and the religion/science tension. *American Psychologist, 43,* 607–613.

Sperry, R. W. (1993). The impact and promise of the cognitve revolution. *American Psychology, 48,* 878–885.

Spiegel, D. M. (1993, April). *Does living better mean living longer? Effects of supportive group therapy on cancer patients.* Paper presented at the Society of Behavioral Medicine's Fourteenth Annual Scientific Sessions, San Francisco.

Spirito, A., Overholswer, J., & Stark, L. J. (1989). Common problems and coping strategies II: Findings with adolescent suicide attempters. *Journal of Abnormal Child Psychology, 17,* 213–221.

Spirito, A., Stark, L. J., Grace, N., & Stamoulis, D. (1991). Common problems and coping strategies reported in childhood and early adolescence. *Journal of Youth and Adolescence, 20,* 531–544.

Spiro, M. E. (1978). Supernaturally caused illness in traditional Burmese medicine. In A. Kleinman, P. Kunstadter, E. R. Alexander, & J. L. Gale (Eds.), *Culture and healing in Asian societies* (pp. 219–234). Cambridge, MA: Schenkman.

Spruit, I. P. (1982). Unemployment and health in macrosocial analysis. *Social Science and Medicine, 16,* 1903–1918.

Spurell, M., & McFarlane, A. (1993). Post-traumatic stress disorder and coping after a natural disaster. *Social Psychiatry and Psychiatric Epidemiology, 28,* 194–200.

Stark, L. J., Spirito, A., Williams, C., & Guevremont, D. (1989). Common problems & coping strategies: Findings with normal adolescents. *Journal of Abnormal Child Psychology, 17,* 204–212.

Sternberg, R. J. (1990). Wisdom and its relations to intelligence and creativity. In R. J. Sternberg (Ed.), *Wisdom: Its nature, origins, and development* (pp. 142–159). Cambridge, England: Cambridge University Press.

Steward, M. S. (1993). Understanding children's memories of medical procedures: "He didn't touch me and it didn't hurt!" In C. A. Nelson (Ed.), *Minnesota Symposium on Child Psychology: Memory and affect in development* (Vol 26, pp. 171–225). Hillsdale, NJ: Erlbaum.

Stone, A. A., Greenberg, M. A., Kennedy-Moore, E., & Newman, M. G. (1991). Self-report, situation-specific coping questionnaires: What are they measuring? *Journal of Personality and Social Psychology, 61,* 648–658.

Stone, A., & Shiffman, S. (1992). Reflections on the intensive measurements of stress, coping, and mood, with an emphasis on daily measures. *Psychology and Health, 7,* 115–129.

Stouffer, S. A. (1949). *The American soldier.* Princeton: Princeton University Press.

Suls, J., & Wan, C. K. (1989). Effects of sensory and procedural information on coping with stressful medical procedures and pain: A meta-analysis. *Journal of Consulting and Clinical Psychology, 57,* 372–379.

Surtees, P. G. (1989). Adversity and psychiatric disorder: A decay model. In G. W. Brown & T. O. Harris (Eds.), *Life events and illness* (pp. 161–198). New York: Guilford Press.

Swartz, L., Elk, R., & Teggin, A. F. (1983). Life events in Xhosas in Cape Town. *Journal of Psychosomatic Research, 27,* 223–232.

Szasz, T. (1961). *The myth of mental illness: Foundations of a theory of personal conduct.* New York: Hoeber–Harper.

Tageson, C. S. (1982). *Humanistic psychology: A synthesis.* Homewood, IL: Dorsey Press.

Tart, C. (1987). *Waking up.* Cambridge, MA: Shambala.

Taylor, S., & Brown, J. D. (1988). Illusion and well-being: A social psychological perspective on mental health. *Psychological Bulletin, 103,* 193–210.

Taylor, S. E., Lichtman, R. R., & Wood, J. V. (1984). Attributions, beliefs about control, and adjustment to breast cancer. *Journal of Personality and Social Psychology, 46,* 489–502.

Temoshok, L., Heller, B., Sagebiel, R., Blois, M., Sweet, D., Diclemete, R., & Gold, M. (1985). The relationship of psychosocial factors to prognostic indicators in cutaneous melanoma. *Journal of Psychosomatic Research, 29,* 137–155.

Thoits, P. (1983). Dimensions of life events that influence psychological distress: An evaluation and synthesis of the literature. In B. Kaplan (Ed.), *Psychosocial stress: Trends in theory and research* (pp. 33–103). New York: Academic Press.

Thoits, P. (1986). Social support as coping assistance. *Journal of Consulting and Clinical Psychology, 54,* 416–423.

Thompson, P. S., Dengerink, H. A., & George, J. M. (1987). Noise-induced temporary threshold shifts: The effects of anticipatory stress and coping strategies. *Journal of Human Stress, 13,* 32–38.

Totman, R. (1979). *Social causes of illness.* New York: Pantheon.

Townsend, A. L., Noelker, L., Deimling, G., & Bass, D. (1989). Longitudinal impact of interhousehold caregiving on adult children's mental health. *Psychology and Aging, 4,* 393–401.

Tseng, W. (1978). Traditional and modern psychiatric care in Taiwan. In A. Kleinman, P. Kunstadter, E. R. Alexander, & J. L. Gale (Eds.), *Culture and healing in Asian societies* (pp. 311–328). Cambridge, MA: Schenkman.

Turner, V. S. (1969). *The ritual process: Structure and anti-structure.* Chicago: Aldine.

Underhill, E. (1961). *Mysticism.* New York: Dutton.

Ursano, R. J., Wheatly, R., Sledge, W., Rahe, A., & Carlson, E. (1986). Coping and recovery styles in the Vietnam era prisoner of war. *Journal of Nervous and Mental Disease, 175,* 273–275.

Vaillant, G. (1977). *Adaptation to life: How the best and the brightest came of age.* Boston: Little Brown.

Vaillant, G. E. (1983). *The nature of alcoholism.* Cambridge, MA: Harvard University Press.

Vaillant, G. E. (1993). *The wisdom of the ego.* Cambridge, MA: Harvard University Press.

Vaillant, G. E., Bond, M., & Vaillant, C. O. (1986). An empirically validated hierarchy of defense mechanisms. *Archives of General Psychiatry, 43,* 786–794.

Villarino, M. E., Geiter, L. J., & Simone, P. M. (1992). The multidrug-resistant tuberculosis challenge to public health efforts to control tuberculosis. *Public Health Reports, 107,* 616–625.

Vingerhoets, A. J. (1985). *Psychosocial stress: An experimental approach: Life events, coping, and psychobiological functioning.* Lisse, Netherlands: Swets & Zeitlinger.

Vingerhoets, A. J., & Marcelissen, F. G. (1988). Stress research: Its present status and issues for future developments. *Social Science and Medicine, 36,* 279–291.

Virchow, R. L. K. (1863). *Cellular pathology as based upon physiological and pathological histology.* Philadelphia: Lippincott.

Virella, G. (1993). Diagnostic evaluation of humoral immunity. In G. Virella (Ed.), *Introduction to medical immunology* (pp. 275–310). New York: Dekker.

Visintainer, M., & Casey, R. (1984, August). *Adjustment and outcome in melanoma patients.* Paper presented at the annual meeting of the American Psychological Association, Toronto, Ontario, Canada.

Visotsky, H. M., Hamburg, D. A., Goss, M. E., & Lebovitz, B. Z. (1961). Coping under extreme stress: Observations of patients with severe poliomyelitis. *Archives of General Psychiatry, 5,* 423–448.

Vitaliano, P., Russo, J., Carr, J., Maiuro, R., & Becker, J. (1985). The Ways of Coping checklist: Revision and psychometric properties. *Multivariate Behavioral Research, 20,* 3–26.

Vitaliano, P. P., DeWolfe, D. J., Maiuro, R. D., Russo, J., & Katon, W. (1990). Appraisal changeability of a stressor as a modifier of the relationship between coping and depression: A test of the hypothesis of fit. *Journal of Personality and Social Psychology, 59,* 582–592.

Vitaliano, P. P., Russo, J., Maiuro, R. D. (1987). Locus of control, type of stressor, and appraisal within a cognitive–phenomenological model of stress. *Journal of Research in Personality, 21,* 224–237.

Vogele, C., & Steptoe, A. (1992). Emotional coping and tonic blood pressure as determinants of cardiovascular responses to mental stress. *Journal of Hypertension, 10,* 1079–1087.

von Bertalanffy, L. (1969). *General systems theory: Foundations, development, applications.* New York: Brazilier.

Wagner, B. M., Compas, B. E., & Howell, D. C. (1988). Daily and major life events: A test of an integrative model of psychosocial stress. *American Journal of Community Psychology, 16,* 189–205.

Walker, E. H. (1970). The nature of consciousness. *Mathematical Biosciences, 7,* 131–178.

Wallace, A. F. C. (1956). *Tornado in Worcester: An exploratory study of individual and community behavior in an extreme situation* (Disaster Study No. 3). Washington, DC: National Academy of Sciences–National Research Council.

Wallace, A. F. C. (1966). *Religion: An anthropological view.* New York: Random House.

Wallerstein, J. S., & Blakeslee, S. (1989). *Second chances: Men, women, and children a decade after divorce.* New York: Ticknor & Fields.

Wallerstein, J. S., & Kelly, J. B. (1980). *Surviving the breakup: How children and parents cope with divorce.* New York: Basic Books.

Ward, C. (1988). Stress, coping, and adjustment in victims of sexual assault: The role of psychological defense mechanisms. *Counselling Psychology Quarterly, 1,* 165–178.

Watson, D., & Clark, L. A. (1984). Negative affectivity: The disposition to experience aversive emotional states. *Psychological Bulletin, 96,* 465–490.

Watts-Jones, D. (1990). Toward a stress scale for African-American women. *Psychology of Women Quarterly, 14,* 271–275.

Weidman, H. H. (1979). Falling out: A diagnostic and treatment problem viewed from a transcultural perspective. *Social Science and Medicine, 13B,* 95–112.

Weinberger, M., Hiner, S. L., & Tierney, W. M. (1987). In support of hassles as a measure of stress in predicting health outcomes. *Journal of Behavioral Medicine, 10,* 19–31.

Weisman, A. (1979). *Coping with cancer.* New York: McGraw-Hill.

Weisz, J. R. (1986). Understanding the developing understanding of control. In M. Perlmutter (Ed.), *Minnesota Symposium in Child Psychology: Vol. 18. Cognitive perspectives on children's social and behavioral development* (pp. 219–275). Hillsdale, NJ: Erlbaum.

Weitz, R. (1989). Uncertainty and the lives of persons with AIDS. *Journal of Health and Social Behavior, 30,* 270–281.

Wells, R. D., & Schwebel, A. I. (1987). Chronically ill children and their mothers: Predictors of resilience and vulnerability to hospitalization and surgical stress. *Developmental and Behavioral Pediatrics, 8,* 83–89.

Werner, E. E., & Smith, R. S. (1982). *Vulnerable but invincible: A longitudinal study of resilient children and youth.* New York: McGraw-Hill.

Werner, E. E., & Smith, R. S. (1992). *Overcoming the odds.* Ithaca, NY: Cornell University Press.

Wertlieb, D., Weigel, C., & Feldstein, M. (1987). Measuring children's coping. *Journal of Orthopsychiatry, 57,* 548–560.

White, R. W. (1961). *Lives in progress: A study of the natural growth of personality.* New York: Holt, Rinehart, & Winston.

White, R. W. (1974). Strategies of adaptation: An attempt at systematic description. In G. V. Coelho, D. A. Hamburg, & J. E. Adams (Eds.), *Coping and adaptation* (pp. 47–68). New York: Basic Books.

Whiteside, T. L., Bryant, J., Day, R., & Herberman, R. B. (1990). Natural killer cytoxicity in the diagnosis of immune dysfunction: Criteria for a reproducible assay. *Journal of Clinical Laboratory Analysis, 4,* 102–114.

Whiteside, T. L., Bryant, J., Day, R., Herberman, R. B., Havens, D. M., & Zink, R. (1993). Tuberculosis: A reemerging and alarming public health problem. *Journal of Pediatric Health Care, 7,* 93–95.

Wiener, H. (1977). *Psychobiology and human disease.* New York: Elsevier.

Wilder, H. B., & Chiriboga, D. A. (1991). Who leaves whom? The importance of control. In D. A. Chiriboga & L. S. Catron (Eds.), *Divorce: Crisis, challenge, or relief?* (pp. 224–247). New York: New York University Press.

Wilson, J., Harel, Z., & Kahana, B. (1989). The day of infamy: The legacy of Pearl Harbor. In J. Wilson (Ed.), *Trauma, transformation, and healing* (pp. 129–156). New York: Brunner/Mazel.

Wolfe, J., Keane, T. M., Kaloupek, D. G., Mora, C. A., & Winde, P. (1993). Patterns of positive readjustment in Vietnam combat veterans. *Journal of Traumatic Stress, 6,* 179–191.

Wolff, H. G. (1950). Life stress and cardiovascular disorders. *Circulation, 1,* 187–203.

Wolfle, L. & Ethington, C. (1985). GEMINI: Program for analysis of structural equations with standard errors of indirect effects. *Behavior Research Methods, Instruments, and Computers, 17,* 581–584.

Wolin, S. J., & Wolin, S. (1993). *The resilient self: How survivors of troubled families rise above adversity.* New York: Ullard Books.

Women's Action Program (1976). *An exploratory study of women in the health professions schools: Vol. 2. Medicine* (Contract No. HEW OS-74-291). Washington, DC: Department of Health, Education and Welfare.

Worland, J., Janes, C., Anthony, E. J., McGinnis, M., & Cass, L. (1984). St. Louis Risk Research Project: Comprehensive progress report of experimental studies. In N. F. Watt, E. J. Anthony, L. C. Wynne, & J. Rolf (Eds.), *Children at risk for schizophrenia: A longitudinal perspective* (pp. 105–147). Cambridge, England: Cambridge University Press.

Wortman, C. B., & Silver, R. C. (1989). The myths of coping with loss. *Journal of Consulting and Clinical Psychology, 57*, 349–357.

Wyman, P. A., Cowen, E. L., Work, W. C., & Parker, G. R. (1991). Developmental and family milieu correlates of resilience in urban children who have experienced major life stress. *American Journal of Community Psychology, 19*, 405–426.

Yeager, C., & Janos, L. (1985). *Yeager: An autobiography.* New York: Bantam Books.

Zajonc, R. B. (1984). On the primacy of affect. *American Psychologist, 39*, 117–123.

Zarit, S. H., Todd, P. A., & Zarit, J. M. (1986). Subjective burden of husbands and wives as caregivers: A longitudinal study. *The Gerontologist, 26*, 260–266.

Zatzick, D. F., & Dimsdale, J. E. (1990). Cultural variations in response to painful stimuli. *Psychosomatic Medicine, 52*, 544–557.

Zautra, A. J., Reich, J. W., & Guarnaccia, C. (1990). Some everyday life consequences of disability and bereavement for older adults. *Journal of Personality and Social Psychology, 59*, 350–361.

Zautra, A. J., & Sandler, I. (1983). Life events needs assessments: Two models for measuring preventable mental health problems. *Prevention and Human Services, 2*, 35–58.

Zautra, A. J., & Wrabetz, A. B. (1991). Coping success and its relationship to psychological distress for older adults. *Journal of Personality and Social Psychology, 61*, 801–810.

Zborowski, M. (1952). Cultural components in responses to pain. *Journal of Social Issues, 8*, 16–30.

Zola, I. K. (1966). Culture and symptoms: An analysis of patients' presenting problems. *American Sociological Review, 31*, 615–630.

Zuckerman, M. (1979). Atttribution of success and failure revisited; or, the motivational bias is alive and well in attribution theory. *Journal of Personality, 47*, 245–287.

Index